Making Waves

Making Waves

Michigan's Boat-Building Industry, 1865–2000

SCOTT M. PETERS

UNIVERSITY OF MICHIGAN PRESS

ANN ARBOR

Published in the United States of America by the
University of Michigan Press
Manufactured in the United States of America
⊗ Printed on acid-free paper

2018   2017   2016   2015   4   3   2   1

A CIP catalog record for this book is available from the British Library.

ISBN 978-0-472-07257-6 (cloth : alk. paper)
ISBN 978-0-472-05257-8 (paper: alk. paper)
ISBN 978-0-472-12098-7 (e-book)

Preface

In Michigan, we are surrounded by water. Recreation on our Great Lakes, inland lakes, rivers, and streams is a way of life, and for many of us it involves owning or spending time on boats. Perhaps not surprisingly, our state also has a rich history of boat-building, and investigating how this craft developed can help us better understand why we value recreation on the water so much. This book is intended to provide an overview in the context of the development of the boat-building industry in Michigan, the opportunities and challenges it faced, the nature of the products and their significance, and how Michigan boat builders changed the industry in general. The industry's visionaries, promoters, failures, and entrepreneurs who called Michigan home played a vital role in producing boats to meet the desires and needs of hundreds of thousands of people over a century and a half.

I have attempted to identify the names of individuals and firms of boat builders of Michigan who intended to build and sell boats as a commercial endeavor, so it does not include the people who built boats primarily for their own use, such as commercial fishermen or the backyard builder. By setting the story grouped roughly by decades, I hope to show major transitions in the industry driven by technological changes such as the development of the internal combustion engine or the economic crises of the 1890s and 1930s and national and international events such as World War II. Depending on their longevity, some companies only appear in one decade while others appear in several. To the extent that I could, I have tried to identify the communities the builders worked in and the date ranges during which they existed in the business.

I used a great deal of data from non-maritime sources, such as the *Michigan State Gazetteer and Business Directory*, corporate annual reports at the Archives of Michigan, genealogical information, newspaper stories, maps, and state and federal censuses, to draw conclusions about where people gathered to build boats, who they established relationships with, and how they built the industry from small workshops to enormous factories, all focusing on people, processes, and products.

The patterns of growth in both the automobile and boat-building industries in Michigan took much the same path after the introduction of the internal combustion engine. An explosion in growth followed by consolidation in hard economic times before yet another expansion is a pattern repeated constantly over the decades. In a few instances, especially in Detroit among the engine builders, the same players led the way in each field.

Michigan became a national leader in the boat-building industry during the early twentieth century. I have tried to show what was happening in Michigan not so much from a geographically myopic viewpoint but more as a representative microcosm of what was going on nationally in a broader context. Michigan boat builders transformed the boat-building industry in many ways, with new subsectors such as knock-down pattern boats, folding canvas boats, and mahogany-planked runabouts. Innovations in the organization of boat production also led the world. Without landing craft built in Michigan, World War II might have lasted much longer than it did.

Michigan boat builders earned fame and fortune with racing performance, endurance runs, design and engineering prowess, creative advertising and marketing, business acumen, and all of the other things that lead to success in commercial endeavors. The failures (which by far outnumbered the successes) all taught the remaining manufacturers more about the nature of the market and the need for products targeted to meet its demands. It is my hope that this work will prove to be a springboard for the further study of historic boat builders around the state, and that boat enthusiasts will find interest and enjoyment, like a good cruise, in what they read herein.

Principle Boat-Building Communities of Michigan

Fig. 1. Principle boat-building communities of Michigan. (By author.)

Acknowledgments

Putting together a book is actually the work of many people: the people who inspired me, the people who took the time to respond to research inquiries, and the production team that assembled it into a proper work.

For inspiration LeRoy Barnett and Rose Victory, former colleagues at the Michigan Historical Center, along with Kenneth Pott of the museum staff, provided me with the encouragement and periodic cajoling that only best friends can supply. I thank you for your persistence in pushing me past the research phase and into getting the work written and published. The inquisitive passion of the late Robert Speltz in discovering a story likewise gave me the enthusiasm to pursue the ones about Michigan builders in greater detail.

To the staffs of the Library of Michigan and Archives of Michigan, from reference to technical services, I am indebted to you for all your hard work in keeping the materials available for research and directing my hundreds of inquiries to the proper sources. Your gracious professionalism is deeply appreciated. To the family genealogists and boat historians who have collected information on well over fifteen hundred Michigan boat builders, I salute your work and your willingness to share it with me. Special thanks to Anthony S. Mollica Jr., Stan Grayson, Steve Harold, C. Patrick Labadie, John Polacsek, Robert Graham, Dr. John Halsey, Don Fostle, the late Ralph Roberts, Jim Wangard, Jill Dean, Caitlyn Perry Dial, Keith Steffke, Michael Dixon, Ron Bloomfield, Richard Durgee, Robert Price, Robert Sintz, George Graff, Dr. Paul G. Spitzer, Andreas Jordahl Rhude, Jerry Conrad, Chad Mayea, Erin Lopater, Louisa Watrous, and many, many others over the course of the past thirty years who have helped with photos and information.

Geoffrey Reynolds of the Joint Archives of Holland kindly gave me access to hundreds of articles and stories about Michigan boat builders and took the time to review the work in progress. Many thanks for saving and sharing this most important part of our maritime heritage, and I hope all your efforts and materials are represented well in this work.

To Scott Ham and the staff at the University of Michigan Press, I thank you for the opportunity to put my hobby interest into print. It was always an ambition of mine, and together we made it happen.

Finally, to my late father Wayne and my mother Virginia, thanks for taking me on innumerable boat rides and travels to historical sites around the country. To my children, Mark, Laura, and Andy, I thank you for your patience with an often distracted father. Most of all, to my wife Mary, I thank you for the enormous sacrifice of time and energy that allowed me to pursue this project and for reading every word of the manuscript. It could not have been accomplished without your help.

Scott M. Peters
Flint, Michigan

Contents

CHAPTER ONE

Beginnings, 1865–95

Introduction

There they are in many of the earliest paintings of Michigan lake and river scenes—small boats scurrying around larger ships, out fishing, or even taking their passengers for leisurely cruises. For the most part, they are anonymous, perhaps drawn in by the artist mostly to make his or her scene come alive. Nevertheless these representations show a presence on Michigan waters that very likely existed in real life, by the hundreds at first and by the thousands just a century later.

In the book *Frontier Metropolis*, Brian Leigh Dunnigan has collected scenes and maps of early Detroit, and the number of small boats in the paintings is larger than one might have thought possible for the time.[1] Certainly the rest of the state's infant villages had similar fleets of small craft plying their waterways. Many of the earliest Michigan boat builders were anonymous or assembled their boats as part of another job as a soldier or fisherman. Still, the products of their efforts capture the imagination. Who were these people, and where did they acquire their skills? Where did they come from? Who were their customers?

Workboats

The origins of recreational boating cannot be accurately determined. It probably dates back to an occasion when two fishermen decided to end their workday early and take a leisurely cruise back home. In the early and mid-nineteenth century, workboats served a variety of industries such as

Great Lakes shipping, the fur trade, commercial fishing, and lumbering, and in its infancy recreational boating emerged out of this world. As the need for boats built specifically for pleasure increased, the recreational boat industry evolved, slowly overtaking the building of workboats and eventually becoming one of the significant manufacturing industries in the state.

Native American canoes, the earliest small craft built in Michigan, existed long before the fur trade and the military establishment that sustained it for the Europeans. Birchbark canoes carried loads of furs and trade goods between the western collection points on the Great Lakes and Montreal. Already a large business by the end of the fur trade era, multiple generations of families engaged in building the craft, continuing the specialties and skills learned since time immemorial. Canoes of the fur trade era were refined to a number of standardized types based on where and how they were used. Some had high ends for handling the large swells of open-water lakes and rapids. For river work others featured low sides so as not to snag overhanging tree branches.[2] Timothy J. Kent, in *Birchbark Canoes of the Fur Trade*, notes that all the major settlement sites in Michigan shared by Europeans and Native Americans, such as Michilimackinac, Fort Pontchartrain (later Detroit), Fort St. Joseph, and others, served as Native American canoe production centers for trading with the French. Jacques Sabrevois de Bleury, the commandant of Fort Pontchartrain between 1714 and 1717, referring to the villages established nearby by the Hurons, Ottawas, Ojibwas, and Potawatomies, noted, "All these nations make a great many bark canoes, which Are very profitable for Them. They do this Sort of work in the summer. The women sew these canoes with Roots, the men cut and shape the bark and make the gunwales, cross-pieces and ribs; the women gum Them. It is no small labor to make a canoe, in which there is much symmetry and measurement; and it is a curious sight."[3]

Europeans brought the bateau to the region, a flat-bottomed, double-end craft with longitudinal planking, similar to a dory, commonly used for hauling cargo. French versions tended to be more heavily built, while British ones were slightly larger. Generally the French name applied to all varieties of the craft of the type.[4] One interesting type of boat merged both New World and Old World designs. Unique lapstrake canoes, presumably constructed by Native Americans in the St. Marys River, were used both for fishing and for taking tourists on a run through the river's rapids in the early twentieth century.

Michigan's Vernacular Watercraft

Mackinaw boats evolved as a unique regional type of small craft used for commerce, primarily in commercial fishing, but also for general transportation on the Great Lakes. James W. Milner, in his report to the U.S. Fish Commission on commercial fishing on the Great Lakes in 1871–72, described the Mackinaw boat.

> The famous "Mackinaw" of the lakes has bow and stern sharp, a great deal of sheer, the greatest beam forward of amidships and tapers with little curve to the stern. She is either schooner-rig, or with a lug-sail forward, is fairly fast, the greatest surf-boat known, and with an experienced boatman will ride out any storm, or, if necessary, beach with greater safety than any other boat. She is comparatively dry, and her sharp stern prevents the shipment of water aft, when running with the sea. They have been longer and more extensively used on the upper lakes than any other boats, and with less loss of life or accident . . .[5]

Based on the design of the Drontheim boats of Northern Ireland, in turn derived from Norwegian craft, these ubiquitous marine versions of pickup trucks of the nineteenth century in the Great Lakes region hauled cargoes and delivered passengers from place to place. The Mackinaw boat's double-end design made it an excellent compromise of sturdy construction, cargo capacity, and maneuverability for the Lakes.

One of the earlier builders of Mackinaw boats, Hyacinthe Chenier of St. Ignace, listed his occupation as boat builder in the 1850 U.S. Census, one of the few individuals to identify himself in the profession.[6] Jesse Wells Church, of Sugar Island near Sault Ste. Marie in the St. Marys River, likewise built several of the Mackinaw boats in the mid-nineteenth century.[7] Roy Ranger of Charlevoix, credited as being the last of the Mackinaw builders, began building Mackinaw boats in the 1890s and continued the tradition of producing these amazingly seaworthy craft until shortly after World War I.[8]

Another important form of transportation crucial to the settlement of the state's interior consisted of the first crude pole boats on the inland rivers, quickly followed by river steamers.

Michigan's impressive population surge, encouraged by inexpensive,

Fig. 2. Mackinaw boats at Leland, Michigan. The Mackinaw boat earned a good reputation as a workboat in commercial fishing and general cargo carrying in the Great Lakes region, paving the way for the recreational watercraft of the future. (Historical Collections of the Great Lakes, Bowling Green State University.)

readily available land for sale to encourage settlement, lured over 212,000 people to the state by 1840. The southern tiers of counties filled first, as well as lakeshore communities near the river mouths. Pole boats carried people and their possessions upstream into the south-central areas of the state and hauled their harvested crops and goods back to the river port villages. Literally propelled by pushing long poles against the river bottom, pole boats such as the *Young Napoleon* and the *Davy Crockett* made early commerce possible in the state's interior.[9]

Steamboats plied the rivers to carry on the business as soon as steam engines became available, quickly replacing the pole boats. Sandbars and snags challenged all river navigators, and passengers occasionally were called upon to help pull the boats off the obstacles. Plans for canals to be dug across the southern tiers of counties to avoid the long trip by lake around the Lower Peninsula were proposed early in the settlement era, with stock companies formed to build them. All quickly came to a halt with the financial Panic of 1837. On the proposed 216-mile Clinton-Kalamazoo Canal, intended to connect Lake St. Clair and Lake Michigan, workers only excavated 12 miles before the money ran out, and the completed portion quickly fell into disrepair.[10]

Michigan's burgeoning lumber industry also required large numbers of boats, ranging from crude homemade dugouts to large steam-driven tugs, to move logs on the rivers and lakes. Although the builders of the smaller boats are seldom identified, these boats played an important role in transporting the logs to sawmills and working around the sorting booms at their destinations.

Creating the Market

Many separate trends and contributing factors led to the emergence of the recreational boat-building industry after the Civil War. Increased amounts of leisure time and wealth, the growth of rowing and yachting as competitive sports, the creation of the resorts with hunting and fishing opportunities, and advances in marketing and advertising all played important roles in the transition of the industry from strictly building workboats to building recreational watercraft.

Finding the Time: The Emergence of Leisure

In the 1860s and 1870s, boat builders began to find a few new customers with sufficient time and money to devote to recreational boating. When the twelve-hour workday started to give way to the ten-hour day, workers found more time for recreation. Donna R. Braden, in *Leisure and Entertainment in America*, suggests that leisure time was linked directly to growing industrialization and the need to balance it with time off.

- For centuries, leisure was primarily identified with a "leisured" class, a group free of any obligation to work. The changed meaning of leisure to relate to everyone rather than to a privileged few is integrally connected with economic, technological, and social changes; above all, it relates to changes in the nature of work and the workplace.
- In America this shift was set in motion in the 19th century with urbanization and industrialization. As rapid technological innovation and the spread of the factory system made workers' tasks more routine, they tried to find new forms of relief from the monotony of re-

petitive work. Inherent in the factory system was a strict adherence to the clock. By the mid-19th century, the intrusion of "clock time" separated "work" from "not work" more clearly than ever before.

• Mechanization, the more efficient use of time, and the growing demand for better working conditions eventually led to the reduction of hours in the workday and workweek . . . By the end of the 19th century, social reformers of the Progressive era, building on earlier attempts to breach the stern Calvinist work ethic, were trying to persuade Americans of the value—indeed the necessity—of leisure time. They recommended this as the way for workers to renew their physical energy, attain mental health, and solidify family relationships.[11]

Increased Wealth

The boat-building industry grew substantially because new customers with better paying jobs also had the money to afford the boats. Most of the larger boats built for recreational purposes could only be purchased by salaried professionals, managers, or owners of companies. Occasionally a group of men would join together to invest in a yacht on which they would share the expenses. Working-class laborers saw increases in their wages to over a $1.50 a day by the late nineteenth century, not enough to buy much more than a rowboat but enough to rent a boat from a livery on occasion for a fishing trip or sailing excursion. For skilled trades, even $2.50 or more a day was feasible, but unless their skill sets included the necessary talents to build their own boats, the chance of owning one outright remained marginal.

By the 1880s and 1890s, a small skiff or rowboat might retail for about $15 to $35, or well over half of a workingman's monthly wages depending on the amount of decorative woods, finishes, and hardware desired. A fast sailing sloop could run from $800 to $1,500, a steam launch about $3,500. The 135-foot wooden steam yacht *Sigma*, built by John Craig of Trenton, cost owner Martin Smith about $45,000 when it was built in 1883.[12] An elegant steel steam yacht such as Merrill B. Mills's *Cynthia*, built in 1895 by the Detroit Boat Works at a cost of $70,000, represented the high end of recreational yachts built in the state in the late nineteenth century.

The Growth of Resorts

For a growing number of people in the middle class, the number of forms of recreation began to increase, and many found solace in the great outdoors. For decades businessmen traveled to the far reaches of the state and discovered the wonders of the natural environment. Looking for ways to merge their business with pleasure, they would frequently do a little exploring at nearby natural attractions and points of interest. Artists and writers soon followed, describing the beauties of their surroundings in widely read journals and books, which in turn led to further travel to the places mentioned.

As the cities grew and industries supporting them flourished, the desire to get away from the crowds and noise, the foul smoke of the factories, and disease in the big cities to a place of relaxation and quiet led to a seasonal migration to the great outdoors. Michigan offered scenic beauty, with beaches on the Great Lakes, quiet inland lakeshores, mountains in the Upper Peninsula, rivers and streams, and abundant opportunities for hiking, hunting, and fishing. Sailing ships, passenger steamers, and railroads conveyed the tourists to their destinations. The middle-class residents followed in the footsteps of the wealthy when they could. Working-class families forced to stay closer to home because of the costs of travel or lack of time found recreational resources nearby, such as picnic groves on a lakeshore, an island, or a park setting, appealing. A family outing to a nearby scenic location served as enough of a change of pace in the daily routine to make the experience valuable for a small sum of money.

By 1880 railroad trunk and connecting lines crisscrossed in a slowly sprawling web in the Lower Peninsula below a line connecting Saginaw and Ludington. Two railroads under construction raced northward to the Straits of Mackinac, the Grand Rapids & Indiana Railroad, known as "The Fishing Line," and the Michigan Central, both arriving at the Straits in 1881–82.[13] The Detroit & Mackinac, "The Turtle Line," traversed the Lake Huron shore by the mid-1890s. The now familiar patterns of Chicago area residents flooding northward in summer up the west shore and Ohio and Indiana residents joining Detroiters to head up the east and central routes by boat or train were well-established by the 1890s. As the railroads spread their steel tentacles across the state, they launched impressive marketing campaigns to encourage passenger traffic. In their literature they stressed the outstanding natural beauty of the region and the health benefits of visiting the resorts. The railroads connected with Great Lakes passenger steamer lines to help the travelers get to their preferred vacation spots.

In their symbiotic relationship, railroads, resorts, and boat builders all fed on the desire of the traveler to visit the great outdoors. The railroads needed new and larger markets to support their growing passenger traffic and complement their freight trade. The resort owners and developers provided the destinations for the railroads in the form of hotels and amusement parks, and the boat builders provided part of the entertainment needed to keep the tourists at the resorts by supplying watercraft for fishing, hunting, or pleasure boating. A leisurely day on a lake or river made for a good deal of repeat visitation, which in turn kept the resort owners and railroads in business.

The resorts provided boat builders with the opportunity to prosper in smaller communities. In many late nineteenth-century photographs showing a resort, one can see a small fleet of skiffs and sailboats tied to the dock, most presumably made by a local builder or purchased from one of the larger factories. Sometimes a builder would associate with a particular hotel or resort, either as the local boat livery operator or as the owner or manager of the resort who built boats during the off-season.

Gone Fishing and Hunting

The growing numbers of waterfowl hunters and sport fishermen gathering at the resorts and sportsmen's clubs along the Great Lakes, inland lakes, and rivers needed specialized watercraft for their particular interests, and a cottage industry grew to fill that need. Christopher Columbus Smith and his brother Henry Smith of Algonac worked as boat builders, fishing guides, and market hunters to serve the boating needs of the resorts along the lower St. Clair River, with Chris later settling down to operate a boathouse and livery.[14] Nate Quillen, a guide and boat builder at the Pointe Mouillee Shooting Club, built shallow draft punt boats and monitor boats for navigating the estuary waters of Lake Erie where the Huron River flows in. Guides used his long, narrow punt boats to set out the decoys and floating blinds and to assist the hunters in retrieving their catch. Quillen's monitor boats were custom made to the size and weight of the individual club members. He carefully selected tamarack stumps to carve into frames and clear white pine for planking his boats.[15]

Specialized boats for inland river fishing also emerged such as the Au Sable River boats, a type of guide boat indigenous to Michigan, used for trout fishing. A long, double-end drift boat with a rockered flat bottom, the boats are propelled by poles and the river current while chains of different weights are dragged behind the boat to control the speed. Thaddeus Norris described an early example in *Scribner's Monthly* in 1879:

The boat used on my first trip is worth description. It was built of white pine; bottom, 1 inch thick; sides, 5/8; 16 feet long, 2.10 wide on top, 2.4 at bottom, and with a sheer of three inches on each side. The bottom was nearly level for eight feet in the center, with a sheer of five inches to the bow and seven inches to stern. The live-box was six feet from bow, extending back two feet. The sides were nailed to the bottom. Its weight was eighty pounds, and it carried two men—the angler and the pusher—with 200 pounds of luggage. With two coats of paint it cost about fifteen dollars. The angler sits on the moveable cover of the live-box, which is water-tight from other portions of the boat, and has holes bored in sides and bottom to admit of the circulation of the water to keep the fish alive, and as he captures his fish he slips them into holes on the right and left sides. An ax was always taken along to clear the river of fallen logs and sweepers.[16]

One of the earlier known Au Sable boat builders, Edwin D. Alger, was born in 1830 in New York, the son of David Alger and Merilla Brown Alger. The family may have moved to Oakland County, at Algerville, now Holly, Michigan. During the Civil War, Alger served in the Twenty-Sixth Michigan Infantry. After his discharge from the army, he worked as a carpenter in Cohoctah. He moved north to Crawford County in 1881, living in the vicinity of Burton's Landing, building boats for fishermen and their guides.[17] He passed his knowledge on building the boats to Arthur E. Wakeley, who started building boats in about 1900. Alger moved to Bay City in 1908, where he died in 1914.[18] The Peter Stephan and Reuben Babbitt families built Au Sable boats for several generations in the Grayling area. These boats were often customized to the owner's individual taste with beautifully crafted decks and functional yet decorative elements such as rod holders. These unique boats are still produced to this day by several contemporary builders.

Folding and Collapsible Boats

Hunting and fishing also led to the growth of a regional center for the folding and collapsible boat industry in the Kalamazoo and Battle Creek area that lasted for close to a hundred years. Most of the activity took place in the late nineteenth and early twentieth centuries. The lightweight boats, made with a waterproofed canvas skin and a collapsible wooden frame stuffed into a box or bag, could be carried by packhorse along with camping gear to remote lakes or streams. While by no means a large industry, the folding canvas boats represent one of the first geographic concentrations in Michigan of a particular type of boat manufacturing. The knock-down boat industry in the Saginaw Valley and the building of mahogany-planked runabouts in the Detroit and St. Clair River districts constituted other concentrations in decades to come.

Nathaniel A. Osgood

A jeweler by trade in Battle Creek, Nathaniel A. Osgood must have appreciated the outdoor sporting life. He invented a folding canvas boat for hunting and fishing, patented on February 26, 1878. The canoe-style boat, a two-seat, 12-foot-long craft with oars located approximately amidships and ribs spaced approximately twelve inches apart, was made in four different weights depending on the user's needs. A version for trout fishing with stretcher, sideboards, and paddle weighed only twenty-five pounds, and the heaviest, a boat equipped with bottom board, sideboards, gunwale, stools, and oars, weighed fifty pounds. Jointed oars and paddles could be packed in a wooden chest with the boat. Osgood set up sewing machines in the back of his jewelry store to stitch the heavy canvas skins.[19]

By 1893 Osgood had sold the Osgood Portable Boat Company to Samuel A. Howes, who moved the company to his father's wholesale fruit and coal business on Canal Street. The Osgood Portable Boat Company was acquired and merged into the Michigan Consolidated Boat Company, Ltd., in 1903. Harry P. Lewis, himself of M. M. Lewis & Sons Company, general construction contractors and builders of both the Bullard steel and Osgood canvas boats, managed the firm.[20] The Michigan Consolidated Boat Company closed sometime after 1910.

King Folding Canvas Boat Company

A short distance away, in nearby Kalamazoo, Charles W. King developed a folding canvas boat of his own, obtaining the first of several patents for a sectional boat frame in 1882 and later ones for a portable boat. King started his business building the boats in about 1885, working out of his home on Rose Street. He eventually decided to get out of the business, selling out around 1898 to George Winans, a carriage manufacturer. Winans acquired

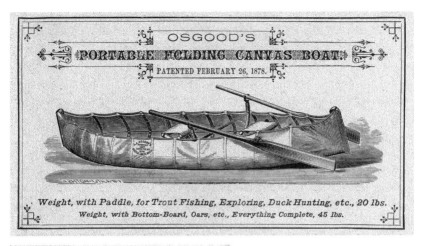

Boat Ready for Packing.

Fig. 3. Nathaniel A. Osgood patented a folding canvas boat in 1878 that could be carried in a box by hunters or fishermen to remote lakes and streams. Other builders in the Battle Creek and Kalamazoo area created similar collapsible boats to form the state's first boat-building niche industry. (Bentley Historical Library, University of Michigan.)

the patents and construction rights and began producing the boats, keeping the name as the King Folding Canvas Boat Company in Kalamazoo. Winans advertised the company widely in national periodicals such as *Recreation*, *Cosmopolitan*, and others with small runner ads. One early ad promoted three boats used by Lt. Frederick Schwatka for his exploration of the Yukon River in 1891. The Yukon gold rush of the late 1890s popularized the boats as easy-to-assemble, durable but lightweight craft that could provide ready transportation to the mining districts. The boat also received first-prize awards at the Columbian and St. Louis expositions in 1893 and 1904. The King Folding Canvas Boat Company employed ten men in 1898 at an average daily wage of $1.25. By 1905 the company's workforce consisted of five men and four women, with the women sewing the canvas hulls.[21] Winans married Pauline S. Peterson, and after his death in 1927 she managed the firm, renaming it the Kalamazoo Canvas Boat Company. The company survived under her guidance for decades afterward, lasting until the 1970s.

Life Saving Folding Canvas Boat Company

The Life Saving Folding Canvas Boat Company, one of the later short-lived folding boat manufacturers, was formed in 1903 and incorporated in Kalamazoo on September 6, 1906. The company built a boat patented by its founder, Ira O. Perring. The craft included air chambers at the bow and stern to keep it afloat even if it was full of water. Perring managed the company at first but was later replaced by John D. Schell, the secretary and treasurer.[22] The Life Saving Folding Canvas Boat Company tried hard to set itself apart in the small market, disparaging its unnamed competitors' faulty or inadequate designs and claiming its own as superior. Perring pointed out in the company's catalog some of the faults in the "old time ponderous canvas boats that required a guide to set up or knock down . . ." The catalog went on, "The inventor of our boat with his long experience in manufacturing and selling, thus being in a position to learn all the faults found with the old time boat, which was the bolted keel running through the center of the boat, rising 5 or 6 inches above the rest of the bottom, making the bottom of the boat very rough and unhandy, also the pounding out of bolts in a tensioned keel is very hard and difficult, and the loose bottom boards not having sufficient strength and firmness to give satisfaction to stand and shoot or cast from. Another great fault was the sorting out of cross ribs which made it very difficult in setting up the boat."[23] All the complaining turned out to be for naught as the Life Saving Folding Canvas Boat Company failed and forfeited its Michigan charter in 1912.[24]

Rowing and Yachting

Boat and yacht clubs sprang up around Michigan in the late nineteenth century, driven not only by an interest in competitive rowing and sailing but also out of the desire to create social organizations for people of common interests and economic status.

Membership in the yacht and boat clubs gave the builders links to potential new customers and often supplied them with the capital to demonstrate their talents when individual members or small groups wanted a fast boat. The competitive aspect of the clubs judged a boat's performance against that of others, as much testing the work of builder against builder as sailor against sailor. Word-of-mouth advertising of a builder's boats and their performance could reach all over the region. The mostly genial club atmosphere served as an important forum for presenting ideas about design and experimentation with hulls and rigging forms. Occasionally the debates pitted older traditions against new. Captain William J. Partridge, a member and boat builder with the Detroit Yacht Club, protested when the ideas seemed impractical. "Take those plans to a box factory; don't insult a boat builder by asking him to carry them out," he once commented.[25]

The sport of rowing began in Michigan in the late 1830s and eventually became an essential element in the formation of the boat-building industry in the state. The Detroit Boat Club achieved distinction as the oldest continually active boat club in the nation from the time of its formation in 1839 to the present day.[26] A reflection of the positive use of leisure time for the physical improvement of its participants, rowing on a competitive basis caught on gradually throughout the nation. Michigan's wide rivers and inland lakes made it a natural location for the sport to survive and prosper. Regattas pitted club against club in a rich tradition that carries on to this day. Several Michigan boat clubs achieved a bit of special fame in the late nineteenth century. The Sho-wae-cae-mette Boat Club crew of four from Monroe nearly won their event at the Henley Regatta in England in 1878 but failed when Joe Nadeau collapsed because of illness.[27] Periodic swells in the popularity of rowing, followed by dormant periods, marked the first half century of the sport. Twenty-one rowing clubs existed in Michigan in 1892, and a number of the early-twentieth-century boat builders in Michigan, such as Carl Schweikart of Detroit and Edward Bryan of Wyandotte,

discovered their interest in constructing watercraft while members of rowing crews for the clubs.[28] Lightweight rowing shells evolved, demanding
exceptional skill from the boat builder, who had to find the best compromise among minimal weight, structural integrity, and speed.

Competitive sail racing and steam yachting for leisurely cruising also
played a significant role in the growth of the boat-building industry.

Competitive sailing was well established and growing as an organized
sport in Michigan by the 1880s. Small groups of yachtsmen would bring
together sailboats of several different types, rigs, and lengths to compete in
any way that seemed fair, sometimes for simple prizes or money. While the
activity was still confined primarily to the larger Great Lakes port cities,
with their substantial rivers, and inland lake resort communities, the number of boat and yacht clubs statewide grew significantly between 1870 and
1895 to encompass over forty organizations of variable duration. By 1900
most yacht clubs had joined larger regional organizations, which provided
the competitive structures for racing with a myriad of rules that could assess one boat's success compared to another's on the basis of hull form and
sail area. In the Great Lakes, one of the largest such organizations was
the Inter-Lake Yachting Association, formed in 1895 for the purpose of
fostering yachting on the Detroit River, Lake St. Clair, and Lake Erie. On
the western side of the state, several clubs belonged to the Lake Michigan
Yachting Association.

As the racing game became more sophisticated, Michigan boat builders
competed, usually unsuccessfully, with East Coast builders to obtain contracts for racing yachts. Yachtsmen would often buy a used boat that had
been successful on the eastern racing circuit after a season or two and bring
it to the Great Lakes to clean up on the competition. Overall, however, the
local yacht and boat clubs provided important relationships between builders and owners that nurtured the infant recreational boat industry both ec-
onomically and socially in a way that no other form of organization could.

Marketing

In order to maintain a customer base or increase the size of the business,
boat builders needed to attract or retain a number of new or repeat customers seeking newer or larger boats. After the Civil War, boat builders
around the state began to advertise their profession and products. The first
to advertise were those builders in the cities who had access to newspapers and city directories. D. G. Cunningham of Detroit and Wilfred S.

Campbell of East Saginaw, among the earliest boat builders to advertise statewide, appeared in the *Michigan State Gazetteer and Business Directory* in 1860, followed by John Jenkins and David Perrault, both of Detroit, in 1863. In 1870, Alcott Caldwell of Grand Rapids and Elliott & Jacobs of Saugatuck started advertising statewide. One of the earlier Upper Peninsula boat builders, Louis Grenier, lived in Escanaba on Ludington Street in 1875.[29] Boat builders' advertisements frequently mixed with those of shipbuilders, especially in the earlier directories, as shipbuilders also built some smaller recreational craft. Moreover, most builders produced working craft such as yawl boats and rowboats for larger vessels. John Oades of Detroit, a well-known shipbuilder, also advertised as a boat builder in 1873. Oades had built rowing shells or barges while living in Clayton, New York, and continued to build small craft once he moved to Michigan.[30]

Print advertising passed through three gradual stages. Initially, most builders advertised in their local newspapers and city directories or the *Michigan State Gazetteer and Business Directory*. When national general-interest periodicals started accepting advertising and the press began focusing on outdoor interests with *Outing, Forest and Stream*, and other magazines, Michigan boat builders could get their products before the eyes of a much larger national audience. Catalogs offered in the advertisements in national periodicals could be purchased for the cost of postage or a small fee. Once the prospective customer saw something of interest in the magazine advertisement, he might then order the catalog for a more detailed examination of the builder's product line. Then as now, advertising subjects generally revolved around speed, quality of materials and craftsmanship, comfort, and safety. Having stock boats on hand and readily available also served as a selling point. In a third form, the gradual emergence of the regional and national yachting press with *The Rudder* after 1890, followed later by *Sail and Sweep* and *Fore N' Aft*, offered a better opportunity for builders to target their advertising to those who desired it most. Nathaniel Osgood advertised his portable canvas boat in the first issue of *The Rudder* in May 1890, as did Edgar Davis of the Davis Boat & Oar Company.[31]

Builders also took their boats to fairs and expositions as exhibits for additional exposure. James Dean & Company and the Davis Boat & Oar Company of Detroit exhibited their boats at the nearby Michigan State Fair. Davis Boat & Oar Company even set up a working exhibit at the Detroit International Exposition in 1892 with twenty men demonstrating their prowess in building rowboats, steam launches, and canoes from the keel up.[32]

Organizing the Businesses

Small Shop or Factory? Early Forms of the Business

What led a traditional builder to try to go the factory route? Boat builders in the late nineteenth century faced many choices about the direction
of their businesses, whether they remained in the small, traditional craft
workshop with a couple of helpers, custom building each boat, or con-
versely, designing identical boats according to a pattern and using factory-
type manufacturing processes to build them. Opportunities for starting a
factory abounded, including a growing number of customers and increasing
demand for boats, as demonstrated by the growth of the cities and resorts.
Michigan's many shipyards served as both customers for workboats and a
source of skilled labor with framing and woodworking skills. The state's
foundries and machine shops could likewise provide numerous varieties of
engines and boilers for steam launches along with hardware castings and
training for the machinists needed to operate the production equipment.
Access to a supply of capital came from wealthy lumber barons, industrial-
ists, professionals, and members of the wider business community who had
the available time and money to invest in a boat-building firm. Most were
located in the cities. Personal drive and ambition to create something big-
ger and better than the small shop, while intangible, played a significant
role in the growth of the factories. On the other hand, the disadvantages to
starting a factory would have included a relatively small marketplace, lack
of marketing capability, and inexperience in creating product designs that
lent themselves to standardization as opposed to handcraft and customization to fit the client's desires.

Well over half the boat builders in the state in the mid-1890s lived
in rural and small community settings where it would seem that the difficulty of finding capital to fund a factory operation and the lack of a
skilled labor force would essentially relegate them to the path of the small
traditional boat shop rather than the factory. To the contrary, the leading
counties in capital outlay for boat-building firms in the 1894 State Census were Charlevoix County, which led the state with $21,000 in capital
investment, followed by $11,000 in Ottawa County, $10,000 in Berrien
County, and $6,400 in St. Clair County, all mostly rural. Wayne County,
where Detroit is located, only had $1,200 in capital invested, and none
was listed for Kent County, where Grand Rapids is located.[33] While the

numbers may be skewed based on the locations of the twenty-one firms surveyed, or because the survey was conducted shortly after the financial Panic of 1893, the amounts are very different from what one would expect. Nonetheless, the pattern of small traditional-craft boat shops coexisting with small, medium, and large factories remains the norm to this day. Then as now, for every factory there are still a handful of small shops, often in the same communities, where men still make a good living building and selling custom-made boats for customers who want something slightly different.

Individual Craftsmen

The traditional individual boat builders, often located in a resort community, constructed complete boats on their own, usually without the assistance of a sailmaker or other tradesman. They worked directly with the customer/client, taking his rough ideas about a boat and creating a plan. With the eye of an artist and craftsman, they then built fine wooden boats harmonious in form and function, often with meticulous detailing and ingenuity, in what small craft historian Joseph Gribbins called "beauty and truth together."[34]

In many cases, the individual boat builders also operated boat liveries to help make ends meet. Boats rented to visitors desiring an enjoyable day of fishing or simply being out on the water rowing or paddling made up an important part of their income stream. The livery boats could be repaired and refinished during the long Michigan winters or new boats added to their fleets. Some builders diversified into other manual skills, doing blacksmithing, house carpentry, or cabinetry on the side.

Victor E. Montague

Boat builder Victor E. Montague of Traverse City represented the individual working in a resort community. He started working as a farmer with his father near Old Mission, building a boat for himself as a youth and a few for neighbors, but he did not start boat-building as an occupation until he was thirty-one, having moved from the farm to Traverse City in 1890. He developed a widespread clientele, building boats for C. W. Pierce, E. L. Springer, and Allen R. Bancroft of Chicago; William A. Greeson of Grand Rapids; Z. T. Aldridge of New York; and E. V. Reynolds of New Haven, Connecticut, as well as many local families in his surrounding area.[35]

Charles F. Plass

Charles F. Plass, an urban boat builder, was one of the young men who started rowing competitively and decided to go into boat-building after constructing one of the first racing shells in Detroit. Plass had been deaf since 1861, but he worked in Detroit as a boat builder as early as 1870 at the age of twenty-seven. He was born in Michigan and had a personal worth of $300, according to the 1870 U.S. Census. He worked in a shop on Atwater Street with his brother-in-law, saloonkeeper turned boat builder William J. Partridge. By 1879 he had moved to a shop at the foot of Chene Street.[36] In later years he moved around frequently, seeking work outside the city. which included building the steam yacht *Roberta* for Edwin R. Egnew at Mount Clemens in 1888.[37] In the mid-1890s, Plass worked at his craft at Orchard Lake in Oakland County where he built a number of sailboats for resort visitors and local yachtsmen, including a yacht named *Keewahdin*, known locally as the "Champion of Champions."[38] He died in 1917 in Detroit.

Small Shops

Many of the smaller boat-building shops and factories started out as partnerships. Usually these firms lasted a short time, with the individual partners breaking up and forming new partnerships with other builders or going out on their own. The shop would consist of a couple of men, sometimes as many as four or five, all still using basically traditional methods of construction with hand tools and turning out small numbers of boats each year.

Samuel E. Burnham and Frank L. P. Fish

Fish & Burnham represent the small, two-man, short-lived boat-building partnerships typical of the late nineteenth century in Michigan. Samuel E. Burnham, a wounded Civil War veteran originally from Maine, settled in the Saginaw area in the fall of 1865. He initially teamed up with Frank L. P. Fish in the Saginaw City Boat Company. The men split up after two years with Burnham subsequently working with Talbert Slenou but only for a short time, as Slenou decided to become a physician and went off to the University of Michigan to study medicine. Burnham moved to Bay City in 1881 and two years later to West Bay City where he worked on his own or with helpers on occasion. Like many boat builders, he operated a livery with twenty-five boats for pleasure seekers.[39] Frank L. P. Fish

Fig. 4. The Spring Lake Clinker Boat Manufacturing Company on Michigan's west side built rowboats in the 1890s in a board-and-batten shop with a clerestory for lighting. Access to rail transportation and the lakefront was important for deliveries of finished boats. (Tri-Cities Historical Museum, Grand Haven, Michigan.)

worked as a blacksmith in addition to boat-building. Fish also specialized in making tools for the local sawmills, salt blocks, and log booms such as peaveys, pike poles, poles for salt blocks, and parts for wagons. Later in his career, Fish operated a boat livery business and also a ferry between East Saginaw and Saginaw City employing several other family members to work for him. Both Fish and Burnham also catered specifically to the new rowing clubs and yacht club members, building rowing shells and crafting "spoon" oars.[40] Despite living in an urban area fueled by Michigan's lumbering boom, neither Fish nor Burnham saw fit to expand his operation into a large-scale factory. Burnham moved to Duluth, Minnesota, in 1894, operating a ferry and tending the harbor lights and buoys for the federal government.[41]

Spring Lake Clinker Boat Manufacturing Company

The Spring Lake Clinker Boat Manufacturing Company, another small shop, began in 1887 at Spring Lake in Ottawa County. The company produced a clinker-type (lapped planking) Whitehall-style rowboat designed by shipbuilder Harrison Pearsons. One of the earlier boat companies to incorporate in the state of Michigan, the company issued an annual report for 1889 with the amount of capital stock listed at $10,000, with $4,800 actually paid in. Credits of the corporation were listed at $1,901.64 and debts of $732.47. Principal stockholders in the firm included C. Alton Pearsons, son of the designer Harrison Pearsons; Cyril P. Brown; Frank C. Bury; and Herman F. Harbeck. Brown served as the company's president, Harbeck as secretary, and Bury as treasurer.

The future looked bright—the company expected to turn out one hundred boats in the 1891 season. In 1893 the company employed five men.[42] In 1895 William Barrett joined the company as vice president and manager. Although the Spring Lake Clinker Boat Manufacturing Company went out of business in 1903, Barrett took over the operation of the firm and renamed it Barrett Boat Works, which survives today as a marine services firm.

Early Factories

Most of the early boat factories started in the cities and small towns with substantial waterfronts, usually on a large river or lake and sometimes in close proximity to shipyards or boat clubs. To be successful, they needed a large potential market with a growing population, access to capital, and a talented or experienced work force. Setting up the factories required a great deal of organizing, from finding the capital and selecting the site to hiring the workers, purchasing production machinery and construction materials, and developing the marketing materials. Three Detroit area factories all started out in different ways, but they shared common successes with evidence of early marketing skills and a penchant for innovation. By the same token, each faced difficult problems such as fire, work force problems, and an economic downturn that forced their failure or hampered their business for a long time afterward.

James Dean & Company

James Dean and Alfred Seymour of James Dean & Company were longtime Detroit boat builders beginning about 1878 with their shop on Atwater Street close to the Detroit Dry Dock Company. Dean, the elder of the partners, was born in England on December 12, 1825, and had been in the boat-building business for thirty-eight years, most recently in a partnership with Peter Myers, as Dean & Myers, building catamarans.[43] Alfred Seymour was born in Canada in 1844 and began building boats around 1866. He had moved to the United States two years prior. James Dean &

Company was the largest firm of its kind in the city in 1880. It built one hundred boats annually, shipping about five a week, and made on average five hundred pairs of oars. The business had grown rapidly, increasing by an estimated 300 percent during the past year. The company operated in a large building fifty by eighty feet in size and regularly employed up to ten hands. Dean had added steam power to run the machinery in order to prepare for the anticipated increase of business.[44]

James Dean patented a diagonal-planked boat (U.S. Patent no. 249461) in 1881, which he submitted to the U.S. Life-Saving Service for potential use as a surfboat. His hull construction technique called for diagonal planking that used a water-resistant canvas lining between the planking layers.[45] Whether this served as the prototypical construction method for later Michigan builders using a similar fabric lining between the layers in the mahogany runabout era is debatable, but it illustrates one of the many innovative practices that professional builders of the day experimented with.

Advertisements in the 1881 and 1883 *Michigan State Gazetteer and Business Directory* stated that the firm kept yawl boats of all lengths on hand and built pleasure boats, barges, and sail and steam yachts to order. With the sport of rowing attracting interest in boating, James Dean & Company advertised that it had spoon-blade oars on hand. It also noted that repairs could be made promptly. R. L. Polk & Company for many years duplicated a lithographic cut of Dean's five-seat rowboat called the "Favorite" under other companies' advertising in the same periodical.[46] By 1883 the company was selling boats collectively worth nearly ten thousand dollars annually, including shipping a vessel's yawl boat to Baltimore among its many products.[47]

Most important, James Dean & Company served as a training ground for boat builders who later formed their own new businesses in the city. After a fire in 1884 destroyed its boat house, the partnership broke up a year later. Alfred Seymour left the firm in 1885 to become a principal of Granger, Seymour & Company and later manager and superintendent of the Detroit Boat Works.[48] John Bolio, another employee, would work for a number of Detroit firms over the span of his career.

In the late 1880s, James Dean & Company relocated to a shop on Selden Avenue building lifeboats, yawl boats, rowboats, sailboats, and steam and sail yachts. The firm also became agents for Woolsey's Patent Life Raft.[49] In March 1895, it employed five men, operating 60 hours per week with an average monthly payroll of $180. By the late 1890s, James Dean appeared to be working on his own, probably close to retirement, as the "and Company" had disappeared from the directory listings. He died August

8, 1905, in Detroit at the age of eighty, at a time of great change in the boat-building industry he had helped create. Reade Motor Boat Company acquired his shop at 381 Selden and continued operation.[50]

Detroit Boat Works

One of the larger and most intriguing boat-building firms in Michigan in the late nineteenth century, the Detroit Boat Works specialized in constructing steam yachts. A company that represented transition in many ways, it built literally everything from commercial passenger steamers to rowing shells for individuals. The company, originally formed by Neil McMillan and Alfred Seymour, formerly of Granger, Seymour & Company, was located at the corner of Guoin and Dequindre in Detroit in 1887. The company later relocated on Jefferson Avenue at the foot of Helen Avenue. McMillan served as secretary and treasurer and Seymour as manager and superintendent of the firm in 1889.[51]

The firm incorporated on April 21, 1890, with capital of twenty-five thousand dollars. Frank E. Kirby, consulting engineer of the Detroit Dry Dock Company and an extraordinary naval architect, served as president. Robert Lorimer was secretary and treasurer, Frederick A. Ballin was the general manager, and Alfred Seymour remained as superintendent. In an advertisement in the 1891 *Michigan State Gazetteer and Business Directory*, the Detroit Boat Works claimed to be "the largest manufacturer of all kinds of steam and sail yachts, launches, row, hunting and racing boats, canoes, etc." The company offered a catalog of its products for ten cents.[52] Kirby and his people designed and built steam yachts in both wooden and steel hulls for wealthy yachtsmen, as well as some smaller passenger steamers and commercial craft. In 1892 they built the 120-foot *Saucelito* for Mark Hopkins of St. Clair at the cost of twenty-five thousand dollars. The yacht could make an estimated sixteen miles per hour.[53] Other steam yachts included the *Princess*, built for O. W. Potter of Chicago; the *Helen* for Joseph L. Hudson, the department store founder; and the steel-hulled *Cynthia* for Merrill B. Mills.[54]

Kirby as an innovator took the company in several different directions in the early 1890s, which included building one of the earliest American internal combustion motorboats, Michigan's first submarine, and electric and steam launches for the 1893 Columbian Exposition. As early as July and August 1891, the company experimented with one of the earliest internal combustion engine launches with a gasoline or naphtha engine acquired from Clark Sintz of Springfield, Ohio, and later of Grand Rapids, Michigan. Testing took place on the Detroit River: "General Manager Ballin and Supt. Seymour took a short spin on the river yesterday afternoon with the little craft, and barring the fact that the engine rattles a good deal and that it needs regulating, it worked to a charm."[55] A foreshadowing of things to come, the motorboat would go on to change everything in the infant industry. One novel project, the construction and testing of George C. Baker's 46-foot cigar-shaped submarine, gained the firm national attention. Using the combination of an electric motor powered by a bank of batteries and a Willard steam engine for propulsion, Baker tested the craft in April 1892 in the River Rouge, submerging it completely on one trip for ten minutes.[56] He took the submarine to Chicago for further demonstrations and testing, competing with John Holland's *Fenian Ram* for the U.S. Navy's proposed submarine contract, but he died of appendicitis before the navy could make its decision. The navy awarded the contract to Holland in 1895.[57] The Detroit Boat Works built four electric launches under a contract with the Electric Launch and Navigation Company for the 1893 Columbian Exposition in Chicago for officials to use and a 36-foot steam launch for Captain Frederick M. Symonds, the man in charge of the Exposition's fleet of fifty-five electric launches traversing the Jackson Park lagoons.[58]

When the Michigan Bureau of Labor and Industrial Statistics inspected the company on November 6, 1893, the firm employed thirty-five males, one of whom was under the age of sixteen. Laborers typically worked a ten-hour day with a thirty-minute lunch break. Business picked up slightly after the financial Panic of 1893. By 1895 the company was running only part time on April 1 of that year, at about fifty-four hours per week, compared to sixty hours per week when running full time. The company had an average payroll of nineteen hundred dollars per month spread among fifty employees, which increased to eighty people when the firm was running full time.[59]

The Detroit Boat Works started to fall apart in the late 1890s. In 1898 Frederick Ballin, the firm's naval architect, moved to Portland, Oregon, with Charles A. Desmond replacing him as manager and designer. Alfred Seymour, the plant superintendent, disagreed with Michael and Neil Mc-Millan, complaining about Michael McMillan's advancement to the secretary position without having been voted in. McMillan also got the company involved in expensive lawsuits with Mark George Davis, an employee, which went all the way to the Michigan Supreme Court. Seymour left to go to work for Ora J. Mulford at the Michigan Yacht and Power Company, formed in late 1899. He forced the company into receivership in

Wayne County Circuit Court in 1901. The Detroit Trust Company sold off the company's assets at public auction on October 28, 1901, and the company was dissolved on May 19, 1902.[60] In its last year, the firm had over forty powerboats under construction and twenty more completed in stock, which would have made it one of the fastest-growing motorboat firms in the region had it survived.[61]

Davis Boat & Oar Company

Edgar A. Davis of Detroit was a young boat builder who decided to follow his passion for building boats and pursue the craft as a factory owner-operator, making the transition from his father's commercial fishing business. Davis used standardized designs, patterns, and machine tools to build large volumes of boats and mass-marketing techniques to advertise them. Born in Detroit on September 24, 1862, Davis was the son of fisherman Samuel Davis. His education in the Detroit public schools suffered because of his interest in boating. Davis penciled sketches of boats in his schoolbooks. He eventually dropped out of school at age fourteen, after his mother's death, to work as a sailor on the Great Lakes despite his father's efforts to keep him in school. After two years as a sailor, he joined his father in the fishing business. Davis worked in the fishery for eight years, the last four of which he managed his own boats and fishing operations. He sold out most of his fishery interest in 1885, although he maintained a small interest in it. The following year he started his boat-building business. On October 4, 1890, he incorporated the company and simplified the name of the firm from the Davis Boat and Oar Manufacturing Company to Davis Boat & Oar Company. Davis served as the firm's president and general manager while Charles S. Davis served as the secretary and treasurer. It was originally located at 12 and 14 Atwater East. Also in October 1890, Captain Edgar A. Davis was elected commodore of the Detroit River Rowing and Yachting Association. At some time prior to 1891, he reportedly controlled the pleasure boats at Belle Isle, "the largest boat station in the world, containing 250 boats," according to one biographical sketch.[62]

Like the Detroit Boat Works, Davis Boat & Oar Company made a wide variety of watercraft ranging from steam yachts to standardized 13-foot rowboats, all represented in a ninety-page catalog with thirty-two different models illustrated. Oliver M. Hepburn, a famous naval architect in Toledo, worked as the chief designer for the firm.[63] Davis moved the Davis Boat & Oar Company to an eight-acre site in Wyandotte in 1893, but he kept the sales office and showroom in Detroit. His plans presumably came crashing to a halt with the financial Panic of 1893. The company doubled its capital stock from thirty to sixty thousand dollars in January and had several large yachts under construction in April, including a 118-footer for Michael Cudahy of Chicago. The firm entered receivership in November 1893 when Cudahy's own company failed, as Detroit banks would not extend credit to the Davis firm because Cudahy's brother John was a vice president. Combined with a 75 percent drop in business, the effect was fatal. The factory appeared idle when inspected on November 21, 1893.[64] Undaunted, Davis helped launch a new venture with the formation of the Wyandotte Boat Company in 1894, this time with Davis as general manager instead of president. The Wyandotte Boat Company held on for nine years before ceasing business on February 28, 1903.[65] Edgar A. Davis got out of the boat-building business and returned to commercial fishing, taking over his father's interests as president of the Detroit Fish Company.[66]

Family Tradition or Apprenticeship

The acquisition and transfer of skills for construction and the business side of boat-building often took two forms, family tradition and the apprenticeship system. Fathers passing skills to their sons contributed to the development of some factories on the managerial level such as the Thomas H. Truscott & Sons Company. Hyacinthe Chenier of St. Ignace trained his son of the same name to build Mackinaw boats. Seth F. Mason likewise passed his skills to his son, Oscar Day Mason, in Charlevoix before the father drowned in a boating accident in 1870.[67] The John Bross family in Dexter remained in the boat-building business for a couple of generations, as did Joseph Pouliot and his son Russell in Detroit. The relationship between ship carpentry and boat-building shows up occasionally between the generations since the older men tended to start as ship carpenters and move into the less physically demanding work of boat-building in their later years.

Michigan's strong craft tradition, in which a worker could learn a trade as an apprentice and work his way up to journeyman and master craftsman, was carried on in small shops as well as early factories. The apprentice system, feasible in the communities large enough to support multiple builders, seems to have been especially strong among boat builders in Detroit and Grand Rapids. A group of unidentified Detroit boat builders responding to a Michigan Bureau of Labor and Industrial Statistics questionnaire regarding wages in 1885 reported the wages paid and the ratio of apprentices to journeymen and masters (table 1). The very clear order of the wages probably reflects the seniority and presumably the skill levels of the employees and distinguishes approximately the wage level at which an apprentice became a journeyman.

Working in the factories still included a great deal of hand cutting and shaping of wooden pieces before fitting them together, again by hand. Steam engines powered band saws, planers, and other mechanically operated woodworking equipment in only about one-third of the boat-building shops and factories in 1884. According to the State Census of 1884, only six factories out of the eighteen surveyed used steam power with a total of 115 horsepower in use statewide. By the mid-1890s, steam power was being used in half the shops, and the other half were driven by water, wind, horse, or treadle-type foot power. State census data for 1894 stated that of the twenty-one boat-building establishments surveyed, ten operated steam-powered equipment with a total of 153 horsepower statewide, one used water-powered equipment of 20 horsepower, and nine used horse, hand, or wind power.[68]

Invention and Innovation

Patents can be looked at as one measure of the creative life of an industry. Invention, with all of its trials and tribulations, leads to advancement in a business. Michigan inventors received a very small number of the overall bulk of patents issued under the classification of boats, although many filed and received patents for boat equipment such as rowlocks, footrests, and other devices. The patent improvements to hull forms mostly dealt with

Table 1. Boat builders in Detroit

Daily wages	
Apprentices	Boat builders
2 at $1.00	2 at $2.50
3 at $.75	2 at $2.25
4 at $.50	2 at $1.50
Average daily wage	
$.69+	$2.08+

Michigan, Bureau of Labor and Industrial Statistics, *Second Annual Report of the Bureau of Labor and Industrial Statistics, February 1, 1885* (Lansing: Bureau of Labor and Industrial Statistics, 1885), table 148, 282, 317.

the elimination of caulking, a continual maintenance job in wooden boats, or eliminating the typical rib structure. A surprisingly large number of the boat patents were for lifeboats, perhaps attributed to the large numbers of shipwrecks in the area or the possibilities of widespread adoption of a design. Robert Dimond Mayo, a former U.S. Life-Saving Service surf man who lived variably in Grand Rapids and Frankfort, received several patents for a rolling lifeboat with a double-cylinder design of one cylinder rotating inside another. He tested a prototype of the device on the beach at Muskegon and advertised it for a short time under the auspices of the Rescue Life Boat Company.[69] Only a handful of the patents issued were to professional boat builders such as James Dean of Detroit. The rest of the inventors made their livings in other trades or professions, and their ideas often reflected the naïveté of people who do not make their livings building small craft. The bicycling craze of the 1890s inspired Edwin Verburg of Grand Rapids to patent a bicycle-powered boat as an alternative form of propulsion in 1898, an idea that achieved success only much later.[70]

Conclusion

By the mid-1890s, Michigan's boat builders stood poised at the beginning of a great revolution in motive power that would dramatically change their profession in ways no one could foretell. As daily wages increased and leisure time became more generally available, the customer base for recreational boating grew larger. The social structures necessary for boating to grow, leisure activities such as hunting and fishing or organized aquatic competitive sports, steadily passed through their formative period in Michigan. By the mid-1890s the yacht and rowing clubs and vacation resorts were well established and developing rapidly.

Even though boats would become more readily available, their high cost made ownership unobtainable for most ordinary workers, relegating them to the wealthy only. Boats would continue to be produced in relatively small numbers by individuals in a traditional manner with careful handcraftsmanship and attention to detail. Traditional boats distinctive to the Great Lakes and Michigan's inland waterways, such as the Mackinaw boats and Au Sable River boats, matured in their forms and, in the case of the Mackinaw boats, reached their zenith by the end of this era. At the same time, and even in the same cities, rudimentary factories with systems for manufacturing boats with standardized hull designs began to flourish.

CHAPTER TWO

Experiments, 1895–1905

Introduction

Boat-building in Michigan rapidly transformed from a small, workshop-based industry into a nationally significant, factory-based industry between about 1895 and 1905, mostly because of the development of the internal combustion engine. While the transition occurred rapidly over the course of a little more than a decade, it was not uniform across the whole industry but rather sporadic geographically and chronologically. The change was largely due to the pioneering work of a few creative designers and engineers operating independently. Many of their earliest efforts more often resulted in failure than success.

Flashes of marine gasoline engine-building innovation showed up all over the world prior to 1895, with most of the development taking place in Europe. The American marine gasoline engine industry had its roots in 1884 with the work of Daniel S. Regan in San Francisco, preceded more than two decades earlier by that of Jean-Joseph Etienne Lenoir, Nikolaus Otto, Gottlieb Daimler, and Wilhelm Maybach in Europe. Stan Grayson, a marine engine historian, establishes the pioneer period as being 1884 through 1898, with the first production period following from 1899 to 1912.[1] While it is not the purpose of this work to recount the early development of the marine gasoline engine, a look at a few early Michigan inventors is helpful to understanding the growth of the boat-building industry within its statewide context.

Commodore Otto F. Barthel, an attorney and Detroit yachtsman, commenting on the growth of motor boating in 1905, noted that the first powerboats on the Great Lakes were exhibited at the Detroit International

Fair and Exposition in 1892 by the Davis Boat & Oar Company, consisting of a 22- or 25-foot open boat equipped with a Monitor engine, complete, for six to seven hundred dollars. By 1905 the same boat could be bought for two to three hundred. A 16-foot rowboat with a 1-1/2 to 2-horsepower motor could be purchased for the remarkably low price of one hundred dollars, while the engine alone, complete with batteries, switch, propeller, and shaft could be had for forty-nine.[2] While he might have been off on the earliest starting date, or even the engine builder, the question remains, what made this cost transformation possible? Strong competition between boat builders and engine suppliers, combined with a tremendously growing demand for the new boats led to improved methods for delivering the wide range of new motorized products.

Marine gasoline engines offered convenience and immediacy of the experience over the operation of steam launches. With a steam launch, one had to be patient before starting out on an excursion. The operator had to get the fire in the boiler going, then wait until steam pressure built up to a sufficient level to provide power for the engine before starting out. Noisy and dirty with coal dust, smokestack soot, and escaping steam, the ride could sometimes be less than pleasurable. The machinery alone could take up to one-third of the space in a small boat, and when coal was added, little room was left for passengers. Steam launches could be expensive to operate, as a 30-foot launch could burn half a ton of coal on a 100-mile trip. Steam yachts and launches were required by law to have a licensed engineer to operate them, and mandatory inspections of the machinery were demanded by the Steamboat Inspection Service. An owner could get a gasoline engine started almost immediately and head off on his outing. Early gasoline engines, despite being heavy and large, slow in overall speed, and occasionally difficult to start, with temperamental ignition systems, still offered the owner or operator a better, more cost-efficient propulsion alternative.[3] Early gasoline engine advertising for the Truscott Boat Manufacturing Company in 1898 pointedly proclaimed the differences between its product and the steam launch: "No Fire, Smoke or Heat. Absolutely Safe."[4]

The new owners of powerboats must have had more than their share of accidents, such as damage from fires and engine backfires, loss of control from errant use of power, or more design-related problems caused by leakage from vibration and the use of propellers of improper size for the engine to which they were connected. Add poor quality fuel and poor carburetor adjustment to the mix and it could make the planned river or lake excursion into a veritable nightmare of grease and oil on clothing, worn-out muscles

Fig. 5. Steam launches took a long time to raise steam to prepare for an outing such as this one by a waterfowling party. The supply of coal needed often left little room for the occupants, and it sometimes covered them with soot or dust. By law, steam launches required a licensed engineer to operate them. Marine gasoline engines could be started readily, and no engineer was needed. (Michigan Historical Museum.)

and back strain from trying to start the engine, and frustration and anger on the part of the owner toward the engine manufacturer. Reliability and dependability came in time, but the early years of marine gasoline engines came at a high cost in operational satisfaction. Early powerboat owners had to be mechanical tinkerers—grinding the carbon out of valves, changing the oil, and fussing with the adjustable carburetor and ignition parts were an essential part of the new powerboat-owning experience, as well as the regular hull maintenance of painting, varnishing, and caulking.

The two hotbeds of invention in Michigan for marine engine building consisted of Grand Rapids on the west side of the state in the mid-1890s and Detroit on the east side by the late 1890s. As demand for motorized watercraft grew, machine shops and foundries throughout the state responded by building engines on their own, sometimes infringing on the patents of pioneering inventors in the process.

The Grand Rapids Builders

Grand Rapids could have become a large boat- and engine-building capital in the early twentieth century if only the principal innovators had stayed in town. The city was blessed with an abundant supply of capital generated from lumbering and the mass production of furniture, and it had a number of machine shops and foundries for carrying on the work that would be needed for the boat-building industry. Instead, the city served as the starting point for some of the largest and most diverse boat businesses in the state but gradually lost them when they were acquired and moved to Detroit or other regions of the country.

Clark Sintz and the Sintz Gas Engine Company

Clark Sintz is best known as the creator of the two-cycle gasoline engine and was the first one to succeed commercially, at least in the short term, in the gasoline engine business. Overwhelmed by patent infringements and poorly timed business decisions, his story turned out to be a tragically common one, but his inventive mind gave motorized transportation an important boosting step.

Sintz was born in Springfield, Ohio, in about 1850, the son of Peter Sintz, a gristmill and sawmill owner. Mechanically inclined, he became interested in steam engines as a youth, learning from steam engine mechanics and blacksmiths in machine shops. Sintz built a tiny engine using the barrel of an old black-powder pistol when he was twelve. At age eighteen, he started building his own full-size steam engine. At the Philadelphia Centennial Exposition in 1876, he saw an early internal combustion gasoline engine built by Nikolaus Otto, which changed his life. Because Otto had a patent on the four-cycle concept (intake, compression, combustion/explosion, exhaust), Sintz began to experiment with the idea of a two-cycle type, and by 1884, according to his own recollection, had built his own marine gasoline engine with a horizontal cylinder. Sintz received U.S. Patent 339,225, for a "Gas Engine" on April 6, 1886.

The earliest report of a boat with an internal combustion engine in Michigan describes Clark Sintz testing his engine on the Detroit River in 1884. In Sintz's own account, written in a brief article published in *Power Boating* in 1914, he stated, "My first gasoline engine for marine work was made in Springfield, Ohio, in the year 1884, and tested on the Detroit River. It was of the horizontal type, two-cycle, with compound trunk piston expanding to twice the original volume. The crankshaft was vertical and the flywheel [was] on the lower end of the shaft." The engine was installed in a 25-foot boat with a 5-foot beam and turned an 18-inch two-blade propeller.[5] Sintz's son placed the event in 1887. A similar account appeared in the *Detroit Free Press* on August 11, 1891, which described Sintz testing a two-cylinder engine purchased by the Detroit Boat Works for use in a 30-foot launch. The article states, "It is the invention of Clark Sintz, of Springfield, O., and although patented in 1877 has never before been tried as a marine engine until this year," so either the Detroit River may have been a popular place for him to try his invention or he was grossly wrong on the date of the testing.[6] Although no details of the earlier test seem to exist, Sintz continued experimenting on both stationary and marine gasoline engines in Springfield throughout the late 1880s.

Sintz temporarily allied himself with John Foos, a Springfield businessman, along with Phineas P. Mast, a windmill manufacturer, in 1888, and established the Gas Engine Company, but he quickly left the venture and organized the Sintz Gas Engine Company in Springfield in 1890.[7] In the next couple of years, he improved his engine design and began marketing and manufacturing it as a marine engine. By November 1891, he was advertising the device in *Scientific American*.[8] He moved the company to Grand Rapids, Michigan, and incorporated it as the Sintz Gas Engine Company on December 21, 1892, joined by Addison A. Barber, Henry A. Winter, and Fred D. Hills as stockholders.[9] Sintz's sons Guy and Claude worked with him in the business, learning the trade that they would take up later in their lives. Addison A. Barber, a local furniture manufacturer, purchased a Sintz engine with a 5-inch bore and 6-inch stroke. He urged Sintz to move the company to Grand Rapids where he subsequently became its treasurer and manager. The city made a good fit for his business. The furniture industry was going strong, and capital was abundant. Nearby machine shops provided a talented labor pool, and the Grand River running through the city proved to be a good place to test the engines in boats. Sintz had developed his two-stroke, three-port engine, with an electrical make-and-break ignition system, receiving U.S. Patent 509,255 on November 21, 1893. On September 26, 1893, when the company was inspected by a State of Michigan factory inspector, the firm employed fifty men and one woman, building both gasoline engines and boats.[10]

Clark Sintz found a great opportunity to exhibit his engine at the Columbian Exposition in Chicago in 1893. He arranged to show the engine in two venues, one in an exhibit with a launch named *Dainty* and the second a working model of a 14-foot yacht tender or launch built by the Truscott Boat Manufacturing Company and operating in the lagoon. The exposition's twenty-five million visitors added a tremendous amount of visibility for the firm, and an article in *Scientific American* about the engine as represented at the exposition brought it to a huge national and international

Fig. 6. Clark Sintz, creator of the two-cycle gasoline engine, in 1892. Sintz played a leading role in early marine gasoline engine production in Michigan with the Sintz Gas Engine Company of Grand Rapids and subsequently the Wolverine Motor Works. (Courtesy of Robert Sintz.)

audience. The placement at the exposition would have far-reaching consequences, as hundreds of other inventors saw the Sintz engine and were inspired to buy one or build their own.

Sintz sold his interest in the Sintz Gas Engine Company, and he and his sons decided to go their own way, forming the Wolverine Motor Works, competing directly against his former firm in the same city.

On February 4, 1902, the company changed its name to the Sintz Gas Engine Company of Detroit, Wayne County; changed its incorporation to that city; and merged with the Michigan Yacht & Power Company, formed in 1899 by Ora J. Mulford. The Sintz Gas Engine Company of Detroit, Michigan, filed notice of its dissolution on May 8, 1905.[11]

Wolverine Motor Works

Clark Sintz's second effort at marine engine manufacturing, the Wolverine Motor Works, became one of the best-known names in the early twentieth century for marine engines. Started in Grand Rapids after Sintz sold his interest in the company of his own name, Clark Sintz and his son Claude worked on improvements to his engines, forming the company while Claude was still a teenager. Claude filed for a patent in December 1894, and the company was in business the following year. Wolverine Motor Works was incorporated a few years later on January 21, 1899.

Rugged and dependable, Wolverine engines powered larger launches and could be started using a reverse lever. Like the Sintz Gas Engine Company before it, Wolverine Motor Works was primarily a builder of marine engines, but it also constructed boats for its engines, employing builders such as Charles L. Greene.[12]

Wolverine Motor Works also opened a plant in Holland, Michigan, in 1900, where it built boats. It might have intended to build engines there as well, but it is unclear if it ever did. The president and treasurer of the firm in 1901 was Charles L. Snyder, with A. C. Denison serving as vice president and Claude Sintz as secretary. Again, leaning more toward invention than the operation of the firm, Clark Sintz sold his interest in the Wolverine Motor Works to Charles L. Snyder by 1901 or 1902, with Snyder subsequently serving as president and treasurer and Louis I. Snyder as vice president and secretary. The Snyders were heavily involved in the formation of the United Fruit Company, and Charles Snyder had purchased some Sintz engines earlier to power small banana boats.[13]

An advertisement in the 1903 *Michigan State Gazetteer and Business Directory* stated, "Wolverine Gasoline Marine Engines and Launches [illustration of a canopied launch]. The 'Wolverine' is the only Reversing and Self-Starting Gasoline Engine on the Market. Lightest Engine for the Power Built. Practically no vibration. Absolutely safe. Single, double and triple marine and stationary motors from 2 to 85 H.P. Write for Catalogue. Wolverine Motor Works, 128 S. Front Street, Grand Rapids, Mich." The officers remained the same in 1903, with the addition of George E. Clark as superintendent of the plant at Holland. Clark was previously an independent boat builder in Holland in the late 1890s. The company built eleven launches in 1905, valued at fourteen thousand dollars.[14]

Later, in 1906, Snyder moved the Wolverine Motor Works to a new plant in Bridgeport, Connecticut, where it remained a prominent engine manufacturer into the post–World War II era. Grand Rapids had lost another marine engine manufacturer, this time to a different part of the country.

After the sale of Wolverine, Clark Sintz spent two years in Panama working for the United Fruit Company. Returning to Michigan, he and his sons invented an automobile and started Claude Sintz, Inc., to build them. The venture failed after building only about six automobiles, closing in 1904. Clark Sintz continued to invent parts for automobiles, such as a hydraulic transmission and floatless carburetor for the Ford Model T. He died after being struck by an automobile in Bay St. Louis, Mississippi, in July 1922. Both sons went on to become successful marine engine manufacturers, Claude with the Sintz-Wallin Company in Grand Rapids and Guy with the Guy L. Sintz Company in Marshall, Michigan.[15]

Monitor Vapor Engine and Power Company

Of the combined boat-and-engine-building firms that emerged in Michigan in the 1890s, one that had a great deal of potential but failed to live up to its promise was the Monitor Vapor Engine and Power Company. Well capitalized and led by an experienced group of managers, the company started off strong, but like the other early Grand Rapids engine manufacturers, it found another home elsewhere.

The Monitor Vapor Engine and Power Company was incorporated on October 15, 1894, at Grand Rapids to build boats and two-cycle gasoline engines under the Monitor and Mogul brand names. It was considered one of the pioneering businesses in what later became the marine engine industry. Officers of the firm included Thomas Stewart White, president of the White & Friant Lumber Co., as the company's president; William S. McCay, president of the Union Foundry Co. and W. S. McCay & Co., as the vice-president; and George H. Gere, a manufacturer's agent, as secretary and treasurer. Of the three men on the management team, Gere was probably the one most involved in the building of boats. He later went on to become a yacht builder at Reed's Lake in East Grand Rapids and patented a combustible-vapor engine of his own design in 1898.

The company initially offered a 16-foot launch with a 3/4-horsepower engine and advertised launches from 16 to 40 feet long with engines from 3/4 to 10 horsepower to propel them. One of its boats was a two-piece sectional that was bolted together. The engines had a tall exhaust stack similar to the naphtha engines of the time, perhaps to visually assure new owners that the gasoline engine was a proven technology.[16]

A year later, in 1896, Thomas White left the firm and William McCay assumed the presidency. Maurice Shanahan, treasurer of the Bissell Carpet Sweeper Company, became vice president of the firm, filling McCay's former position. The company also added a sales office at No. 2 Sunny

Side Drive in Ludlow Station, New York, a Yonkers post office, to generate interest in its products on the East Coast.

When the Michigan Bureau of Labor and Industrial Statistics inspected the company's factory, located at 6–8 Erie Street, in January 1896, the firm employed eight males and one female and had an average monthly payroll of $835. At the time, the company was growing fast. A year later, in the 1897 inspection, the factory employed twenty-three men and one woman and had an average monthly payroll of $1,145.

Among the employees were Philip Hain and Ralph B. Hain. Philip was a carpenter for the firm, possibly working on the boats, and Ralph was a mechanical engineer and later superintendent of the firm. Ralph Hain was the engine developer, having invented a combustible-vapor engine patented in 1894. Another patent awarded to him for a multiple-cylinder vapor engine in 1898 was assigned to Monitor.

Because of its growth, Monitor may have become an acquisition target. The company was sold in 1900 to the Automobile Company of America, which controlled about forty patents on gasoline engines, propellers, and other equipment. The company intended to build a large factory on the Hackensack River in New Jersey. George Gere moved the enterprise to Newark, New Jersey, and began building knockdown boat frames and completed boats under the Monitor name. The Monitor Vapor Engine and Power Company filed notice of its dissolution on December 5, 1903.[17]

What the Sintz family, George Gere, the Hain brothers, and all of their business partners could not do was keep the marine gasoline engine businesses growing in Grand Rapids. Other engine builders would come and go in the city, but never again would it have the opportunities it had in the earliest years of motorboating. The work of the early pioneers was not totally in vain as it spread their mechanical art and design to a wider national panorama of marine engine manufacturing and boat-building.

Detroit Area Builders

Unlike the Grand Rapids story of early marine gasoline engine innovators, Detroit was an accumulator city for gasoline engine manufacturers and boat-building firms, collecting expertise from other cities in the state but also cultivating and nurturing its own homegrown talent. The city had a long tradition of building foundry-based items, particularly railroad cars and cast-iron stoves, and numerous machine shops and steam engine builders had created the foundation for the forthcoming explosion in marine gasoline engines and the matching demand for boat hulls to put them in. With the plethora of partnerships, mergers, and breakups that marked the beginning of the early auto industry, growing up side by side with the marine engine building that in essence slightly preceded it, Detroit was a place that was on the move for motoring, be it on the water or on land.

Charles Brady King

Charles Brady King made a great effort to develop internal combustion engines for boats. Had not the Spanish-American War interfered with his plans, he might have been the nationally recognized pioneer of the boat-building industry. Instead, he became best known for his automotive work.

Of the millions of people who visited the Columbian Exposition in Chicago, another young inventor, Charles Brady King of Detroit, picked up a number of good ideas while working there. King studied mechanical engineering at Cornell University in 1887, but was forced to leave the following year after his father died. Returning to his home in Detroit, he began working for the Michigan Car Company as a draftsman. In 1890 he invented a pneumatic hammer used for riveting and caulking in shipyards.

King also created a brake beam for railroad cars. Russel Wheel & Foundry Company, owned by his cousins George and Walter Russel, sent him to the Columbian Exposition to take charge of its exhibits in the Transportation Building, where he had the opportunity to study a multitude of engineering displays. While there he closely examined the Sintz gasoline engine and later ordered one for himself to power a motorized tricycle he had designed. King became dissatisfied with the Sintz engine and started to design his own two-cycle, two-cylinder engine. By 1894 he had concluded through further experimentation that a four-cycle engine would be more practical.[18] He organized the Charles B. King Company in 1894 at 112–114 St. Antoine Street in Detroit to manufacture pneumatic hammers and marine engines, selling his brake beam patent to the American Brake Beam Company of Chicago to finance his new venture. In 1895 he created a four-cycle, four-cylinder gasoline engine based on measurements taken from a Herreshoff marine steam engine.

King became better known as the builder and driver of the first automobile to run on the streets of Detroit on March 6, 1896. This event marked the starting point for the growth of the auto industry in the city. The Charles B. King Company was reorganized with John S. Newberry and Henry B. Joy a year later. The company focused on two-cylinder

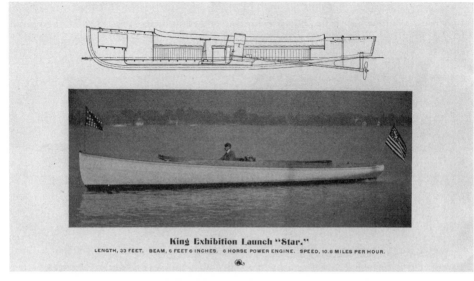

King Exhibition Launch "Star."
LENGTH, 33 FEET.   BEAM, 6 FEET 6 INCHES.   6 HORSE POWER ENGINE.   SPEED, 10.6 MILES PER HOUR.

Fig. 7. Charles Brady King of Detroit tested his early four-stroke gasoline engine in the launch *Star* in 1898, leading to the growth of the powerboat industry in Michigan. Clark Sintz, George H. Gere, and Thomas Truscott all developed gasoline engines on the west side of the state around the same time. (Courtesy of Robert B. Price.)

marine engines and, in 1898, issued a catalog for them, complete with photos of its demonstration launch, *Star*.

Heading off to serve the nation during the Spanish-American War, King temporarily gave up working on the engine but returned to work on it afterward. A boat he was building for a Boston owner, the *Lady Frances* (U.S. Official no. 141654) was left to be finished by the Vernon Company of Detroit, a carpentry contractor located near the water.[19] King returned to Detroit and started work on a new engine with overhead valves activated by rocker arms and an aluminum crankcase, but he never completed it, much to his regret in later years. In 1900 he sold the King engine business to the Olds Motor Works, builders of the first mass-produced automobiles in the United States, and joined them as the superintendent of their marine engine division. After a fire destroyed its Detroit factory, Olds sold the marine engine business to the new Michigan Yacht & Power Company, and King joined that firm as its mechanical superintendent. He stayed with Michigan Yacht & Power until August 1903, when he left to design automobiles for the Northern Manufacturing Company. King became a well-known automobile manufacturer in the city, lending his name to the King Motor Car Company, but he was better known for his work on the Northern and Maxwell automobiles.[20]

Michigan Yacht & Power Company

The Michigan Yacht & Power Company of Detroit was a short-lived boat-building firm at the turn of the twentieth century, yet it was significant in that it brought together the two leading marine gasoline engine types, four-cycle and two-cycle, developed by two different inventors. Attempting to cover all the bases with an emerging new technology when no apparent winner was evident at this stage, the firm brought together the design work of Clark Sintz and Charles Brady King, Sintz with the two-cycle engine, and King with the four-cycle.

The company had a confusing and tumultuous beginning. The business was first incorporated on January 3, 1900, at Detroit, for the purpose of building gasoline launches and other boats. Olds Motor Works purchased Michigan Yacht & Power from Charles Brady King in February 1900, only a month after its creation.[21] The company was reincorporated on November 1, 1900. Officers in the firm were Ora J. Mulford as president and general manager, William A. Pungs as vice president and treasurer, and John C. Mulford as secretary. Pungs was the majority stockholder with 1,500 shares, followed by Ora Mulford with 1,480, John Mulford with 10, and W. A. Stock with 10.[22]

Ora J. Mulford had made his fortune in the streetcar advertising business, at first in Los Angeles and later in Detroit with the Michigan Street Car Advertising Company. He became sales agent for the Sintz Gas Engine Company and when the Sintz firm could not supply enough engines to meet the demand, he purchased the company and moved it to Detroit. William A. Pungs was born in Germany and came to America in 1852. He started working in the railroad supply business and later founded the Anderson Carriage Company. Pungs was president of the Central Savings Bank between 1898 and 1900. Both Ora Mulford and William Pungs were active yachtsmen in Detroit.[23]

For the boat-building side of the Michigan Yacht & Power Company, Mulford hired Alfred Seymour away from the Detroit Boat Works. Seymour became irritated with the way Michael and Neil McMillan and Frank Kirby were running the Detroit Boat Works and filed suit to force his former firm into receivership. The two firms had been competing strongly in the market for smaller launches. Seymour's long experience in boat-building attracted workers such as John Bolio and others to follow him to the new firm.[24]

In the spring of 1901, Olds Motor Works sold the Michigan Yacht & Power Company because Olds needed to raise capital quickly after a disastrous fire at its Detroit factory in March 1901, unfortunately just as the Curved-Dash Olds runabout automobile was gaining in popularity.[25] The firm's Jefferson Avenue plant, when running at full capacity, employed up to sixty people. When State of Michigan factory inspectors visited the plant in 1900, it had twenty-five employees working ten-hour days at an average daily wage of two dollars. Like many industries, the company employed a few youths to perform menial tasks. The plant typically operated twenty-six days per month but for only an average of seven months out of the year.[26]

Alfred Seymour designed several of the Michigan Yacht & Power Company's craft, including the *Wilanna* (U.S. Official no. 81831), a twin-screw, 68-foot motor yacht built in 1902, and the *Lotus* (U.S. Official no. 141849), a 76-foot motor yacht built in 1903. George "Kid" Wilds designed the *Detroit*, a 47-foot trunk cabin racing sloop built to challenge for the Canada's Cup in 1902. Sometimes the firm worked very closely with the owner on the boat's design. Walter S. Russel, Charles Brady King's cousin, reportedly designed and owned *Fleur de Lis*, a 35-foot motor launch built by the company in 1903.

For power plants, the company built the King-designed four-stroke, two-cylinder engine for *Bab*, launched in 1900. The same year it installed a triple-expansion, three-cylinder steam power plant in *Mohawk*, thereby working with both gasoline and steam engine designs as the market demanded.[27]

The Michigan Yacht & Power Company had merged with Sintz Gas Engine Company by 1902, with advertising listing both firms for a while. By 1905 the firm was merged yet again to form the Pungs-Finch Auto and Gas Engine Company, which Pungs created with his son-in-law Edward Finch and others, to build automobiles and gasoline engines.

The Michigan Yacht & Power Company filed notice of its dissolution on January 11, 1904.[28]

Mulford subsequently became president of the Gray Motor Company, working his advertising magic to make it one of the world's largest marine engine manufacturers. Pungs retired from the boat and automobile industry after the Pungs-Finch Auto and Gas Engine Company failed.

Automobile pioneers Ransom Eli Olds and David Dunbar Buick, while both better known for their work on early horseless carriages, built some of the earlier marine gasoline engines. Olds built some of his gasoline engines at P. F. Olds & Son in Lansing to power launches, according to the *Scientific American* of March 14, 1896. In May 1901, *Rudder* described Olds marine engines as having 30 percent more power than their specified rating, with their exceptionally large cylinders, and observed that the designers were recording a most efficient type of propeller to use in a race given the lines and general dimensions of the boat.[29] First operating in Lansing, then Detroit, and eventually returning to Lansing after its Detroit plant burned, Olds's marine engine work helped build the reputation for reliability that the concurrently built Curved-Dash Olds automobiles thrived on.

Likewise, David Buick started building gasoline engines by the mid-1890s and later collaborated with Walter L. Marr. Buick, an avid sailboat yachtsman, sold a 20-foot gasoline launch with a 3-horsepower engine to Albert Stegmeyer, a fellow Detroiter, in 1898, which turned out to have a more reliable engine than most. Two years later, when Stegmeyer approached the Buick Manufacturing Company about building a 30-footer, he stated, "I wish to say right here that I consider your gasoline engine the best there is on the Detroit River . . . Whenever you go down to the livery [Stegmeyer converted his former bathhouse into a gasoline launch livery] you will see several owners of the different boats fixing up their engines, and it seems that there is always something the matter with them. For your benefit I would say that I have had absolutely no trouble at all with my engine, except putting on a larger wheel, as the engine was too powerful for the wheel that originally came with the boat."[30] Buick transferred his interest in marine engines to those used to power an automobile, and soon the brand became famous, obscuring the marine origins of its success.

Unlike Grand Rapids, a host of other marine gasoline engine builders emerged at nearly at the same time in Detroit, including the Charles A. Strelinger Company, United Manufacturing Company, M. O. Cross Engine Company, and Belle Isle Motor Company. Also the demand for hulls grew with the steadily increasing number of engines produced each year. By 1906 about eight manufacturers of marine engines were well established in the city, with others soon to join them.[31]

Outstate Builders

Engine building was not just confined to large cities like Detroit and Grand Rapids; it also appeared in some of the smaller cities, occasionally as part of a larger firm. For instance, the Regal Gasoline Engine Company in Coldwater, while primarily known as a stationary engine manufacturer, built marine engines in large quantities.

One Upper Peninsula engine builder who achieved a bit of fame was Carl H. Blomstrom of Marquette. He worked as the superintendent and manager of the Lake Shore Engine Works and presumably designed the engine for the first motorized lifeboat used in the United States. Born in Grand Rapids in 1867, he received a degree in mechanical engineering through the International Correspondence School of Scranton, Pennsylvania. He briefly worked as a mechanic at the F. C. Wells Pump Company in Chicago before moving to Marquette and the Lake Shore Engine Works, where he built the "Superior" engine.[32] The U.S. Life-Saving Service looked to integrate the newest relevant technologies into the tools of its work, and it selected the Lake Shore engine because of its "lightness per horsepower, simplicity of construction, compactness and its unfailing ability to run under adverse conditions." Keeper Henry Cleary of the Marquette Life-Saving crew tested the engine, a 12-horsepower, two-cylinder, 1,500-pound model, in a 34-foot lifeboat in 1899, trying it out in all kinds of weather, including severe storms on Lake Superior. The engine's successful trials led to the adoption of motorized lifeboats throughout the U.S. Life-Saving Service in due course.[33] Blomstrom moved to Detroit, where he formed the C. H. Blomstrom Motor Company to build boats and eventually even automobiles. Blomstrom built two hundred boats in 1905, valued at twelve thousand dollars.[34]

The Smalley Motor Company, Ltd., operated in Bay City on the Saginaw River where it empties into Lake Huron. This company represented just one of a handful of engine builders that started in the Saginaw Valley. Smalley's new plant, built in 1903, consisted of a two-story brick and concrete fire-resistant factory, with the office on the second floor of the main building overlooking the entire plant. The main building housed the pattern shop, forge shop, and finishing and shipping rooms. The entire facility was electrically powered by a single Westinghouse generator with three motors. For testing its engines, the company built a test stand of concrete 7 feet deep, capable of holding fifteen engines at once. The engines were connected via shafting to a number of propellers in a huge water tank, creating a constant load on the power plants. Three rail lines and the river made for excellent shipping facilities for deliveries to customers and the handling of incoming materials. Smalley would eventually enter the racing game, and its high-speed engines powered several championship-winning boats.[35] The Erd Motor Company and Stork Motor Company, both of Saginaw, likewise became important marine engine suppliers for boat-builders in the Saginaw Valley.

Challenging Traditions

What happened to traditional small-scale boat builders as gasoline-powered engines become increasingly available and demanded by their customers? All had to follow suit and produce the products that people wanted, but suddenly there were new issues of weight, engine placement, shaft logs, fuel tanks, and a host of other problems to work out. Some of the work translated easily from steam launch and yacht design, but other elements, such as hull designs for the highest speed, remained more challenging.

Joseph A. Pouliot of Detroit was one of the small-scale boat builders caught in the middle of the transition from sail and steam-powered boats to marine gasoline-engine-powered craft. Pouliot got his start in boat building with the Detroit Boat Works in 1889.[36] Working independent of that firm later on, Pouliot earned a reputation as a talented racing sailboat designer as the builder of the *Juanita* and *Viking*. By 1900 he had leased an 8-foot deep, 1,100-foot long slip on the Detroit River on the south side of Jefferson Avenue, between Hibbard and Holcomb Streets, and had a boat shop, marine railway for launching and retrieving boats, and a good anchorage.[37]

A few years later, in 1904, Pouliot was involved in a new venture in Wyandotte at the old Davis Boat & Oar Company plant. Bankrolled by Emory Leyden Ford (treasurer of the Michigan Alkali Company), H. B. Moran, and Otto Barthel (the Detroit attorney), and aided by a young naval architect, Carlton Wilby, the company intended to build racing boats as a specialty.[38] Unfortunately, Detroit area yachtsmen were often more likely to purchase a sailboat that had been designed, built, and successfully raced on the East Coast than they were to buy locally designed and built craft. A steady stream of contenders or winners of the Seawanhaka Cup, Canada's Cup, and other trophies made their way westward to the Great Lakes to continue their racing careers. Designs by Small Brothers, Charles D. Mower, the Herreshoffs, and other prominent eastern designers and builders made up the majority of the racing fleet. Of the six sailboats based in Detroit in the 21-foot restricted class that were racing in 1904, only one, the *Pirate*, built by Pouliot, was both designed and constructed locally, although another, *Eyota*, was designed by Burgess & Packard of Boston but built by Edward C. Bryan of Wyandotte.

Pouliot eventually moved into powerboats, but not in Michigan. He formed the Pouliot Boat and Power Company in Sandusky, Ohio, at the site of the former John Monk shipyard, incorporated September 7, 1904, with twenty-five thousand dollars in capital, just months after the new Wyandotte venture was launched.[39] Like his earlier efforts, this one, too, ended in failure by 1906.

Pouliot returned to Detroit and started yet another company. The Pouliot Boat Company was incorporated on November 2, 1907. Officers of the firm included William E. Scripps as president and Joseph A. Pouliot as general manager. The company's shop was originally located at the foot of Bowen Avenue. By 1909 the company was located at Park Place at the foot of Parkview Avenue. Officers of the firm by this time consisted of William E. Scripps, president; Henry LeGroue, vice president; Volney Copeland, secretary and treasurer; and Joseph A. Pouliot, manager. Scripps, a newspaper magnate, was treasurer of the Evening News Association and secretary and treasurer of the James E. Scripps Corporation. The Pouliot Boat Company filed notice of its dissolution on December 30, 1911, and Pouliot then joined John L. Hacker to form the Hacker-Pouliot Boat Company.[40]

Among the boats built by the Pouliot Boat Company were four rowboats used by Julius F. Stone on his famed expedition down the Colorado River in 1909. The boats may have been rushed for delivery, as Stone complained that when they arrived the canvas cockpit covers were not waterproofed, nor were the iron upright brackets for them installed, as per the contract. Of the four boats, all survived, although one was left in the canyon with a local resident. One of the remaining three boats is owned by the National Park Service's Grand Canyon Museum in Grand Canyon, Arizona.[41]

Not everyone was thrilled with the new marine gasoline technology. Some older builders at the end of their careers, such as William J. Partridge, never got into powerboats and even expressed disdain for the changes the engine had forced in the trade.[42]

Competition for Factories

Throughout the early years of the boat-building industry, Michigan cities actively competed against one another and against cities in other states to lure factories to settle in their communities. Local boards of trade and chamber of commerce groups, using funds raised by subscription, membership, or other methods, appealed to manufacturers of all kinds to get them to locate plants in their cities. The internecine rivalries, fueled by financial and real estate incentive packages, led the manufacturers to demand more for relocating as the cities bid fiercely against each other to build their industrial base. Plants that reached their maximum capacity or lacked expansion room for additions caused much of the movement.

In one of the earlier attempts to lure a boat and engine company away from its home, the city of Benton Harbor tried to get the Sintz Gas Engine Company to move from Grand Rapids for an incentive of twenty-five thousand dollars in 1896, albeit unsuccessfully.[43]

Muskegon successfully lured the Racine Boat Manufacturing Company away from Racine, Wisconsin, when the latter city could not offer land to replace and enhance what the company lost when a fire destroyed its factory in May 1903. Incentives in the form of twenty thousand dollars, free land on the lakeshore, and tax relief motivated the company to relocate in Muskegon a year later.[44] Saginaw's Board of Trade likewise stole the rapidly growing Brooks Boat Manufacturing Company away from Bay City with financial incentives, as well as acquiring Valley Boat & Engine Company from Baldwinsville, New York. The Board of Trade also worked hard to link related industries, such as gasoline engine manufacturers, to the boat builders.

Not all incentives proved enough to force a move. Monroe attempted to snag the Matthews Boat Company from Bascom, Ohio, but was unsuccessful, as the firm ended up in Port Clinton, Ohio.[45] Niles tried to lure the Outing Boat Company from Kankakee, Illinois, but likewise without any luck as it landed in Chicago.

Cities also needed to be wary of scams. The Muskegon Steel Boat Company was incorporated on September 22, 1904, at Muskegon to build steel boats. J. Harvey McCracken, founder of the firm, was also vice president of the Racine Boat Manufacturing Company for a short time. An agreement provided that a bonus of ten thousand dollars was to be paid for the new boat building company. A year later McCracken applied for half the bonus, but the application was denied by the Chamber of Commerce on the grounds that the incorporation was clearly a subterfuge, and that all operations, including payment of bills and payrolls, were being met by the Racine Boat Manufacturing Company.[46]

Occasionally a city would also try to recover from the loss of a factory by forming a new boat- or engine-building organization to take over the old plant. This appears to have been the case with the Bay City Boat Manufacturing Company when the Brooks Boat Manufacturing Company moved to Saginaw, and also with the formation of the Holland Launch and Engine Company when Wolverine Motor Works left for Bridgeport, Connecticut. Trying to capitalize on former success often did not work. Usually these operations would run for a couple of years after the departure of their better-known, better-organized predecessors, and then die out.

Operating the Boat-Building Factories

The Truscott Boat Manufacturing Company, one of the largest operations in the state, serves as a good example of the modern, high-volume boat manufacturing plant of its time. After leaving Grand Rapids, Truscott moved its factory from one site to another in St. Joseph during the 1890s, starting with a single building of about 65 by 125 feet near the intersection of Main and Ship Streets in 1891. By 1896 the company's plant was in a different structure, a two-story building near the St. Joseph River, where it was served by a spur of the Chicago & West Michigan Railway. As the business was going strong, a new facility was erected on the Morrison Canal at the former site of the Morrison Tub and Pail factory. In a letter to the *Marine Review*, a trade journal, the company reported enthusiastically on the outlook for its potential growth.

> We have reason to believe that next season's business will be the best in the history of small launch building. We are at present and have been for some time past working a good force of men, and are putting on more at the rate of several every day. We have on our books orders for over twenty-five launches, in sizes ranging from 16 feet to 50 feet in length, which we will ship to all parts of the world, and which are almost exclusively for pleasure purposes. We are also working on a line of stock boats. The excellent outlook for next year's business has been sufficient to warrant our making extensive additions to our plant. In fact we have added three buildings.[47]

Unfortunately, it was not to be. This factory was destroyed by fire in September 1899 at a loss of seventy-five thousand dollars to the building and machinery, of which only twenty-five thousand was covered by insurance. After an extraordinary effort to rebuild, the company was back in operation within ninety days.[48] For Truscott building a replacement factory after a major fire gave it an opportunity to reconfigure its operation to make it more efficient and to plan for expansion. The new plant was illustrated in the Sanborn Fire Insurance Map of St. Joseph in July 1902, which provides a number of clues about the operation.[49]

Factory Sites and Buildings

The Truscott Boat Manufacturing Company, like others in its class, such as the Davis Boat & Oar Company in Detroit and its successor, the Wyandotte Boat Company in Wyandotte, had significant amounts of real estate associated with it. In most instances, the plants of companies such as these were located on large waterfronts on rivers feeding into the Great Lakes and with substantial rail facilities for bringing in the raw materials and sending out finished products.

Like most industries, the boat-building factories evolved organically, usually from a single building with additions or separate buildings added as demand grew or product lines changed. Boat factory layouts depended on many considerations, such as site size and location in relationship to the water and the rail lines. Launching ways and marine railways for hauling boats out for maintenance and repair had to run directly in and out of the factory, which could also affect the site plan. Rail sidings had to be accessible for the inflow of raw materials such as lumber or iron for castings, as well as for shipment of finished boats to market.

Larger boat plants, such as Truscott's, had numerous departments for organizing the work, usually arranged by craft or trade. Work on the boats was performed in a specific department, and the tasks for that operation were completed before the boats were moved to another department, usually on carts or other carriage-like vehicles.

Outbuildings often included a shed or small building for boat storage prior to shipment and lumber sheds to house raw materials. Depending on the size of the plant and its output, the factory may have had a boiler for steam bending of frames. Lighting with clerestories or cupolas in the upper level of the building provided the workmen with natural light to do their work. At Truscott the plant was heated and powered by steam and fueled by coal and scrap waste, and electric lighting supplemented the natural light.

Offices at Truscott were located on the second floor of the main building, above the tool and stock rooms. The boat carpentry shop was a relatively narrow room about 200 feet long by 40 feet wide running nearly the full length of the factory on its west side. A second boat carpentry shop, possibly a later addition, was located on the Morrison Canal waterfront, overhanging it slightly and separated from the main plant by a double-track siding of the Illinois, Indiana & Iowa (or Vandalia) Railroad. This building also was connected to a large lumber storage shed on its north

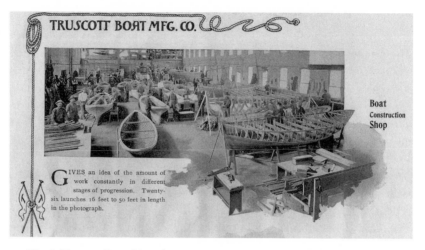

TRUSCOTT BOAT MFG. CO.

GIVES an idea of the amount of work constantly in different stages of progression. Twenty-six launches 16 feet to 50 feet in length in the photograph.

Boat Construction Shop

Fig. 8. Truscott Boat Manufacturing Company in St. Joseph, Michigan built all types of models on the production floor at any one time. Workers took materials and tools to the boat rather than having the boat move through them as with later assembly-line methods. (Courtesy of the Heritage Museum and Cultural Center, St. Joseph, Michigan.)

side. Woodworking machinery, presumably for constructing parts or sectional pieces, was located in the southeast portion of the building, between the blacksmith shop and boat painting operation.

Truscott apparently did not have a designated space for design and lofting of its boats, implying that the company was either working on the boat designs with naval architects off-site or relying on its master carpenters to build the standardized design patterns and did that work more informally in-house.

Companies that decided to go into the business of building their own marine gasoline engines, as Truscott did, needed much more floor space than those plants that brought in their engines from elsewhere. At Truscott the foundry and casting shop required a brick building with a cupola and a combination earth and cement floor for fire protection, with the rest of the plant essentially built around it. Adjacent to the foundry to the south was a blacksmith shop, and to the north of it was the machine shop. The metalworking trades essentially took up about one-half of the main building of the plant.

The boat-painting shop was located at the southeast end of the main building, as far from the foundry as possible but within the same building. Finished boat storage was in two places, one a combined finishing and warehouse building detached from the main building but connected by a platform, and a second a large waterfront warehouse building with 20-foot ceilings. Truscott's plant had a marine railway that could handle up to 15 tons, launching into water 8 feet deep. But given their volume, it appears that the majority of the boats left the company by rail rather than water.[50]

Smaller operations, such as the Detroit River Boat & Oar Company in Wyandotte, had a single building in 1895, two stories in the center and one story on the north and south ends, projecting slightly into the Detroit River. The factory was almost square in the shape of its footprint. Two sheds north of the main building were presumably used to house raw materials or finished boats. In 1900 the plant was shown a few feet back from the water but with a dock extending out to a boathouse. The company had no lights or power, so presumably the equipment was human powered, probably with pedal-driven jigsaws, hand-cranked drill presses, treadle-powered lathes, and similar machinery.[51]

Manufacturing Processes

The first step in the manufacturing process, materials acquisition, required ready access to mill-cut lumber in huge quantities. With white oak frequently desired for keels and frames, Michigan sawmills had already harvested most of the largest and most plentiful stocks decades earlier during the era of large-scale shipbuilding in the state, so the boat builders may have had to look to Canada and other regions for stocks of oak.

Lumber for planking was also imported in the form of red cypress from Louisiana by the railcar load. Other exotic woods such as Philippine or Honduran mahogany and cherry for decks and covering boards and interior panels made for a nice finished appearance on the interiors. Clear white cedar, used for planking by some builders, came from the Upper Peninsula and elsewhere in the state.

Depending on how large the plant was, hardware and fixtures such as brass railings, iron cleats, and other accessories may have been provided by national suppliers or even cast locally or internally if the manufacturer had its own foundry.

Early Truscott factory photos show that much more emphasis was placed on a high volume of overall production than on standardization of production to a particular model for efficiency. Boats of all sizes are shown scattered all over the factory floor, with everything from rowing skiffs to 50-foot cabin cruisers in various stages of completion. The diversity of models under construction at the same time was likely generated as orders came in as opposed to any plan of production for a specific kind of boat. This approach probably resulted in inefficiencies in supplying materials and organizing the labor to perform the work.

Organizing the work by trades meant that the company employed a large number of carpenters but also painters, plumbers, glaziers, mechanics, and even electricians. Construction of a large cabin launch involved the installation of many glass windows, plumbing for the toilet room and galley, and even electric lighting if the boat was equipped with an auxiliary generator system.

Product Lines

The large plants produced an amazing diversity of craft types, with models designed for work and pleasure, large and small, inexpensive and expensive, sail and motorized. From small dinghies to very large, glass-cabined cruisers, the larger plants featured standardized craft that could be customized to the owner's desires, often with different kinds of sterns that were popular in the day such as torpedo sterns, flat transoms, or overhanging fantails.

Truscott's product line went from thirteen models listed in its 1898 catalog to over thirty models of boats, and several of these came in various sizes or multiple stern forms, as described in the advance catalog for 1905.[52] Its boats were used exclusively at the Louisiana Purchase Exposition in St. Louis in 1904, winning the grand prize and three gold medals for merit. Boats from the company were shipped all over the world, as typified by two craft, a 40-footer and a 25-footer, shipped to the Honduras Mahogany Company in British Honduras in 1904.[53]

Production techniques in boat factories as opposed to smaller boat shops required different approaches to building when it came to customization to fit the owner's wishes. A small-scale builder of custom boats had the luxury of getting specific details on design preferences from the prospective owner and then incorporating those changes into the boat as construction went forward. In the factory setting, the options for customization were of more of a gingerbread nature where the detailing was added to an existing structure, and even then in limited quantity as a steady rate of production had to be maintained. More flexibility was granted to the customer in selecting power plants, with multiple ranges of size and horsepower options and manufacturers to choose from.

Statistically, the number of small craft under 5 tons reportedly built in Michigan was undoubtedly woefully undercounted in the federal census. For the year 1900, Michigan boat builders created twelve steam launches totaling 79 gross tons and 44 net tons, having a value of $16,400, ranking third in the nation behind New York (fifteen launches, 248 gross tons, $56,975) and Massachusetts (seven launches, 61 gross tons, $23,850). Connecticut was actually the leader in the number of launches built with twenty-two, and second in tonnage with 189 gross tons, but fourth in value with $13,050.

Michigan's production of sailboats under 5 gross tons, used for both fishing and pleasure, amounted to 215 boats with a value of $51,393. Production of rowboats of all kinds, including pleasure, fishing, lifeboats, racing, ships' boats, hunting, and canvas canoes totaled 454 boats with a value of $18,212.

For power launches using engines other than steam, including both gasoline and electric, Michigan produced 327 with a value of $171,405, more than twenty-seven times as many powerboats as steam launches, with over ten times more value financially. It ranked second behind New York (552 boats valued at $454,643) and ahead of Wisconsin (241 boats valued at $89,780).[54] By 1905 the number and value of small powerboats under 5 gross tons built in Michigan had shot up to 771 boats, valued at $268,449. For rowboats, canoes, and small sailboats, the state produced 4,447 such craft, valued at $146,134.[55] Michigan builders firmly established the state as the national leader in the volume of small craft produced, ranking only behind New York in the total value of boats built.

The Work Force

In looking at the size of the work force in the Michigan boat-building industry between 1895 and 1905, it is difficult to assess exactly how many people were in the industry, as statistically it was merged with the wooden shipbuilding industry in the federal statistics. The Census of Michigan for 1894 listed twenty-one manufacturers of boats, launches, sail and steam yachts, and canoes employing an average over the year of 147 males and 1 female statewide, with businesses located in fourteen counties. Capital invested in the firms totaled $63,100 in personal and real property.[56]

As representative examples, however, Michigan factory inspectors listed the plant employment figures for small boat manufacturers in 1895 (table 2).[57]

Women started to enter the boat-building work force after about 1900, primarily in clerical work and sewing for upholstery on seat cushions and canopies. In the folding boat industry, around Kalamazoo especially, women made up a significantly larger percentage of the work force because of their seamstress skills in manufacturing the canvas boats.

The differential in pay for workers in the boat-building industry was slightly different between those working on the west side of the state from those working on the east side. Detroit area workers received more on an average daily basis than a worker at Truscott in St. Joseph. In 1897 Truscott had an average payroll of $2,400 a month spread among its 60 male employees, or about an average of $1.53 per day. A year later, it employed 88 males, with average daily pay of each at $1.59 for a ten-hour workday. In 1899 average daily pay had shrunk to $1.50 for the 155 men employed before bouncing back up to $1.67 per day for 80 employees by 1900. By comparison, workers at the Detroit Boat Works in 1897 made about $1.60 per day for the same work, but with only 24 males; at the Wyandotte Boat Company they paid $1.61 on average per day in 1899. Carl Schweikart of Detroit paid an average of $1.80, albeit with only 4 employees. By 1900 Schweikart's 5 men averaged $2.40 per day, reflecting a significant increase from even the year before, but Detroit Boat Works' 22 men only received $2.00 on average in the same city.[58] Clearly the boat-building business was beginning to boom, and wages slowly rose with the trend as sales increased.

Seasonality had a significant effect on plant operations. Factories would slow down in the late summer months and frequently lay off workers until work picked up again, sometimes in winter but more often for a spring rush. At Truscott the firm laid off sixty workers on July 28, 1900, described as "primarily transient help," at the beginning of the slow season.[59] Contingent on economic conditions and overall demand, some Michigan plants would shut down for several months at a time during the worst financial crises, always hoping that the spring rush would pull them through the rest of the year. The Michigan Yacht & Power Company worked only seven months in 1900, and the Beauvais Boat and Canoe Company in Charlevoix was idle at the time of inspection. Likewise, plants operated at less than full capacity most of the time, or at least they indicated as much to factory inspectors as

Table 2. Plant employment figures for small boat manufacturers in 1895

Company name	City/Village	No. of males employed	No. of females employed	Total number of employees
Coller Steam Yacht & Engine Works	Detroit	4	0	4
Spring Lake Clinker Boat Manufacturing Company	Spring Lake	3	0	3
Sintz Gas Engine Company	Grand Rapids	45	0	45
Wyandotte Boat Company	Wyandotte	50	0	50
James Dean & Company	Detroit	5	0	5
Detroit Boat Works	Detroit	50	0	50

Source: Michigan, Bureau of Labor and Industrial Statistics, *Third Annual Report of Inspection of Factories in Michigan* (Lansing: Bureau of Labor and Industrial Statistics, 1896), 16–17, 30–31, 38–39, 74–75, 156–57.

the numbers of employees offered for "number of persons employed when running full capacity" appeared to be significantly higher than the number actually employed. In 1900 the larger plants appear to have been working at only half their capacity or less in terms of numbers of employees. The Detroit Boat Works employed only 22, while at full capacity it operated with 100. The Truscott Boat Manufacturing Company employed 80 out of a capacity for 250. About the only larger firm working at capacity was the Wolverine Motor Works in Grand Rapids with 23 employees.

Unlike the shipyards, where the Ship Carpenter's Union and other unions became active, there does not appear to have been any form of early organized labor in the larger boat plants, mostly because there were so few large operations, and the smaller ones relied on other means to satisfy their workers. Close family ties among the boat builders, particularly in the smaller firms, further negated the need for organized labor. Paternalism in the larger firms also played a role in maintaining a loyal work force. Truscott presented each one of its married employees with a fine turkey for Thanksgiving in 1900. Apparently, unmarried workers were not so fortunate.[60] Health and safety issues, such as sanitation in the workplace and protection from dangerous equipment, were just starting to be monitored by factory inspectors as a way to reduce on the job accidents and illness. Inspectors typically cited companies for lacking guards for saw blades and emery wheels, low-water alarms for boilers, and signage for the male and female restrooms. They also checked for underage youths in the workplace, forcing the companies to discharge them if they were not eligible to work.[61]

State of the Industry, 1905

Michigan-made boats sold and delivered worldwide by its manufacturers by 1905 made the state a national leader in the boat-building industry. In what clearly was a decade of flux with the transition of the marine gasoline engine industry from Grand Rapids to Detroit and other parts of the country, the state nurtured many important innovators in the formulation of their machines through the support of its yachtsmen, promoters, and capitalists. Michigan factories grew rapidly in size to support the new demand for boats, increasing their workforces and providing employment opportunities in the growing trade.

Motorboating began as a recreational trend that, while affordable mostly only for the wealthy for the time being, would set the stage for future growth for all classes in the future.

CHAPTER THREE

Growth of the Giants, 1905–15

Introduction

The story of boat-building in Michigan between 1905 and 1915 is essentially one of fluctuation, with a great wave of expansion and contraction as a large number of boat- building firms created to cash in on the motor-boating phenomenon were formed and eventually collapsed. At the end of the era, boat-building in Michigan found itself in a very different place than in the beginning.

The period reflected two changes, one in growth in the overall number of firms building boats, with an increasing degree of stratification between large and small companies. Large companies became very large, but the small ones remained small, with not very many in the middle range transitioning from small to large. Second, diversification into different methodologies for constructing and marketing boats, as represented by the knockdown boat-building sector of the industry, brought the Saginaw Valley into the limelight as an internationally recognized center for boat-building.

Several of the pioneering inventors of the rapidly growing gasoline engine technology, such as Charles Brady King, moved into automobile manufacturing as opposed to marine work, while at the same time, many new developers in the marine engine field changed the emphasis to high-speed engines of greater reliability and durability. New companies emerged that focused specifically on marine engines as opposed to the mix of stationary, automotive, and marine of the earlier generation, represented by the Scripps Motor Company, Van Blerck Motor Company, and Kermath Motor Company, and each became an emerging leader in the field during this era. Between 1905 and 1915 the horsepower-to-weight ratio of marine engines improved dramatically through ingenious engineering and practical experience, reducing the weight of individual parts and gaining more compression in the cylinders to create more power.

At the intersection of the worlds of the new, more powerful marine engines and the market's demand for faster boats stood the naval architects and designers, who had to figure out how to harness the motive power in hull forms that best suited the owner's speed desires while still making boats that were safe and comfortable. Young professionals such as the self-taught John L. Hacker and Christopher Columbus Smith, the apprentice-trained Carlton Wilby, and university-trained Stuart Kingsbury designed ever-faster boats for both racing and leisurely cruising.

Growth

Growth in the boat-building industry began in the sheer number of incorporations of new firms all over the state around 1904 and after. By 1907 the boat-building industry in Michigan had developed to the point that it could support four large factories sending forth a huge volume of standardized small craft, as well as about one hundred smaller companies or individual operations.

Driven by the skyrocketing demand for gasoline launches and cruisers, the recreational boat market increased in size at first because of the novelty of the powerboating experience but also because it expanded into the classes that previously could not afford to own a boat, making ownership of a small, low-powered launch a possibility for middle-class families.

For the largest firms to emerge as national leaders in boat manufacturing, vertically integrated manufacturing became the key to their success. These companies built their own engines as well as boats, giving them a marketing and pricing advantage that few other builders could compete with. Second, extensive marketing and promotion, driven by large advertising budgets and catalog sales, made them highly visible in the marketplace. Prominent product placements at national motorboat shows and expositions likewise promoted the firms.

Racine Boat Manufacturing Company

One of the largest firms to operate in Michigan in the early twentieth century arrived from across Lake Michigan. The Racine Boat Manufacturing Company kept its Wisconsin city name despite having moved to

Muskegon, Michigan, in 1904, making it the newest large boat-building firm in the state. Fred W. Martin started the company in 1893 in Racine, Wisconsin, after his former business, the Racine Hardware Manufacturing Company, closed during the financial crisis of that year. Throughout the 1890s the company expanded and started building large steel steam yachts and fin keel racing sailing yachts, quickly establishing a regional, then national reputation for excellence. The company lost its original home in a fire on May 31, 1903, which destroyed all the equipment, tools, patterns, and paperwork and over 400 boats. The firm had built on land leased from the Chicago, Milwaukee and St. Paul Railroad. When it could not acquire more land for expansion after the loss, the company took up an invitation from the Muskegon Chamber of Commerce to relocate in that city, with an offer of 10-1/2 acres of waterfront property and twenty thousand dollars in cash as an incentive. Like many other formerly lumber-based communities, Muskegon desperately needed to rebuild its economic base in the face of the dwindling supply of timber to feed its sawmills. On August 18, 1903, the company announced its departure from Racine, and it began building its new plant in Muskegon in 1904, temporarily building boats away from the plant while it was under construction. Racine reportedly turned out 3,005 boats valued at three hundred thousand dollars in 1905, only a year after constructing its new plant. This proved to be a volume over five times larger than that of the Truscott Boat Manufacturing Company, but built with only a third greater size work force of 322 people compared to Truscott's 204 workers. The boats sold were presumably smaller than Truscott's, as their value totaled far less than Truscott's half a million dollars for 600 boats. Clearly, a new giant in boat-building had come ashore in the Great Lakes state, changing the competitive environment for everyone in the region.

The Racine Boat Manufacturing Company's enormous new plant covered more than 68,000 square feet, with part of it built on three piers extending out over Muskegon Lake. Pilings sunk into the lake bottom more than 100 feet supported the piers. The factory included an office building, a machine shop of 116 × 60 feet, an iron and brass foundry of 104 × 116, a power plant of 40 × 70, a saw room of 60 × 80, a woodshop of 200 × 66, a storage room of 200 × 60, and a steel erecting shop of 200 × 80. The woodshop occupied one pier there and a second pier by the storage building. Departments for finishing, upholstering, testing, and shipping made up other important parts of the plant. The powerhouse, equipped with a 300-horsepower Nordberg-Corliss steam engine directly connected to a 250-horsepower Northern Electric generator and a 400-cubic-foot air compressor, drove all the electric motors on the machines and all the air tools. A modern heating and lighting system made the workers more comfortable and safer with improved visibility.

The company's unusual setup for building both wood and steel boats set it apart from many other large builders of the period, and it reflected the growing demand for steel small craft. The plant and equipment investment amounted to nearly half a million dollars, and the company could build anything from a rowboat up to a $200,000 steel yacht.[1]

For Racine's boat-manufacturing process, customers sent in letters or postcards requesting a catalog with the company responding by delivering an illustrated booklet showing all its products. If the customer inquired further about a specific model, the company followed up by sending blueprints and specifications, and sometimes special designs created to individualize an otherwise standardized boat. A flurry of paperwork preceded and followed each boat through the building process. Upon the sale of a boat and acceptance of the specifications, the order was attached to the specifications and copies provided to the purchaser, the superintendent, and the office. The superintendent filled out an order for the engine department for a motor (or motors), and he placed a similar order with the construction shop for the hull and one with the finishing shop for the fittings and completion of the boat.

The superintendent of construction supervised the setting up of the patterns or forms for a particular boat, the laying of the keel, and the steam bending of the frames to shape. Planking and caulking of the hull followed. After the forms were removed, the boat was ready for the decking and cockpit construction. To obtain the construction materials, workmen presented requisitions from the superintendent of construction to the lumber room foreman for the lumber. Types of wood stocked included oak, ash, cedar, cypress, butternut, mahogany, black walnut, pine, maple, and spruce, ordered by the foot. A requisition form submitted to the stock room foreman for the fasteners listed the size and number of pounds of each type. Racine used copper clout nails, wire nails, and tacks, as well as iron wire nails and iron tacks on the planking and ribbing. Requisition forms for fasteners used by the hull builders differed from those used by the joiners working on the cabins and decks. The stock keepers approved the requisitions and forwarded them to the cost department, where other workers kept the files for figuring the cost of the completed boat.

Once the hull was completed and the gasoline tank installed, the boat moved to the engine-installing department, where workers placed the engine in the boat, the gasoline system was piped, and the necessary engine fittings were attached.

Racine tested all powered watercraft by running a three-mile course mapped out on Muskegon Lake, operating at maximum speed, taking up to half a day or more to make sure the motor ran properly. After the testing, workers removed the boat from the water by means of the marine railway or cranes. It continued on to the finishing department, where the deck fittings, awning, icebox, cushions, railings, mooring lines, anchor and cable, flags, and flagpoles were added as specified on the original order. Workers applied paint, varnish, and enamel and repolished metal parts. After a minute final inspection, the workers crated the boat for shipment by rail. Boats could also be launched into Muskegon Lake for delivery by way of Lake Michigan. Managers recorded labor costs for the hull on a job ticket listing the workers' names, pay rates, time spent, and materials used to make the boat.

Racine treated the engine department almost as a separate business, keeping separate time cards for the operation. Standardized engine products enabled it to make various parts in large quantities, such as shop orders for a hundred cylinders at a time. Numerous tasks necessary to create an engine, including boring, planing, shaping, drilling, milling, laying out, vise work, erecting, filing, grinding, polishing, testing, painting, and inspecting, required a great deal of coordination. The company purchased some materials to assemble the engines, such as screws and piping, from outside suppliers. Racine charged defective castings and resulting time lost to the foundry and defective workmanship to the machine shop. By recording the total cost of manufacture, materials purchased, supplies, and labor, and adding the machine-hour rate and a percentage of the shop's overhead expense, the firm understood its costs for a complete engine and how it compared to previous costs, so that variations in costs or supplies could be located and investigated.[2]

Fallen Giants

Advertising brought the Racine and Truscott companies greater fame than most Michigan boat builders enjoyed. Both firms advertised in several national journals, initially with small runner ads but later with larger, more visible box ads. Both companies promoted extensive catalogs of their products available for a few cents and postage, showing potential buyers the wide range of available boat designs they had to offer. Combined with low prices for their products and high volume, the increased name recognition helped create an idea in the public's mind about the size and stability of the firms, as well as the inexpensive nature of their products. Truscott and Racine developed a level of stratification, sizewise, well above that of the smaller builders based on business size and advertising budgets.

By 1910 the boat-building market had changed considerably, and the competitive environment had matured to the point that in order for larger builders to increase market share, some consolidation would be required. Similar attempts in the auto industry, such as William Crapo Durant's creation of General Motors in 1908, tried to pull together a large number of different firms, including a mishmash of both auto manufacturers and parts suppliers, to form a new corporation that would lead the way to future growth. "I was for getting every car in sight, playing safe along the line," Durant later claimed.[3] The first version of General Motors ran into financial trouble in 1910, costing Durant his presidency. A short time later, the west shore Michigan boat builders all too hastily followed in his footsteps. A similar ill-fated effort to merge several boat and engine firms into a large conglomerate, however well intentioned, turned into a destructive disaster that completely ruined both Racine and Truscott and changed the state's west-shore boat-building scene for decades to come.

In November 1910, Walter J. Reynolds, Racine's president, announced the formation of the National Boat & Engine Company, capitalized at ten million dollars, with himself as president; James M. Truscott, vice president; and Michigan's lieutenant governor, John Q. Ross, of Muskegon, secretary. The companies incorporated into the new firm included the Racine Boat Manufacturing Company, Muskegon, Michigan; Truscott Boat Manufacturing Company, St. Joseph, Michigan; Pioneer Boat and Pattern Company, Bay City, Michigan; Pierce Engine Company, Racine, Wisconsin; Inland Lake Boat Company, Lake Geneva, Wisconsin; Pope Boat Company, Fond du Lac, Wisconsin; Outing Boat Company, Ashland, Wisconsin; Shell Lake Boat Company, Shell Lake, Wisconsin; and West Mystic Boat Company, West Mystic, Connecticut. As originally envisioned by Reynolds, the National Boat & Engine Company could control 90 percent of the boat-manufacturing industry from Maine west to the Mississippi River. With the large amount of capitalization, Reynolds anticipated that several other boat and engine manufacturers would be lured in to build an even larger firm.

From the beginning the company may have been fatally flawed because of what it *did not* include. All the companies hailed from Wisconsin and Michigan with the exception of the West Mystic Boat Company, perhaps reflecting Reynolds's Wisconsin business relationships. He may have attempted to simply reduce competition in the Midwest. Most of the companies were small or weak, and only one represented the East Coast, leaving out the large, important plants in New York and New Jersey such as the Electric Launch Company, Gas Engine & Power Company, and Charles L. Seabury & Company, Consolidated. The Matthews Boat Company of Port Clinton, Ohio, a large midwestern cruiser builder with a big advertising budget, wasn't included. This company could have captured a larger share of the regional market.

The company authorized bond issues of four million dollars to cover the cost of the mergers and to take over the mortgages of the old companies, but the whole affair collapsed by late 1911 because of a tight money market for its bonds. Trusts became suspect, and investors, uncertain about the new laws governing combines, feared anything that tried to corner a market. Only fifty thousand dollars' worth of bonds were sold, an inadequate amount to pay off the debts of the old companies. In the subsequent fallout, the entire company, including both Racine and Truscott, fell into receivership. A judge in Portland, Maine, where the company had filed for incorporation, appointed Walter I. Woodman to serve as receiver. The bondholders appointed William H. Mann of Muskegon as trustee to operate the plants.[4] Pioneer's management filed suit, unsuccessfully attempting to back out of the contract forming the deal. Creditors of the Truscott Boat Manufacturing Company accused Reynolds and Lieutenant Governor Ross of gross fraud, claiming that the merger should have been set aside because the men had received half a million dollars in stock without paying in anything. Lawsuits abounded in the courts for years afterward to try to clean up the mess.

In an attempt to salvage some of the new organization, Walter Reynolds, James Truscott, and others formed a committee to purchase three remaining viable firms. The group formed the Racine–Truscott–Shell Lake Boat Company in early 1912 with J. M. Smith, president of the Shell Lake Boat Company, as president and treasurer, Paul Findlay as vice president, and James Truscott as secretary, with offices in Shell Lake, Wisconsin.[5]

Part of the motivation for starting over was contracts with the U.S. Lighthouse Service for several lightships, which kept the company operating for a while, but trouble persisted. One of the lightships, *Light Vessel No. 95*, sank at the company's dock on December 26, 1911, with the builder raising the craft on February 20 of the following year. Another brand new one, *Light Vessel No. 82*, delivered to the Lighthouse Service unfinished in July 1912, was wrecked and sank in the Great Storm of 1913 with the loss of all six hands off Buffalo, New York.[6] The Racine–Truscott–Shell Lake venture ended completely in 1915. The Michigan Trust Company, appointed as receiver, foreclosed on the property and sold the former Racine Boat Manufacturing plant in Muskegon to the Harris Brothers Company of Detroit and Chicago in 1916 for one hundred thousand dollars.[7] Rumors floated for years afterward that the plant would be reopened, especially after America's entry into World War I, but it never functioned in the same way again. The Truscott plant remained open as the Truscott-Pierce Engine Company, taking over the Pierce Engine Company of Racine, Wisconsin, but the company no longer operated at the level it did prior to the failures, building washing machines and engines for a while in the early 1920s before getting back into the boat business.[8]

Michigan Steel Boat Company and Detroit Boat Company

An enormous operation of a different sort emerged in Detroit, the Michigan Steel Boat Company and its sister firm, the Detroit Boat Company, part of a larger collection of firms operated by Hugo Scherer and Frederick E. Wadsworth. The Michigan Steel Boat Company originated in Kalamazoo and was organized in 1900–1901. Officers of the firm included Chandler G. Bullard, Lewis H. Bullard, N. J. Bullard, and Arthur E. Chambers.[9] The company manufactured steel boats under a patent (U.S. 681,363) issued to Chambers. The patent was assigned to the Western Novelty Company of Kalamazoo, owned by Chambers and the Bullards, makers of slot and amusement machines. He also designed and patented the machinery to build the boats. Resembling a stove pipe joint, the double seam edges of the steel interlocked to keep water out. The lightness and durability of the new steel hulls proved attractive to buyers and offered less annual maintenance than a traditional wooden hull.[10]

Acquired by Scherer and Wadsworth, the company was incorporated on December 27, 1901, with capital of $37,500, and moved to Detroit in January 1902, initially intending to employ one hundred men and build twenty boats a day.[11] In 1905 the company acquired new facilities, consisting of a group of existing and new structures covering 8 acres, or 500,000 square feet under one roof, including the former Detroit United Railway interurban car barns owned by Olds Motor Works adjacent to the boat

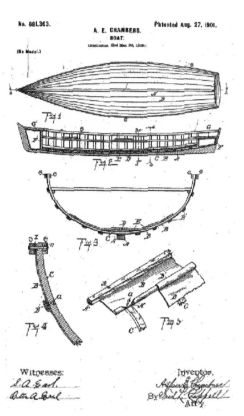

Fig. 9. Arthur E. Chambers devised a unique approach to steel boat construction wherein the seam edges interlock to form a waterproof joint. The Michigan Steel Boat Company, which Chambers helped found in Kalamazoo, moved to Detroit and became one of the state's larger boat-building firms in the early 1900s. (U.S. Patent Office.)

company's plant. The company boasted of having the largest boat-building plant in the world.[12] The firm flourished as a large combine of boat builders, marine engine manufacturers, and automotive parts and body suppliers, including the Detroit Boat Company and Michigan Steel Boat Company, with several affiliated engine manufacturers, including the Detroit Engine Works, Thrall Motor Company, Detroit Motor Supply Company (makers of the Sandow motor), and other firms under the umbrella of the Wadsworth Manufacturing Company. The arrangement appeared to be unusual because the companies operated independently as individual private companies under the partnership of Scherer and Wadsworth. The Michigan Steel Boat Company grew to be a sizable firm for the same reasons that Truscott and Racine became successful, with abundant advertising, aided further by a contract to supply Sears, Roebuck & Company with its White

Flyer launches.[13] Its most prominent advertising offered "This Magnificent Steel Launch," a 16-footer with a 2-horsepower engine, for a mere ninety-six dollars. Boat livery operators frequently purchased the Michigan Steel Boat Company boats for their durability and relatively low maintenance. The Detroit Boat Company, its sister firm, built wooden boats and made a specialty of canoes, hiring W. L. Luke, formerly superintendent of the Old Town Canoe Company, to manage that aspect of the business.

Despite its claim that "We are the largest builder of boats and launches in the world," the company sold only 1,200 boats in 1905 compared to Racine's 3,005 in its own state, making it a distant second in terms of production, as opposed to plant size.[14] Wadsworth's flair for selling boats knew virtually no limits. For the opening of the Actor's Fund Fair at the Seventy-First Regiment Armory in New York in May 1910, Wadsworth proposed sending a 30-foot motorboat donated by the Detroit Boat Company down a greased track from a high platform above an 80-foot circular tank, with the front seat occupied by the actress Mabel Taliaferro, who would crash a bottle of wine over the prow as the boat was released. President Taft was invited to witness the novel boat launch and christening ceremony.[15] While it is unclear whether or not the spectacle actually happened, Wadsworth's imagination for marketing boats certainly could attract attention from the press. Cleverly named demonstration models such as the Silver Fizz, Lemon (a bright yellow racing boat), Rabbit's Foot (for navigating the Niagara River rapids and whirlpools), and the uniquely shaped, fan-propelled Bat helped to promote the company's products in a crowded marketplace. In 1911 the company offered forty-seven different models, including one called the International Special, an 18-footer with a 3-1/2-horsepower Detroit motor marketed specifically for export.[16]

Despite the apparent success of their boats, the Wadsworth Manufacturing Company got out of the boat-building business shortly before World War I, turning its attention instead to the growing stamped auto parts and auto body manufacturing businesses, serving the Ford Motor Company and other Detroit auto plants as a major supplier. The Columbia Motors Company leased the boat company's portion of the plant in 1916. The Michigan Steel Boat Company filed notice of its dissolution on December 8, 1920.[17] Hugo Scherer continued to work with Frederick E. Wadsworth on a variety of real estate and manufacturing ventures until shortly before his death in 1923. Wadsworth moved to Palm Beach, Florida, where he died a millionaire in 1927.[18]

Smaller Outstate Builders

Companies that typified the new small-scale startup boat builders all around the state included firms such as the Holland Launch and Engine Company, which got its start as the Valley City Gas Engine & Launch Works in Grand Rapids. Herman Garvelink, the firm's manager, needed to find a place with larger quarters and better shipping facilities than what he had in the larger city, so the firm was organized in January 1907 as the Holland Launch and Engine Company with capital stock of fifteen thousand dollars. Garvelink took over the former plant of the Wolverine Motor Works on Macatawa Bay after Wolverine moved to Bridgeport, Connecticut. The skyrocketing demand for motorboats did not necessarily mean one could make easy money in the business, especially over the long term. Within two years the firm had failed, although Garvelink and Hugh Bradshaw repurchased the property and planned to reopen the factory after it closed. Fire seriously damaged the factory in July 1914, but the company continued to build or repair boats until after 1916.[19]

Undercapitalized and poorly marketed businesses, sometimes selling boats mostly in their immediate area, soon reached market saturation as larger powerboats remained relatively expensive toys for a small number of wealthier patrons. The St. Joseph Boat Manufacturing Company in St. Joseph was organized in 1903 to build both electric and vapor launches. The company found it necessary to increase its working capital within two years after a rapid start to its business. It reorganized with capital of twenty-five thousand dollars to build required additions to the plant and leave a sufficient working fund for efficient operation of the concern. Unlike the Truscott firm of the same city, the company had a short life. The St. Joseph Boat Manufacturing Company was dissolved on August 19, 1908.[20]

New companies grew in the resort communities of the northern Lower Peninsula as well, driven by the seemingly insatiable demand for motorboats. The Traverse City Motor Boat Company showed great promise at the time of its formation in November 1905. With several of the town's leading citizens backing the venture, the company acquired Thomas W. Stanton's existing boat-building operation, giving him stock in exchange and retaining him as superintendent. The company acquired a large block of land with buildings that it intended for use as its plant, and the purpose of the corporation was "to manufacture gasoline launches, sail boats, row boats and kindred water craft, including a repair business of all classes of boats and to reach out for extended trade in the markets of the country." A delay of several months in the startup of the two-story Bay Street factory while the company tried to get it into shape did not seem at first to cause any harm. A very successful first season concluded with a substantial volume of new orders on the books to carry the operation through the winter. At the company's annual meeting in January 1907, a selection committee was formed to look for an office manager to solicit orders and business. A year later it lured F. M. Miller, formerly of the Lozier Motor Company, to serve as the designer and builder by the end of 1908, having apparently bought out Stanton's stock interest. The company voted to double its capital to twenty thousand dollars, but it was all for naught as it fell on hard times and went into receivership, eventually declaring bankruptcy.[21] One contributing cause of the failures of 1907–8 may have been the reverberating effects of the financial Panic of 1907, leading to a short but sharp national recession and the resultant loss of consumer confidence.

In a few instances, individual builders or very small companies could survive and prosper for years, sometimes far longer than incorporated companies. In northern Michigan, George M. Obenauf, an expert boat designer from Chicago, set up shop at Mullet Lake in Cheboygan County in 1908. He rapidly established himself as a quality builder, carefully selecting the seasoned wood he used in his boats, which were mostly rowboats of lapstrake design with cedar planking. When he first started, he sold a 14-foot rowboat for the "huge sum" of thirty-five dollars with a single pair of oars. "Obie Boats," as they were called by the locals, sold throughout the northern Lower Peninsula, and Obenauf continued to build them until shortly before his death in 1958.[22] Bert Ginman of Muskegon, another example of a small-scale or individual builder, likewise carried on the trade for decades after the huge Racine Boat Manufacturing Company in the same city failed.

In the small resort village of Algonac on the St. Clair River, Christopher Columbus Smith and his brother Henry started building motorboats after many years of building rowboats and duckboats. They purchased a secondhand 2-horsepower Sintz engine from Isaac Colby, a local resident who could not get it to run properly. By 1906 Chris Smith could build a 26-foot boat capable of 18 miles per hour. In resort communities boat builders sometimes came in contact with people with serious money. In 1910 Smith met John J. "Baldy" Ryan, a Cincinnati movie theater owner and gambler who spent his summers at nearby Harsens Island. Ryan looked him up to build a boat to beat the fastest one on the river, another Smith-built boat named *Dart*. Together they formed the Smith-Ryan Boat and Engine

Company in 1911. With Ryan providing the financial backing, Chris Smith created a series of boats for J. Stuart Blackton, the owner of Vitagraph Studios, named *Reliance* and *Baby Reliance*.[23] Smith built the first, *Reliance III*, as single-step hydroplane based on the idea of William H. Fauber's patented multistep hydroplane concept of 1908. The step in the bottom of the hull permitted the boat to ride on a substantial amount of air when at high speed, breaking the drag and resistance of the water on more than two-thirds of the hull. When they did not capsize, burn, malfunction, or sink, the *Reliances* won local races and attracted national attention. Eastern yachtsmen at first could not believe that western boat builders could make such fast craft, but they soon discovered that the claimed speeds were for real when the boats came east and beat them soundly in their own events.[24]

Concentrated Talents: Builders at Motor Boat Lane, Detroit

More than any other single place in the country, the foot of Motor Boat Lane in Detroit became the influential development center for powerboating in the period between about 1905 and 1915. In an industrial district formed roughly around the intersection of Jefferson and Parkview Avenues, and encompassing Holcomb Avenue, extending to the Detroit River, a small number of boat-building firms quickly grew, first in fame, then in size. These firms drew from an unusual talent pool of boat builders, naval architects, and engine designers sharing their knowledge to create some of the fastest and most powerful motor craft in the world, ranging from speedboats to cruisers.

The innovative work that began at Motor Boat Lane started with William B. Gregory, who had his hand in a string of firms that established the location's significance in the boating industry. Gregory started in the boat-building business through the marine engine side of things. He, along with Earl Ryno and Richard H. Franchot, incorporated the Belle Isle Motor Company in 1907 with $40,000 in capital to build automobile and marine engines, their primary product a single-cylinder, 2- to 3-horsepower marine engine named the Skidoo. They worked with Howard A. Pike, a naval architect of Providence, Rhode Island, to design and build an 18-foot gasoline launch to help promote the new engine. Ryno became entangled in a federal mail fraud trial over the delivery of automobiles, but he sold the business to Gregory, Belle Isle's vice president, who reinvented the firm under the name New Belle Isle Motor Company in March 1909, with his son, Edgar M. Gregory, leading the organization.[25] The New Belle Isle Motor

Company merged with the Collapsible Steel Form Company of Detroit and Carson City in 1911 to create the unusual combination of the Concrete Form & Engine Company, incorporated with capital of $150,000, which built marine engines as well as steel forms for constructing roadway culverts.[26] The Gregorys formed the Belle Isle Boat & Engine Company in 1917, a very influential firm in the development of mahogany-hulled runabouts. Motor Boat Lane today remains the home of the Gregory Boat Company, a sales and marina operation but no longer a boat builder, after well over one hundred years in the same location.

John L. Hacker, one of the world's leading twentieth-century naval architects, found his interest in boats at an early age, fascinated by what he found on Detroit's waterfront. Working as the bookkeeper for his father's ice and coal business, he found time to learn boat design and naval architecture through correspondence courses and night school. Hacker built his first boat at age fourteen in about 1891. One of his earliest racing boats, *Au Revoir*, built in 1903 for Willard Murray Smith, quickly drew national attention as a fast racer. Hacker formed the Detroit Launch & Power Company with local boat builder Louis Mayea in 1907, with Hacker's father, John F. Hacker, as president of the firm, presumably having bought Cyrus B. Merriam's Belle Isle Launch and Power Company.[27] At first the company enjoyed a good deal of success with orders, building several boats for members of the Detroit Motor Boat Club, including *Comet*, a speedboat built for Dr. William Sanborn, three new catboats for the Edgemere Yacht Club, and nine launches of between 21 and 36 feet. Nine men were kept busy working for the company in 1908.[28]

Hacker enjoyed much greater success at designing boats than at running companies to build them, as his lack of business skills led to his company's failure. Hacker sold out his interest in the Detroit Launch & Power Company to Mayea in early 1911 and temporarily allied with Joseph Pouliot, forming Hacker-Pouliot Boat Company in March 1911; however, the collaboration did not last as Hacker suffered a nervous breakdown while at the peak of his success with racing craft. His father wound up the affairs of the business with his son in August 1911.[29] A year later *Kitty Hawk II*, designed by Hacker and built by his partner Mayea, became the first boat in the United States to surpass 50 miles per hour.[30]

Their neighbor at the foot of Holcomb Avenue happened to be Joseph Van Blerck, an engine builder, and the men eventually collaborated to build *Van Blerck II* for Wayne County road commissioner and brickyard owner John S. Haggerty, a 28-foot boat with two 6-cylinder Van Blerck engines, producing 160 horsepower together. Van Blerck, a Dutch immigrant who arrived in Detroit in 1902, started out as a backyard engine builder working in his woodshed. Eventually Van Blerck's engines grew in size first to 6-cylinder and then 12-cylinder behemoths. Over the next few years, they powered some of the fastest racing boats in the nation. Both John L. Hacker and Chris Smith used Van Blerck engines in their racing boats, quickly earning a reputation for their exceptionally light weight, durability, and speed. In 1911 Chris Smith used an 80-horsepower 6-cylinder Van Blerck engine in *Reliance III*, the first single-step Smith-Ryan hydroplane. The Hacker-designed, Van Blerck–powered *Kitty Hawk V*, the fastest boat in the world in 1913 at 53 miles per hour, held a 12-foot long, 12-cylinder in-line engine that weighed about 1,900 pounds, but its efficiency of an estimated 7.6 pounds per horsepower far exceeded the typical runabout engine ratio of 28:1. Van Blerck's 250- to 270-horsepower monster made the racing world take notice.[31] Soon boat owners and builders from all over the country came to Van Blerck for his incredibly powerful engines to drive both their racing boats and fast cruisers.

After his departure from the Detroit Launch & Power Company and Hacker-Pouliot Boat Company, John L. Hacker worked for Joe Van Blerck as his business manager for a short time until June 1912 when a fire at the factory forced the Van Blerck business out of its leased home. The company relocated to Monroe, Michigan, in 1913. Hacker continued working as a freelance designer in Detroit and kept using Van Blercks to power his boat designs. At one point in 1913, Hacker made an arrangement with the Van Blerck Motor Company to market his designs and build the engines with Valley Boat & Engine Company of Saginaw to supply the hulls under royalty for his Stroller model. Louis Mayea moved his firm to Fair Haven in 1914, where it continues to this day.[32] In 1915 Hacker temporarily moved the Hacker Boat Company to Watervliet, New York, working with L. L. Tripp, before reestablishing his business a year later in Detroit. Tripp carried on the Watervliet business as the Albany Boat Corporation.

Other prominent figures emerged as denizens of Motor Boat Lane, such as Max Dingfelder, who started building boats in 1904, creating a racing winner named *999*. He later moved into the automobile and aircraft engine building business as Maximotor Makers. Henry C. Bosserdet formed the Bosserdet Yacht & Engine Company in 1905, working with naval architect Carlton Wilby to design cruisers for several wealthy Detroit area customers. These included *Josephine H. II* (U.S. Official no. 210215), a 64-foot motor yacht built in 1912 for August P. Kling; *Toyship*, a 42-footer built in 1913 for Frank W. Sinks; and *Vantage*, a 35-footer built in 1914 for Alexander I. McLeod. In 1906 the Marine Manufacturing Company, owned and operated by James H. House, produced gasoline launches such as *Sunbeam*, built for Henry Bosserdet before he entered the boat-building business. Alfred G. Liggett, a noted stock runabout and cruiser builder and brother to Louis K. Liggett of the Rexall Drug fortune, started at Motor Boat Lane and later operated a yard with his son at Trenton. The American Boat Company, formed by Emmet P. Gray and others, built the American Beauty brand of small launches and catboats. It also constructed the large cabin cruiser *Silver Heels*, designed by its manager Charles G. Davis, formerly of *Motor Boat* magazine. This organization later merged with Gregory's Belle Isle Boat & Engine Company.

Diversification

Knockdown Boat Building in the Saginaw Valley

In the heart of the Saginaw Valley in the cities of Saginaw and Bay City, Michigan, there rose the small but relatively unique boat-building development of "knockdown" or pattern boat manufacturing. While other states had individual plants that built these products, nowhere else in the nation could there be found such a concentration of this particular type of factory as was found along the Saginaw River.

In many ways the knockdown boat building industry in the Saginaw Valley represented a spectacular microcosm of what was going on with the boat-building industry nationally. Just like the burgeoning automotive and powerboat industries, the knockdown boat-building business started with recognition of an invention, followed quickly by the phases of rapid growth, a sorting-out period of movements of personnel and mergers, overexpansion, collapse, and finally a slow decline with periodic resurrections. But there was never a complete abandonment of the concept.

The question "Why Saginaw and Bay City?" can be answered in part by the decline of the local lumber industry. As major lumbering ports in the last half of the nineteenth century, the cities' sawmills converted huge stands of white pine and hardwood forests into building materials. After 1900 timber tracts along the nation's West Coast attracted the lumbermen to new opportunities, and the exodus from the Saginaw Valley began in earnest. Shipbuilding, initially of wooden vessels and later of steel ships, employed a large portion of the community.[33] Desperately searching for new employment sources in the wake of closing sawmills at the end of the white pine lumber era, the communities found that by building wood-related products such as furniture, doors, sashes, carriages, and boats, large numbers of the skilled machinists, woodworking equipment operators, and unskilled laborers could be kept gainfully employed using the material they were most familiar with. The concerted efforts of local promoters to lure woodworking manufacturing jobs to the area and retain those already there became critically important to the survival of the cities' industrial base. The availability of large quantities of venture capital locally from fortunes built on the older lumber industry also played a significant role in attracting business investment.

Marine and gasoline engine manufacturing in the region, with a few builders in the valley itself but many more in the Detroit area and throughout southeastern Michigan, proved to be an important secondary factor in the development of boat-building in the Saginaw Valley. Cheap, convenient transportation of finished products by ship or railroad to other transportation centers or regions made the location even more attractive for boat-building.

Brooks Boat Manufacturing Company

The story of "knockdown" or pattern boat-building started in a significant way with Clifford C. Brooks, a former newspaperman, advertising agent, and sailor from Bay City. In 1901 Brooks worked as a sailor, making his living on the water. About 1902 Brooks decided that he wanted to get into the launch-building business. He did not have much cash to start the venture, but one day he came up with an idea. Watching his wife, Blanche, use some paper dressmaking patterns, he came up with the concept of doing the same thing to build boats. He took the idea to his friends, one of whom was a practical boat builder, who laughed at him and told him he could not make a financial success of it. Eventually he scraped up two hundred dollars, rented a workshop for four dollars a month, and went to work on the plan. At night he set up his office on the dining room table and used the pantry shelves for filing his papers. He turned to William G. Schindehette and Alonzo L. Arnold, presumably his doubtful boat builder friends, of the Bay City Yacht Works for help in developing the idea.[34] They built boats of different sizes and drew patterns from each separate piece as it was ready to put in the boat. Brooks studied the methods of putting the boat together, down to the smallest detail, so that he could prepare printed directions for rebuilding the boat. Brooks arranged to have the patterns printed on large rolls of paper, a separate pattern, full-size, for each piece of wood used in the boat, allowing the builder to mark the shape on a piece of lumber and cut it himself. The directions included an order sheet showing the exact quantity of each piece of lumber needed, the number of pounds of nails of each size, and the quantity of screws to be used. The "pattern system" of boat-building as devised by Brooks became a startling success.

The Brooks Boat Manufacturing Company was incorporated on November 18, 1903, with capital of $100,000 with Clifford C. Brooks as president, Leon J. Weatherwax as vice president, and John O. Pierce as secretary and treasurer. According to a 1902 Bay City city directory, Pierce worked as a merchant tailor, and Weatherwax was proprietor of The Parra, a millinery company.[35] Using Brooks's marketing skills, the company began advertising in national and international periodicals such as *Scientific American* as early as April 1903, offering a 23-foot-long open gasoline launch with a 5.5-foot beam: "To build this boat requires 250 ft. of oak, 475 ft. of pine or cypress, $4.50 in hardware and paints, and a set of our $15 patterns. We sell Row Boat Patterns for $3." All of this could be built for one-tenth the factory price.[36] "Build Your Own Boat" soon became the company's advertising headline and suggestion, asking readers to send in a postcard and a quarter to order a catalog. A new subdivision of boat-building was off and running.

After a slow start in the first two or three years, orders continually increased at an accelerating pace. The company began manufacturing complete boats and "knockdown" boats, for which all the different pieces were cut to the proper shape, bundled into a package, and shipped to a customer by mail order. Soon a factory was required. The Brooks Boat Manufacturing Company made a deal to merge with Bay City Yacht Works, with partners Arnold and Schindehette joining the company as stockholders. Arnold signed on as the designer and superintendent of construction, and Schindehette took charge of the motor department.[37] Orders came in from the Hawaiian Islands, Honduras, Japan, China, South Africa, and Australia for the unique boats that saved immensely on the cost of building and shipping a complete boat.

In 1905 the Brooks Boat Manufacturing Company produced not just a few hundred boats but *thousands*, building 6,000 boats valued at $240,000, comparatively about twice the volume of the Racine Boat Manufacturing Company and tenfold more than Truscott, but only about half of the value of the Truscott output and about three-quarters that of Racine.[38] A year later Clifford Brooks claimed to have sold boats to 10,686 novices, most

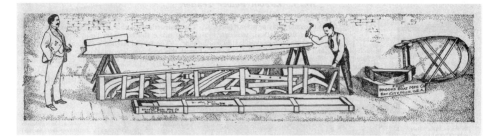

Fig. 10. The Brooks Boat Manufacturing Company's packaged knockdown frames could be shipped virtually anywhere. Backyard owner-builders could save about a third of the cost by building the boats themselves. The Defoe Boat & Motor Works and Pioneer Boat & Pattern Company soon followed Clifford C. Brooks's successful idea with their own products. (Bay County Historical Society.)

of whom had no experience with tools. Over 50 percent of these customers had already built a second boat.[39] The company employed thirty-four workers, eight of whom were women, in 1905. A year later the work force swelled to ninety-seven. The plant was initially located at 1113–1115 Washington Avenue in Bay City, adding a second location in 1906 at the northwest corner of 1st and Jefferson. By the fourth year, four factories were operating at full capacity, and the company had paid-in capital of $76,000.[40] People in the area paid close attention to the amazing quantity of boats, frames, and plans leaving the factories and began looking for opportunities of their own. Competitors started lining up quickly to cash in on the new phenomenon of knockdown or "K-D" boats.

Modern Boat Pattern Company, Ltd., and Pioneer Boat and Pattern Company

The Modern Boat Pattern Company, Ltd., one of the first of several companies to get in on the act, was incorporated on February 1, 1904, in Bay City. In 1905 William N. McLennan served as chairman of the company, Frank McDonell as manager, Mrs. Mary D. McDonell as secretary, and Samuel P. McDonell as treasurer. McLennan worked in the lumber business in addition to his managerial capacity at Modern. The McDonell family owned the McDonell Hardware Company. The Modern Boat Pattern Company, initially located at 817 N. Water Street, soon found that it needed a larger building, contracting with Heumann & Trump of Bay City in August 1904 for a new facility of 40 by 200 feet at the corner of 10th Street and North Birney.[41] Modern traced its roots back as early as 1872 to the work of local boat builder Frank A. Carpenter, the company's superintendent, who wrote "F. A. Carpenter's Improved Method for Amateurs" and sent a copy out with his plans as a guide to building the boats. Modern reported a total of forty-two employees (thirty-eight males, four females) when inspected on May 12, 1905, by state factory inspectors, making it slightly larger than even Brooks, but it was not to last. The Modern Boat Pattern Company was dissolved on April 18, 1906.[42]

Emerging out of the Modern Boat Pattern Company was the Pioneer Boat and Pattern Company, incorporated February 24, 1906, in Bay City with some of the same stockholders and management as Modern and initially capitalized at fifty thousand dollars. The new firm took over Modern's relatively new Birney Street factory. Pioneer became one of the larger manufacturers of knockdown boats, although never of the size or duration of Brooks. William N. McLennan, former chairman of the Modern Boat Pattern Company, served as president; Octavius A. Marsac, secretary; and Albert U. Hoyt, treasurer. Henry K. Gustin of Alpena provided significant financial backing.[43] The company's work force was presumably carried over from the Modern firm as well, as on May 16, 1907, the firm employed thirty-three workers, consisting of twenty-five men and eight women.[44] The firm enjoyed success in its earliest years, increasing its capitalization in 1908 to seventy-five thousand dollars, issuing preferred stock to raise the additional capital for a new building and equipment.

Pattern boats offered by the Pioneer Boat and Pattern Company in 1909 included some fifty-two different models, most organized into seven product lines arranged by stern type. The "100" line consisted of transom stern launches, the "200" line of round stern or fantail launches, the "300" line of pointed torpedo stern launches, the "400" line of full torpedo stern launches, the "500" line of compromise stern cabin cruisers, the "600" line of Norman stern launches, and the "700" line of Norman stern cabin cruisers. Miscellaneous other boats included rowboats, dories, racers, sailing yachts, tunnel boats, and powered rowboats. Variations in canopy and cabin configurations offered more appearance and comfort selection options for the customer. Advertising for the company reached international markets with catalog 40, produced in 1909 and printed in Spanish for foreign distribution. The company mentioned customers in the "thousands" that year.

The firm hired Alonzo L. Arnold, the designer who assisted Clifford Brooks in developing the pattern process for boat construction while he was superintendent of the Bay City Yacht Works. He worked as a designer for Brooks until that company moved to Saginaw. Deciding to remain in Bay City, he worked for Weatherwax's Bay City Boat Manufacturing Company, but the firm closed in 1908, so he started with Pioneer the following year.

As indicated earlier in the chapter, the Pioneer Boat and Pattern Company got caught up in the ill-fated attempt to merge a number of boat builders into a large corporation or conglomerate, the National Boat & Engine Company. After the failure of the National Boat & Engine Company, the Pioneer Boat and Pattern Company fell into receivership and downsized its work force by nearly half, leaving only eighteen people by 1912. In 1913 Arnold remained as general superintendent and designer at Pioneer, but Albert Hoyt moved to Harrisville and Octavius Marsac became the county clerk. Marsac apparently retained his interest in the firm but left the operational aspect to Arnold. The Pioneer Boat and Pattern Company filed notice of its dissolution on April 9, 1915, as an incorporated company, but the firm apparently continued for a couple more years. Further decline of sales forced a further reduction to six employees by 1916. The company probably kept going until about 1917 when the plant was converted to building auto body tops.

Defoe Boat & Motor Works

One of the future industrial giants of Bay City over the long term started by building knockdown boats. Harry J. Defoe, a school principal, decided to take a chance on the new development in knockdown boats, starting the Defoe Boat & Motor Works in 1905, picking up on the success of Brooks's idea. Frederick W. Defoe, his brother, and their brother-in-law, George H. Whitehouse, joined him in forming the new startup. Defoe's first yard was located at the foot of 5th Street on Bay City's east side, but after three years, when the city needed the property for the new Wenonah Park, the company moved the buildings onto vessels and relocated them at the foot of State Street across the Saginaw River next to the Michigan Central Railroad bridge, where the factory remained until 1921.[45] Defoe offered an 18-foot open launch with a 2-horsepower motor complete for $130 in 1908.[46]

Soon most of Bay City joined in the "K-D" craze. The knockdown boats led to another new industry, selling knockdown houses. William J. Sovereign, a draftsman for Brooks, saw the value in the idea and with his brother, Otto E. Sovereign, formed the North American Construction Company in 1906. At first he had trouble convincing Otto of the possibilities, arguing that boats could be sold only near navigable water, whereas

Fig. 11. A Defoe knockdown boat frame preassembled prior to shipment. The company evolved from a builder of knockdown boats to a full-fledged shipyard by the late 1930s. (Bay County Historical Society.)

a knockdown house could be put up virtually anywhere. "Aladdin Homes" sprang up across the nation, often advertised in the same publications as the knockdown boats. By 1918 the approximately 2,800 Aladdin homes sold represented over 2.37 percent of the nation's housing starts for that year. Sovereign, like Brooks before him, soon had another flock of companies following to build knockdown houses.[47] Knockdown in all its forms became a big business trend for the city and region.

Other firms statewide and nationally tried to get a piece of the action in knockdown boats. Larger advertisers included the Niagara Motor Boat Company of North Tonawanda, New York; American Gasolene Motor Company of Baldwinsville, New York; and Sparks Machine Company of Alton, Illinois, among many others.

Brooks Moves

Meanwhile, the Brooks Boat Manufacturing Company became a target for acquisition by another city. In 1906 Saginaw, a few miles from Bay

City on the Saginaw River, offered Brooks's company a clear title-deed to an immense 20-acre plant that had been recently vacated by the Bay City–Michigan Sugar Company. The deal, arranged through the Saginaw Merchants and Manufacturers Association, represented an investment of $750,000 if the firm would maintain an average payroll of $60,000 annually for five years.[48]

Clifford Brooks and John Pierce decided to take the offer and relocate in Saginaw, much to the chagrin of the Bay City community. They parted ways with Leon Weatherwax, who later formed the short-lived competitor the Bay City Boat Manufacturing Company in 1907, became its president, and took over the former Brooks plant at 1113 Washington in Bay City for its operation. Lon Arnold also remained in Bay City with the new firm as its designer, so Brooks and Pierce sought the services of Charles Desmond, formerly of the Detroit Boat Works and Racine Boat Manufacturing Company, to work as their designer and naval architect.

The new Saginaw plant was located on the south side of Rust Avenue near South Jefferson Avenue, and it appears to have been a two-story brick structure. Brooks evidently took over managerial responsibility for the operation in addition to being president. By 1908 the work force had grown to 142, making it one of the largest boat-manufacturing firms in Michigan during the decade.

Beginning in 1910–11, the company began to diversify in several ways. That year the company was renamed the Brooks Manufacturing Company with its capital increased to four hundred thousand dollars. It became a knockdown furniture manufacturing business, building Mission-style pieces in addition to boats. As early as 1905, the company had been using surplus lumber from the boat-building operation to build the furniture.[49] In 1911 the Brooks Aeroplane Company was incorporated on January 26 with capital of five thousand dollars, Clifford Brooks as president, and John Pierce as secretary and treasurer. Six months later, on June 8, the Brooks Motor Wagon Company was incorporated with three hundred thousand dollars in capital, Frank G. Palmerton as president, Brooks as vice president, and Pierce as secretary and treasurer. Palmerton also took over the vice presidency of the Brooks Manufacturing Company. He was also chairman of the F. G. Palmerton Woodenware Company. Palmerton died March 16, 1913, causing a managerial problem of several years' duration. All three companies shared the same address on the south side of Rust Avenue near South Jefferson Avenue. The expansion into other interests turned out to be a failure. By 1915 only the Brooks Manufacturing Company remained in business and was listed only as a furniture manufacturer rather than a boat-building firm, although it may still have constructed both kinds of products.

Beginning about 1919, a series of management changes occurred at the Brooks Manufacturing Company. Founder Clifford C. Brooks left the firm to become vice president of the Klemm Manufacturing Company, which made a phonograph that could repeatedly play a recording. Working with Edwin O. Klemm, with whom he patented the device, Brooks moved to Fenton, Michigan. At the Brooks Manufacturing Company, they continued to manufacture phonographs and boats at their Rust Avenue plant. By 1921 Eva S. Palmerton, Frank's widow, became president, but another shakeup a year later had Ora R. Fowler, a former Palmerton associate, as president, I. Schaitberger as vice president and assistant treasurer, and Fred J. Schmidt as secretary-treasurer. Without a clear direction or leadership, the Brooks Manufacturing Company fell into bankruptcy.

In 1923 buyers found the company's valuable elements and split it up. The phonograph business changed its name to the Brooks Company, with James T. Wylie in the leadership role, and apparently the company remained in the boat business for part of the year. In October 1923, the Brooks Boat Co., Inc., was incorporated with capitalization of forty thousand dollars and a new lease on life. Joseph Pelon, a former foreman and later department superintendent of the shop beginning about 1919, became president; his son, Wilfred J. Pelon, managed the sales end as vice president; and Charles W. Forsyth started as secretary-treasurer. The boat company moved to 416 Salt Street in Saginaw.

Over the next twenty years, the Pelon family held a controlling interest in the firm, with Joseph Pelon serving as president until his death, Wilfred J. Pelon taking over in 1930, and Joseph's wife, Melina, becoming vice president. In 1929 the company moved to 2200 S. Hamilton Avenue, remaining there throughout the Great Depression. Charles Forsyth left the firm about 1938. By 1940, Wilfred was running the company by himself, and by 1942 he had moved on to be a carpenter at the Palace Travel Coach Company.[50] The end of one of the pioneer pattern boat companies passed virtually unnoticed in 1951. Clifford C. Brooks continued in the phonograph business for a while and eventually became a clerk at the Ford Motor Company in Dearborn in 1928. An auto accident left him an invalid in about 1936, and he died in 1941, a far fall from his early career as one of the greatest boat salesmen of all time.[51]

Valley Boat & Engine Company

Picking up Brooks was not enough for Saginaw. The Saginaw Merchant and Manufacturers Association next pursued the new Valley Boat & Engine Company of Baldwinsville, New York, and persuaded the firm to relocate in the city in late 1909. The Valley Boat & Engine Company, formerly the American Gasolene Motor Company, was a knockdown boat-building firm that used designs created for it by naval architect Charles Desmond. It built and shipped erected frames nested in two sections, an idea picked up from one of its customers. It even experimented with selling knockdown marine gasoline engines that the buyers could reassemble.[52] The company made for a nice fit in the existing industrial expansion plans for Saginaw, as the boats would also need engines made locally by the Erd Motor Company or Stork Motor Company, other firms the association had lured to the city.

The Valley Boat & Engine Company of Saginaw filed articles of association in January 1910, with capital of twenty thousand dollars subscribed and paid in. The original stockholders included Dwight S. Simpson and Reed H. Hubbell, both of Baldwinsville, as well as a host of Saginaw businessmen. A year later the firm increased its capitalization to thirty thousand dollars in order to make improvements, including a new office building, finishing room, and pattern loft. This doubled the capacity of the plant and increased the work force by some thirty employees. The company built a smaller variety of open launches of 16, 18, and 20 feet in length, as well as a 25-3/4-foot cruiser.[53] Newell Barnard, formerly of the Barnard & Barnard lumber business, became president of the company in 1911 or 1912, having also served as a partner in Lockwood & Barnard, a banking firm. The Barnards and the Lockwoods had intermarried, making the business more of a family-run operation, with Andre G. Lockwood serving as the firm's vice president.[54] Like Brooks and several other Michigan boat builders, the Valley Boat & Engine Company tried and failed to get into the automobile business, building the "Faultless" cyclecar in 1914, an expensive and energy-consuming diversion from their primary product line.[55]

The Valley Boat & Engine Company filed notice of its dissolution on March 13, 1915, and reinvented itself as the Valley Boat Company, incorporated on the same day, with Newell Barnard remaining as president. In the end, the company never really took off again because World War I intervened. The plant was eventually sold in 1919 to the Lockwood Manufacturing Company to make "Store at Your Door" delivery trucks, a kind of grocery store on wheels. The Valley Boat Company filed notice of its dissolution in May 1924.[56]

Advertising Knockdown Boats

Brooks claimed to be the "originator of the pattern system of construction," which may have been true for patterns, but the concept of knockdown boats had been around for quite some time prior to the startup of the Michigan contingent of companies. The American Boat Building Company, located in St. Louis, Missouri, advertised knockdown boats in *Forest and Stream* in 1897. The Fred Medart Company, a playground equipment manufacturer, also of St. Louis, advertised "knockdown" boats in *Marine Engineering* a year later.[57] The Yukon gold rush in 1898 gave the few builders of the era a quick boost when demand jumped for a boat that could be quickly assembled, especially in a timber-poor area with waterways for the best routes to the gold fields.

The companies advertised in the national popular journals of the day in order to target specific audiences. General interest magazines such as *Muncey's*, *Pearsons'*, and the *Saturday Evening Post* appealed to a broad and diverse group of readers. For more limited targets of hands-on, do-it-yourself men, *Popular Mechanics*, *Popular Science*, and *Scientific American* made good choices for placement. For sportsmen, the yachting journals *Rudder*, *Motor Boating*, *Power Boating*, and *Sail and Sweep* made sense, as well as *Forest and Stream* and *Outing* for people more interested in hunting and fishing.

The companies took diverse approaches to marketing their products. Clifford C. Brooks personalized his sales pitch, showing his portrait and guaranteeing that "Whether you buy boats, engines or furniture of me, I absolutely guarantee that you will be satisfied. I will refund your money if you are not. I stand back of every statement made in this advertisement. I have made them as strong and convincing as I know how. The goods warrant it." By establishing a personal connection with the customer, he added a new dimension to boat advertising seldom seen before, and it dominated his company's advertising for years. Pioneer's advertising placed the emphasis on quality, claiming, "You can easily build this boat yourself with Pioneer Perfect Frames, the ONLY frames having ribs bent to EXACT SHAPE, SET UP, TRUED, TESTED and BEVELED for PLANKING before being knocked down for shipment to you." On the subject of its completed boats, Pioneer stated in its 1909 catalog 39, "Pioneer completed boats are models of strength, beauty and seaworthiness; nothing but the choicest material throughout is used. We make no second-grade boats, nor allow second-grade material of any kind in our factory. They are finished in the highest style of the boat builder's art. They are made to use and to last; neither money nor labor is spared to make them not only staunch, but seaworthy." Names such as Pioneer "Perfect" frames and Valley "Fault-less" frames further assured potential owners that what they planned to purchase was well made and complete, the two things any builder of a kit would essentially want. Defoe's advertisements stated that it built com-pleted boats for both business and pleasure, and that it derived its patterns from "tried and tested" boats.[58] At most of the companies, each frame was advertised as being carefully set up and assembled in the factory to assure that it was complete and fit well together before being dismantled and shipped to the buyer. How well that process worked in actual practice is unknown, as the boating industry press seldom ventured into consumer complaint reporting.

The companies competed fiercely, challenging everything their opposi-tion did in the advertising. Defoe claimed in an obvious bash on Brooks, "We are not the originators of the pattern boat system, but we have been building boats for a time considerably longer than the pattern business has existed."[59] Anything was fair game, from the thickness of the paper on which the plans were printed to the numbering or marking of the frames and the quality of the workmanship. Buyers who were essentially purchas-ing a product sight unseen, other than a catalog illustration of the over-all appearance of the boat, needed a solid guarantee of satisfaction, which most companies provided. The manufacturers effusively described the ease and simplicity of construction and claimed it was difficult to make mistakes when using their instructions. How could anyone go wrong working with their very detailed plans? If the purchaser got stuck, the literature encour-aged him to write for further advice, which would be cheerfully supplied free of charge.

Catalogs were filled with testimonial letters and photos of successful construction stories by people all around the world, many stating that they had either built or intended to build multiple boats. Abundant photographs accompanied the letters, showing that the sometimes massive undertaking could be easily accomplished by a reasonably skilled man with the available time. The market to which the knockdown builders appealed most were those in the economy class of potential buyers, workmen used to work-ing with their hands at manual arts and trades, or those of lesser financial means but potentially highly skilled in construction methods or at least in the use of tools. Younger people who may not yet have found jobs that generated the significant income needed to buy a complete, factory-built boat probably formed a specific target audience. The boat manufacturers tried to make boats affordable to those who could least afford to purchase a luxury item by having the customer supply the bulk of the labor.

The international market served as a very important niche for the knockdown boat builders as they could gain a clear advantage on shipping costs for customers in remote places where no boat factories existed but a skilled work force of builders could be found within the native population to assist the owner in constructing the craft. Boat builders also made potential customers. "Boat builders are mistaken when they figure that our business hurts theirs," Brooks stated. "As a matter of fact I think we help them. In the first place, there are very few of the men who buy boat patterns or frames from us who do not hire the local boat builder to do part of the work. A man will get a knock-down frame and the patterns for his planking and then hire his local boat builder to cut the planking and put it on . . . A lot of small builders use our frames, too. We buy oak in large quantities and have all the facilities for bending it to the right shape, and it is cheaper and more satisfactory for a good many builders to buy their frames right from us than it is to get them out themselves. On the whole I do not think boat builders have any quarrel with us."[60]

The knockdown boat-building industry in Michigan peaked in about 1910 and slowly went downhill after that point for a number of reasons. Market saturation may have been part of the problem, as not enough do-it-yourselfers existed to sustain the vast number of boats or builders after they had built their first one or two boats. People with the wherewithal, time, talent, or economic motivation to complete such a project then, as now, are relatively few and far between. Mismanagement characterized another possible reason for the failures, as Brooks went too far into diversification away from its core business by diverting into automobiles, airplanes, furniture, and finally phonographs. The Pioneer Boat and Pattern Company collapsed with the failure of the National Boat & Engine Company fiasco.[61] Other possible causes for the downturn may have included the decline in international sales after the outbreak of World War I in Europe or increasing price competition from large-output manufacturers of completed boats. Of the survivors, only Defoe went on to substantially increase its size and production, using knockdown boats as a springboard into the larger-scale cruiser- and pleasure-yacht-building business.[62]

As a concept, knockdown boat-building never really went away. Some-body always wanted the satisfying experience of building a boat with his own hands. Louis E. Germain, for instance, formed the Germain Boat Company in Saginaw shortly before World War I and continued building boats after 1950.[63] Harry J. Defoe, later a builder of palatial yachts, never really got out of the business, having formed Bay City Boats, Inc., during the height of the Great Depression but operating well into the 1960s.[64] The interest in knockdown boats continues to ebb and flow even to this day as new generations discover the fun of building one's own boat, using plans or kits produced by the Glen-L Company or others.

More Power

Cameron Waterman and the Outboard Motor

Cameron Beach Waterman, a Detroit and Grosse Ile resident studying law at Yale University, came up with the concept of an outboard motor, an in-vention that would revolutionize boating by making virtually any rowboat a powerboat. While Waterman was not the first to conceive of the idea, he was the first to mass produce and successfully market the device. As early as 1896, the American Motor Company of Long Island City, New York, produced twenty-five air-cooled outboards, and Harry Miller, the automo-tive pioneer engine builder, likewise had the idea to mount an engine on the transom of a boat, though he soon dropped the concept after 1898.[65]

It wasn't that he did not like rowing—he was the captain of the Yale University crew. According to his personal recollection, Waterman pur-chased a Regal motorcycle, taking delivery in February 1902. He drove it around until late fall. In September 1903, he removed the engine and hung it over the back of a desk chair in his room to clean and overhaul it. It was a four-cycle, air-cooled motor that weighed about 20 pounds: "It occurred to me that I could hang it on the transom of a rowboat, attach a propeller to it, and drive a boat. If I hinge the engine to the back of the boat, it could be used to steer as well as propel it. Then in my mind, I provided it with a tiller and mounted a gasoline tank (idea from an oil lamp base) near the tiller to make the whole a self-sufficient unit."[66]

After graduating from law school, Waterman worked for James Whit-temore's law firm, which specialized in patents. When he showed his col-leagues the sketches, they asked him, "Have you made one yet?" He created a series of sketches describing the features and took the drawings to a boiler shop in Detroit run by George Thrall, who agreed to build it if Waterman could get the motorcycle engine. Waterman purchased a 3-horsepower, four-cycle engine from Glenn Curtiss. In February 1905, Waterman and some friends took the prototype to Grosse Ile, an island in the Detroit River, and attached it to a 15-foot steel rowboat: "Although the river was full of ice cakes, the try-out was a complete success except for the fact that once a piece of ice got caught between the chain and sprocket causing the chain to run off the sprocket. We rowed ashore to replace the chain." That day R. McDougal Campau in the party called it an "outboard motor." Others nicknamed it "Coughing Sarah." Thrall and Waterman modified the design to replace the chain drive with an open drive shaft and bevel gears.

Waterman submitted a patent application on December 6, 1905, and was eventually granted U.S. Patent 851,389 on April 23, 1907, for a "Boat-Propelling Device." In the meantime, to refine the design and prepare the motor for production, Waterman took it to Oliver E. Barthel, a consulting engineer in Detroit, to prepare plans. The Caille Brothers Company, Detroit slot and vending machine makers, built the first air-cooled production models in its tool room. Waterman promoted the new product at the February 1906 National Boat and Sportsmen's Show in New York, garnering enough interest from the audience to indicate that the product would be a commercial success. The early air-cooled version overheated, so Waterman and Barthel changed the motor to a water-cooled design in fall 1906 for spring 1907 production.[67]

Waterman formed the Waterman Marine Motor Company on November 5, 1906, with capital of forty thousand dollars to produce the new motor, building a new factory at 1506–1512 Fort Street West with a capacity of twelve to fifteen motors a day. Waterman advertised the "Waterman Porto" motor in popular magazines such as *Colliers*, *Popular Mechanics*, *Rudder*, *Scientific American*, and *Outdoor Life* and soon orders took off. The company sold three thousand motors in 1907, about as many in 1908, and doubled its sales in 1909. Cameron B. Waterman himself did not stay in the business for long, returning to his law practice because of the inability to secure enough patent protection on the invention. Competitors soon flooded the market, and the Waterman Marine Motor Company sold its manufacturing rights to the motor in 1917 to the Arrow Motor and Marine Company of New York.

Waterman was the first to use the term *outboard motor* in advertising, and his motor is considered the first mass-produced outboard to be successfully marketed. His contribution of making an inexpensive rowboat into a powerboat opened up a new audience for boats, changing the marketplace in the process for decades to come.

Many other engine builders played an essential role in the growth of the powerboat industry, supplying the enormous motive power necessary to push boat hulls up out of the water and onto plane. Like Van Blerck, their names became legendary. Gray, Kermath, Scripps, Caille, and a host of others put Detroit and Michigan on the map as the center for marine engine manufacturing. Without them, the boat builders of Michigan would never have become famous in their own right.

Building Materials

Wood

The large amount of wood used in small pleasure boats in the state often came at a high price. Of the ten most common species of wood used by boat builders, white oak constituted more than one-quarter of all the wood consumed in the state. Most of it formed the frames and heavy timbers of boats, but the species was also used for flooring, planking, and finish. By 1912 white oak harvested in Michigan amounted to only about 185,000 board feet of the 1,205,000 board feet consumed annually by the boat- and shipbuilding industry, with the remaining volume shipped in primarily from West Virginia and Kentucky. Cypress, the second most commonly used wood, with an annual consumption of 916,500 board feet, or about 20 percent of the total, was often purchased for planking and came exclusively from the South, mostly from Louisiana. The third, northern white cedar, accounting for about 11.65 percent of the total, came primarily from Michigan. Other woods making up the remaining top ten in 1912 included Douglas fir, often used for masts and yards; sweet birch; swamp white oak (exclusively from Michigan); shortleaf pine; longleaf pine; white pine; and mahogany. Mahogany in 1912 accounted for a mere 1.67 percent of the wood used in boat-building in the state, a figure that would rapidly change over the course of the following decades. Twenty other species, such as redwood, Sitka spruce, butternut, and tamarack, made up between 1 and 2 percent each of the remaining varieties of wood used in boat construction. Most of these woods were used for trim and decoration or for a specific element such as tamarack for knees. In total the state produced only about one-third of the wood used in the ship- and boat-building industry. By far the most expensive of the woods was the mahogany at an average cost of $153.07 per 1,000 feet. By contrast, white oak could be purchased for $49.36 per 1,000 feet and cypress for $45.65 per thousand. Northern white cedar came as low as $37.00 per 1,000 feet.[68]

Steel

By the early 1900s, the production of steel progressed to the point where sheet steel could be cheaply made and incorporated into numerous products, including boats. Steel offered great strength and durability and relatively light weight as a material. Its ductility and resistance to impact or abrasion made it even more desirable for boats with extreme service requirements.[69] With a fresh coat of paint applied annually to minimize corrosion, the boats could be very low in maintenance and could last virtually indefinitely with proper care.

In addition to the Michigan Steel Boat Company of Detroit, several Michigan manufacturers started in steel boat-building, most of them smaller firms that soon failed but also a couple that survived with notable longevity.

Frank H. Darrow, an Albion sportsman, came up with a concept for building a flat-bottomed steel boat of roughly canoe shape and size for hunting and fishing. Patenting the idea in 1911 (U.S. Patent 1,000,766), he formed F. H. Darrow Steel Boat Company in 1912. He soon advertised his product in *Popular Mechanics*, first as a kit boat built from a pattern. As a boat that "Can't Leak, Shrink, Warp or Swell," Darrow hulls featured galvanized sheet steel reinforced with oak and cypress frames, with riveted ribs, gunwales, and keelsons. One of the more popular models, a rowboat or outboard-driven three-section boat that could be nested (bow and stern fitting into the midbody) and transported on the running board of an automobile, earned a reputation as an easily assembled craft that could be taken virtually anywhere. The company offered eight models in numerous sizes in 1926. It operated in Albion until 1951.[70]

In Ludington, William L. Gile started building boats in 1909 as general manager of the Gile Boat & Engine Company, having formerly worked for Cass T. Wright in Greenville. Gile's boat company, bankrolled by lumberman and industrialist Justus S. Stearns, became a regional manufacturer and one of the few builders in the medium-size range in terms of work force, with fifty-six men and two women employed when it opened.[71] Its boats tended to be small and medium-size launches from 16 to 20 feet, and it built its own engines of Gile's design to power them. In 1911 the company started building larger steel boats in the 40-foot range designed by Stuart B. Kingsbury, one of the first naval architects to graduate from the University of Michigan.[72] By the winter of 1913–14, the operation was running night and day, with the capacity to turn out about fifty engines a day.[73] As the market grew tighter over time, the company moved out of boats and into building farm tractors, increasing its production as World War I loomed.

CHAPTER FOUR

Rum-Running, Racing, and the Rise of the Runabouts, 1915–29

Introduction

Despite an initial decline after World War I, the boat-building industry in Michigan reemerged in a period of tremendous growth during the "Roaring Twenties." Most of the growth can be attributed to the desire for high-speed runabouts, fed by three general factors: recreation, rum-running, and racing. All were intertwined as both the rumrunners and rum chasers needed fast boats for avoidance and pursuit, and the general public viewed the racing results as indicators of higher quality and performance in boats, which in turn led to greater sales of watercraft for recreational purposes. Feeding those desires for a fast, comfortable, safe boat, the boat builders became more adept at building boats quickly with new assembly line methods, and shifting the task of marketing and selling the boats from the factories to the advertising agencies and growing dealer networks. By the eve of the Great Depression, Michigan boat builders had created the fastest boats in the world, produced them in the greatest volume ever, and made them available for purchase by buyers of virtually any income.

Military Work during World War I

Boat-building in Michigan before America's entry into World War I in 1917 was largely in a state of flux. The two largest west shore builders, Truscott and Racine, had fallen into bankruptcy in 1915 with the collapse of the National Boat & Engine Company. Truscott emerged as the sole survivor from the failure through the perseverance of its family owners in remaining in the marine engine business. The knockdown boat-building industry in the Saginaw Valley peaked in popularity and subsequently entered a period of slow decline. The Detroit area builders likewise went through an era of transition, but their fortunes rose because of their racing successes, particularly with the growing fame of Chris Smith, whose firm built the fastest boats in the world, and Gar Wood, the industrialist and racer who financed construction of his boats and drove them. John L. Hacker, with his ingenious designs for V-bottom, forward-cockpit-controlled runabouts and racers, likewise became famous for his fast boats and classic styling.

As national hysteria grew about the new submarine menace after the sinking of the British passenger ship *Lusitania* in 1915, Michigan boat builders, like others across the country, tried to come up with ideas to defeat the threat. Chris Smith submitted a design for a 75- to 100-foot torpedo boat capable of 30 to 40 miles per hour to the Navy Department at its request in March 1917. The boat could carry a single torpedo tube and one or two 3-pound guns.[1] Sometimes practicality had little to do with the inventive rush to solve the submarine problem. C. W. Meeker, a boat builder in Oden, Emmet County, spent forty years working for E. I. Dupont de Nemours creating explosives before he started building boats. He conceptualized a weapon in which a ship would tow a torpedo or other explosive device behind it for defense against pursuing U-boats. An antisubmarine board invited Meeker to a Washington conference to present his idea.[2]

As the push for American entry into the war progressed, many yacht and pleasure boat owners showed their patriotism by loaning or selling their yachts to the navy for use as Section Patrol craft for coastal defense. A few citizens also commissioned new boats for use in the service, some designed to appear as warships and armed with light guns. The Dachel-Carter Boat Company of Benton Harbor built *Miss Toledo* for Robert M. Ellery of Toledo, Ohio, in 1917, specifically for this purpose.[3] The government took the initiative in purchasing or temporarily leasing all kinds of cruisers for patrol craft. The Defoe Boat & Motor Works had three of its recently built private yachts requisitioned for coastal patrol duty in 1917.[4]

Michigan shipbuilders and boat builders hoped to secure some of the flood of contracts issued by the government after the nation declared war on Germany. Despite the enormous initial demand for new ships to replace those lost to submarine warfare, small boat construction during World War I in Michigan ended up being a relatively minor endeavor, consisting mostly of small-scale orders for the navy, the army, and the Emergency Fleet Corporation of the United States Shipping Board. Most of the contract work in the state went to the large steel shipyards, the Detroit Shipbuilding Company, Great Lakes Engineering Works, and Saginaw Shipbuilding Company for "Laker" cargo ships. The smaller or older wooden shipbuilding yards, often with new names or ownership, received contracts for wooden barges and repair work to make older boats serviceable. Among the hardest hit in Michigan were the up and coming runabout and cruiser builders, including the Belle Isle Boat & Engine Company, Brooks Manufacturing Company, Church Boat Company, Dachel-Carter Boat Company, John L. Hacker Boat Company, Renaud Boat Works, C. C. Smith Boat & Engine Company, and Valley Boat Company. Each of these firms was listed as either idle or underutilized plants that could conceivably be converted to aircraft or aircraft parts production.[5] Unlike other, larger boat-building firms in the Great Lakes region, Michigan boat-building companies failed to obtain the contracts for the 440 wooden, 110-foot submarine chasers, one segment in defensive small craft where they could have excelled.

A lack of contracts for small boats was not the only hindrance to Michigan boat builders. Congress imposed a luxury tax of 10 percent on any new "yachts or motor boats not designed for trade, fishing or national defense; and pleasure boats and pleasure canoes if sold for more than $15" under section 900 of the Revenue Act of 1918, which hampered the new boat market for years after the war ended. In addition, an annual use tax of ten dollars for any motorboat under five gross tons and larger amounts for bigger boats on a length-per-foot basis impacted the boat owners.[6]

Rumors of rehabilitating the Racine Boat Manufacturing Company's old plant for shipbuilding appeared in July 1917. A new company named the Peninsular Shipbuilding Corporation, formed by George R. Ross and others, attempted to revive the plant. Planning to start with capital stock of five hundred thousand dollars, a work force of five hundred people, and the strong prospect of government contracts, the company seemed poised to make a success as a renewing entity. Unfortunately, it incorporated in the last week of October 1918, just weeks before the war ended with the Armistice.[7]

In 1918 the Defoe Boat & Motor Works received a contract to build five 40-foot wooden torpedo chasers, used to retrieve the expensive weapons after practice firings.[8] Harry and Fred Defoe joined with Otto and William Sovereign of Aladdin Homes to incorporate the first version of the Defoe Shipbuilding Company as a new steel shipbuilding plant separate from Defoe Boat & Motor Works in September 1918.[9] Defoe's transition to steel shipbuilding benefited from an abundance of experience in steel shipbuilding in Bay City. F. W. Wheeler & Company and its successor, the West Bay City Ship Building Company steel shipyard, in operation since the 1890s, had closed a decade before, but many skilled workmen remained in the area. The firm contracted to build eight steel 98-foot "junior" harbor mine planters for the U.S. Army Transport Service, but only four were started before the war ended.[10] Problems in obtaining the necessary steel prevented the mine planters from being finished until 1921, years after the war was over. The Defoe Shipbuilding Company was dissolved a year later, but the Defoe Boat & Motor Works remained in the steel boat-building business, changing its focus to luxury cruisers of both steel and wood. Smaller Michigan boat builders found a niche in building boats for life-saving purposes. The Perry Boat Works of Pearl Beach received orders for 126 U.S. regulation lifeboats and a smaller number of U.S. workboats in July 1918.[11] One factory that converted to war work, the Detroit Vapor Stove Company, changed its plant from building stoves to building lifeboats for the Emergency Fleet Corporation ships under construction in nearby shipyards. Its work represented one of the earlier versions of an assembly line for boat manufacturing with the plant building about eight boats a day. A track system extended from end to end of the 700-foot building. The boat shell was built on the track. As it was completed, it moved along to another workman or group for the next part of the process. Each boat needed eighteen thousand rivets. A paint finish was baked onto the hulls as they passed through a huge japanning oven on a conveyor. Next the boat traveled on for lifelines and floats. Sails, oars, and even rations and water were put in before the boats left the plant, equipping them for immediate service in the war zone.[12] In another form of boat for saving lives, the Belle Isle Boat & Engine Company built one of its fast new mahogany-hulled runabouts to perform rescue work at Selfridge Field in Mount Clemens, retrieving airmen who crashed into Lake St. Clair during the course of their flight training.[13]

New processes for boat-building and shipbuilding emerged during the war years. In 1916 Henry Haskell of Ludington, creator of the Carrom board game, invented a process to make molded veneer canoes. The method used three sheets of California redwood veneer glued together with waterproof albumin glue and then squeezed together in a huge 60,000-pound press capable of exerting 500 tons of pressure. The process formed an extremely sturdy hull and eliminated the ribs used in traditional canoe construction, forming a smooth interior bottom. Haskell's process led to important weight reductions, added strength in aircraft-building technology, and even later led to the introduction of molded plywood boat hulls.[14] Using another novel material and technology, the Grayhaven Shipbuilding Company of Detroit used the "Torcrete" process to build 150-foot steel-reinforced concrete barges for service on the New York state canal system at the end of the war.[15]

The sudden cancellation of contracts by the government at the conclusion of hostilities caused a great deal of chaos in the shipbuilding and boatbuilding industry. Virtually all builders with government contracts faced immediate financial hardship because materials purchased in anticipation of deliveries scheduled into the next year sat unused in their yards with no orders to fill. Typical of the companies hit hardest by the government's decisions, the Sydney C. McLouth shipyard in Marine City received a contract for ten tugboats worth 2.5 million dollars from the United States Shipping Board. When the federal government canceled the shipbuilding contracts, McLouth, left with three unfinished tugs under construction and a yard full of 600,000 feet of lumber, faced the new problem of trying to sell the tugs to private customers with a glut of new construction already on the market from builders in similar circumstances. With nothing moving on the tugs, McLouth built 16-foot, $250 "Moto-Row" motorized rowboats for the Belle Isle Boat & Engine Company for a short time in 1922. Undoubtedly stressed by the burden of trying to revive his company, Sydney C. McLouth died suddenly of heart failure in September 1923, forcing his son Peirce to take over the operation.[16]

An extremely sharp deflationary recession in 1920–21 created additional hardships for many of the boat builders as they struggled to find their new niche in the marketplace. Many factors caused the recession, such as an irregular supply of raw materials diverted from their normal inventory streams, combined with a tangled railroad transportation system generated by the poorly planned mobilization for the war. Soldiers returning to civilian life at home found a high unemployment rate and few opportunities for work. Labor strife in the iron, steel, railroad, and coal industries likewise negatively affected the national economy. Of the ninety boat-building firms listed in the *Michigan State Gazetteer and Business Directory* for 1917, only sixty-five remained in the 1923 edition, and several of those reflected changes in ownership. The casualties included the Central Lake Boat Manufacturing Company of Central Lake, which was dissolved in June 1921, as well as the Marquette Launch & Motor Works and Michigan Boat Works of Petoskey, among several others.[17]

Mass Production and Standardization

As the most ambitious experiment in the early mass production of boats and ships in the history of shipbuilding, automobile manufacturer Ford Motor Company learned many lessons building the Eagle boat submarine chasers during World War I. Encouraged by the federal government at the highest levels to put its massive production capacity to use, Henry Ford launched a huge project to mass-produce steel submarine chasers of an intermediate size between the 110-foot wooden sub chasers and full-sized destroyers. In planning the 204-foot oceangoing "boats" armed with 4-inch guns, Ford worked with the navy to design the revolutionary craft using assembly lines and factory workers, unlike any ship construction method developed to date. He insisted on using flat plates to minimize the curves typical in a ship in order to reduce production time, resulting in a slab-sided, unattractive appearance as a trade-off for faster framing and plating. Ford persuaded the navy to accept steam turbines instead of the typical steam-reciprocating engines for greater speed, but otherwise the design remained the U.S. Navy's. U.S. Secretary of the Navy Josephus Daniels telegraphed Ford on January 17, "PROCEED WITH ONE HUNDRED SUBMARINE PATROL VESSELS . . . DETAILS OF CONTRACT TO BE ARRANGED AS SOON AS PRACTICABLE."[18]

Ford erected a huge new plant designed by Albert Kahn at River Rouge with three assembly lines each a third of a mile long, each line capable of carrying seven boats and employing some eight thousand workers at one time during the height of production. The first keel, laid on blocks on May 7, 1918, was quickly transformed into a completed boat launched July 11 on schedule. Ford found out the hard way that shipbuilding did not lend itself as well to assembly line techniques as automobiles did, as none of the following boats could be delivered on time. Numerous riveting and welding problems appeared in the first few boats, caused by an undertrained work force lacking experience in shipbuilding. Ford's contract called for 112 Eagle boats (12 were added for the Italian navy) to be delivered by December 1, 1918, yet only two made it to the Atlantic coast before Armistice Day. At the conclusion of the war, the government slashed Ford's contract to 60 boats, with the last one commissioned on October 15, 1919. The Ford experiment in mass production of boats ended in failure, as it never revolutionized shipbuilding technology, but it clearly illustrated the difficulty of transferring the high-volume processes of automobile manufacturing to those in the low-volume, handcrafted shipbuilding tradition.[19] Small boat-building, on the other hand, lent itself well to assembly line manufacturing techniques and in a decade became the standard method for building large numbers of watercraft. Edsel Ford, Henry Ford's son, briefly experimented with building small craft in 1924–25 with a boat driven by a Fordson tractor engine, but the company soon abandoned the tractor business, which in turn eliminated the source for engines, halting the project.[20]

Efforts at standardization of boats and marine engines started to gain momentum after World War I, but even before the war, as early as 1916, the Executive Committee of the National Association of Engine and Boat Manufacturers encouraged the engineers of its member companies to apply for membership in the Society of Automotive Engineers. The society, the leading organization for standardization, formed a Motorboat Division within its Standards Committee to focus on developing complete sets of standards for construction and installation. Coming up with standards and best practices to find economies in production and simplification in assembly and service caught on slowly in the boat-building industry. Standardization, even by the mid-1920s, usually only meant "standard" within the individual shop in which the boats were built. The S.A.E. Motorboat Division within the Standards Committee confined its work primarily to the mechanical side of the boats, such as the engines, reverse gears, and standardized control levers, for safety in operating boats as opposed to hull design and construction techniques.[21]

The Liberty aircraft engine represented one of the better examples of standardization driven by the war effort. Engineers designed the basic concept of the engine over six days in a Washington hotel room. Automobile manufacturers Packard, Buick, Ford, Lincoln, Marmon, and Cadillac stepped in to build them, and within seven months engines were streaming off the assembly lines by the thousands. For decades the engine played an important role in the boating industry, particularly racing. The quick end to the war created a huge surplus stock of engines that far exceeded the U.S. Army Air Corps and the U.S. Navy's future needs.[22] Speedboat racer Gar Wood formed the Detroit Marine-Aero Engine Company to purchase over 4,500 of the war-surplus Liberty engines and other types new in their crates for just pennies on the dollar. He used them in his own racing boats and high-speed pleasure boats sold for years to other private individuals.[23]

Rum-Running: Prohibition and the Boat Builders

Beginning as a wartime measure in May 1918, well ahead of the rest of the nation by nearly two years, Michigan started on its long, fateful journey through Prohibition, during which the state became renowned for its extremely leaky border with Canada for the smuggling of alcoholic beverages. As the dark side of Michigan's rise to eminence in the boat-building industry, Prohibition played a pivotal role in the rate of growth of the companies building fast boats as demand skyrocketed for anything that could carry booze across the Detroit River, the St. Lawrence River, and other, narrow waterways dividing the two countries. Just as the fame gained by the fast boats in racing spawned new sales, the opportunities for fortune building through rum-running proved just as compelling for the same market.

With a border several thousand miles in length, in many areas separated by a mile or less of waterway, the problem of halting the flow of liquor was essentially insurmountable. Approximately 75 percent of the liquor smuggled into the United States crossed Michigan's border with Canada, mostly in a 28-mile stretch of the Detroit River from Lake Erie to Lake St. Clair jokingly referred to as the "Detroit-Windsor Funnel." Dotted with islands and inlets, the Detroit River offered hundreds of hiding places in which to elude government patrol boats. Smugglers could make the run across the river in less than five minutes in the narrower areas.[24] Boathouses lining the river concealed transfers from boats to shore-based transportation behind closed doors. Likewise, farther north, the St. Clair River and even the St. Marys River in the Upper Peninsula offered similar geography suitable for smuggling, although a much smaller volume passed through these areas than through the Detroit and Downriver Detroit areas because there were fewer export docks.[25]

Prohibition provided a great opportunity for the boat builders to cash in on the two warring factions, smugglers (or rumrunners or bootleggers) and law enforcement. Essentially acting as arms dealers in the struggle, the boat builders caught in the middle of the conflict served both sides equally as speed merchants to the rumrunners and contractors to the government for rum chasers, often to their great profit.

With the passage of the Volstead (National Prohibition) Act in February 1920, matters became even more difficult for the law enforcement community. At first the rum-running operations were small family and friends affairs, a matter of bringing a few cases over the border from Canada and collecting handsomely on the added value of the illicit product in the United States. After just a few trips, enough profit could be generated to buy a new, faster boat. Over time the fabulous fortunes generated from many trips across the river attracted the attention of organized crime, which moved in and pirated the trade away from the individuals and families, frequently leaving floating bodies behind as a reminder for anyone

LOOKOUT ON
AMERICAN SIDE

RUNNER WITH GLASSES
AWAITING SIGNAL

LOADED OUTBOARD
SPEED BOAT

Fig. 12. A rumrunner watches for a signal that it is safe to cross the Detroit
River from Sandwich, Ontario, to the American side at Detroit in 1929.
The narrow channel could be traversed in about five minutes or less,
making it virtually impossible for law enforcement agents to catch the
smugglers. (Courtesy of the *Detroit News* Archives.)

who crossed it or got in the way. The so-called Little Jewish Navy, a faction
of Detroit's notorious Purple Gang, ran about a dozen fast boats across the
river, leading, in part, to the rise of organized crime in the city.[26]

Smugglers used just about any kind of watercraft imaginable to move
the booze, from rowboats to fast runabouts to freighters, barges, tugs, passenger ships, iceboats, and even torpedo-like devices. More than anything
else, they desired speed, along with carrying capacity to a lesser degree,
easily obtained with the products of the burgeoning boat industry, especially those of the companies conveniently located near Detroit. The Belle
Isle Boat & Engine Company, C. C. Smith Boat & Engine Company, Gar
Wood, Inc., Dee-Wite, Inc., and Hacker Boat Company all built extremely
fast runabouts in the area, and the Purdy Boat Company, Corsair Boat
Company, A. G. Liggett & Son, and others built high-speed cruisers in
the post–World War I era. Not all the boats needed to be extremely fast.
Louis Mayea of Mayea Boat Works built a 30-foot boat with good carrying capacity nicknamed a "bathtub bootlegger." Large plugs in the bottom

could be pulled to intentionally sink the boat and its lucrative cargo if the pursuing authorities got too close.[27]

A dichotomy for the early rumrunners in high-speed boats so legendary in the many romanticized stories about Prohibition has to do with boat ownership and who was actually involved in the business. On the one hand, stories abound about fast boats crossing the river by dark of night, waiting for a signal light from the other side indicating that this was a safe time to cross and evade passing patrol boats and shore-based enforcement. On the other hand, very few of the Michigan boat manufacturer histories even mention the use of the boats as rumrunners, particularly the ones located in the Detroit area. Early sales ledgers for Chris Smith in the 1921–24 era are filled with the names of prominent community businessmen and professionals, most of whom do not seem to have been the kind of people originally engaged in rum-running. The same goes for known early Hacker boat buyers. Obviously the people with the fastest boats were not the ones getting caught, so the criminal records and news articles only represent those unlucky enough in the timing of their runs to be caught on shore. While the assumption is that everybody was doing it, little is known about who actually purchased the boats used as rumrunners, be it otherwise honest, well-known citizens who were letting their fast boats be used or were themselves using the boats for illicit purposes or unrecognizable buyers who were fronting for organized crime gangs or other illegal independent operators. According to historian Larry Engelmann, "Successful rum-running involved coordination and speed as well as bravery, bribery and luck."[28] The boat builders must have known a little about who they were selling to, but like most Michigan citizens, they either chose to ignore the issue or made no effort to halt the transactions as it was none of their business how the boats were used after their sale.[29]

Shocked and appalled by the public's lack of respect for the new law, governments on all levels, federal, state, and local, slowly responded by buying boats to defeat the rum traffickers, but the boats acquired proved to be far too few in number and too slow in performance to effectively fight the smuggling. Usually the fastest boats in the law enforcement agencies' fleets were those they had confiscated during shore-based raids.

Congress did not even officially authorize the Coast Guard to enforce Prohibition until 1923 after rumors of an "army" of twenty-five thousand smugglers hauling over 100,000 gallons of liquor a day across the Detroit River, in addition to stories about other national hotspots of illegal activity, forced it to act.[30]

Fig. 13. U.S. Coast Guardsmen dumping cases of beer into the Detroit River during Prohibition after the seizure of a rumrunner. Michigan boat builders profited by serving both sides of the rum war over the course of the 1920s and early 1930s by building fast boats. (Courtesy of the *Detroit News* Archives.)

"I am going to blot Ecorse and other smuggling centers completely off the map," said Lieutenant Laurence A. Lyons, head of the Michigan State Police river patrol in 1924. "Hitherto our department has maintained only a shore guard. They have held down the liquor traffic, but with the river patrol in operation, smuggling will be at a standstill."[31] Lieutenant Lyons's woefully over-optimistic assessment of his troops' capabilities reflected the attitude of the law enforcement community, which was initially undeterred by the volume of boat traffic it needed to stop. The Michigan Department of Public Safety (Michigan State Police) decided to take a different approach to rum chasing in 1924. In setting up Lyons's marine unit on the Detroit River, it purchased four Chris-Craft runabouts for twelve thousand dollars and serviced them with a mother ship, the cruiser *Aladdin*, purchased from William J. Sovereign of Bay City. For a short time the new, faster boats slowed down the rumrunners, but soon the traffic increased to normal levels and beyond.

As time went on, the fleets were updated with faster runabouts for the police and U.S. Border Patrol. The U.S. Coast Guard commissioned a number of larger "rum chasers" from a couple of different builders in the state. The Dachel-Carter Boat Company and Defoe Boat & Motor Works received large contracts as both firms had earned a solid reputation with the government for their wartime production during World War I. In June 1924 Dachel-Carter received a contract valued at $250,000 for 10 wooden, 75-foot, "six-bitters" class of patrol boats for rum chasers. Defoe did even better with 15 of the same boats for a contract price of $21,000 each. Nationally the Coast Guard purchased 205 of these boats. The "six-bitters," with a top-end speed of about 17 miles per hour, turned out to be far too slow to pursue fast runabouts capable of twice that speed, and their large size did not make them particularly effective in patrolling the Detroit River, although they were more adept at offshore work along the nation's ocean coastlines.

The inability of law enforcement to control the epidemic of lawbreaking inspired Gar Wood, a prohibitionist, to suggest the construction of two hundred speedboats equipped with Liberty engines, which he offered to build at cost, to help the federal government enforce prohibition laws. The proposal, never taken seriously and doomed to failure for lack of interest, could have gone a long way toward reducing the problem. Congress, torn between recognizing the failure of its policies and the need for strong law enforcement when so many were ignoring the penalties, could never supply sufficient funding to solve the problem.[32]

In addition to new boat construction, the boat builders also cashed in on the large amount of repair work for both sides. Rumrunner boats shot up during run-ins with law enforcement boats or by rival gangs during hijacking attempts required repairs that demanded confidentiality and speedy workmanship. Inexperienced crew members handling the law enforcement boats often wrecked their craft in shallow waters during high-speed chases. Engines ruined by misuse and abuse likewise constantly added to the equipment problem for the government agencies.[33]

Just as the creation and attempted enforcement of Prohibition led to the greatest years of mass-market boat-building in the state to date, the abandonment of Prohibition in 1933 created negative consequences for the industry, making matters worse right at the height of the Great Depression. Not surprisingly, Michigan residents led the nation as the first state to approve the Twenty-First Amendment, repealing Prohibition. For well over twelve years, the boat builders had made the best of the rare opportunity to serve two separate and opposing markets, the bootleggers' need for fast runabouts and cruisers and law enforcement's need for faster pursuit craft with which to chase them. Now the bootleggers no longer needed to purchase fast boats, and the Coast Guard and other government agencies no longer had the funds or the mission to purchase rum chasers. Combined with the financial malaise of downward-spiraling sales and lower repair volume, the demise of Prohibition probably helped cause the failure of some of the Michigan boat-building companies, although the real impact can never be realistically known.

Racing: Gar Wood and the Search for Speed

Gar Wood of Algonac and Detroit epitomized the search for speed on the water. In a series of racing boats named *Miss Detroit* and *Miss America*, built by the capable hands of Christopher Columbus Smith and subsequently Joseph Napoleon Lisee, Wood dominated high-speed racing on a national and international scale with his conquest and defense of the American Power Boat Association's Gold Cup and the British International Trophy, also known as the Harmsworth Trophy. Known as the "Gray Fox of Algonac" for his silvery white hair, Wood could be characterized by the press as either a cunningly fierce competitor or an honorable racing gentleman, depending on the event.

Wood's racing success spawned a public interest in motorboating that would last for decades. Roaring down the waterways first at 60, then at 80, and finally upwards of 120 miles per hour, his racing exploits captured the imagination of a nation craving speed. Events in which he raced drew hundreds of thousands of spectators lining the banks of the Detroit River, making them some of the largest sporting events of their time. For many, a thrilling glimpse of the fastest racing boats in the world roaring down a straightaway, going head-to-head in competition, made for a strong desire for fast boats of their own.

Garfield Arthur Wood, named after two presidents, was born December 4, 1880, in Mapleton, Iowa. He was one of thirteen children raised by a ferryboat captain and his wife. The family moved to Minnesota, where the young Wood learned about gasoline motors while working on an inspection boat along an interlake railroad construction project. While living in St. Paul, he invented a device that would later earn him a fortune—the hydraulic dump-truck hoist. With his new product in high demand by road builders and the construction trades, Wood moved to Detroit in about 1913 to be closer to the truck manufacturers.[34]

With his wealth accumulating rapidly, Wood started investing in powerboat racing. One of his first acquisitions, in 1916, brought him into con-

tact with Chris Smith. *Miss Detroit*, financed by subscription by the Miss
Detroit Power Boat Association, succeeded in winning the Gold Cup for
Detroit in 1915, but the builder, Smith, had not received the final payment
on the boat, a battered hull after a hard season of racing. John J. "Baldy"
Ryan had gone bankrupt earlier, and the boat company badly needed some
quick cash to make ends meet. At a luncheon auction, Wood, a relative unknown in town, bought the boat and went to Algonac to check out his new
purchase. Wood met Smith and his son Jay, and by the end of the day Smith
had found a new financier for the C. C. Smith Boat & Engine Company.[35]
Over the next few years, Smith built Wood a string of boats named *Miss
Detroit II, III*, and subsequent numbers, winning the American Power Boat
Association's Gold Cup in 1917, 1919, 1920, and 1921 with Wood driving,
earning him wide acclaim as one of the finest drivers in the nation. As the
world's fastest man on water, Wood sought something even greater, winning in international competition.

For many years, the British International Trophy, also known as the
Harmsworth Trophy after its donor, Sir Alfred Harmsworth, represented
the epitome of speed in the international arena of boat racing. Rules for
the race stipulated that the boats could be no longer than 40 feet and the
component parts and crew's nationality had to be from the country represented. Wood ordered two boats built for the 1920 Harmsworth race, the
38-foot *Miss Detroit V* and the 26-foot *Miss America*. Both were equipped
with modified Liberty aircraft engines. A third American contestant's boat
burned up in trials shortly after its arrival in England. The British competitors, the *Maple Leaf V*, *Maple Leaf VI*, and *Sunbeam-Despujols*, were powered by Rolls-Royce and Sunbeam engines. Wood and his brother George
drove the boats, assisted by mechanics Jay and Bernard Smith, sons of
Chris Smith, their builder. In the August 20 and 21 races, the American
boats beat their British opponents, with Gar Wood winning the prestigious
Harmsworth Trophy in *Miss America*. He returned to the United States less
than a month later and established a new world water speed record in one
lap at the Lake George One-Mile Championship trials at 78.2 miles per
hour, faster than anyone had ever traveled on water before.[36]

Just before the 1921 racing season began, Wood formulated plans for
a unique race and endurance run. He intended to race his 50-foot express
cruiser, *Gar Jr. II*, against the Atlantic Coast Line's Havana Special train,
from Miami to New York, in an effort to prove that a cruiser could travel
long distances in the open sea at high speeds in relative comfort and with
only minor maintenance. *Motor Boating* magazine editor Charles F. Chap-

man promoted the race and served as Wood's navigator. On the night of April 24, they left Miami on a forty-one-hour trip, arriving in New York on April 30, twenty minutes ahead of the train.

Wood continued to defend the Harmsworth Trophy for over a decade in the 1920s and early 1930s in the face of ever-increasing competition from Great Britain. In the late 1920s, the British government helped subsidize engine development in order to push for speed supremacy on land, sea, and air. It assisted companies such as Rolls-Royce and Napier to create more powerful engines, which private sportsmen in turn placed into boats, automobiles, and aircraft. The British challengers for the Harmsworth Trophy kept coming, only to suffer defeat because of structural or mechanical failure or Wood's racing skill . . . or luck. A superstitious man, Wood carried two toy teddy bears, "Teddy" and "Bruin," for good fortune when racing. Not that he completely trusted his luck. Wood told writer William S. Dutton in an interview, "In life's experiences there may be a chain of circumstances that seem to cause the fickle Goddess of Fortune to smile upon someone, but as for luck, I believe in most instances it follows preparedness and the person who leaves anything to luck is taking a long chance."[37]

Once Wood ran out of luck and very nearly missed the 1928 Harmsworth event himself. Running tests on the St. Clair River in *Miss America VI* with mechanic Orlin Johnson by his side, the boat hit a submerged object and went to pieces at over 70 miles per hour. Wood was thrown clear, but Johnson hit an exhaust stack, slicing his neck and breaking his jaw. When he regained consciousness about an hour later, he told his boss, "Guess we'll have to build another boat." Wood told his crew to start work on a new boat immediately, and after four days of searching, divers located the engines under six feet of muck in the river bed and salvaged them for the new boat. Fifteen days later Wood launched a new contender, *Miss America VII*, just in time for the race. Johnson accompanied him in the event with his jaw in a cast. The race turned out to be anticlimactic. The British challenger, Marion Barbara "Betty" Carstairs, heiress to the Standard Oil fortune, raced her *Estelle II* against Wood's *Miss America VII* in the contest for the trophy, but her boat dove into the wash of Wood's boat when rounding the first turn, throwing her and mechanic Joe Harris from the craft. Carstairs emerged battered and bruised, but Harris suffered broken ribs and a spine injury.[38] Carstairs returned to Detroit in September 1929, racing against Wood before half a million spectators lining the riverfront, but her *Estelle IV* hit a log, damaging the boat. With her boat repaired but with no chance to win, Carstairs gamely raced the next day but inevitably lost to Wood's faster boat.[39]

One of the best competitions in boat-racing history pitted Kaye Don, a Brooklands track race car driver, against Wood in a boat named *Miss England II*. The boat was wrecked in a previous world water speed record attempt by Sir Henry Segrave on Lake Windermere in England in 1930, killing its driver and a mechanic. Salvaged and reconditioned, Kaye Don drove the boat with a vengeance, trading world water speed record leads with Wood between 1930 and 1932 and raising the record by 21 miles per hour. The 1931 Harmsworth race against Don cost Wood dearly. On the first day, Don swept the first heat, beating both Gar Wood in *Miss America IX* and his brother George in *Miss America VIII* by a considerable margin. During a spectacular beginning on the second day, the gun sounded for a flying start. Both Gar Wood and Kaye Don crossed the starting line ahead of the gun by over five seconds. During the first turn, Wood swung his boat wide of the course-marking buoy. Don followed but was forced to cut across Wood's wake in order to catch up. Don's boat entered the wash along the line of the trough and capsized, spilling the crew into the river and sinking the boat. Both Kaye Don and Gar Wood were disqualified, leaving George Wood to finish the race alone, although officials declared that "no match resulted." The sporting press exploded, accusing Wood of a premeditated "Yankee trick" to lure Don into a false start and unsportsmanlike conduct. Wood vehemently denied the charges, but they continued to haunt him for years afterward.[40]

Competing against the British with their subsidized engines came at a phenomenal expense for Wood as a private citizen, working directly with the Packard factory to further the development of its engines for his boats. At one point, he figured he had spent over a million dollars on his hobby. During a 1931 interview, he lamented, "My boat, *Miss America IX*, has two Packard engines of 1,060 horsepower each and weighing 1,500 lbs. apiece. *Miss England II* has two Rolls-Royce engines, no heavier than mine, but delivering 2,000 horsepower each, just twice the horsepower of *Miss America IX*. There are no engines in this country to compete with them." Wood's final defender, *Miss America X*, exceeded all prior boats in terms of sheer horsepower. A 38-foot mahogany-hulled behemoth equipped with four supercharged Packard engines totaling 6,400 horsepower, the boat contained more power than three railroad locomotives of the day.[41] Skeptics warned that the engines would tear the boat apart, but Wood persisted, creating special gearboxes that splined the shafts of the engines together in tandem pairs. His defenses of the Harmsworth Trophy and the world water speed

Fig. 14. Gar Wood, the "Gray Fox of Algonac" (*left*) with Orlin Johnson. Wood raced the series of boats named *Miss America* to break world water speed records throughout the 1920s and early 1930s. Packing in as much power as a hull could hold, *Miss America X*'s four Packard engines totaled 6,400 horsepower in 1932. (Kettering University Archives, Flint, Michigan.)

record near the height of the Great Depression clearly demonstrated the technological changes in advanced racing boats. The British contender in 1933, *Miss Britain III*, designed, built, and driven by Hubert Scott-Paine, featured a 24-foot aluminum-clad hull powered by a single Napier Lion engine of 1,370 horsepower. Wood won the race in a tight contest, but the era of boats like his ended as the Great Depression deepened. His final world water speed record, set on September 20, 1933, on the St. Clair River, of 124.91 miles per hour stood for five years before Malcolm Campbell's *Bluebird K3* set a new record in 1937.[42]

Runabouts: Building Mahogany Classics on the St. Clair and Detroit Rivers

By the 1920s, Michigan builders along the Detroit and St. Clair Rivers had become the nation's speed merchants for fast runabouts. No other area of the country experienced the proliferation of so many firms, nor did any achieve the tremendous commercial success of the Michigan builders. Contributing factors accounting for the rapid rise in the industry, all of which coalesced in the 1920s, included rum-running across the Detroit River and other border waterways, racing success (particularly that of Gar Wood's, Chris Smith's, and John L. Hacker's boats, with their attendant publicity), and significant increases in the power of the engines provided by Detroit area builders such as Van Blerck, Gray, and Scripps, all of which fueled the growth of the industry. Combined with exceptional design talent for hull configurations, marketing prowess, and a highly skilled work force, the formula for success made Michigan firms the international leaders for speed on the water.

Runabouts, a general term for fast motorboats propelled by powerful engines, with long foredecks and open cockpits, became the boats of choice for the public for their speed, the ability to carry a small party of passengers, and an attractive appearance for a price affordable to the business and professional classes. The builders were transformed into mass producers of watercraft out of necessity to keep up with a thriving business, adding people and large quantities of machinery to cut out and shape individual wooden parts, resulting in faster assembly times and lower production costs. The transition was complicated because not everyone wanted an identical stock model boat, so the customization of individual boats in many instances still met the broad demands of the marketplace. Builders experimented with different construction approaches such as the level of sustainable customization because there was plenty of room in the marketplace due to the unprecedented demand. Most of the advances in mass production of the boats emerged out of organizing the work environment in the factories into efficient progressions from process to process rather than speed of line assembly. Like early automobile manufacturing, boats moved on carts from station to station rather than on moving assembly lines. The efficiencies came at the expense of craftsmen with well-rounded boat-building skills. Where before a group of men would work on a boat from start to finish, now the assembly-oriented builders trained them to perform one very specific series of tasks before the boat moved on to the next station, with the men performing the same operation day in and day out. Standardization of a limited variety of models, essential to mass production, meant fewer choices for customers, but the builders offered an increasing number of models with greater variations in size and power over time to reach the broadest portion of the market.

Creating Chris-Craft

At the C. C. Smith Boat & Engine Company, building hydroplanes created an enormous amount of interest in these fast boats, but Chris Smith and his financial partner, Gar Wood, differed on the direction the company should take in the future. Smith's philosophy called for building smaller, more affordable boats in higher volumes for a larger customer base, and Wood wanted to build larger, faster, more powerful boats for a more limited, affluent clientele. In the end, each man decided to go his separate way.

Chris Smith and his sons split from Gar Wood in February 1922, renaming their business the Chris Smith & Sons Boat Company. The Smiths sold their former shop to Wood, using the proceeds from the sale to purchase 20 acres of land at Pointe du Chene, building a new factory just outside the village of Algonac. Initially the parting seemed amicable, only a business deal between partners who decided to go in different directions. The Smiths continued to build the 33-foot Baby Gar model boats for Wood's new firm, Gar Wood, Inc., through 1925. The initiative behind the shift to make the business independent of Wood's financial control probably came from Smith's sons, particularly Jay and Bernard, ages thirty-seven and thirty-three, compared to Chris Smith, who turned sixty-one in 1921. His son Hamilton coined a new name, "Chriscraft," originally nonhyphenated, to identify the boats of the new firm.[43]

One of the contributing factors leading to the eventual rivalry between Wood and the Smiths happened when the Smiths built the racing runabout *Packard-Chriscraft* for Colonel Jesse G. Vincent, the chief engineer at Packard, who in turn beat Wood in the 1922 Gold Cup Race. Wood dominated the Gold Cup event for so long that the American Power Boat Association rewrote the rules to prohibit stepped-bottom designs and limited engines to 625-cubic-inch displacement. Another point of contention was the loss of talent. Wood and the Smiths surrounded themselves with a number of extraordinary designers and builders, who, like the businesses, ended up going in the two different directions. Joseph Napoleon "Nap" Lisee, an extremely talented designer and carpenter for several of the Smith racers, went to work for Wood, serving as the lead designer of all of his racers, including *Miss America X*. George Joachim also joined Wood, becoming the lead stylist of his production boats. The Smiths suffered from their loss, but they also gained some business-changing help of their own. Joining the Smiths in the spring of 1922, A. William ("Mac" or "Bill") MacKerer initially did not stay with the Smiths, having butted heads with Napoleon

Fig. 15. Christopher Columbus Smith earned a reputation for building fast racing boats for J. Stuart Blackton, John "Baldy" Ryan, and Gar Wood. Wood financed Smith's company in the early years before the men went their separate ways. Smith decided to build smaller, less expensive boats while Wood built larger, fast boats for the wealthy. (© Mystic Seaport, Rosenfeld Collection, no. 2998S.)

Lisee, but he returned to them after Lisee started working for Wood. A New York native who spent time working for George Crouch, and later in Michigan working for John L. Hacker, the Purdy brothers (he married Gil Purdy's daughter Dorothy), and the Belle Isle Boat & Engine Company, MacKerer became a driving force in the factory, demanding quality construction and unrelentingly seeking new ways to make the plant more efficient any way he could. MacKerer and Jay Smith created the "straight line" production method, leading the company to great cost reductions in building its boats.[44] Unlike other boat-building operations, where one crew worked on a boat from start to finish, MacKerer organized the boat-building work of the C. C. Smith & Sons shops into a station-by-station work environment, where a small group of workers performed a number of construction tasks before the boat moved on to the next operation in a linear fashion. The Smiths and MacKerer borrowed some of their ideas from the Fisher Body Corporation in Detroit, the well-known automobile body manufacturers.[45] MacKerer stayed with the company with only a couple of breaks in service for over forty years, eventually retiring as vice president in 1965.

The Smiths in their new organization and factory slowly built an interesting product line and production technology. Production in the first season in 1922 started out quite slowly, averaging about 1 powerboat and 1 rowboat a week, presumably due in part to the lingering effects of the 1921 recession. In the first nine months of the year they produced 22 26-foot standardized powerboats and 22 rowboats for delivery. The 26-foot boat retailed at $3,200, plus tax, including a Curtiss OX-5, 90-horsepower marine conversion aircraft engine. The boat did not yet have a windshield (a feature added in 1925), but wicker chairs in the stern cockpit offered comfortable seating for passengers. Typical early buyers in 1922–24 included Charles E. Allinger, secretary and treasurer of the Charles A. Strelinger Company (invoice no. 1); Vincent Bendix, the four-wheel brake manufacturer; and Eral C. Chute, superintendent of the Ainsworth Manufacturing Company, according to the company's financial ledger.[46] Chris Smith & Sons produced 33 motorboats in 1923 and 48 units in 1924, with sales of $165,485 in the latter year. Production more than doubled in 1925 to 111 units, and in 1927 the Smiths generated revenues of over $1 million dollars from sales of 447 units.[47]

The Smiths also concentrated on building a dealer network, starting with the E. J. Mertaugh Boat Works in Hessel, Michigan, in the eastern Upper Peninsula, which signed on with them in February 1926. The deal-

Fig. 16. Constructing runabouts at the Chris Smith & Sons Boat
Company in Algonac in 1925. Jig-cut standardized parts fastened in place
with electric screwdrivers sped up production, but many workers still used
a discerning eye, hand tools, and careful craftsmanship to achieve a tight fit
before the boat moved to the next assembly station. (Mariners' Museum,
Newport News, Virginia.)

erships played a critical role in the growth of the firm, nurtured by the
arrival of John E. "Jack" Clifford, formerly of C. H. Wills and Company,
makers of the Wills Sainte Claire automobile, in Marysville. Clifford up-
graded the quality and distribution of the company's advertising by making
it attractive and similar to the high-end automotive advertising he knew
best. Dealerships needed to display at least one boat and sell a minimum
quantity during the year.[48]

When MacKerer returned to the Smiths in March 1926, he wrote home,
"Some changes at Smith's—you wouldn't know the place. It's grown to become one of the biggest plants in the country—building a boat a day now,
and plans for two a day. I have complete charge of the production end."[49]

In the record-breaking year 1927, the Chris Smith & Sons Boat Company plant experienced tremendous growth, ending the year with 114,517

square feet of floor space in twenty-six different buildings, warehouses, and sheds under cover. An article in August 1927 in *Motor Boating* described the efficiency of the operation: "If any one should doubt the efficacy of this machine method over the cruder, slower, time wasting hand methods ordinarily used one has but to watch this phase of the work and follow it to completion to discover how absolutely precise and to exact measurement each piece fits into every other piece with the same accuracy that is to be found in articles made of metal, such as engines and machine parts."[50] The company's new Cadet model, introduced in 1927 and priced at $2,250, initiated the practice of offering a runabout that families of more modest means could purchase and enjoy. The family-run business changed its management as well, with Jay Smith taking over as president and general manager of the company in 1927, and the elder Chris Smith, age sixty-six, taking a less-demanding role as chairman of the board. Daughter Catherine kept the books and dealt with the business correspondence, and son Bernard served as vice president and treasurer.

In 1930 the company became known as the Chris-Craft Corporation, named after its products, worldwide in the scope of its product distribution and the undisputed leader of standardized boat construction in the world. Like Truscott and Racine long before it, a new giant in boat manufacturing had emerged in Michigan, only this one would literally change the industry worldwide by virtue of its dominant size and incredible output, making boats available to virtually all at a price they could afford.

Gar Wood, Inc.

Aside from his racing career, Gar Wood's boat-building company grew rapidly at the same time as the Smiths'. Advertised as "The Commodore's Fleet," Wood concentrated on building more powerful, stylish, racing-capable boats, named Baby Gars, for wealthier sportsmen between 1922 and 1929. The 33-foot boats, propelled with war-surplus Liberty engines acquired by Wood's Detroit Marine-Aero Engine Company, attracted buyers such as William Randolph Hearst, Robert Ringling, Philip Wrigley, and other famous clients. While Wood only sold 67 of the Baby Gar boats during the seven years, in 1927 he built and sold 103 26-foot Baby Gar Jr. boats in a single year.[51] The dramatic upsurge in sales forced the company to use every bit of space in the old factory that Wood had purchased when he split with Chris Smith. He constructed a new factory at Marysville in 1929 to handle the ever-expanding volume.

John L. Hacker and the V-Bottom Hull Runabout

While Chris Smith led the world in the production of standardized runabouts, another man took a different approach, believing that craftsmanship counted more than sheer production numbers. His boats became known for the excellence of their construction and beauty, so much so that the company name remains alive and well today. Like the Smiths and Gar Wood, John L. Hacker's boats achieved fame because of their racing successes, but as a designer he transformed that fame into a notable boat-building manufacturing business because he carefully balanced the competing demands for a high-quality boat of fine workmanship with the need to produce large quantities of standardized boats in order to remain competitive in price. Hacker boats earned a reputation as the finest runabouts of their time, combining excellent ride characteristics, remarkably light but staunch construction, and very elegant lines. Hacker's eye for a sleek, well-proportioned, attractive design made his boats timeless classics to this day, nearly one hundred years later.

In 1918 Hacker designed and built six standardized runabout boats at his John L. Hacker Boat Company, located at 323 Crane Street in Detroit. Three were sold to Edward W. Gregory of the Belle Isle Boat & Engine Company, who named them Belle Isle Bearcats after the powerful Stutz Bearcat automobile. The Bearcat brought together in one standardized boat several concepts developed individually by Hacker and others. The boat featured a V-bottom runabout hull, with the driver's controls and steering wheel located in the forward cockpit, a passenger cockpit at the stern, and the engine in the middle. Each idea had appeared in boats years prior. Both Hacker and William H. Hand Jr. advocated the V-bottom hull as one of the best hull forms for powerboats as modern engines could easily push the boat onto plane, reducing the friction of the wetted surface.[52] Hacker felt that by moving the controls to the forward cockpit, drivers would have better visibility, where spray and the rising of the bow as the boat gained speed would be less of a problem. Hacker claimed that *Dough Boy*, built for John W. Stroh of Detroit in 1918, was the first stock runabout to have the forward controls. The forward cockpit controls layout established by Hacker remained the most prominent design in runabouts for decades. The success of the Belle Isle Bearcats and Hacker's own stock 40-mile-per-hour runabouts powered by six-cylinder Hall-Scott engines earned him an additional degree of fame.[53]

Flush with the success of his racing boats, Hacker incorporated the

Fig. 17. John L. Hacker of Detroit (*right*), a self-taught naval architect, designed some of the fastest and most beautiful boats in the world. He formed the Hacker Boat Company to construct high-quality runabouts, and after leaving the firm, he collaborated with several Michigan builders to construct cruisers. (© Mystic Seaport, Rosenfeld Collection, no. 36125F.)

Hacker Boat Company in 1920 with capital of one hundred thousand dollars, with Hacker himself as president; Paul Strasburg, a dance studio owner, as vice president; and Hugh F. Palmer as secretary and treasurer. Hacker moved a portion of the business to Mount Clemens, Michigan, in 1920, constructing a new cinder block factory at 9 Judges Street on the Clinton River. Strasburg bought the first boat produced by the new company, a twelve-thousand-dollar displacement boat named *Sure Cure*, powered with a Liberty aircraft engine.[54] The company built Hacker Dolphin stock model boats, and the Baby Dolphin, a smaller size, soon followed.

Hacker tried several different methods for selling his boats and designs in a succession of marketing ventures. He first established a marketing arrangement with the Central Marine Service Corporation, a Detroit firm that also carried Chris Smith's new boats and Elco cruisers. When that company failed, Hacker formed two new ventures to aid in marketing the boats. Starting in February 1925, he joined with Ed Gregory of the Belle Isle Boat & Engine Company and Leonard H. Thomson to sell both Hacker boats and Belle Isle Bearcats as the Belle Isle-Hacker Boat Sales Company.[55] Three months later, in May 1925, he formed Hacker & Fermann, Inc., with fellow naval architect William P. Fermann, formerly of the Matthews Boat Company of Ohio, to concentrate on designing and marketing larger cruisers in a yacht brokerage but not in competition with the Hacker Boat Company.[56]

Hacker moved all operations to the Mount Clemens plant in 1923. The factory expanded throughout the 1920s. In 1925 the company turned out three Dolphins a week. That year S. Dudley McCready joined the firm as secretary and treasurer, replacing William Fermann and N. B. Washburn. McCready's father, Corwin P. McCready, of Akron, Ohio, invested heavily in the company. Hacker remained as president and Strasburg as vice president.

The Hacker Boat Company employed about seventy men in 1928 and built between 125 and 130 boats that year in the spring and summer months, consisting of three lengths, the 24-foot Baby Dolphin, 26-foot Dolphin Junior, and 29-foot Dolphin, the latter in both runabout and sedan styles.[57] Depending on the size, the boats used Sterling Petrel, Scripps H-6 or Scripps F-6 Gold Cup engines. Prices ran from $2,975 to $5,850.[58]

As the product of a nationally renowned designer, Hacker's work found its way into many different boats produced across the land, including magnificent mahogany cruisers at the Robinson Marine Construction Company in Benton Harbor, Michigan, but also in licensed or contractual design/build relationships with Fellows and Stewart in California and Bayboro Marine Ways in Florida. Even the king of Siam, Praja Dhipok, ordered a Hacker cruiser-commuter in 1930, a 38-footer capable of over 63 miles per hour, complete with solid gold fixtures in his cabin and the boat itself paid for in gold bullion.[59] Michigan-built Hacker-Craft, literally fit for a king, like Chris-Craft and Gar Wood boats, ruled the world's waterways with speed, comfort, and style.

Horace E. Dodge Jr., Automotive Scion and Boat Builder

Horace E. Dodge Jr., son of the auto magnate Horace Elgin Dodge of the Dodge Brothers, tried to closely follow in his family's footsteps by racing fast boats. His father and uncle, John F. Dodge, prominent yachtsmen in the earlier days of motorboating, raced boats built for them by Peter H. Studer of Detroit. Together the brothers built a fortune as a parts supplier to Henry Ford's Ford Motor Company, but in 1913 they broke away from Ford to start their own automobile-manufacturing company. Aimed toward the more economical end of the market, the Dodge Brothers' automobiles achieved phenomenal success in a very competitive marketplace. By 1919 their firm ranked third in sales behind the Ford Motor Company and the companies under the corporate umbrella of General Motors. Michigan's largest steam yacht, the 257-foot *Delphine*, named by the elder Horace Dodge after his daughter, designed by Henry J. Gielow, and built locally in River Rouge by the Great Lakes Engineering Works, reflected the family's new wealth and prestige, although the elder Dodges never had the chance to enjoy its launch in 1921. Neither Horace nor John Dodge lived long after earning their fortunes; both men died less than a year apart, first John, age fifty-five, in January 1920, and then Horace, age fifty-two, in December 1920.[60]

After his father's death, young Horace Dodge Jr. started experimenting with building small-scale fast runabouts, constructing a few prototypes in a corner of the Dodge automobile factory. The Dodge "Watercar," like Dodge automobiles, ran toward the lower-priced end of the cost spectrum, trying to make the boats accessible for average working families and using the Dodge Brothers' dealership network for distribution, parts, and service. Dodge formally introduced the 22-foot, $2,250 boats to the public at the National Motor Boat Show in 1924 and incorporated the Horace E. Dodge Boat Works, Inc., in late February 1924, with financial help from his mother, Anna Thompson Dodge. Constantly under his mother's financial control and supervision because of his propensity for parties and a spendthrift attitude, Horace Dodge Jr. could never be what he wanted to be, a successful boat racer like his hero Gar Wood. Not that he didn't try—he spent a small fortune on racing boats with very few significant achievements, often because he did not take the time to prepare the boats properly to prevent mechanical failure or because he lacked the necessary driving experience, gained only through continual practice. As a boat builder, however, he could attract talent around him with his considerable charm and financial influence. He lured George Crouch, one of the finest naval architects of the day, out of a comfortable teaching role at the Webb Institute in December 1924 to guide his boat company as vice president.[61] Styling turned out to be a Dodge strong point. With a flush-deck design and long foredeck, Dodge boats made the Gar Woods and Chris-Crafts look slightly dated with their boxy topside cockpit structures.

Dodge's company, unlike Chris Smith's, never could bring the price of the boats down far enough to reach the working family's disposable income. It tried to sell a stripped-down, 20-foot runabout called the Sport-a-Bout in 1928, with no windshield or ventilators and a painted rather than varnished finish, but lackluster sales reflected the fact that potential buyers considered it too plain. Dodge's plan to market and service the boats through the Dodge automotive dealer network likewise faded after the dealers, leery of taking on a product unrelated to their core business, decided against stocking the boats on a regular basis.[62]

Horace Dodge Jr. decided to launch a new boat company in 1929, starting the Horace E. Dodge Boat and Plane Corporation. Building a new factory in Newport News, Virginia, with the intention of building both boats and amphibious seaplanes in a warmer climate, he left Michigan, with his mother once again supplying the financial backing for the new venture. Unfortunately, with the new, state-of-the-art plant opening within months of the stock market crash in 1929, and Dodge as an absentee owner spending most of his time in England, the company's days were numbered. He celebrated a rare racing victory when his boat *Delphine IV* won the Gold Cup in 1932 with his factory production manager, William Horn, driving. The boat Dodge himself piloted, *Delphine V*, dropped out in the first heat because of mechanical failure. The new factory closed in 1935, although it briefly reopened for the production of military boats during World War II before being sold to Gar Wood, Inc., its owner the man Dodge so desperately wanted to beat in the racing world.[63]

The mahogany runabouts of Chris Smith, John Hacker, Gar Wood, and Horace Dodge found copiers all over. One company, the Atlas Boat Corporation of Menominee in the Upper Peninsula, was formed in 1929 by Edmund P. Smith, Mae Smith, and James Gram. For a brief time, it built multiple sizes of boats, including some 30-footers with twin-engine installations capable of 45 miles per hour, before folding during the Great Depression. The Atlas boats, with their white oak frames, double-planked mahogany bottoms, and fasteners of bronze and brass, incorporated most of the same features offered by the largest firms in the industry. Atlas offered a wide selection of upholstery colors and customizing options to purchasers, all available at a moderate cost.[64]

Building Express Cruisers in the Downriver District

Cruisers became a popular form of boats in the Great Lakes region starting in about 1910. Once marine gasoline engines became powerful and reliable enough to withstand long journeys without catastrophic failure, boat owners no longer needed a live-aboard engineer to lubricate the moving parts and make constant adjustments to the engine in order to keep the boat running smoothly. Instead they relied on their own skills as the sole pilot and operated the craft from a console or dashboard station. The concept of the "commuter" cruiser evolved out of the desire to speed down a waterway from a distant summer residence to one's workplace. Amenities of home also found their way into the larger boats, such as electrical lighting plants, improved galleys, and larger or better-laid-out sleeping accommodations. Michigan-built cruisers, particularly those built in Detroit and the communities downriver from the city, such as Wyandotte and Trenton, established speed records and proved the durability of the express cruisers in long-distance endurance runs, as well as more leisurely cruising.

The express cruiser's speed and range made possible many a long weekend journey from Detroit to Lake Huron's Georgian Bay in Canada. During the Prohibition years, the region became a very popular destination for both its natural beauty and the alcoholic beverages easily obtainable in Canada.

Church Boat Company

Austin Church, part of the Arm & Hammer family fortune members Church & Dwight, worked for his father as vice president of the Sibley Brick Company at Sibley, near Detroit. Long interested in high-speed boats, in 1907 Church owned an early high-speed cruiser, *Rainmaker*, and actively participated in Detroit's yachting scene as a member of several clubs. He started his own boat-building factory, the Church Boat Company, at Sibley in about 1909. One of his first boats, *The Sibley*, was designed by Clinton H. Crane of New York and carried a six-cylinder Scripps engine of 50 to 60 horsepower.

Around 1913 Church began working with Carlton Wilby of Detroit, a talented young designer and pioneering naval architect involved in developing what became known as the express cruiser. Wilby had earned a local reputation earlier, designing boats for Henry Bosserdet in his Motor Boat Lane shop. Charles W. Kotcher, a wealthy Detroit coal dealer and prominent yachtsman who demanded speed in all his boats (and he had many), commissioned Wilby and Church in 1915 to design and build *Betty M.*, a racehorse of a cruiser that beat other boats in its class at the 1916 Miami Regatta. Kotcher followed up his racing success with orders for *Betty M. II* (a section patrol craft during World War I) and *Betty M. III*. Detroit yachtsmen Arthur M. Buhl and David C. Whitney soon turned to Church for their cruisers.[65] World War I turned Wilby away from cruisers as he went to work for the large shipbuilder Great Lakes Engineering Works and later the United States Shipping Board's Emergency Fleet Corporation office in Cleveland. After the war, Wilby moved to New Jersey and did design work on the municipal ferries of New York City.

Purdy Boat Company

Church sold his factory to Edward Dowling "Ned" Purdy and James Gilbert "Gil" Purdy, of Miami Beach, Florida, boat builders bankrolled by Carl G. Fisher of Indianapolis. The Purdy brothers originally worked at the Gas Engine & Power Company and Charles L. Seabury & Company, Consolidated, plant in Morris Heights, New York City, where they built several boats for Fisher, gaining his trust and respect for their craftsmanship. Fisher, owner of the Indianapolis Speedway and the real estate magnate who founded Miami Beach, lured them away from Consolidated to relocate their boat-building operation first to the Indianapolis Speedway infield grounds, then to Miami Beach in December 1914, and eventually to Michigan in May 1919. The move to Sibley made sense in part because of the lack of skilled labor and the difficulty of finding supplies in Miami Beach, combined with an increasingly wealthy local clientele. After acquiring Church's factory, they found it too small, moving instead to a new factory a short distance farther downriver in Trenton.[66]

The Purdys built customized cruisers and runabouts tailored very closely to the customers' requirements, determining exactly what they wanted for space, power, and amenities in conversations and correspondence. Carl Fisher's *Shadow F* (72-foot, 1919), *Shadow H* (46-foot, 1923), and *Shadow J* (52-foot, 1924), all built in Trenton, reflected Fisher's desire for fast cruisers of ever-increasing power with different engine combinations. For the three boats, Fisher selected a pair of Allison engines, a marine conversion of a pair of Fiat aircraft engines, and finally a pair of Packard engines. Richard P. Joy, the Packard Motor Car Company executive, and James A. Allison, the engine builder who Fisher likewise sponsored, also commissioned the Purdys to construct cruisers and runabouts for themselves.

Fisher's creative marketing mind led to some odd products built by the Purdys, such as six Venetian-style gondolas raced at the Miami Mid-Winter Regatta in 1921. A series of one-design 18-foot racers, named "Biscayne Babies," raced by Indianapolis Speedway drivers, including Louis Chevrolet, Tommy Milton, and Ray Harroun, competed against each other in March 1925 after being rushed to Miami from the Trenton shop. Too lightly built for the rough conditions of Biscayne Bay, several boats capsized or were otherwise damaged. Fisher, irritated by their poor performance, had the engines removed and the hulls burned in a bonfire.[67]

Fisher frequently changed his mind about where the Purdys should build their boats, often in tandem with the place where his latest real estate venture was located. In 1925 the Purdy operation moved to Port Washington, New York, where Fisher developed the Bayview Colony. The company changed its focus from express cruisers to racing craft, building several racing runabouts for Walter P. Chrysler, the 1929 Gold Cup and President's Cup winner *Imp II* for Richard F. Hoyt, and the 1930–31 Gold Cup winner *Hotsy Totsy* with Victor Kliesrath driving. The company continued to operate until 1950 in Port Washington.[68]

A. G. Liggett & Son Company

The A. G. Liggett & Son Company was incorporated in March 1917 with capital of $15,000 and moved from Motor Boat Lane in Detroit to Wyandotte near the foot of Sibley Road. Alfred Liggett's brother, Louis Kroh Liggett, built the Rexall Drug Company fortune. Building cruisers and runabouts of its own design and the designs of others, mostly in the 30- to 50-foot range, the company established a solid reputation for excellence in construction using standardized designs. It produced a 28-foot stock cruiser designed by William H. Hand Jr. in 1922. In 1928 the company built three sizes of standard model cruisers. Their best seller, a 34-footer, generated more demand than the company could meet. It built about twenty-five that year, selling for $10,500 each. A second standard cruiser, a 40-footer, sold for $24,000 and was built only to order. A third, a 52-footer selling for $38,000, also built to order, found less demand because of its size, and only four were built the year before. Like many cruiser builders, the company also constructed runabouts and planned to build five hundred in 1928.[69]

Louis G. Liggett operated the boat company for decades after the passing of his father, moving the operation to nearby Trenton in 1943. Like many boat companies, the Liggett firm became a dealer for Chris-Craft when it could no longer compete head-to-head with the giant company, working instead in sales, repairs, and marina services. The Liggett company finally closed with Louis Liggett's retirement in 1965.

Defoe Boat & Motor Works, Yacht Builder for the Auto Barons

In the period following World War I, the Defoe Boat & Motor Works of Bay City quickly established a reputation as a major Great Lakes luxury motor yacht builder. By now experienced in working in steel as well as wood, Defoe's yard could offer a wider array of large yachts. Its clientele demanded yacht designs similar to what the East Coast yards could deliver but for a reduced price in labor. Like many in Michigan with "new money," the men who made their fortunes in the automobile manufacturing and parts supply businesses wanted to enhance their newfound wealth with the trappings of the rich in the form of large, elegant homes, yachts, and fast automobiles. Buyers in the mid- to late 1920s included Charles E. Sorensen of the Ford Motor Company; E. T. Strong, president of the Buick Motor Company of Flint; Ransom E. Olds of the REO Motor Car Company in Lansing; and Aaron DeRoy, a Detroit auto dealer. William C. Rands of the Motor Products Company became a repeat customer and a Defoe booster for more business with his 79-foot *Rosewill*, delivered in 1926, and 126-foot *Rosewill II, delivered* in 1931.[70] Charles F. Kettering's *Olive K* served as a testing bed for Kettering's personal interest in diesel engine technology, and he could often be found belowdecks tinkering with the power plant. Most of the Defoe boats were in the 50- to 100-foot range, produced at a rate of about five or six a year.

Defoe built designs from Hacker & Fermann, Inc., Cox & Stevens, and

John H. Wells, as well as other notable designers and firms. In addition to its pleasure craft, Defoe constructed workboats for the Ford Motor Company rubber plantations in Brazil.[71]

During the late 1920s, a couple of the larger East Coast yacht-building companies established offices in Detroit, presumably to cash in on the wealth of the auto industry executives but also to be closer to Defoe as their local builder. Henry J. Gielow, Inc., was incorporated in Michigan in the week of July 28, 1928, with offices in the Dime Bank Building in Detroit, to "design and build ships, sailing vessels, boats, submarines, launches, yachts, life boats, rafts, etc." Alfred G. Mueller, Robert O. Newell, and Vera M. Presher, all of New York, capitalized the firm with five thousand shares of no par value. Cox & Stevens, Inc., followed suit by incorporating in Michigan in the week of February 23, 1929. William E. Fermann, formerly of Hacker & Fermann, established a Cox & Stevens branch office in the Barlum Tower in Detroit with capital twenty-five thousand dollars.[72]

State of the Industry

Boat-building in the state during the 1920s mirrored the tremendous growth of the cities in the southeastern Lower Peninsula because of the rise of the automobile industry, capturing a share of that prosperity in dollars spent on recreation. Further fueled by racing and rum-running, production efficiencies, and marketing, the boom times for the boat builders led to fortunes for a few.

Nationally, the boat-building industry fell into a serious slump during World War I. According to Bureau of the Census data collected in that era, the number of establishments in the United States building boats of 5 gross tons or less, performing both construction and repair, dropped from 588 in 1914 to 294 by 1919. Likewise, the total size of the industrial work force went from 2,749 in 1914 down to 1,951 by 1919.[73]

For powerboats of less than five gross tons, Michigan ranked fifth nationally in 1916 and seventh in 1919 among the leading states producing them. In 1927, however, the state rebounded to lead the nation with 821 powerboats, more than triple the number produced in second-place New York, a number that skyrocketed to 2,976 powerboats in 1929.[74]

Regionally, the largest and arguably the most influential builders were located in the southeastern portion of the state, but smaller firms abounded in the resort communities throughout the Lower Peninsula and Upper Peninsula, frequently following the leaders in design and construction but never approaching them in the sheer volume of production. Had the Purdys and Horace Dodge decided to remain in Michigan, the competitive environment of the boat business in the state could have turned out to be significantly different. While neither firm dominated the marketplace in its Michigan years, both were influential in shaping the industry nationally after their departure, the Purdys with their successful racers and cruisers and Dodge with his innovative factory and assembly line processes at Newport News, Virginia.

In the end, the 1920s turned out to be a shining moment on the edge of a financial precipice, as all the builders had to deal with the trials of the following decade.

CHAPTER FIVE

The Great Depression, 1929–39

Introduction

For years throughout the 1920s, widely available credit for boat buyers made purchasing decisions extremely easy and affordable. Compounded by overvalued stocks and rampant speculation in the stock market, a high price would soon be paid for the exceptionally good times. Recreational boating in the United States reached a peak in April 1930 with some 1,424,924 motorboats registered nationally. According to an estimate by the National Association of Engine and Boat Manufacturers, one boat existed for every fifteen automobiles and eighty-one people at the time.[1] After the stock market crash in October 1929, panic set in among investors, who withdrew their money from the banks and stock markets, causing business failures of epic proportions. Consumer credit, necessary for most boat buyers, became increasingly difficult to obtain.

Without a doubt, the Great Depression devastated Michigan's boat-building industry. In the years following the stock market crash, Michigan boat builders were forced to make major adjustments to their production plans, something that only a few ended up doing successfully. Slightly over half of the ship- and boat-building establishments in the state failed or at least temporarily closed during the first half of the era. In 1929 a total of thirty establishments were located in Michigan according to the Bureau of the Census. By 1931 the figure had shrunk to eighteen firms. It fell to fourteen in 1933 before rebounding to sixteen in 1935–37.[2] For many builders, the transition through the financial crisis was a terrible experience often ending in failure, but those firms that survived at least had fewer competitors and the opportunity to prosper later on. Rebuilding the market turned out to be no small feat, as the long, drawn-out recovery was hampered by setbacks such as a recession in 1937–38, when the production of durable goods dropped precipitously.

Buildup of Plant Capacity

Virtually all of Michigan's major builders completed large new additions or entire new buildings just before the stock market crash to accommodate the rapid expansion of product lines in 1928 and 1929. Some firms even added buildings after the crash before the effects were felt. In most cases the companies needed to replace old, inefficient, or small structures built years earlier before the unprecedented demand generated the need for more space.[3]

Among the largest firms, Chris-Craft, already with twenty-six buildings in 1927, added two new wings 100 by 60 feet to its main building. The Hacker Boat Company constructed a new steel addition to its factory in 1928. Gar Wood opened a brand new, 63,000-square-foot factory on 6 acres with 650 feet of water frontage on the St. Clair River at Marysville in 1930. The Dwight Lumber Company's boat division moved from a space of just 3,000 square feet in a lumber company building to a new, 30,000-square-foot facility. Among the four major builders alone, enclosed floor space exceeded 250,000 square feet, not to mention several acres of yards, docks, and outdoor facilities. Many new startups and smaller firms also leased older buildings for plant space. The Pouliot Boat Company leased the former Alboy Manufacturing Company factory in St. Clair in 1928 and Jack Beebe's new Beebe Boat Works leased the Walker Electrical Refrigeration Company factory in Port Huron a year later.[4]

The debt load of all the new construction and purchases of new production machinery and equipment within the buildings dragged down the bottom lines of many companies after the stock market crash and probably caused more than a few failures.

Sales Jump, Then Slump

At first there was a sense of disbelief that anything terrible was happening. Sales of boats were particularly strong in 1929 and even going into 1930, after the stock market crash, with consumer confidence still high. Many in the industry believed that the market was still solid and sales would grow, if anything. *Motor Boat*, the trade periodical, conducted a survey of the boat-building and marine engine industries in 1930 and felt that the national industry was ready for expansion: "Summed up we believe that, a year from now, when we make the 1931 survey we will find a total of at least 30,000 employees in the two fields. We believe that we will see the production figures increased by at least 25%. We feel positive that the report will show that the average dealer is being offered 25% to sell boats and that the distributor gets a 40% discount from the maker. We expect that the overhead figures will come down about 5% and the advertising go up to a figure of about 8%. All of these things are in line of progress and we shall watch the results and draw the comparisons for your benefit."[5] Clearly the industry tried to put its best face on what looked to be a quickly deteriorating situation.

Production of powerboats of under five gross tons in Michigan rose to 2,976 (or roughly one-fifth of the nation's 14,930 powerboats of under five gross tons) in 1929. The total for Michigan had decreased to 2,041 out of the nation's 6,214 powerboats by 1931, down by nearly a third from the 1929 total, and production continued to drop rapidly thereafter. By 1933 national production had sunk to a mere 796 inboards and 1,337 outboards for a total of 2,133 powerboats, or slightly more than what Michigan alone had built two years earlier.[6]

With the Chris Smith & Sons Boat Company still growing by all appearances and sales seemingly climbing, the company started the process of incorporation as part of a financial deal. In April 1930, Jay Smith negotiated with the Wall Street investment banking firm of Childs, Jeffries & Company for the option to purchase a third of the family business for $1,125,000. A clause in the contract called for a deposit to be paid to the Smiths of $250,000, which they would keep in case the bankers wanted to back out of the deal. As part of the deal, the Smiths formed the Chris-Craft Corporation in 1930 and bought the stock of the Chris Smith & Sons Boat Company in exchange for its own new stock. The Smith family made a series of legal and financial maneuvers, forming the Smith Investment Company, to insulate itself from the federal taxes on the windfall profits from the sale.[7]

The 1930 fleet offered by Chris-Craft contained something for virtually everyone of any pocketbook size. A two-page advertisement in the December 1929 issue of *Motor Boating* proclaimed, "Chris-Craft offers for 1930 The Greatest Fleet in Boating History—New Lines, New Values, New Models, New Smartness, New Refinements, New Smoothness." With twenty-four different models of boats ranging from a 20-foot, eight-passenger runabout for $1,895 to a 48-foot cruiser able to carry thirty passengers for $35,000, the company's models surpassed those of any other manufacturer in the boating industry in terms of sheer volume. In addition, the company had moved into the engine-building business a year earlier, producing its own V-8, the Chris-Craft A-120, which could push a runabout to speeds of over 40 miles per hour. As Truscott, Racine, and other boat builders had learned long before, if a company could control the cost of the engine in a powerboat, it could control a greater percentage of the boat's cost overall and reduce its price accordingly.

The company's dominance in the marketplace by the late 1920s and the brand's name recognition became synonymous with excellence in performance and styling at a low price. By the end of 1928, the Chris Smith & Sons Boat Company claimed that more of its boats had been purchased in 1927 and 1928 than the production of all competitors combined. The competitors were offering models virtually identical to Chris-Craft boats. A key part of this accomplishment can be attributed to the company's tremendous growth in its dealerships. By 1929 the company's dealership network encompassed 108 agencies in the United States and many more internationally, a few of them former competitors.[8]

At the National Motor Boat Show in New York in January 1930, shortly after the stock market crash, sales for Chris-Craft alone jumped to a record of 497 boats valued at over $2.2 million, making up more than a third of all the sales at the show. Shortly afterward, dealers began to cancel many of the orders, with some customers backing out of their purchase agreements and forfeiting their deposits, a startling indication that the crisis had finally reached a dangerous point for the builders. Chris-Craft discovered it had lost over $100,000 just in the last quarter of 1930.[9]

Gar Wood in 1930 also looked to expand its offerings, adding a smaller 22-foot runabout on the low end of the product spectrum but finished with the same quality and materials as its larger boats. The company also introduced new enclosed cabin top styles in sedan, landau, and limousine forms to its standard 28-foot runabout hull for greater quiet and comfort.[10] The Hacker Boat Company experienced the same sales increases that most of the industry witnessed right up to 1930. Deliveries for Hacker peaked at ninety boats in June 1930.[11]

A year later the nature of the crisis became painfully apparent. At the National Motor Boat Show in 1931, orders for Chris-Craft reached 316 boats, both runabouts and cruisers, valued at $1,012,854. This still represented a reduction of over half of the sales volume of the prior year's show.

At the same event, Gar Wood, Inc., managed to sell one of its boats to industrial designer Raymond Loewy, and two of its best dealers, Fitzgerald and Lee of Alexandria Bay, New York, and Stearns Marine of Boston, ordered three boats each, a major disappointment for all the effort President Ed Hancock expended trying to get the dealers to order more boats. Boat production at Gar Wood for the entire year, for all models, totaled only 32 units, with all deliveries taking place in May, June, and July, and more than half of these had been left over from the prior model year's production.[12]

Chris-Craft, the largest of the boat builders, lost nearly $200,000 in 1931. Childs, Jeffries & Company, the Wall Street investment firm, forfeited its deposit and withdrew its offer to buy a third of Chris-Craft, leaving the Smiths with a $250,000 bank balance that would carry them through the worst of the Depression's early years. Decades later Jay Smith admitted that the firm probably would have failed without the cash windfall.[13]

Bottoming Out

Sales at all of the builders fell sharply through the latter portion of 1931, and by mid-1932 consumer confidence and the demand for boats reached their low point. The business failures at first consisted of newer, fledgling firms that folded rather quickly for lack of brand name recognition and a customer base.

Dee-Wite, Inc.

Dee-Wite, Inc., a boat-building subsidiary of the Dwight Lumber Company of Detroit and River Rouge, Michigan, exemplified one the new firms and the largest failure of a mahogany-hulled runabout manufacturer in Michigan. Although the exact start date for the company's production of boats is unclear, by the late 1920s, it was building boats, first as a small operation in the lumberyard. Soon it expanded into a full-fledged boat-manufacturing plant called the Dwight Lumber Company Boat Division, selling boats under the trade name Dee-Wite, a modification of the parent company's name.

The driving force behind the boat-building effort was Joseph Berry Lodge, son of the physician and surgeon Edwin Lodge and his wife Alice Dwight Berry Lodge. The elder Lodge was president of the Dwight Lumber Company, but he also managed the affairs of the Berry Brothers

Varnish Company after his father-in-law passed away. Joseph B. Lodge was the nephew of John C. Lodge, the mayor of Detroit in portions of the 1920s. Lodge became an avid yachtsman on soft water and hard water. He collaborated in the creation of the DN 60 (Detroit News) class of iceboats with Archie Arroll and Norman Jarrait.[14]

In the fall of 1928, the Dwight Lumber Company Boat Division began to organize and equip the small boat-building shop for volume production, trying to become a national leader in the production of standardized runabouts designed for use with outboard motors. A number of talented people prominent in Detroit area boat-building were associated with the firm in 1929. Russell J. Pouliot, a noted boat designer and formerly a foreman at the Belle Isle Boat & Engine Company of Detroit, joined the company as its naval architect. Pouliot was the son of Joseph Pouliot, a prominent Detroit boat builder. Ambitious to start his own boat-building business after Belle Isle's Gregory family decided to go into boat brokerage instead of boat-building, he started the Pouliot Boat Company at St. Clair in 1928, but it evidently failed a year later. Pouliot subsequently went to work for the Dwight Lumber Company. Jan Smits, formerly the owner of the Algonac Machine and Boat Works and later service manager of the Chris Smith & Sons Boat Company, became the firm's director of service and assistant sales manager.[15]

By April 1929, the Dwight operation had expanded from under 3,000 square feet to more than 30,000, with plans being prepared for a still larger group of buildings to contain production facilities, physical testing laboratories, and experimental departments for development work. A year later the firm added another 10,000-square-foot building and a monorail system to convey the boats from building to building. Average monthly production had already increased to more than 325 boats after the New York Boat Show in 1929. "When the new addition is completed," said T. F. Rogers, the sales manager, "our average production will be in excess of thirty boats a day."[16]

Russell Pouliot created a unique outboard motorboat design by developing an enclosure for the motor, presumably to reduce the noise and fumes but also to enhance the boat's appearance by making the head of the motor visually disappear. He filed for a U.S. patent in June 1929 for an outboard motorboat. It was issued two years later in 1931, Patent 1,818,273, which he assigned to Dee-Wite, Inc. A cutaway well with a transom forward of the stern for the outboard motor's shaft was concealed by the hull framing, and a hinged hatch cover with ventilating holes hid the head of the motor, giving the boat the appearance of a more expensive inboard runabout.[17] Dee-Wite presented eleven models for 1930, from 16-feet through 19-feet, ranging in price from $1,185 to $2,700.[18]

Typical of most boat builders of the time, the Dwight Lumber Company turned to racing and endurance runs to build name recognition for the firm. One advertising stunt conjured up in 1930 consisted of sending two women, Miss Peggy Radcliffe of Philadelphia and Miss Maude Hughes of New York, on an endurance run from Detroit to Florida by way of the Atlantic Ocean, using two stock 22-foot triple-cockpit runabouts, each powered with a 135-horsepower Lodge engine. Dressed in white racing togs with the Dee-Wite label prominently displayed, the ladies left Detroit on October 24, stopping at Cleveland and Buffalo on the Great Lakes before landing in New York City at the Columbia Yacht Club. By December 31, the two boats were skirting the coast, bound for Florida. A factory crew took over the final leg from Florida to New Orleans, and then up the Mississippi River to Cairo, Illinois.[19]

Joseph B. Lodge had the 40-foot multistepped hull, *Miss Dee-Wite*, designed and built as a racer in 1929. Called a torpedo-shaped hull, the boat's streamlined, elegant stern tapered to a point, similar to the Cord and Auburn boat-tailed automotive speedsters of the same era, and it served as a model for the future appearance of part of the company's product line. The boat finished last out of three boats in the Dick Locke Handicap race held in conjunction with the Harmsworth contest that year. Dissatisfied with the boat's performance, Lodge asked Russell Pouliot to design a new 35-foot triple-cockpit runabout for him. Lodge planned to use *Miss Dee-Wite II* in Gold Cup competition.[20]

Dee-Wite, Inc., filed for incorporation in late October 1930, with Alice D. Lodge, Joseph B. Lodge, and Harold H. Bowman as incorporators with fifty thousand shares of stock at no par value, intending to "manufacture, buy, sell, repair, fit out, equip, operate and maintain ships, vessels and boats." Its business address was 1016 Book Building in Detroit, although the manufacturing plant was located in River Rouge. The timing of the formal creation of the firm, just a year after the stock market crash in October 1929, turned out to be remarkably bad.[21]

Boat sales became more difficult as the economy worsened, and attempts to diversify Dee-Wite's products led to some interesting efforts. The Bendix Aviation Corporation licensed Dee-Wite, Inc., to sell "Stow-

Away" folding laminated wood boats under its patent. The boats reportedly found wide use in England and the rest of Europe. Dee-Wite claimed that "they are light enough to be carried by one man, can be stowed away on an automobile, easily set up or folded by one person, have a capacity of several passengers, and are suitable for use with outboard motors."[22] Following Chris-Craft's lead in moving into the engine business, Joseph B. Lodge formed yet another subsidiary of the Dwight Lumber Company, Lodge Motors, Inc., to build engines for the Dee-Wite runabouts and possibly other makes. Lodge motors came in four-, six-, and eight-cylinder varieties.

Unlike most other builders, who shifted to constructing smaller boats and downsized product lines as economic conditions worsened, Dee-Wite, to the contrary, expanded its line to fourteen models of boats in 1932, offering more size and power options than ever. The company offered the Lodge Torpedo, which became a huge success, so much so that in 1933 the company announced a 300 percent increase in sales over the previous year.[23] Despite its apparent success with broader product lines and diversification into other boating ventures outside its core business, the expansion decisions turned out to be fatal. Dee-Wite, Inc., continued to suffer losses, racking up large debts as sales declined. According to the firm's 1933 annual report, the company owed notes to Joseph Lodge's family and other creditors for over $117,000. With the owners unable to sustain further losses, the company closed its doors in late 1934 or early 1935, ending the run of one of Michigan's larger runabout builders.[24]

Corsair Boat Company

The financial malaise cut a wide swath through all sectors of the boat-building industry, causing business failures and plant closings among small boat builders and cruiser manufacturers alike. The Corsair Boat Company, a stock cruiser builder with offices in Detroit and construction facilities in the old Purdy shop in Trenton, was formed out of the merger of Chenevert & Company and Davis Boat Company in April 1929. Charles T. Chenevert served as the distributor in Detroit for American Car & Foundry Company cruisers, and Seth C. Davis had previously worked as manager of the American Boat Company of Detroit. Together they produced the 30-foot Corsair "Cruisader" stock cruiser, designed by Eldredge-McInnis, Inc., of Boston. The partners later renamed their company after their product and incorporated in 1930.[25] A new 36-foot Corsair introduced in December 1929 featured an automotive-style deckhouse designed by LeBaron. With the deepening damage to the economy, the company sought government work and received a contract for six 38-foot picketboats for the U.S. Coast Guard in 1931–32. The additional work could not sustain the firm, which closed shortly thereafter, although Seth Davis later decided to build boats again on his own, incorporating the Davis Boat Company in September 1939.[26]

Figuring Out What to Do

Most of the boat builders, at least the major firms, came up with several different ways to minimize the financial disaster appearing on their balance sheets. The three most critical changes usually included (1) downsizing and changing the product lines, eliminating models that did not sell well; (2) introducing new, generally smaller, inexpensive boats or models with fewer features or unique new designs; and (3) deeply discounting the products that did sell.

Companies that downsized their product lines to offer boats in smaller sizes and with simplified finish levels needed to carefully balance the appearance and quality of materials in what they marketed. If too many corners were cut, the few remaining customers would find a nicer boat elsewhere. Those companies that tended to survive also generally needed a mix of runabouts, cruisers, utilities, and custom work, appealing to the broadest clientele. Chris-Craft introduced its 1932 fleet of "Level Riding" runabouts but cut the number of models from twenty-one to only twelve. It also dropped its new Custom Commuter and 48-foot yacht to concentrate on building smaller 31-foot and 36-foot cruisers. The company eliminated the advertising budget, catalog, direct mail campaign, and show expenses, but even with these changes and cuts, the company suffered losses in 1932 of $263,730, cutting its reserves to a dangerously low level.[27]

Utility boats, introduced by the Horace Dodge Boat & Plane Corporation of Newport News, Virginia, in 1932, represented a new idea in boat styling and functionality. The 19-foot All-Purpose, or Model 202, utility sold for only $695 and represented a clever product born of necessity during the Depression. The boat's open interior hull plan with a large box covering the engine could be cheaper to build than full-decked runabouts, and passengers could more easily move around. Utilities created more flexibility for boating activities as they tended to work better for fishing, aquaplaning, and picnics than traditional deck-and-cockpit-style runabouts. In time they replaced them.[28] Chris-Craft quickly adopted the concept, following Dodge's lead by modifying its 1931 model 24-foot runabout with a large open cockpit in the stern half of the boat. Gar Wood and Hacker, on the other hand, did not offer a utility until three years later, in 1935, after the style caught on.[29]

Bouncing Around: Movement of Personnel within the Industry

Corporate casualties of the Great Depression turned into human casualties on a grand scale. For the workers in the boat plants, layoffs and part-time work became the order of the day, and work of any kind became even harder to find. Almost two-thirds of the wage earners working in the boat-building industry in Michigan were unemployed by 1933, going from annual average employment figures of 1,803 workers in 1929 to 926 in 1931 and a low of 351 in 1933. In 1935 employment rebounded to 660 on average, and later 1,660 in 1937, but it dropped again, to 872, in 1939. Wages paid went from $3,019,225 in 1929 to a low of $432,000 in 1933 before rebounding to $2,376,195 in 1937.[30]

The layoffs frequently followed skill levels, with those in the unskilled positions going first, then those in the skilled trades. To some extent the most skilled workers could find jobs by moving from company to company if they lived in an area with multiple builders. The best boat builders at Gar Wood's barely operating new plant in Marysville found temporary work constructing a new racing boat for their company's wealthy owner in preparation for the 1932 Harmsworth Trophy defense, transferring to the old Algonac plant to build *Miss America X*.[31]

Salaried employees suffered just as much, with employment ranging from 226 people in 1929 to just 70 in 1933. Company managers often gave up or deferred portions of their salaries in the early years in hopes of reducing the losses, according to corporation annual reports of the period. The managerial talent pool became a merry-go-round of people looking for any opportunity they could find in the business during the hardest times.

William A. MacKerer and John E. "Jack" Clifford, two of the most talented managers at Chris-Craft, bounced around the industry during the worst of the crisis. Both men lost their jobs at Chris-Craft in the late summer of 1931 following drastically dropping sales. MacKerer, the driving force behind the design and manufacturing operations at Chris-Craft, briefly went to work for Glen Robinson at the Robinson Marine Construction Company for about a year before moving in the summer of 1933 to

Long Island, New York, to work at Co-Mac Seacraft with Cecil Cohrone on building cruisers. Needing their right-hand man more than ever before as Chris-Craft recovered, the Smiths rehired him in 1935.[32]

Jack Clifford, former sales manager for Chris-Craft and creator of its large dealer network, joined Dee-Wite, Inc., as vice president and director of sales in August 1931. In true salesman form, a week after his appointment was announced, Clifford cheerily reported that Dee-Wite's August sales were larger than any August in the company's history. Shipments were 96 percent of the figures for June, which was ordinarily the peak month for boat sales, and were 89 percent greater than those for August 1930.[33] After Dee-Wite failed, Clifford found work at Chris-Craft's rival, Gar Wood, Inc., whose wealthy owner could subsidize the operation of the boat company with his other businesses. Clifford remained for many years as its sales manager, helping the firm get through the Depression with his outstanding advertising talent.

Company owners themselves were not immune. One of the victims of the Great Depression turned out to be John L. Hacker, who lost control of the company bearing his name in 1934. In a buyout agreement dated December 31, 1934, made with S. Dudley McCready and his family, Hacker and his son John A. Hacker surrendered all of their stock and complete operational management of the firm and its name in payment of his debt to the company.[34] Although he remained bitter about the loss for the rest of his life, Hacker continued to design boats for the Hacker Boat Company but preferred to work out of an office in Detroit. He renewed a prior agreement with McCready that allowed him to continue to design and build cruisers over 28 feet and racing or special custom boats, but he could not design or market runabouts in competition with the Hacker Boat Company.

Hacker found a construction partner for his cruisers in Benjamin H. Huskin of Bay City, who had built a number of cruisers designed by Hacker since 1929. Huskin's and Hacker's most beautiful collaboration, *Thunderbird*, a streamlined 55-foot cruiser/commuter built in 1939 for real estate magnate George Whittell, was used on Lake Tahoe at Whittell's Thunderbird estate.[35] The cruiser's Honduran mahogany hull contrasted sharply with the aviation-inspired stainless steel cabin house. The boat became famous enough to inspire a 2007 U.S. postage stamp with its image many decades after its creation.

For the boat-building factory worker, layoffs lasted for months at a time, even for the most skilled production people. Workers became res-

Fig. 18. John L. Hacker's *Thunderbird*, built in 1939 by Ben Huskin of Bay City, epitomized the streamlined look with its graceful, aircraft-inspired, stainless steel deckhouse and mahogany-planked hull. Owner George Whittell used the boat at his Thunderbird Lodge on Lake Tahoe in Nevada, where it remains today. (Mariners' Museum, Newport News, Virginia.)

tive, seeking any kind of protection from the economic storm they could find. Unionization offered one form of protection that appealed to a few workers, especially when they saw the results achieved by the United Automobile Workers of America in the nearby auto-manufacturing plants, such as the gains made following the sit-down strike in Flint in 1936–37. About 150 of the 600 workers at Chris-Craft organized a strike in March 1937 over wages. Although the company had given workers a 5 percent increase only a year earlier, in June 1936, the addition of four cents to a thirty-five- to forty-cent-per-hour wage did not mean much. The company caved in to the union's demands for recognition, reduction in the work week from forty-eight to forty-four hours, and a wage increase of an additional 5 percent. The strike left a bitter relationship between the workers and management that the firm never completely overcame. Algonac was a small town where most of the managers and workers were friends and neighbors, and the anger and distrust caused by the labor strife would have future ramifications.[36] One of the long-term consequences of the strike turned out to be the spreading out of the corporation to more business-friendly communities where the labor unions were weaker or nonexistent. When Chris-Craft added new plants, the communities it turned to would be far from the village of Algonac, such as the city of Holland on the west side of the state.

Changes for Small-Scale Builders

How did the small boat builders hang on and survive? Sometimes they had to move their focus away from solely building to a variety of related businesses. The Jesiek family of Holland struggled on by providing boat storage and repair, serving primarily as a marina rather than relying entirely on boat-building. When boat-building became unprofitable for the small builders as mass production drove down the price of boats, many shifted into the more labor-intensive marina services because they did not require the capital investment that boat manufacturing did. Marine railways and storage buildings could be built reasonably by families. Boat services such as seasonal cleaning and repairing, storage, and fueling could still be offered locally to the customers they knew the best. With few alternatives available for boat-building, it was "join 'em" rather than trying to "beat 'em" to save what they had of their valuable waterfront properties, which in many cases also served as their homes.

By offering sailboat and speedboat rides, making a run to Saugatuck every Saturday night in summer for the entertainment of tourists, the Jesiek family helped make ends meet by offering services to those who still had money to play with. Like many boat builders, the Jesieks evolved to become boat and marine equipment dealers or distributors. Throughout the Depression, the family found customers for boats, working first as dealers for Hooton hydroplanes and Johnson motors, then Chris-Craft boats after 1930. The Jesieks also built their own 13-1/2-foot Crescent class one-design sailboats for the yacht clubs around western Lake Michigan, selling them for $135 each. Lois Jesiek, the daughter of Adolph "Otto" Jesiek, won the 1939 Western Michigan Yachting Association Crescent Skipper's Regatta in that class.[37]

Another survival mechanism was to merge with another firm or serve as a supplier. The Mayea Boat Company formed a joint venture with the Allen Boat Company of Detroit to supply its boats to the Allen firm in the early 1930s. Louis Mayea designed and built the Seaboat line for Allen, a seven-passenger craft with a wood-framed windshield, ranging in size from 16 to 26 feet. The Mayeas equipped each one with a Gray Phantom engine and all the necessary gear before delivery to Detroit.[38] The economic situation also caused hardships for the elderly. Peter H. Studer, the small-scale builder who built boats for the Olds Motor Works and John and Horace Dodge in Detroit around the turn of the twentieth century, tried to sell his boatyard in 1930; consequently, the Riverside Boat Company was incorporated by LeRoy W. Forrester and others in 1930 to take over his operation. A year later, in 1931, toward the end of his career, Studer helped incorporate another new venture, the Windmill Pointe Boat Company, presumably to find another buyer for the yard.[39]

Diversifying into creating other kinds of boats worked well for some builders. Finnish immigrant Waino Wiinikka Sr. established the Wiinikka Boat Works of Portage Entry, near Chassell in the Upper Peninsula, in about 1910. Building sturdy fishing tugs designed to deal with the severe weather and icy conditions on Lake Superior, the company branched out occasionally into cabin cruisers and heavy-duty launches. Some of the Wiinikka fishing boats were double-ended craft, powered by Ford Model A engines converted to marine use. In 1934 the company reported that it was running full time and had several orders in hand. At the time, they were building a 38-foot fishing tug for Charles Jamsen of Gay, and orders for future work included another tug of about the same size, a large cruiser launch, and two boats for the U.S. Department of Commerce to be used in the lighthouse service.[40] After his death in 1937, his sons Waino Jr., John, Omni, and Sulo carried on the work.

Charles Kauppi commissioned the Wiinikka brothers to build a ferry, the *Copper Queen*, to transport passengers to the new Isle Royale National Park. William B. Gertz, a professor at the Michigan College of Mining and Technology and amateur boat designer, drew the boat, and Kauppi, a commercial fisherman, asked the Wiinikka brothers to build it for him in 1936 as he already operated the fish tug *Water Lily*, built by the same firm. With a white oak keel and cypress planking carefully clench nailed with hot-dipped galvanized nails over 2 by 2 inch ribs, the *Copper Queen* made for a resilient boat, but the craft suffered from serious stability problems according to the federal government marine inspectors. Kauppi fought with them for years to license the boat to carry passengers but was forced to register it as a private yacht. In the end, he sold it to Stan Sivertson in the spring of 1953, who eventually used the boat, renamed *Voyageur*, in the ferry service as originally intended. He added a pilothouse atop the main deck to slow the boat's rolling. The boat made many the long, occasionally treacherous trip across Lake Superior, keeping the vital tourist trade to the island thriving.[41]

Gerald Mallon, an aspiring twenty-two-year old boat designer and builder, formed the Tawas Bay Boat Works in the depth of the Great Depression with Carl Babcock in 1934 in Tawas City, with plans to build fishing tugs and pleasure craft up to 70 feet in length. Mallon learned carpentry as a cabinetmaker in a nearby railroad car shop and took correspondence courses to learn naval architecture. Both young men had sailed competitively on Tawas Bay on Lake Huron for years and wanted to try their hand at building boats. One of their first products was a 30-foot Sparkman & Stephens–designed racing sloop for Charles and Harold Moeller of Tawas City, named *Yucatan*. Mallon bought out his partner and renamed the firm the Mallon Boat Company. As business slowly picked up, he built a number of other sailboats, including the Arrowhead class 21-foot *Gale*, a Philip Rhodes–designed boat. Although his passion for sailboats remained, he also built rowboats for inland lakes recreational fishermen to maintain an income. Forced to move his shop with the U.S.-23 highway expansion in 1940, Mallon planned to build a new shop in East Tawas with a rotunda in front for displaying his boats, a shop area in the rear, and living quarters above. World War II intervened; therefore, Mallon never completed his shop before entering the navy.[42]

Eugene L. Eckfield owned and operated a small boat-building firm, the Eckfield Boat Company, at Algonac, in the same community as Chris-Craft. Eckfield graduated from the University of Michigan with a bachelor of science in engineering degree in 1923 in naval architecture and marine engineering. As a relatively new startup firm, aided by his father's financing, he purchased Jan Smits's former Hess Motor Company facility when Smits went to work for Chris-Craft as its service manager. Eckfield designed a number of his own small craft, including the "Jazz Bug" and "Jack Snipe" outboard hydroplanes and runabouts. He soon found that he could not sustain himself with the low volume of boats sold. Eckfield eventually went to work for the Smiths at Chris-Craft in 1930 and became an important member of its engineering and design team for forty-five years after his own firm closed.[43]

Changes in metal-fabricating techniques, especially in welding steel, enabled a couple of small Michigan boat builders to develop new products for the industry. The Gil-Boat Company of Holland developed a novel manufacturing process by which sheet steel could be quickly rolled and shaped into concave and convex forms, then welded at the seams to form a very simple, inexpensive, durable rowboat. Captain Mark L. Gilbert of New York City headed the startup of the new company in June

1934 and claimed the basic patent design on the boat.[44] Instead of a conventional boat bottom of flat or V-hull design, the Gil-Boat incorporated a series of reverse curves, resulting in a rigid, ribless boat with no stem, keel, or frames. Using a steel sheet roller, sheets were first cut to pattern and then rolled in the form of a tube. Each tube was then broken in three places, the center break forming the keel. The formed sheets were then matched to a pattern and the bow also cut to a pattern. All was welded into place. The same process was used for the stern. Three seats, welded into place, served as both air tanks and the supporting bracing.[45] An 11-foot boat weighed only 84 pounds, complete, and could easily plane with a 3-horsepower motor. Plans called for manufacturing twenty-five boats a day in three different sizes, 11, 12, and 14 feet in length. Because of its speed of production and simple design, the Gil-Boat Company could fill orders very quickly. An order for one hundred boats shipped in one weekend to flooded areas in southern Indiana at the request of the State of Indiana in January 1937.

Captain Mark Gilbert seemed to be a man of vision, even if his dreams never quite came to fruition. He predicted that "volplaning" (Gilbert's term) ships would skim their way across the Atlantic between New York and London in eighteen hours at a cost of twenty-five dollars per person. He also predicted that ships no longer than 200 feet but capable of carrying a thousand passengers and 3,000 tons of cargo would someday be crossing Lake Michigan in a little more than an hour. Gilbert had a new boat designed to test some of his revolutionary ideas for larger craft in 1939. Claiming his new boat to be "the fastest commercial ship in the world," Gilbert's "Sea-Hydro," named the *Nassau Clipper*, looked something like a boat hull with an airliner fuselage on top, sloped at the stern, an ungainly example of futuristic streamlining. The 80-foot-long, double-decked, steel-hulled boat with Dowmetal sides was built at a Brunswick, Georgia, shipyard. Powered by no less than seven engines, testing performed at Brunswick in early July 1939 reportedly produced a speed of 65 miles per hour.[46] Although the boat operated for a while as a commercial carrier in the southern fruit trade, it never achieved the success anticipated by the owners. Gilbert and the Gil-Boat Company eventually ran into trouble with the Securities and Exchange Commission while trying to sell undivided interests in the *Nassau Clipper*.[47] The firm fell into receivership, and the assets were liquidated in 1942.

Milo L. Bailey of Detroit designed, built, and promoted electric arc-welded steel cruisers in the late 1930s as a lower cost alternative to traditional riveted steel hulls or even wooden hulls. Bailey, a naval architect and boat builder who worked on both the east and west sides of the state throughout his career, got started in the boat-building industry in 1929 as one of the incorporators of the short-lived North Star Marine Construction Company of Holland, along with Gordon B. Hooton and Adrian Van Putten. After that company failed, he moved to Detroit and began designing and building welded steel cruisers under the name Bailey Boat Works in 1931–32 and subsequently the Bailey Steel Shipbuilding Company in January 1937. He wrote in the late 1930s about the advantages of arc-welded steel cruisers as being lighter and more cost efficient to build than riveted steel hulls, and that the maintenance cost of an arc-welded steel hull could be a quarter of the cost of a wooden hull.[48] Bailey worked his way through the Great Depression by advertising his pioneering standardized steel cruisers, taking the concepts of knockdown boat design and applying them to steel, offering stock model steel hull frames of 30, 40, and 48 feet.[49] Other yacht builders soon picked up on some of his ideas, and over the course of the next decade arc-welded seams became the standard methodology for steel cruiser hull construction.

For some companies, odd jobs made up a portion of their survival strategies. The Truscott Boat Company of St. Joseph received one such contract for the Century of Progress exhibition in Chicago, building fifty-four boats for the 1933 season. The company contracted for an additional ten exotic boats to decorate the north lagoon in 1934. Officials of the company worked for three months with the artists of the Century of Progress in designing the decorative craft, which were anchored in the lagoon. The new 40-foot boats represented the designs of different countries, decorated in bright colors. These included five Chinese boats, each of different design; two Alaskan boats, like those used by the natives of the north; one Sumatran boat; one Egyptian boat; and one Hawaiian boat. The company imported a truckload of bamboo poles, some six inches in diameter, to be used as masts in some of the oddly designed boats.[50]

Robinson Hangs On

The Robinson Marine Construction Company, a prominent Michigan cruiser builder located in Benton Harbor, turned out some of the most attractive cruisers ever built in Michigan, planked in African mahogany, with glistening brightwork finished in five coats of spar varnish. Young Glen E. Robinson formed the Robinson Marine Construction Company after a broken business deal within the Dachel-Carter Boat Company. Dachel-Carter was incorporated in Benton Harbor on June 19, 1924, with Allan B. Carter as president, Peter Dachel as vice president, and Glen E. Robinson as secretary-treasurer. The new business partnership soon turned into an unhappy combination. Both Dachel and Carter filed suit against Robinson in circuit court in early January 1926, alleging that the he had pocketed over twenty-one thousand dollars in profits from the firm's contract with the U.S. government for the construction of ten rum chasers, built a personal 36-foot boat using company time and materials, and used company funds to purchase materials to improve his home. While the lawsuit was going on, Robinson left the company to form his own boat-building firm, the Robinson Marine Construction Company, also located in Benton Harbor, building a shop at 227 West Main Street.[51]

In January 1927, Robinson announced that he would build twenty-five Hacker-designed standardized "Sea Bird" cruisers for Hacker & Fermann, Inc., the naval architects and distributors. The arrangement with Robinson may have represented a reversal of the usual designer-builder relationship, as the designer in this case also functioned as the retailer. The first Sea Bird boat was shown at the National Motor Boat Show in New York on January 21–29. Glen Robinson attended the show and took charge of the Hacker & Fermann exhibit there. Sales must have been good, as by May 1927 the new company had six boats in progress and one ready to go to the Chicago Boat Show, to be delivered by Carl Kistler, the shop foreman. By the late 1920s, a typical Robinson cruiser would sell for about fifteen thousand dollars. Ransom E. Olds, of the REO Motor Car Company, purchased two Robinson cruisers for his Florida home in February 1928. One of the two, named *Flying Cloud* for the REO automobile of the same name, was described by the *Benton Harbor News-Palladium*: "The Flying Cloud has something of a look of a smart automobile about it. It has long, graceful lines, like a sedan . . . and is equipped for every modern convenience."[52]

Robinson made its way through 1930 and 1931 on the strength of government orders for twenty-two Coast Guard 38-foot picket boats in May 1930, doubling the company's payroll and giving it the best summer in its history.[53] The firm also received an order for five large boats from the U.S. Army Corps of Engineers in 1931. Temporarily flush with cash from the government orders, the company was incorporated on January 5, 1932, with capital of one hundred thousand dollars, consisting of common stock valued at one hundred dollars per share. Robinson filed for the incorporation with his father and William MacKerer, the former Chris-

Craft production superintendent. Glen Robinson remained as president with MacKerer as vice president and Marie Robinson as secretary of the firm. As private orders quickly dwindled, one of the corners the company cut was on wages and salaries accrued as liabilities, according to the company's annual report of 1932. After about a year of presumably very little in pay, MacKerer moved to Long Island to work with Co-Mac Seacraft.[54]

During the worst years of the Depression, Robinson cut its work force from about eighty-three in 1930 to twenty by April 1934.[55] Like others in the industry who bounced from company to company, Carl E. Kistler, the Robinson shop foreman during the late 1920s, found work at the Barrett Boat Works in Spring Lake and Burbach Yacht Company in Grand Rapids in the construction of yachts in the late 1930s. The Robinson Marine Construction Company also found ways to stay open with repair work, such as rebuilding the hull of the fish tug *B & B* for Captain Fred Balow of South Haven.

Passenger excursion operators discovered that the Robinson cruisers could make some money because of their attractive appearance and thrilling speed capabilities of up to 35 miles per hour. For instance, the Union Electric Light & Power Company at Lake of the Ozarks ran two 1931 Robinson cruisers on excursions, the 45-foot *Tuscumbia*, with a capacity of thirty-six passengers, and the smaller 38-foot *Grand Glaize*, twenty-eight passengers, each powered by twin Kermath Sea Wolf engines. With speed and spray, the boats would head for Bagnell Dam or make big waves on the lake for the enjoyment of the passengers.[56] In Michigan E. W. Couchois of the White Star Rapid Transit Company, serving Mackinac Island, commissioned the Robinson firm to build the *Pilot II* in 1935. The Arnold Transit Company purchased the boat in 1942 and operated the craft during the World War II years until the federal government acquired it for patrol purposes.

The company completed contracts for large boats in the mid-1930s from a few very wealthy individuals such as Barney Balaban of Chicago, head of the Paramount Studios, who owned the 54-foot *Judith R*, and Roger Firestone, the tire magnate, who owned a 1934 Robinson Seagull. Although the company's cruiser work slowed down considerably, it was enough for it to survive until government contracts preceding World War II could be obtained.

Government Support

In the early years of the Depression under the Hoover administration, Prohibition enforcement was still a priority. As the responsible federal agen-

Fig. 19. The Robinson Marine Construction Company's crew proudly celebrated the completion of the *Aphrodite* in 1936. While the Great Depression reduced new boat construction to a minimum, the occasional large job helped companies and their workers make ends meet. (Courtesy of the Heritage Museum and Cultural Center, St. Joseph, Michigan.)

cies worked out their enforcement plans in the budgetary process, the boat builders were able to supply desperately needed boats for the work. The U.S. Coast Guard became an important customer for Michigan boat builders, albeit late in the Prohibition era. Like the Robinson Marine Construction Company of Benton Harbor, the Corsair Boat Company of Detroit landed a contract for five 38-foot picketboats in 1931.

The Defoe Boat & Motor Works of Bay City survived the Depression in great part due to government contracting. After building power yachts for the wealthy into 1931, private jobs at the yard slowed to a virtual standstill by 1933. The company received large contracts from the U.S. Coast Guard for building icebreaking 165-foot cutters, the first for the *Escanaba*, delivered in 1932, and a second for the *Onondaga* and *Tahoma*, valued at

$1,227,600, in 1934–35. Defoe erected two new buildings and employed five hundred men to perform the work on the second contract. The company tried to spread the work among the men as best it could, running two shifts a day of five hours each for six days a week.[57] Defoe built the 175-foot lighthouse tender *Hollyhock* and the smaller tender *Elm*. Other unique jobs included a welded-steel-hulled fireboat for the city of Chicago and a mail boat, the *O. F. Mook*, for a private mail contractor to round out the company's government work through the worst of the Depression.

As the financial picture darkened in the early to mid-1930s, the boat builders looked increasingly to government support to make it through the worst times. President Franklin Delano Roosevelt's election and the creation of programs constituting the New Deal increased government spending dramatically, and boat builders were able to win small but substantial contracts for boats for the U.S. Army, Navy, and Coast Guard. The Hacker Boat Company filled a contract with the Coast Guard for seven airplane crash rescue boats at a price of twenty-five thousand dollars in 1935. The Coast Guard used three of the boats on Lake St. Clair and the others in Mississippi and Arkansas.[58] The larger runabout builders sold a few smaller cabin cruisers or runabouts with shelter cabins to a host of the smaller agencies of the federal government, including the U.S. Biological Survey, Fish and Wildlife Service, Public Health Service, and others, which used them as utility and inspection craft for a variety of purposes. As a stopgap measure to closing, the government orders provided essential help for some of the larger companies to keep their doors open during the worst years.

New Incorporations and Startups

While much of the decade consisted of business failures and idled plants, not all was doom and gloom. Most of the companies formed between 1930 and 1933 never had a chance. The Spring Lake Boat Company of Fruitport, Challenge Boat Company of Grand Haven, and American Boat Corporation, houseboat builders of Marysville, all failed rather quickly. Even during the depth of the Depression, Bay City Boats, Inc., incorporated in 1934, renewed the public's interest in knockdown boats as one of the most affordable ways to obtain the boat of one's dreams. Harry Defoe, one of the early proponents of the knockdown business, took advantage of the hard times to bring back to the market the products that made the labor of the owner even more valuable in the construction process. An advertising article in the *Michigan Investor* showed that the company offered a little of everything for everybody: "Sixty different designs—for boats ranging from nine to 100 feet in length—are included in the company's line incorporating everything from a rowboat to a palatial Diesel cruiser, or a 90-foot schooner yacht. The commercial designs offered include tugs, cargo carriers and ferry boats."[59]

As conditions improved in the late 1930s, several more firms were incorporated in 1937, including the Campbell Boat Company of Holland and American Cruiser Company of Detroit. Wayne E. Taylor of Owosso, who started a boat-building operation in a bus garage, built over two hundred boats in a year and by July 1938 was working on another hundred for fall delivery to Florida.[60]

Outboards for Racing and Cruising

As Gar Wood dominated the 1920s and early 1930s with his *Miss America* line of hydroplanes and drew the public's attention to speed, interest grew for the creation of different classes of racing boats, moving the sport out of the realm of the very wealthy and into a range that more of the public could afford. In the twenty-five years following Cameron Waterman's and Ole Evinrude's pioneering outboard motors, builders of the power plants refined the concepts to rapidly improve their horsepower and speed. The American Power Boat Association formed rules for outboard racing in 1924. The Michigan outboard motor manufacturer Caille of Detroit offered the first "racing trim" outboard in 1926, and another important builder, Lockwood of Jackson, earned many trophies for racers with the 11-horsepower Chief and 7-horsepower Ace models in 1928. Unfortunately, both of these firms were on their last legs by the time of the Great Depression. Evinrude/Elto bought out Lockwood in the 1929 merger forming the Outboard Marine Corporation and then eliminated the brand. Caille dropped out of racing motors in 1932 and ceased manufacturing altogether by 1935, giving way to faster machines.[61]

For a young driver, kneeling on the floor of a tiny "shingle" boat speeding across the water made for thrills, chills, and occasional spills that no other form of sport could deliver. Divided into different classes according to motor cubic-inch displacement, racers constantly experimented with alcohol-based fuels with castor oil lubrication and anything that would give them an edge in competition. Most of the small racing hulls could be purchased inexpensively, although many drivers probably spent much more money on modifications to their motors. Michigan boat builders placed a wide variety of outboard hulls on the market, some for racers but many more for family boating.

Century Boat Company

One of Michigan's most important builders of the second half of the twentieth century started out as an outboard racing boat manufacturer. James and William Welch formed the Century Boat Company in Milwaukee, Wisconsin, in 1926, and within a year their venture rose to fame with very successful outboard racers, starting with the Century Kid. The Kid model combined the features of a racer and a runabout, as its unique double cockpits could carry two passengers forward and the driver in the aft cockpit. Drivers raced the Kid in the B, C, and D outboard motor class races, with four owners winning a stunning twenty-six first-place trophies out of thirty races entered in 1927. The Welch brothers immediately introduced the Century Cyclone, a lightly built, single-seat, 12-foot racer capable of 40 miles per hour and selling for only $215, which likewise became a hit with the racers. With $130,000 in boat orders and a very cramped factory, the Welches needed to make a move. Their vice president, William W. Sherman, urged the brothers to move to Manistee, Michigan, where he had worked during World War I for the Manistee Shipbuilding Company and was familiar with the community there. With Manistee's excellent shipping connections, the company bought the former American Woodenware Company factory in December 1928 and started producing boats in February 1929 with about twelve men on the payroll.[62] Within two months, the company fell into receivership in an attempt to stabilize its credit. The Welch brothers decided to sell their interest in the firm in late 1929 and remained in Milwaukee.[63]

George G. Eddy and John A. Hacker, son of John L. Hacker, took over the company in 1930 with Ard E. Richardson of Lansing providing the financing. Soon the company offered a new line of redesigned outboard racers and inboard runabouts attributed to the elder Hacker, including the 17-foot Sea Maid. Eddy, the general manager, contrary to the thinking of most builders of the time, firmly believed that smaller inboards, equal in quality and performance to the larger boats, would find a broader market with their greater affordability.[64] Eddy invented the "Air-Cushion" bottom design for the Century Thunderbolt, a beautiful and successful 14-foot inboard racing boat with an unconventional clapboard type of construction in a V-hull to reduce the amount of wetted surface.

Century struggled through a number of fits and starts in its earliest years. The company shut down for three months in the fall of 1930, followed by an early start for the 1931 model season with 143 men working ten-hour days, producing about ten boats a day by April 1931.[65] The number of dealerships skyrocketed from eleven in 1929 to nearly four hundred by the end of 1931. Expanding too fast into inboard runabouts for the declining market conditions, the company fell into bankruptcy in June 1932 with over $706,500 in liabilities.[66] Ard Richardson, the majority stockholder, purchased the company and reincorporated the firm, bringing in Gates Harpel, the former sales manager of the Johnson Outboard Motor Company, to run the operation. Harpel acquired the company from Richardson in May 1933, remaining as the owner and manager for sixteen years.[67] Over the remaining years of the 1930s, the company diversified into a long line of more family-oriented utility-type boats, but it also experimented with new materials such as Masonite and plywood as the hull material on some of its smaller boats. Harpel managed to stabilize the finances and production of the firm, and Century became one of the larger builders of boats in the state, surpassing many other companies with its longevity.

George G. Eddy, after losing control of the Century Boat Company in the 1932 bankruptcy, ended up moving to Bay City, where he formed the Eddy Marine Corporation in 1935.[68] One of the first steps taken by the new Eddy Marine Corporation was the purchase from the Century Boat Company of the Air-Cushion bottom patents, which Eddy had developed.[69] He worked with naval architect C. Douglas Van Patten to create the Eddy "Aqua-Flow" bottom designs for a line of runabouts powered with marine versions of Ford four-cylinder and V-8 engines. Like Century, Eddy's company slipped into bankruptcy in 1936, but District Court judge Arthur J. Tuttle allowed him to reorganize the outfit, which reemerged with new financing in 1937. George Eddy could be considered either a visionary influence on small boat design or a commercial failure as he started and lost control of several boat companies over his lifetime. He nonetheless remained interested in the design side of the boat business, patenting new ideas into the early 1960s.

Dachel-Carter Boat Company

In 1929 the Dachel-Carter Boat Company decided to move into outboard-powered runabouts to supplement its cruisers, producing a design named the Waterwitch to be sold by the Johnson Motor Company through its dealer network for use with its larger motors. Planked in solid mahogany, the 16-foot family-type runabout incorporated many amenities, such as a folding table for card games or picnic lunches, fold-down seat backs to make an impromptu bed, and electric bow and stern running lights. With a class C, 20-horsepower outboard, the boat could make up to 27 miles per hour. Within a year or so after its introduction, the boat disappeared from Dachel-Carter's advertising, and the company returned to cruiser production.[70]

Gordon B. Hooton

One of the unique figures of boat-building in the late 1920s and early 1930s in Michigan, Gordon B. Hooton of Grand Rapids, built a few fast outboard-powered racing boats. Hooton worked as a designer for automotive and aircraft designer William B. Stout on Stout's Batwing airplane, so he may have transferred some of his experience with the visionary Stout into watercraft. Along with Milo Bailey and Adrian Van Putten, he incorporated the North Star Marine Construction Company in 1929 in Holland to build runabouts. He patented a hydroplane (U.S. Patent 1,762,626) with a spring-loaded forward fin to help prevent skidding in turns at high speed. Marketed as the Hooton Safety Plane, his single-step, sea-sled-type hydroplanes, powered by an outboard motor, achieved some success as racers. One of the boats he designed and built, *Ludolph's Wildcat*, won the national outboard championship for class E racers. In the end, the Depression forced his small operation to close. Hooton lived simply at the local YMCA. Workers in his shop who had not been paid were offered unsold inventory for their compensation.[71]

Hooton advocated a deep V-hull shape with a greater than usual degree of dead rise to reduce the pounding of the ride through waves, according to articles he wrote in *Power Boating* magazine. Naval architect Weston Farmer later discounted Hooton's philosophy as pseudoscience but affirmed that if the engines of the time had been powerful enough he would have achieved the softer ride.[72]

In the late 1930s, the boom in outboard racing began to wane, and the focus of the larger builders changed back to designing and building inboards and cruisers, but the niche for more family-friendly outboard-driven boats would remain for some of the smaller companies.

Sail Racing Flourishes

One-design sail racing experienced a surge in interest in the 1930s, with the yacht clubs leading the way in organizing races and establishing the respective classes. One-design racing offered increasingly cost-conscious yachtsmen a way to stay competitive without the expensive, frequent modifications in hull or gear that the "formula" classes of boats needed to stay within the rules and have a chance of winning. With one-design racers having a uniform hull and sail area, these classes reduced the number of "checkbook champions," promoting racing skill over the affluence from which the formula classes suffered.

After years of working for other boat builders, Russell J. Pouliot decided to go his own way. Pouliot had long been interested in sailing craft, and as captain and owner of the yacht *Bernida* he won the first Bayview to Mackinac boat race in 1925, sailing in stormy conditions but arriving at Mackinac Island in forty-eight hours, well ahead of his competitors. Leaving Dee-Wite, Inc., Pouliot went into business for himself as Russell J. Pouliot, Inc., in Detroit in June 1932.[73] Russell Alger Jr., a prominent Detroit yachtsman and son of the former Michigan governor and U.S. secretary of war, invested heavily in the new operation. Pouliot designed and built a large 46-foot cutter named *Baccarat* for Alger in 1933 that achieved a good deal of fame for its beauty and speed, winning four consecutive Port Huron to Mackinac races and winning the class B race from New London, Connecticut, to Bermuda in 1934.

Pouliot received a commission from a group of yachtsmen of Charlevoix and Harbor Springs in 1933 to work out the final design and build a new class of one-design sailboats, the C-H (for Charlevoix–Harbor Springs) class. LeRoy Kramer, a young local sailor and amateur naval architect, sketched the initial concept for a sloop designed to be both a racer and a cruiser, based on the best features of the 6-meter and 22-square-meter boats already sailing in the area, including a large cockpit with seating for several passengers for cruising but an open area forward where a racing crew could move about. Pouliot built the boats on a subscription basis in Detroit at a cost of about twenty-four hundred dollars per boat. He shipped them by railroad car to the northern Michigan ports. Kramer renamed the class the Northern Michigan (NM) after the Little Traverse Yacht Club asked for the fleet's name for inclusion in the 1935 Lake Michigan Yachting Association Directory. Eighty years later the class remains a classic icon of sail racing and cruising in northern Michigan.[74]

Pouliot secured a long-term lease on the shops and yards of the Detroit Yacht and Motor Boat Basin in 1934, taking over a venture on Motor Boat Lane initiated by the Gladwin Park Realty Company two years earlier.[75] He worked on building Teal and Star class one-design sailboats and was also active in the iceboat-racing community. Pouliot never quite made it on his own. William P. Fisher purchased Russell J. Pouliot, Inc., in 1937, renaming the company Pouliot Boat Works, Inc.[76] About a year later the company changed its name once again to Fisher Boat Works, with Pouliot still working as one of its chief designers and second vice president.

Occasionally the powerboat builders also extended their capabilities into sailboats. The Dachel-Carter Boat Company built six new Eagle or S-class one-design sloops in 1929 for members of the Chicago Yacht Club. Designed by club member Francis Early, Commodore Hollis E. Potter helped finance the boats and resold them to interested parties.[77]

The Century Boat Company constructed the popular one-design Snipe and Comet class sailboats between 1936 and 1939 as a way to enter a new market for small, and more importantly inexpensive, sailboats used on inland waters.[78]

A Slow Recovery

In the late 1930s, Americans regained their confidence as consumers, and the economy slowly began to rally from the depths of the Depression. Gar Wood, Inc., and Chris-Craft Corporation reported record sales for 1936, far surpassing their sales in 1929. The Hacker Boat Company bragged that its sales in 1936 were 800 percent better than in 1935.[79] A few new boat companies were incorporated, hoping to cash in on the renewed prosperity working its way into the leisure and recreational sector. However, the rally faltered when a recession struck heavily in early 1937, immensely slowing down the recovery. Then optimism began to return. The Davis Boat Company, formed by Seth C. Davis, formerly of Corsair Boat Company, and George Sheldon's Sheldon Marine Company of Ferrysburg commenced operations in 1939.

Chris-Craft, the national production leader even before the Great Depression, actually emerged even stronger because much of its competition disappeared during the crisis. The founder, jovial, nonassuming old Chris Smith, died on September 9, 1939, leaving behind a legacy in the firm that forever changed recreational boating. The family now had to carry on without him.[80]

For some, even the last years of the Depression turned out to be dismal times, but for one man, Fred P. Bingham, new perspectives gained and lessons learned after his boat-building business failed actually resulted in making him a better boat builder. The Bingham Boat Works of Detroit struggled through the latter portion of the Depression. Bingham became a proponent of the work of Charles G. MacGregor, a plywood boat-building pioneer. Bingham stated, "In the four-year life of my Detroit boat shop, I built five of MacGregor's designs: five *Norsemen* 15-foot fin keelers, a 27-foot voyaging sloop, *Threesome*, four *Defender* 23-foot fin keelers, three plank-on-frame *Shipmite* cruising sloops, and started a 42-foot ketch when the Depression nabbed me in 1940 . . . He taught me that there were two or more ways of doing almost everything, and that low-cost does not mean cheap." Just as old doors closed for Bingham, new ones opened: "My book larnin' and modest experience enabled me to work with my team of French, Scottish, Swedish and German *artists* in wood. And not only to learn from *them* but to introduce them to this 'new' boatbuilding medium, plywood. Early in 1940 at Fisher Boat Works I was exposed to some of the finest workmanship—experimental torpedo boats, yacht-like submarine chasers, and major yacht repairs. And there for six months I was privileged to hide away in the same drafting room as Nelson Zimmer, N.A., a talented yacht designer and meticulous craftsman."[81]

With one crisis slowly concluding, a second was about to begin, this one with more dramatic changes for Michigan's boat-building industry as clouds of war darkened Europe and Asia.

CHAPTER SIX

Building for the Arsenal of Democracy, 1939–49

Introduction

By the late 1930s, the boat-building industry in Michigan was slowly beginning to recover from the devastating effects of the Great Depression,
but the deteriorating political situation in Europe under the growing
power of Adolph Hitler began to cast shadows over the Atlantic in preparation for a conflict to come. World War II challenged the boat-building
industry in Michigan as no other market factor did before or since. Everything that represented normal operations in the business was soon turned
upside down. Skilled labor and construction materials became scarce. Making deliveries on time presented management with logistical nightmares
unimaginable only years earlier. The government-requested changes in
specifications and designs could make for volumes of additional paperwork
with no extra compensation. Interference by government inspectors verify-
ing the costs and quality of the contractual work brought in new, often un-
welcome visitors to peek at all areas of the operations, upsetting the private
nature of the business. Despite the difficulties, boat builders, along with
other Michigan industries, like those across the nation, rose to the challenge with remarkable innovations, persistence, and individual trials and
triumphs to make the state the center of the "Arsenal of Democracy" for
wartime production. Michigan boat builders contributed to the war effort
by constructing huge numbers of wooden small craft and small steel fighting ships. Without landing craft from Michigan, the invasions of Europe
and the Pacific islands would have been long delayed, if not impossible.

Michigan wooden boat builders made up the largest sector among the state's maritime, wartime construction firms. Long a center for cruisers and runabouts, when the government needed thousands of small boats to perform hundreds of tasks, the Michigan builders provided the military with a high-quality, well-constructed boat, delivered quickly and in great volume when needed. The steel shipbuilding industry in Michigan had downsized immediately after World War I, leaving only the Great Lakes Engineering Works for large Great Lakes bulk carrier construction, as the Detroit Shipbuilding Company and Saginaw Shipbuilding Company had disappeared decades before. The Defoe Boat & Motor Works, a relative newcomer in the steel shipbuilding business, constructed small cutters for the U.S. Coast Guard and large steel yachts until that market evaporated during the Depression.

The Prewar Situation

Pleasure boat plants began to come back to life in Michigan after the worst of the Great Depression. According to the 1939 U.S. Census of Manufactures, Michigan was home to eleven boat-building establishments that built boats of less than 5 gross tons of all types. This branch of the industry employed approximately 986 people and distributed salaries and wages of nearly $1.3 million. Nearly one-third of the nation's boat-building work force of 3,009 people was located in the state at the time. The industry's products were valued at $4,113,913 in Michigan alone out of $10.8 million nationwide.[1]

Hints of the increase in business showed up virtually everywhere. Chris-Craft, the largest manufacturer of small craft in the world, celebrated a banner year in 1940. Introducing ninety-eight models of boats, many of them cruisers, the company finally surpassed the 1929 level of sales in 1940.

Gar Wood Industries likewise rebounded a bit more in 1940 after a good year in 1939. The public seemed to be more interested in cabin utility boats, which offered a combination of room, shelter, and flexibility that standard runabouts could not provide. Called the Trophy Fleet since the late 1930s, Gar Wood's designer, George Joachim, presented even more streamlined and beautiful styling for the 1941 model year with barrel sterns, raked transoms, and lots of chrome on the bow. Roof lines slightly overhung the windshield on the cabin models to create a visor effect. Combined with even more powerful engines, the company intended to add even more fun with style than ever before in boating.[2]

New incorporations in 1940 alone included the Boat Center, Inc., in Grosse Pointe Park; Gull Lake Boat Works, Inc., in Kalamazoo; and The Harbor, Inc., in Detroit. Factory moves and new plant construction also picked up as the economy improved. Edward Brown, owner of the Brown-Bilt Boat Company of Ionia, acquired the former Ypsilanti-Reed building in Lyons, recently occupied by the Booth Manufacturing Company of Chicago, intending to move operations to Lyons later that year. The Raymond Darrow Boat Works of Traverse City built an addition to its plant to double its production of sloops, ketches, and catboats. The Donaldson-Barnes Boat Company of Tekonsha leased a section of the Simons-Leedle building in Marshall and planned to move its operations there at once.[3]

Politically, the nation's attention was focused internally on healing itself after economic chaos, resulting in American isolationism from international issues. In the twenty-seven months between the invasion of Poland and the bombing of Pearl Harbor, the majority of the American people felt unwilling to get involved in the political and military crises in Europe and China, fearing entanglement in affairs that did not seem to be their business. The American public demanded neutrality, but the political leaders, believing that Europe's plight would soon be their own, started thinking about preparations for war. President Franklin Delano Roosevelt, a year before the bombing of Pearl Harbor, stated, "We must be the great arsenal of democracy," and begrudgingly at first, the nation slowly started building a defensive industrialization effort unlike any seen before or since. By late 1940 and early 1941, the automobile industry was already building enormous war material plants in southern Michigan such as Chrysler's Warren Tank Arsenal and the Ford Willow Run bomber plant near Ypsilanti.

Physical Restrictions of the Great Lakes

Geographically, the Great Lakes formed a great inland highway for the movement of boats and ships in its own region by water, but to get larger boats to other coastal regions of the country by water, many restrictions hurt the ability to move them. For the smallest boats, the old Erie Canal or New York State Barge Canal from Buffalo to Albany and the Hudson River made for the shortest, most direct route to the East Coast, but its shallow depth prevented anything large from passing through. For the larger boats, the fourth Welland Canal, connecting Lake Erie and Lake Ontario, was completed in 1932 with eight locks to bypass Niagara Falls and cross the Niagara Escarpment. The lock size of 766 feet long by 80 feet wide by 25 feet deep likewise prevented the Great Lakes builders from constructing large steel fighting ships for lack of a way to get them to the ocean.

Another way of moving boats out of the Great Lakes involved going from Lake Michigan through the Chicago Drainage Canal and Illinois River to the Mississippi River and then out to sea via New Orleans. This, too, posed problems with shallow areas that necessitated the use of pontoons attached to deep-draft vessels to get them through the passage, and masts and upper works on tall superstructures needed to be cut down and stored on deck to get the ships under bridges safely, all of which took a lot of time and effort to put back in place once the journey was completed.

The biggest problem the builders faced was not geography but weather. With the Great Lakes frozen over for at least three months of the year, the boats could only be shipped by rail during the winter, or they had to be held for delivery the following spring, causing peaks and valleys in the flow rate of boats, so many Michigan and other Great Lakes ship- and boatyards ended up being the last resort for contract work when no other sources on the coasts could be utilized.[4]

Building Prototypes

As residents of the largest small-boat-building state in the nation, Michigan builders could draw on an incredible amount of design and construction talent to aid the armed services in figuring out what would work best for the different kinds of boats they needed. Testing different concepts for hulls, power plants, armament schemes, and living and working spaces in prototypes, the military and the contractors could assess by trial and error their performance and change the designs accordingly before settling on a final configuration for mass production.

Although the U.S. Navy had long been unenamored with small boats as fighting craft, President Franklin Delano Roosevelt, after his work as assistant secretary of the navy in World War I, saw their possibilities as useful weapons. Congress passed a supplemental appropriation for construction of experimental small craft of under 3,000 gross tons, and in July 1938 the Navy Department sent out invitations for a design competition for boat builders to submit plans for a 165-foot submarine chaser, a torpedo boat 70 to 80 feet long, and a torpedo boat 54 to 60 feet long.

The largest prewar boat builder in steel, Defoe Boat & Motor Works, with its long experience in the federal procurement system with the U.S. Coast Guard, received a contract to design and build two experimental steel patrol craft (PC)/submarine chasers in 1939, the 163-foot *PC451*, with twin General Motors diesel engines for power, and the 173-foot *PC452* with steam propulsion. "Awarding of the contract," Harry Defoe said of the *PC451*, "will mean the return of a normal crew of men to our plant." Under regulations of the 1817 Rush-Bagot Treaty between the United States and Canada, which governed the construction of warcraft on the Great Lakes, the *PC451*'s keel could not be laid until September 28, well after the award of contract in June. Preliminary work on the ship started immediately as delivery was scheduled within a year. *PC451* was delivered to Norfolk, Virginia, under its own power and commissioned in August 1940. *PC452*'s steam power plant used a flash boiler, which proved unsatisfactory in trials, so Defoe towed the boat to the coast minus the boiler and delivered it to the navy for study and completion with a different power plant. The slightly larger hull design of *PC452*, however, was adopted for the remaining PC fleet. Defoe and Bay City scored $2,412,400 between the two contracts, a major boost to a community trying to pull itself out of the Depression.[5]

The Fisher Boat Works of Detroit got through the later years of the Depression by building semicustom cruisers designed by John L. Hacker, including the *Bismillah* for George Trumbull and the *Lone Wolf* for Ed Wolf.[6] Based on that experience, the company placed a bid on the navy's 54- to 60-foot experimental patrol torpedo (PT) boat. The torpedo boats carried two torpedoes, 50-caliber machine guns, and depth charges. The winner of the design competition would receive a prize of fifteen thousand dollars, a hefty sum in those days. Fisher received a contract for construction of two 58-foot prototype plywood-hull patrol torpedo boats, *PT3* and *PT4*, to be built from a distinctive design by George Crouch but modified by the U.S. Navy's Bureau of Construction and Repair. Packard marine engines powered the boats, which could make 32 knots speed. The original specifications called for a boat small and light enough to be lifted by a crane onto a mother warship or "PT carrier." The concept never worked except in theory, and it was eventually determined that a boat 58 feet long was too small to be of much practical use. Its rear-firing torpedo tubes would not work as well as those of the other designs. After further experimentation and testing, the navy decided to build the larger 78-foot Higgins and 80-foot Elco boats as its standard PT boat designs. The *PT3* and *PT4* were commissioned as part of the navy's Motor Torpedo Boat Squadron One in July 1940, but their mechanical and structural deficiencies forced them to spend the winter of 1940–41 in Florida waters. In the spring of 1941, *PT3* and *PT4* were transferred to the British Royal Navy under the Lend-Lease policy and ended up working out of Nova Scotia for the Royal Canadian Air Force on air-sea rescue missions.[7]

The Fisher Boat Works also built the experimental wooden-hulled submarine chaser *PC453* (later reclassified *SC453*) in 1940, further adding to its reputation as an innovator. One of the earlier small craft of the World War II era, the submarine chaser's keel was laid in September 1940, and the boat was launched on March 5, 1941. The 110-foot submarine chaser used a recently developed General Motors Model 16-184 "pancake" diesel engine from its Electro-Motive Division, a unique design making the best use of the boat's limited space. The sixteen radially-arranged cylinders were stacked in four layers of four cylinders each and mounted on a vertical crankshaft in layers like a stack of pancakes.[8] To assure that everything would work correctly, Fisher created an exact mockup of the engine room and shipped it to Elgin, Illinois, where the engines were built, for installation and testing purposes.[9] The subsequent boats of the design, called the SC-497 class, and generically nicknamed the "Splinter Fleet," primarily served as offshore coastal patrol boats to fight the submarine threat. The boats proved to be versatile in many different roles. Later in the war some of the class was assigned to the amphibious assaults in the European and the Pacific theaters for beach control craft, designated submarine control chasers (SCC). The navy employed others as patrol gunboats and coastal minesweepers, and many went to other nations as part of the Lend-Lease program to help arm the Allied forces.

Despite record business in the civilian sector, the Chris-Craft Corporation planned early on to get into the naval contracting business, assigning Harsen Smith, its vice president, the task of winning a contract for landing craft. In September 1940, the company took its 30-foot prototype of a landing boat to a design and performance competition in Virginia Beach, Virginia. Its most competitive rival, Andrew Jackson Higgins's Higgins Industries of New Orleans, brought its *Eureka* landing boat to the event, which also included two other boats. The Chris-Craft boat, loaded with 4,000 pounds of sandbags to simulate a cargo of men and equipment, performed as well as the *Eureka*, which was loaded with only three men and no extra weight. On the second day of testing, with Charles Smith driving the boat for the first time, the boat made a perfect 90-degree beaching, then a second time beached a full 20 feet farther ashore than the Higgins boat did. With the Chris-Craft crew thinking it had won the contest, the navy added an unscheduled test at the end, a broaching maneuver with motors dead. The Chris-Craft boat, partially filled with water from the surf and with a broken exhaust line from the prior trial, tried to make the maneuver but lost power on the starboard motor from water that had splashed on the ignition system. After repeated efforts to back the boat off the beach with the second engine, the navy officials ordered the *Eureka* boat to tow the Chris-Craft off the beach. The humiliating fiasco turned out to be very costly for Chris-Craft despite the fact that it performed better in the scheduled tests and was a cheaper boat even with two engines instead of the Higgins's one. Higgins received the order for four hundred landing craft. William MacKerer fought the navy's decision but to no avail.[10]

The U.S. Army also needed boats. One of the early prewar military contracts for Gar Wood Industries in 1941 called for a 33-1/2-foot radio-controlled target boat for training gunnery units on fast-moving targets. Gar Wood himself pioneered the technology as early as 1933 with the army coastal defenses, maneuvering a 28-foot runabout with gyroscopic controls and a compressed-air piston system from the aft cockpit. Chris-Craft and the Hacker Boat Company in the summer of 1940 built a similar 34-foot radio-controlled target boat for the navy for towing targets to be struck by bombers in practice runs but also to be loaded with explosives and used as big torpedoes. Both companies went head-to-head with Gar Wood in the navy target boat competition, and the Hacker boat, despite being 1,700 pounds heavier than Gar Wood's, received a slightly better score for ride comfort because its convex hull bottom did not pound so hard in rough seas.[11]

Not all experimental work was generated by the army and navy. Ora J. Mulford, founder and president of the Gray Motor Company, initiated boat-building contracts with the Mayea Boat Works in 1940 for experimental high-speed diesel utility boats, then used those designs to obtain government contracts. The Gray Motor Company tested its firm's conversion of the General Motors 6-71 diesel in a Milo Bailey–designed 49-foot boat named *GM2*. Powered by three 200-horsepower Gray marine diesel engines, the boat could achieve speeds over 40 miles per hour. Mulford kept *GM2* in Florida, where he could test the engines through the winter. After successfully running to his satisfaction, Mulford commissioned a larger, 53-foot boat from Louis and Herbert Mayea in 1941, the *GM3*, this one with four Gray marine diesels and claimed to be the fastest diesel boat in the country. The navy acquired this boat after its launch in October 1941. One other experimental boat that the Mayeas built was *GM6*, another Bailey-designed 65-foot troop hauler built in 1942, again powered by four Gray marine diesels.[12]

The Buildup to War

As it became clearer that the United States would likely be drawn into the war, the army and navy began an extensive buildup of all kinds of munitions and weapons to aid the Allies overseas, including various types of small craft for Lend-Lease projects initiated by the federal government. Michigan's boat-building plants were uniquely suited to wooden small craft production in large volume, and military and civilian production officials saw to it that they were used to maximum capacity. As the new prototypes progressed from their testing to satisfactory designs, the army and navy started generating production orders for boats through early 1941. The navy desperately needed submarine chasers as German U-boats were ravaging the British military fleets and commercial shipping. Both the army and the navy wanted air-sea rescue boats. The services also required minesweepers to keep the shipping lanes clear.

The business community likewise took notice and planned accordingly. Chicago area investors targeted small, struggling boatyards on the Lake Michigan shore for takeover in order to become eligible for the large government contracts that they felt fairly certain would be appearing in the near future.

One nearly dormant operation, the Dachel-Carter Boat Company of Benton Harbor, had managed to survive through the late Depression years by building a few sailing yachts and even rowboats of a new design. Gordon S. Clark, a vice president of Chicago machine tool manufacturer Samuel Harris & Company, bought out the original owners and reorganized the firm into the Dachel-Carter Shipbuilding Corporation in February 1941. Clark became the president and treasurer, with the original company founders Peter Dachel as vice president and Allan Carter as secretary; however, Carter left the company soon thereafter. Joseph Kehoe, a Chicago financier, served on the board of directors. Clark announced that the company planned to spend some ten thousand dollars or more on building modernization, improvements, and new equipment to prepare it for future government contracts for auxiliary naval vessels.[13]

Gordon Clark also planned to build a shipyard for steel ships at Grand Haven on a large island in the Grand River adjoining the industrial sec-

Fig. 20. The Dachel-Carter Shipbuilding Corporation plant at Benton Harbor operating at full capacity during World War II. The company constructed minesweepers, tugs, air-sea rescue boats, and submarine chasers. When it eventually ran into financial trouble, the navy reassigned management of the plant to a Chicago construction company. (Courtesy of the Heritage Museum and Cultural Center, St. Joseph, Michigan.)

tion of the city, although the project never came to fruition. By November 1941, the Benton Harbor plant was operating at capacity, with two minesweepers under construction and contracts for two more, as well as submarine chasers for the navy and air-sea rescue boats for the army, making it impossible to accept further orders from the government and private firms for steel ships, so Clark looked elsewhere for expansion.[14] In the meantime, the company went after new wooden boat business. After the passage of the Lend-Lease Act, Dachel-Carter picked up a contract for a pair of British motor minesweepers (BYMS) during the winter of 1941–42.

Additional Chicago area capital breathed new life into another firm just across the river from Dachel-Carter in St. Joseph. Francis H. Early of Winnetka, Illinois, along with Harold B. Prout of Oak Park, Illinois, and William A. Schaedla of Chicago, resurrected the Truscott Boat Company in March 1941, renaming it the Truscott Boat & Dock Company. The new company purchased the old Truscott plant and leased land from the Ireland & Lester Company for five years.[15] The company soon obtained a contract to build air-sea rescue boats for recovering air crews forced to ditch their aircraft at sea. Francis Early, a naval architect with the United States Shipping Board in World War I, served as president, and Schaedla had headed the Abeking & Rasmussen shipbuilding firm in Vegesack, Germany, designing submarines there, before relocating in Chicago. Charles H. Morse Jr., a millionaire formerly of the Fairbanks-Morse engine group, served as treasurer.

Several new or existing firms sought financial assistance from the federal government to add to their plants and to order construction materials for the first few contracted vessels through loans from the Reconstruction Finance Corporation.

The federal government directed most of the early boat procurement before Pearl Harbor to reduce the German U-boat submarine threat endangering Great Britain. In early 1941, Fisher received a contract for an additional pair of wooden submarine chasers. The American Cruiser Company of Detroit and Trenton, formed in 1937 by Martin D. Riekse, also won a contract to build a pair of wooden submarine chasers, with their keels laid in August 1941.[16] Not everybody initially received a contract. Among the bidders that lost out in the twenty-firm nationwide competition for the 110-foot submarine chasers was Bay City Boats, Inc., the knockdown boat-building firm.

Another Michigan boat concern, the Century Boat Company at Manistee, received a contract award in July 1940 of $111,510 from the War Department for the construction of eighteen hundred small boats to be used by the US Army Corps of Engineers. The order would give approximately one hundred men steady employment for nine weeks, Century officials said.[17]

The automobile industry in general became far too busy with other kinds of war work to deal with boats for the armed services. Airplanes, trucks, tanks, and ammunition consumed huge amounts of its production capacity. General Motors Corporation worked on important marine engine projects, including the GM 6-71 diesel engines used with landing craft and the novel "pancake" diesel for the submarine chasers. The Packard Motor Car Company, drawing on the experience of building Gar Wood's racing engines a decade earlier, supplied modified V-12 marine gasoline engines derived from its aviation versions for patrol torpedo boats, with each PT boat requiring three engines.

One large auto manufacturer noticeably missing from the boat-building programs during World War II was the Ford Motor Company. After its experience in World War I with the Eagle boats, the firm had more than enough on its plate with the problematic B-24 bomber plant at Willow Run and many other products more along the lines of its core business such as the Jeep.

Another large auto manufacturer, Chrysler Corporation, built "water tractors" called Sea Mules for pushing around the multitude of landing craft. Chrysler originally designed the small boat to be built of steel, but the supply of steel quickly dwindled, and the remaining stocks were diverted to more important projects. The corporation approached the Mayea brothers about producing a wooden version of the craft as an alternative. The Mayeas redesigned the craft for plywood and developed a three-stepped keel that could be easily assembled and disassembled for shipment overseas. After demonstrating the design to Chrysler executives, the company asked the Mayeas to build hundreds of them. Unfortunately, the Mayeas had to pass on the opportunity as their six-man shop was far too small for the job. They declined the offer and sold their design to Chrysler instead.[18]

For a few years prior to American entry into the war, the Chris-Craft Corporation planned to expand into cities outside the Algonac area because of a lack of space at its Point du Chene facility and a saturation of the work force at Algonac and Marine City. The increasingly hostile relationship with its workers' labor union could also have been a contributing factor. During the 1937 strike, the company looked into acquiring the Eddy Marine Corporation plant in Bay City but evidently never went through with the deal, or it may have been an attempt to spur the contract negotiations.[19] The company opened one new plant in Holland, Michigan, on twenty-two acres purchased in July 1939, followed by the construction of a three-hundred-thousand-dollar plant measuring 600 by 110 feet, which opened only four months later. Chris-Craft planned to build 15-1/2 to 42-foot boats in the new facility, and the first shipment of boats left the factory by truck in the last week of January 1940, bound for a western distributor.[20] Holland made a good fit for the company with skilled woodworkers from the nearby furniture industry in Grand Rapids and Holland itself.

Less than two years later, in January 1941, the company negotiated an agreement with the city of Cadillac, Michigan, to purchase a vacant factory of 125,000 square feet for a new facility to build its line of 18- to 22-foot utility boats. The company received free use of the land for eight years or until the time when the local payroll exceeded $250,000, after which the city would turn over title to the land. Chris-Craft employed about two hundred workers shortly after the plant opened five weeks later, and a new production line for 30-foot cruisers was in the process of being set up.[21]

In general the boat builders found themselves in the increasingly awkward situation of trying to promote the sales of private pleasure boats in greater numbers while at the same time ramping up production on military contracts to meet those deadlines. Chris-Craft, despite losing out on the initial contract for the landing craft to Higgins, contracted with the federal government in February 1941 to provide engines for the 26-foot motor mine yawls being built by the Wheeler Shipyard in Brooklyn, Palmer-Scott of New Bedford, Massachusetts, and Southwest Harbor Boat Corporation of Maine. In addition, the company sold twenty-seven of its 22-foot utility boats to the army for use in air-sea rescue work. The small contracts helped the company sort out the complexities of the government contracting procedures, and soon afterward it sold four virtually stock cruisers to different federal agencies.[22] Chris-Craft suffered through another strike in October 1941, in violation of its prior two-year agreement, signed January 1. The strike ended on December 2, 1941, but only after company officials and nonstriking workers filed and won a court-ordered injunction to get the men back to work. The strike threatened the company's schedule of deliveries to both the civilian sector for its 1942 model year boats and the army for its boats. In just over a week, the nation would be at war.[23]

After Pearl Harbor: Urgency for Wartime Production

Japanese aircraft launched a bombing and torpedo attack on the U.S. Navy fleet based at Pearl Harbor, Hawaii, in the early dawn hours of December 7, 1941. In some ways, the American public felt a sense of relief that a decision had been made, and with the anger that came from being suddenly and deliberately attacked, a new sense of urgency bent on dealing with the immediate crisis took hold. With the Germans having captured and established control over most of the European countries and the Japanese having taken over most of the island archipelagoes in the South Pacific soon after Pearl Harbor, it was felt that the only way to bring freedom back was with an invasion . . . by boat. And all kinds of boats would be needed for the task.

Landing craft, the amphibious assault transportation boats for sending troops ashore in all of the major theaters of the war, made up the largest quantity of boats produced in Michigan, with Chris-Craft, the world's largest wooden boat builder, acting as the primary contractor. Despite having lost the initial design and build contest to Higgins, Chris-Craft stood in a great position to influence the future procurement of contracts with its huge main plant at Algonac and the new, fully operational plants at Holland and Cadillac. Within weeks after the bombing of Pearl Harbor, Chris-Craft received a contract from the navy for 1,025 of the 36-foot *Eureka*-style landing boats designed by its competitor, Higgins. The production was split between all three plants at Algonac, Holland, and Cadillac. The new boats were to be built of plywood rather than the mahogany planking the firm traditionally used, but the boxy hull form would be simpler to build by comparison. The navy supplied armor plate for the ramp at the bow and for some bulkheads. Chris-Craft's contract called for payment of eight thousand dollars for each boat. Because of the company's existing organizational ability, under William MacKerer, to control each cost and process, it could quickly find cost discrepancies and create savings to pass on to the government. The company set to work immediately on converting its operation to meet the military's needs for the duration. With the new 1942 model year just started, the company quickly sold off its existing stock of civilian boats to concentrate completely on war production.

Orders followed the initial landing craft contract within ninety days for even more, including 725 landing craft personnel ramp boats (LCP(R)), four hundred vehicle landing craft (LCV), and two hundred additional regular landing craft, vehicle and personnel boats (LCVP). The navy supplied its own Gray marine diesel engines or Chrysler Royal gasoline engines for the boats. Shortly after the initial landing craft contracts, the navy issued Chris-Craft another order for 36-foot picket boats, more similar to the cruisers of its prior experience. Chris-Craft constructed these in its Cruiser and Yacht Division facilities. The army soon followed suit with orders for its 42-foot army command boats and 60-foot quartermaster boats.

Over the course of the following years, the navy issued huge contracts to Chris-Craft, such as the ones for 1,200 landing craft personnel, large (LCP[L]) boats; 1,048 landing craft personnel, ramp (LCP[R]) boats; and 4,305 landing craft, vehicle and personnel (LCVP) boats.[24] A Chris-Craft landing craft was the first boat ashore in Normandy on D-Day, June 6, 1944, and by the end of the war the company had built *thirteen thousand* landing craft of all varieties.[25]

Defoe of Bay City conceived an ingenious method for constructing its steel submarine chasers in the shortest time possible. The company built the hulls of the boats upside down as it was easier to weld seams working

Fig. 21. Landing craft built by Chris-Craft Corporation during World
War II made possible the amphibious invasions of Europe and Japanese-
held islands in the Pacific. Workers in Algonac, Holland, and Cadillac built
the boats by the thousands in many configurations. (Mariners' Museum,
Newport News, Virginia.)

downward on the hull than upward, and the quality of the workmanship improved as well. First, a cradle was built to the exact size and shape of the main deck of the craft. Interior bulkheads and frames went on next, erected bottom-side up. Following that operation, the keel and floors and from four to six strakes of shell plating were attached on top of the frames and bulkheads with an overhead crane. The workers finished the remaining plating for the hull. The company then attached a pair of 50-foot, 40-ton semicircular steel eccentric wheels to the hull near the bow and stern, mounted in heavy parallel steel tracks. Cables were thrown around the hull in opposite directions, and using a locomotive crane pulling on one cable and holding back with the other, workers could turn the hull right-side up within three minutes to continue work on the interior. Deckhouses and machinery were installed afterward. The Defoe "rollover" technique, first used on a 173-foot submarine chaser in August 1941, eliminated nearly 90 percent of the overhead welding, and the company could complete boats in up to a third less time than with conventional construction methods. Later in the war the company used the rollover method for building the largest new-construction warships built in Michigan, the 307-foot destroyer escorts and high-speed troop transports. The "rollover" also earned the company additional contracts for work due to the savings in man-hours required to build a ship.[26]

Defoe Boat & Motor Works was renamed the Defoe Shipbuilding Company in 1942 to more accurately describe its operations and products.

Much of the activity at Defoe during the war was reported in the company's employee newspaper, the *Defoe Rollover*, named after its most prominent innovation. Filled with articles that would be considered gossipy and intrusive by today's standards, the newspaper covered the work of the different departments of the shipyard and the hundreds of personalities in each one. The company frequently urged employees to participate in war bond drives and blood drives to aid the greater war effort in addition to their regular work. The women in the yards got their own column, "About the Gals," with notes about female employee engagements, weddings, spouses overseas, travel, office treats, and new jobs in the shops. The company supported its own softball, basketball, and other sports teams as a way to build camaraderie and reduce work-related stress.[27]

Defoe constructed an incredible variety and number of warships for the navy. Starting with the prototype submarine chasers in 1940, the firm built three 100-foot tugs in the remainder of the year, then minesweepers and submarine chasers in 1941, and more 143-foot tugs and submarine chasers

Fig. 22. Defoe Shipbuilding of Bay City invented the technique of constructing a ship hull upside down for easier welding, then rolling it over for completion. This fast attack transport APD 134 is being rolled over in 1945. (Bay County Historical Society.)

in 1942 and 1943. The company received a contract for destroyer escorts in 1943–44. The first was built the traditional way, right side up, but with subsequent boats the company used the rollover technique so successfully used on the submarine chasers. As the submarine threat diminished, the navy modified Defoe's contract to build destroyer transports, high-speed (APDs), using the same hull as the destroyer escorts but enlarging the superstructure to house 162 troops and changing the armament to include heavier antiaircraft weapons. In 1944 the company started building landing craft infantry, large (LCI(L)) vessels, producing 47 of them. Defoe added to its workload to build freight and ammunition lighters in 1945, but as the war closed the contracts for additional minesweepers were canceled, forcing many out of work. The boats partially under construction were eventually scrapped. The company completed 154 fighting and service craft over the course of the war and with its preceding contracts.

Two of the other large builders, Gar Wood and Hacker, built a variety of craft, including the 36-foot and 45-foot picket boats. The Hacker boats had twin engines, but both had right-handed propellers instead of opposed screws because they allowed the engines to be replaced with a single model but at the disadvantage that the boats needed the help of a tug to dock on their starboard side. Gar Wood also built 24-foot plane personnel boats, target boats, and 46-foot towboats, with their production totaling 188 boats between 1942 and 1944.[28] The towboats, built of yellow pine and plywood and painted battleship gray, bore little resemblance in material and finish to the glistening stained and varnished runabouts of earlier years, but the craftsmen building them still used their fine woodworking skills and care in constructing them.

Getting the boats to the ocean early in the war was no simple task either. Robinson Marine Construction Company's recently commissioned *SC540* was ordered to New Orleans in April 1942 by way of the Mississippi River. The *SC540*'s crew had no nautical charts, so they relied on road maps picked up from gas stations along the route. Along the way, they tied up each night to avoid the hazards of what one man described as "logs, trees, houses and barns floating down the Big Muddy."[29] Captain Jay Ottinger ferried Hacker's picket boats in convoys of two or three at a time down the Clinton River to Lake St. Clair and down the Detroit River to Lake Erie. At Buffalo, New York, the boats traversed the Erie Canal to Troy and the Hudson River, entering the Atlantic Ocean and ending their journey at the Norfolk Navy Yard in Virginia, a trip of some 1,250 miles.[30]

Small Builders Participate

Virtually any boat company that could build anything, regardless of size, was inexorably drawn into the vortex of the war effort, and not all government contracts were huge.

Harry G. Foster moved his Foster Boat Company from Grand Rapids to Charlevoix in 1940. He leased and then purchased the former Ferry Seed Company building where before the war his company had constructed plywood rowboats, Snipe-class sailboats, a canoe, an outboard motorboat, and a pontoon boat. The company also picked up a side job producing bowling pin blocks for the Brunswick-Balke-Collender Company of Muskegon. In 1942 the Foster Boat Company received its first wartime contract for about thirty aircraft rearming boats used for servicing seaplanes by attaching torpedoes or bombs under their wings. Orders for other small specialty boats followed, including sailing dinghies for the navy, dinghies for the Coast Guard, and a 27-foot personnel boat for transporting air crews to seaplanes.

Foster's company, working twenty-four hours a day, seven days a week for several weeks, built hundreds of nesting 16-foot storm boats for the army in early 1945, shipping them to Detroit by rail and then ferrying them in aircraft to the front lines in Europe. The boats transported seven fully equipped riflemen, a noncommissioned officer, and two crew members. Designed for crossing rivers, they temporarily replaced the bombed-out bridges for getting men to the other side quickly. The soldiers abandoned the outboard-powered boats as soon as the river was crossed. These boats were far less complex to construct than runabouts and cruisers and had a small enough volume that they did not tie up work at the larger yards. At its peak of production, Foster employed 175 people in the company's three plants, two in Charlevoix and one in Petoskey.[31]

In some cases, small firms could find work as subcontractors. In late 1941, the I. Hemming Larsen Boat Works at Menominee was awarded a contract to build twelve lifeboats for the government subchasers under construction at the Peterson Shipyard in nearby Sturgeon Bay, Wisconsin, across Lake Michigan's Green Bay from Menominee.[32]

Entrepreneurs looked for construction resources with which to win small but lucrative government contracts for military craft. Rudolph W. Bramberg and Irvin. A. Blietz, both of the Chicago area, formed the Victory Shipbuilding Company under a temporary renaming arrangement with the Jesiek Brothers to do their boat-building at Holland on Lake

Macatawa. The Chicago men served as the administrators while Joseph and Adolph Jesiek supervised the construction operations. The company obtained a contract in May 1942 for a pair of 110-foot wooden submarine chasers.[33] It also built four harbor tugs for the navy.

The Traverse City Ship Building Company, formed later in the war in 1942, bid on a contract to build six small (65-foot) harbor tugs at a price of $32,495 each, with the tugs to be delivered without engines. The company set up shop in the former Greilick Furniture Company factory and improved the property to build two tugs at a time. Because construction materials could not be acquired immediately, several weeks passed before the keels could be laid. Around the nation, 106 builders from twenty-one states competed for multiple awards of the contract. In Michigan, the Foster Boat Company of Charlevoix, Love Construction and Engineering Company of Muskegon, Campbell Boat Company of Holland, Truscott Boat & Dock Company of St. Joseph, and Victory Shipbuilding Company of Holland all submitted bids, ranging widely from a high of $86,235 for two boats from Campbell to $31,500 each from Love for six tugs at a fixed price.[34] The Traverse City Ship Building Company and Love won contracts for six tugs each.

The Eddy Shipbuilding Corporation of Bay City, emerging out of the former Eddy Marine Corporation, managed to get contracts for a variety of boats for the army in 1943–44, including 36-foot launches and 85-foot air-sea rescue boats, as well as marine tow launches of different sizes and marine tractors. John L. Hacker worked as the company's chief designer, redesigning the bottoms of some of the company's air-sea rescue boats as one of his contributions to the war effort.[35]

For the Kalamazoo Canvas Boat Company, the war formed the all-time peak of its business when it turned out nearly four hundred boats a year in addition to canvas cots and covers, leggings, knapsack straps, and other canvas and webbing items. Paul Winans, reminiscing in 1964, stated, "We were working two shifts then, and had about fifteen employees. The Navy was using our ten-foot, square stern model, the 'Nimrod,' and the Army bought sixteen-foot double-enders. I met a former Army officer once who told me our boats were used in the crossing of the Rhine River during the assault on Germany. I myself saw one of our 'Nimrods' on Guam during the war when I was in the Marine Corps."[36]

The individual boat builders or very small firms that could not produce the output required for the military contracts settled for custom work for the dwindling recreational market. With the draft occasionally taking away portions of their work force (often family members), and the increasing inability to purchase raw materials diverted to the defense industries, the smallest firms faced the likelihood of shutting down for the duration of the war unless they could find work within an essential industry, such as commercial fishing. The problem of civilian logistics involved keeping essential nonmilitary boat-building operational for the good of the national economy. Commercial fishing boats and workboats were still in demand and played an important role in keeping the population fed.

Faster: Scaling Up Production

During the war, the small craft manufacturers of Michigan built boats with breathtaking speed and an astounding volume of production, although not without great difficulty. Most remarkable was the incredible variety of the types of boats produced. Boats for every conceivable purpose— barrage balloon boats, air-sea rescue boats, beach control craft, submarine chasers, landing craft, minesweepers, assault boats, sounding boats, storm boats, passenger cruisers, tugboats, barges, and many other forms all found their way to the war theaters. Every day they walked through the gates, the workers faced a barrage of new demands for faster work with better quality, all aimed at bringing their loved ones home sooner. The *Defoe Rollover* exhorted the workers to produce more constantly: "Come on EVERY-BODY! Let's go! . . . That MARCH SCHEDULE OF SHIPS MUST BE MET! We'll do it! Sure! Remember how tough our schedules were on the P.C.'s—Mine Sweepers—D.E.'s? Why, they said we couldn't do it and we said—we could, and we did it and turned right around and beat the schedules. So, with the LCI schedules being the TOUGHEST we've had, it's up to all of us to repeat again by beating the LCI schedules. The Navy says: They MUST be on time! We say: They SHALL be on time!"[37]

Relationships with the government procurement and inspection officials could sometimes turn prickly and constantly demanded good communication skills. The friction caused by trying to get a job done in a hurry and meeting the requirements to document the work thoroughly caused more than a few shop floor battles, production delays, or, in at least one instance, the loss of control of the business. At the navy's insistence, Dachel-Carter Shipbuilding Corporation's board ousted its president, Gordon S. Clark, and replaced him with Jacob T. "Jack" Schless, a Chicago construction contractor who had built the Seneca Shipbuilding Company shipyard in Seneca, Illinois. The navy itself took over financial control of the company. The workers called a mass meeting and demanded an explanation from the management to find out what was going on.[38] Dachel-Carter sued Clark for $50,000 over accounting discrepancies for unauthorized spending, claiming that he had diverted part of the money for his personal use. Clark countersued, stating that he should have received a 2 percent commission for each contract he secured for the company, totaling $7,480,000 in contracts, with commissions of $142,120 owed to him.[39] He also contended that a conspiracy between Schless and the board had removed him from the presidency. During the trial in early 1944, both sides brought up varied issues facing the boat company's management during this trying time, illustrating the dark side of the military procurement business, especially on the cost-plus contracts. Clark alleged that "a certain Navy captain directed him to get rid of certain officers and employees and also instructed him to buy the treasury stock with the idea in view of going into business with Clark, because the navy officer in question planned to retire from the navy in three years."[40] Quality of construction on the first two minesweepers exiting the yard may have been the initial issue as problems developed soon after their commissioning. An inspection at a New York shipyard revealed some twenty-five hundred plugs and eighteen bolts missing on delivery, and both boats required about $90,000 in repairs. The trial ended in favor of Dachel-Carter, but Clark fought on with an appeal. He died in 1947 before the lawsuit could be fully resolved.[41]

Government contracts came at the cost of a wide range of new problems for the boat builders. Huge volumes of additional paperwork, regulation, and demands for secrecy and higher levels of security added to the ordinary difficulty of constructing the boats. Rapidly changing design modifications or specification changes needed to be constantly updated on construction blueprints, creating further potential delays in production. The army and navy assigned professional boat builders or designers as government inspectors, sometimes from competing firms, to monitor the quality of the work and production costs at the factories. Depending on the size of the plant, this could be one person or a small office. For firms not used to having someone look over their shoulders and challenge their business decisions, the interference could be more than an annoyance, as contractual penalties and ill-will could hurt the bottom line substantially if ignored. Gerald Mallon, the displaced boat builder from East Tawas, became a navy lieutenant and a supervisor of shipbuilding, inspecting construction work at Gar Wood in Marysville and overseeing Chris-Craft at Algonac. After the war ended, Mallon worked for Chris-Craft, retiring as a plant manager in 1973.[42]

Secrecy and security could cause additional problems. A fine dividing line emerged in the boatyards, where on larger boats much of the work had to be done out in the open. Neighbors and local residents could easily see what was going on at the yard. The government built antipersonnel fences around the plants to keep out potential saboteurs, complete with guard towers and armed Coast Guardsmen patrolling the perimeters at the plants in Algonac, St. Joseph, and Benton Harbor. Employees wore identification pins with their photograph, and visitors needed passes to get through the gates.[43] Companies stressed the need for confidentiality, with reminders such as "loose lips sink ships," but on the other hand, the government expected them to keep morale up among the employees, often by celebrating achievements such as large vessel launches or shop production records. Censorship in the press started in earnest after Pearl Harbor, limiting the number of details about production levels released during the remaining portion of the war.

Material shortages and supply problems played havoc with the production schedules. Often the Maritime Commission, which authorized many of the boats built in the Great Lakes region, had to play second to the navy, for shipments of steel especially, although all the boats were going to the same cause. Shortages of essential boat-building materials soon began to affect production. A minesweeper or submarine chaser took as much timber and wood to build as ten average homes, according to the US Forest Service's Forest Products Laboratory.[44] George Smith, son of Bernard Smith, worked at the Holland Chris-Craft plant and recalled one day, "We had a hundred and seventy of those boats out in the yard, couldn't complete them because we didn't have a piece of armor plate for them, or we didn't have an engine for them, but we were pushing them out every day. We were shipping about ten boats a day, actually."[45] Subcontractors and suppliers to the boat firms faced the same problems. By late 1943, the scarcity of common labor in the foundries at Detroit and Muskegon became critical. The Allied invasion of Europe hung for a time on the ability of the foundries at Muskegon to produce engine blocks for the landing craft under construction. Foundry jobs were dirty, hot, dangerous, and did not pay as well as others, so many workers avoided them if they could find better jobs elsewhere.[46]

The quickly changing nature of the work force added another level of complication for the boat builders. Labor availability became a constant problem for the boat companies in several ways. Enlistments and the draft took away many skilled, able-bodied young workmen early in the war, leaving the boat builders scrambling to find workers to replace them. Collectively, the work forces at the boat companies grew very large very quickly, changing traditional working relationships built over time within each firm. Dachel-Carter received its first contract for a pair of minesweepers in June 1941, and by September the work force had swelled to 200 people. By March 1942, the firm had doubled that number, and it employed 650 people by the end of the year. Its boat-building operations generated a payroll of nearly $1.5 million annually, or $5,000 per day by the end of 1942, and the company spent $438,000 locally on materials, services, and equipment.[47]

Out of necessity the companies hired workers with little or no industrial experience, who had never before worked in factory settings and had to be trained to use even the most rudimentary equipment. As late as December 1944, one out of every five Michigan inhabitants was engaged in war production.[48] All kinds of new workers entered employment with the boat companies. Most notably, women started working as clerks and truck drivers, but some soon found jobs as welders and pipefitters. The women suffered from sexist teasing and harassment in their new workplaces, but in general they were also respected for the outstanding work they were doing. Mrs. Harry Borton of the Truscott Boat and Dock Company of St. Joseph earned a bit of celebrity in the company as she worked in the same firm as her husband and three sons. Workers selected Borton and Mrs. Harry Jones, another Truscott yard worker, by ballot to serve as launch sponsors for two air-sea rescue boats in July 1943 at the plant, believed at the time to be the first christenings by female shipbuilders. Older and disabled persons also found new roles in the boat companies. Harry Daker, age sixty, son of the former superintendent of the Truscott Boat Company, worked for Dachel-Carter on its minesweepers in late 1941 and still enjoyed the tradecraft after forty-one years in the business. "In boatbuilding, from your apprenticeship up, you get to learn the whole thing. You don't become a particular specialist but you become an all-around boatbuilder. You know how to do something from start to finish," he said.[49] The very young also discovered what it was like to work in the boat-building industry indirectly. High school student Mercer Fisher, using his father's drill press and a special drill plug bit given to him by John Granzow, supplied Dachel-Carter with thousands of the wooden plugs used to cover recessed screws in the hulls to minimize corrosion. He was paid by the bushel for the plugs.[50]

With so many inexperienced people in the work force, training in the rudiments of boat-building became an immediate priority. The Robinson Marine Construction Company, Dachel-Carter, and Truscott Boat &

Dock Company all participated in a training program for their employees
on boat construction, offered through the Michigan State Board of Control for Vocational Education in January 1943, a twelve-week program held
at the high school in St. Joseph.[51] As workers became more adept at their
jobs, efficiencies generated by employees finding easier and more effective
ways to do the work led to design modifications of the boats for further
cost savings.

Safety likewise became a critical topic for all of the boatyards to address.
Injuries due to a lack of training or inexperience in materials handling and
fabrication techniques or unfamiliarity with the equipment led to constant
reminders on signs posted everywhere about the importance of working
safely to protect the employees and those workers around them. Articles in
the *Defoe Rollover* even went so far as to list the injuries of individual workers to help make the point. Cartoons and illustrations in the newspaper
focused on workplace safety and the importance of protective gear and
guards on equipment.

Launching ceremonies, particularly the early ones, reflected the pa-
triotic fervor of the communities as well as celebrating the accomplish-
ments of the builders. At the Victory Shipbuilding Company in Holland,
the launch of its first 110-foot wooden submarine chaser, *SC 1063*, in November 1942 made for a festive occasion as it was the first significant naval
vessel ever built in the city. About twelve hundred people attended the
launching ceremony, including naval officials, Coast Guardsmen, and Mrs.
John Gingrich, wife of a US Navy captain, who christened the boat with
champagne. Music by the American Legion Band filled out the program.[52]
Victory Shipbuilding's second launch was more problematic as the company had to dynamite thick ice in Lake Macatawa to launch *SC1064* in
January 1943.[53] In christening ceremonies at Defoe, a bottle of champagne
broken across the bow of a ship by a somber widow or mother dressed in
dark clothing honored her deceased mate or son, for whom the ships were
named. Mrs. Marjorie Rich wore the Navy Cross posthumously awarded
to her late husband during the launching ceremony on June 22, 1943, for
a destroyer escort DE695, the U.S.S. *Rich*, named in honor of Lieutenant
Ralph MacMaster Rich, a navy flyer who died following the Battle of Mid-
way. Five thousand yard workers and citizens witnessed the launch.[54] In
one glorious moment of motion, the "big splash" as the boat hit the water
after slipping down the ways represented the satisfying work of an entire
community in aiding the war effort. In this instance, the joy could only be
temporary as the U.S.S. *Rich* was lost a year later shortly after the D-Day

invasion of Normandy, colliding with mines offshore on June 8 while attempting to aid another vessel.

Testing the finished boats made up a critical part of the construction and contract process. Chris-Craft tested all its boats and landing craft at its main plant in Algonac, shipping them in from their satellite plants in Holland and Cadillac to testing basins and slips adjacent to the plant. To keep the operations going through the winter, the company installed underwater steam pipes off its heating boilers to keep the testing basins free of ice in December 1942.[55]

Companies also tested finished boats in trial runs on the Great Lakes that could range from pleasurable high-speed cruising in midsummer to runs during early winter storms in which huge waves and howling winds caused pitching and rolling in the smaller boats that made the crews seasick at best and fearful for their lives at worst. Defoe nearly lost an unnamed destroyer escort, traveling light without ammunition and stores, on Lake Huron in a snowy, 40-mile-per-hour gale in the late fall of 1943 when the boat fell into the trough of the seas during a turn toward shelter. The ship rolled so far over that when alarms went off the crew donned life jackets and thought they might have to abandon ship. After putting in at Tawas Bay to wait out the storm, the ship continued on its way to Chicago without incident.[56]

Frustration among employees, in both labor and management, likewise grew over rapidly changing roles for workers, new work rules, and the never-ending pressure to build boats faster. Too much overtime and the ensuing exhaustion caused stress for many workers, resulting in high absenteeism. Trying to maintain a family life and keeping up relations with loved ones overseas in harm's way all contributed to the challenges of the home, which found their way into the work environment. Although workers made more money than ever before, they had very little spare time in which to spend it. Simply getting to work could be a challenge with gas rationing and rubber shortages affecting the supply of tires. Many workers lived in rural areas, sometimes quite a distance from the boat builders in the cities. Even a trip to the grocery store could be irritating with the rationing of sugar, meat, and other sundry items. Although organized labor pledged not to strike after Pearl Harbor, labor troubles continued, especially over payment of overtime wages and length of the standard work week. Piecework, especially for parts makers, was still the norm in some companies.

For all of their difficulties of production, the larger firms received recognition for their outstanding war production efforts with the awarding of the Army/Navy E-Flag in formal ceremonies. Both the services appreciated the long hours and difficult work of the civilians in providing them with the boats they needed so badly. Initially the services each presented their own flag, or in the navy's case an "E" pennant, but the programs merged later in the war. The Robinson Marine Construction Company, one of the early recipients, was awarded its E pennant from the navy's Bureau of Ships only about three months after the bombing of Pearl Harbor. Rear Admiral John Downes, commandant of the Ninth Naval District at Great Lakes, Illinois, presented the pennant on March 5, 1942, to Glen E. Robinson, president of the firm. Carl W. Ratter, one of the Robinson workers, accepted the individual E buttons given in turn to each of the 250 employees.[57] Defoe earned an E pennant with five renewal stars for its excellence in production, and Chris-Craft employees at all three plants wore their pins with pride after their company won the award on June 15, 1942.[58]

Wartime profits helped restore the industry after the crisis years of the Great Depression. Sales for Chris-Craft in 1943 totaled nearly $21 million, with profits of $2 million for the fiscal year. Because of restrictions in the War Profit Controls Act, the company renegotiated its contracts and returned $5.6 million to the government.[59]

In 1943 small craft procurement started to slow down. Earlier contracts filled the need for submarine chasers, although the Fisher Boat Works, Dachel-Carter, and American Cruiser continued to fulfill the last of their orders for the boats. As the navy called for different conversions of patrol boats for use as minesweepers, gunboats, and other vessels, the companies modified a few of the boats in process for their new roles before delivery. Defoe also shifted its work on the LCIs to variants of the same boats as flagship landing craft and mortar and rocket batteries.[60] Gar Wood's contract for thirty towboats was canceled in March 1944 with seven boats still under construction.[61]

Preparing for Peacetime

Companies started planning for reconversion back to civilian work soon after the dark days of 1942. In the backs of the minds of company executives, far removed from their present logistical nightmares, planning for the boats of the future in the civilian market started out with sketches of streamlined hulls slinging spray at high speeds for the enjoyment of returning GIs. Some of the ideas started to make their way from dreams into print in advertisements meant to remind potential buyers that their company would be ready and willing to build the boats they wanted when the war was over. At the same time, the companies still had a very important job to do for the duration to assure victory for the Allies with their military production, so the firms gradually placed advertising that showed both facets, for the present and proposed future. In a national survey of boat builders conducted by *The Boating Industry*, a trade periodical based in St. Joseph, Michigan and published in December 1943, a number of Michigan boat builders listed what they were currently building for the military and what kinds of pleasure boats they planned to build after the war, including cruisers, runabouts, and utilities, some even with sizes mentioned.[62] The Truscott Boat & Dock Company produced a brochure, "Truscott's Post War Sketch Book," showing design sketches of its intended postwar boats, including cabin cruisers and sailboats, near the war's end.

Chris-Craft ended its run of building landing craft and other boats when its contracts were canceled after the atomic bomb blasts at Hiroshima and Nagasaki ended the war in August 1945. The company transitioned back to building civilian boats even earlier, delivering its first of the 1946 model year boats in late July 1945.[63]

In early 1945, the government canceled many contracts for boats as the tide of war shifted in favor of the Allies and the need for specific kinds of boats ended, resulting in extensive layoffs and reducing the volume of deliveries. Defoe received the last small craft contract for thirty minesweepers (AM) in 1945, but the contract was soon canceled, and the steel of the last wartime boats, *AM391* and *AM392*, was scrapped by the end of the year. Still, the yard was not empty as a Coast Guard contract needed to be filled, and launching ways had to be prepared for a new 117-foot cruiser Defoe planned to build as its first boat produced for private citizens since it started work for the navy in 1939.[64] Ultimately, the greatest expense of the war was human life. Defoe lost twelve of its former workers as its "Gold Stars," or servicemen killed during the war. The company named an icebreaking shipyard tug that it built for its own use in 1943 after Jack Boyce, the first former employee to lose his life for his country. Mr. Wesley Whitehouse at its launch stated, "Every time you look at this tug, performing the service for which it was built, think of the boy for whom it is named, and, on this anniversary of Pearl Harbor, vow again to put the extra effort into the job which will speedily end this killing. Point your finger at the slacker, absentee, and loafer. Jack Boyce gave his life in the country's service. We are not called upon for so great a sacrifice but we are called upon to produce with honest work and tools and equipment necessary to lessen the suffering and hasten victory."[65]

Postwar

The immediate post–World War II era turned into a challenging sorting-out period for the boat builders of the state. The war created enormous changes in the boat-building industry. In the immediate postwar period, the government canceled 1.5 billion dollars' worth of contracts for war materials after the Japanese signed articles of surrender on the deck of the U.S.S. *Missouri* on September 2, 1945. In the ensuing months and years, Americans transformed the enormous war machine built to defeat the Axis powers into one that returned to producing civilian consumer goods. Trying to figure out what the market wanted proved to be complicated by all kinds of new transitions in leisure, materials, assembly techniques, and styling. Builders in the late 1940s and early 1950s ran head-on into a number of material supply problems, a national economic downturn, and a dramatically changing work force as GIs returned home to work in their former jobs. When the war was over, a few of the companies took their profits and shut down after their usefulness ended. Victory Shipbuilding reverted back to the Jesiek family, and the American Cruiser Company and Traverse City Ship Building Company simply disappeared. A few new small companies soon replaced large firms that failed or closed shortly after the war's end, such as the Sportcraft Manufacturing Company of Ironwood, outboard boat builders, and the Hugh Lee Iron Works of Saginaw, builders of steel-hulled cruisers. Some of these were started by GIs returning from the war with an idea for a business, but material shortages, inadequate or poorly targeted marketing, undercapitalization, or inexperienced management caused most to fail in the postwar era.

The navy disposed of many of its excess boats to the Allies, including Russia, France, Norway, Turkey, and other nations. It sometimes destroyed its boats intentionally, as a cost-effective solution, rather than maintaining them or transferring them to other locations. In the South Pacific, PT boats were burned after decommissioning at Samar in the Philippines because of their poor condition or because their service life had ended abruptly. Others served as targets during atomic weapons tests at places such as Bimini Atoll.

Adding to the confusion in the marketplace was a glut of small military boats on the market as war surplus, with huge numbers of picket boats, cruisers, and workboats constantly being auctioned off at extraordinarily cheap rates. These boats could be inexpensively and easily modified for personal use, converted into private yachts or workboats, a real bargain for do-it-yourselfers or persons with modest incomes. Most of the boats had suffered hard use and abuse during the war, but an almost brand new one could make for a valuable investment.

Michigan's boat builders, in their first offerings of the postwar era, produced models that looked very similar to their prewar craft, only to find out soon that consumer tastes had changed drastically. Shortages of construction materials such as plywood and mahogany created more headaches for company officials and workmen alike. Builders resorted to constructing cedar strip boats with painted finishes instead of the stained mahogany finishes used prior to the war.

Several of the companies that had survived the economic distress of the 1930s and the production pressures of World War II failed within a few years after the war, mostly because they were pinched by the quickly rising prices for most commodities in the postwar years or they expanded into product lines outside their core businesses. Five large Michigan firms, the Gar Wood Industries Boat Division, Truscott Boat & Dock Company, Eddy Shipbuilding Corporation, Robinson Marine Construction Company, and Fisher Boat Works, either failed or got out of the boat-building business by 1949. Each firm had produced large volumes of boats during World War II and employed hundreds of workers. With the cancellation of the military contracts, the firms quickly downsized their work forces and shifted to the work of reconversion to production for the civilian market.

The Gar Wood Boat Division, builder of the Trophy Fleet, departed when its parent corporation, Gar Wood Industries, decided to eliminate its boat division. Long the stepchild of the giant corporation's hoist, dump truck body, and furnace divisions, the boat division lost money for years. When Gar Wood decided to get out of racing in 1935, he kept the boat-building business going, but he gradually left its management to his brother, Logan Wood. When Logan Wood died in 1938, the boat division never recovered from the loss of his leadership and managerial talent. During the war the company made all kinds of boats from picket boats to tow launches. Gar Wood's military boat contracts ended in March 1944 with the cancelation of the 46-foot towboats. The Marysville plant continued to work on other, non-boat projects, such as fabricating winch drums and fiberglass radar housings, but the company's designers found time to plan new postwar boat projects in the interim, starting as early as 1943. The late war years turned out to be a watershed moment in timing for the firm. The company's longtime lead designer and stylist, George Joachim, died early in 1943. Napoleon Lisee, who built the famous racing boats and designed the soft-riding bottoms of the production boats, retired. The company's other designers started thinking about what the company's future products would look like, posting futuristic-looking conceptual sketches on bulletin boards around the plant to help boost morale. Most important, Gar Wood himself retired as chairman of the board of Gar Wood Industries in 1945, eliminating a voice of support in the boardroom for the often struggling boat division. Resentment grew over the years in the other corporate divisions about the boat division's protected status assigned by the former owner, and now the boat division had no sponsorship within the firm to watch over its interests. The company shifted its corporate offices to New York City, far from its Detroit roots. Glen Bassett, the company's new president, set goals for the boat division for sales of four to five million dollars annually, although it had never made more than five hundred thousand dollars in any fiscal year. To meet the sales target would require the boat division to build an estimated four thousand boats in six different sizes, more than the Marysville plant could handle. The unrealistic expectations of a corporate leadership disconnected from the boat-building operations would soon have negative consequences.

The parent company hired the well-known Norman Bel Geddes industrial design firm in 1945 to restyle the firm's entire postwar product line, from bulldozers to boats, and to evaluate the company's facilities.[66] After carefully studying the plant operations and reviewing its seven prototype boats for the next model year, the Geddes firm issued a report criticizing the boat division's cost controls and its general unwillingness to share information with the consultants. The consultants' analysis stated that "the boat plant is basically nothing more than a large, overgrown boat shop. It's a shop where boats are made, not produced." Further criticisms concerned the boat division's skepticism about using new materials and methods. The Geddes report challenged the outstanding quality of construction the boat division insisted on for all of its work: "There is an over emphasis on tradition and craftsmanship that keeps prices too high." The comments hit hard all the values the people of the boat division held dear, and more disturbing changes soon followed.[67]

Gar Wood Industries purchased the former Horace E. Dodge Boat & Plane Corporation plant in Newport News, Virginia, in late 1945 to add capacity to meet the new production goals of the boat division, and it also decided to move the tank division to the new location. At Newport News it produced a single new model, the 16-foot utility boat named the Ensign, an entry-level boat with white-painted sides and a vinyl-upholstered interior. The company took the excellent designs generated by its designers during the war years and added surface treatments of new emerging materials. On larger models the decks were changed to plywood with vinyl covering because of mahogany shortages. From mid-1946 to early 1947, Gar Wood splashed the Norman Bel Geddes name across its advertising as the designer, although the boats actually were designed in-house by the company's own designers. Although the boats appeared markedly different from those of previous years, the designs still originated internally within the Gar Wood firm, but the Geddes firm received the credit as it added a prestigious name at a time when industrial design was flourishing.

As the corporation took direction of the Gar Wood Boat Division into its own hands, division general manager Ed Hancock retired after twenty years and advertising man Jack Clifford resigned. When the Geddes firm recommended that the show models for the 1947 National Boat Show all have painted hulls, visitors walked away wondering if the paint covered inferior wood and poor workmanship. The company produced nine hundred boats in fourteen months, its best year ever despite a brief strike in February 1946. The boat division closed its doors in April 1947, ending a long heritage of beautiful mahogany boats of outstanding quality within the industry, acknowledged by all for their excellence in construction.[68]

The Truscott Boat & Dock Company tried to make two different shifts, one to a new home and another to a new product line. The troubled Dachel-Carter Shipbuilding Corporation closed up shop almost immediately following completion of its wartime contracts in December 1944, long before the war was even over. Truscott, seeing the advantages of larger open sites, leased a portion of the former Dachel-Carter plant in December 1945.[69] It hoped to build a thousand of its 24-foot boats for the 1946 model year, in addition to the other varieties. The company primarily built small cruisers immediately following the war. Howard Conklin, a veteran who worked at the company before enlisting in the navy in 1943, returned to his old employer at the war's end. "Every serviceman I knew of could go back to the company they worked at before the war," he said. "I swung into all phases of the making of pleasure craft and I had the opportunity to learn a lot."[70]

Truscott tried to take someone else's ideas and make them its own. The company offered a new line of utilities and runabouts in November 1947 that strongly resembled the product designs of the recently defunct Gar Wood Boat Division. The boats ranged from 16 to 25 feet, finished bright with mahogany.[71] Ed Hancock, the former Gar Wood general manager, joined Truscott as vice president of operations. J. Gordon Lippincott, the industrial designer who styled the Tucker automobile and the Campbell soup label, designed the 1948 model year boats presented by the company. In April 1948, Charles H. Morse Jr., the company president, announced a new program of streamlining and expansion, moving the production lines of four lines of small boats and their related mill equipment to the former Dachel-Carter plant in Benton Harbor, where the company already built larger cruisers. Custom boats would be built at the St. Joseph facility, and the storage and repair operations located there also.[72] Rising prices for labor and material, compounded by excessive inventory and decreasing demand for luxury boats eventually did the company in. Truscott Boat & Dock Company voluntarily filed for bankruptcy in October 1948 in order to clear its books. Morse blamed the problems on past financial decisions, not the company's current activity, and stated that it intended to build a smaller lineup of boats while going through the bankruptcy process.[73] Howard Conklin thought otherwise about the reason for the company's demise: "Just guessing from a working man's standpoint my inward feeling is that they were top heavy on the administrative end. It was out of kilter and they sunk the boat. That's where I ended my career . . . They went bankrupt and your checks began to bounce . . . I was just married and it was rough. I never worked with a nicer bunch of guys in all my life. No one made any money but it was quite a family."[74]

The Eddy Shipbuilding Corporation of Bay City may have tried to go in too many directions at once. The company built four models of outboard-powered runabouts based on its old Aqua-Flow design. Eddy Shipbuilding took a formerly very successful idea from the knockdown housing industry in its community and decided to go into the prefabricated housing business, building four-room prefabricated Quonset-style houses for British families that lost their homes in the German bombing raids. At first the company seemed to be booming with sales, reporting a backlog of boat sales of $1 million and a backlog of $11.4 million in sales of its Edco prefabricated homes in October 1946. In the next year, when material shortages struck the industry hard, especially for steel for the Quonset homes, the Eddy Shipbuilding Corporation went into receivership with Bay Trust Company as the receiver. Despite attempts to reorganize, the company exceeded $1 million in liabilities and federal judge Frank A. Picard adjudged the firm bankrupt.[75]

The Robinson Marine Construction Company, builders of elegant cruisers before the war, completed its war contracts with a series of 25-foot utility boats. The company received one postwar military contract for 108 motorboats in 1946. Soon afterward the government reduced the number to 29 boats, and then the contract was terminated before even those could be finished. To add insult to injury, the government fined Robinson $7,000 in 1949 for overcharging $27,000 in labor on the $1,134,000 contract, mostly for pay warrants that had not been signed off on by inspectors. The company pled guilty, having long since stopped building boats after the contract canceled.[76] The company leased the large buildings of its plant to the 1900 Corporation (later Whirlpool Corporation) and went into storage and repair work before closing completely in about 1955 when the Wizard Boat Company, fiberglass boat builders, leased the plant. The company went out of legal existence in May 1958.

In a few instances the postwar products did not match the expectations of the buying public. Caught in the transition of a public demanding something new and different, the Fisher Boat Works of Detroit may have mistargeted its boats to an audience that no longer wanted large cruising yachts and sailboats. The company built two experimental PT boats, a prototype of the 110-foot wooden submarine chaser, and eighteen production models of the same during the war. It started out in 1946 offering a beautiful 64-foot Hacker-designed cabin cruiser designed before the war. One of these boats was originally built in 1940 for Lawrence P. Fisher, acquired by the Coast Guard during the war, and used afterward by President Harry S. Truman as the presidential yacht *Margie* on the Potomac River.[77] The company also presented a smaller 53-foot cruiser designed by Milo Bailey and styled by industrial designer Robert Bingman, and a 40-foot Sparkman & Stephens sloop named the Mackinac or Brasil. The company built eight of the sailboats in the immediate postwar era, all named after Santa Claus's reindeer.[78] The company offered a second Sparkman & Stephens sailboat design, the 33-foot Pilot model, slightly later. Despite a profitable year in 1947, sluggish sales may have forced the company to dissolve in 1948.

Even the most highly experienced yacht builder, the Defoe Shipbuilding Company, miscalculated on its postwar pleasure cruisers. The company planned to sell a standardized 117-foot steel cruiser, the Cruisemaster, which it had designed before the war in 1937. The yacht could be easily customized to suit an individual owner's desires. After the war the company could only build and sell six cruisers before having to shelve the project for lack of sales. Defoe, like Eddy Shipbuilding of the same community, also decided to go into the prefabricated housing market, though for domestic distribution, with a whole new Housing Division, building Defoe Homes. Under its plan you could buy a home from a dealer as you would buy an automobile and have it built and ready for occupancy in two weeks. Making the best use of its interior design talent from the yachts, the Defoe Homes "Working Walls" integrated high-density storage and utility functions in organized, highly compact wall units. One of its contemporary home designs appears to have been inspired by Frank Lloyd Wright, with a flat roof, although others resembled more traditional Cape Cod, ranch, and colonial styles. As the *Defoe Rollover* of January 1946 exclaimed about the quality of construction, "Defoe Homes will be thoroughly tested before delivery to the dealer. Just as in the case of every vessel built to meet rigid naval specifications, there will be no 'trial run at the owner's expense.'"[79] Postwar inflation, material shortages and price restrictions likewise forced cancellation of that program.[80] Defoe never returned to the pleasure yacht business it had grown up on. Instead, in the early to mid-1950s, it focused on building new or modifying older large Great Lakes ore freighters for regional use. The company took on more repair work and smaller commercial craft and later built more military vessels for the navy.

As the soldiers returned home, fears grew that there would be huge numbers left unemployed at first. The problem never really materialized, although women left the boatyards fairly soon after the war to start new lives with those returning soldiers. Many gained purchasing power in their boat company jobs that they had never had before, so the transition for some probably was difficult. The returning soldiers also wanted to return to the pleasures they had missed out on during the war years, and the boat builders in their advertising appealed to them to fulfill those dreams of speeding across a lake or cruising on a river.

Learning from their war construction experiences, the builders found thousands of new ways to build or improve their products and cut their costs due to the pressures of the war and the struggle to produce great volumes of boats in a remarkably short period of time. Plywood would also become a boat-building material of choice for inexpensive boats for builders both large and small. Chris-Craft workers became experts in the use of Thiokol, an adhesive sealant, for their Sea Skiffs and Plywood Division boats, formed in the 1950s.[81] More important, aluminum aircraft manufacturing techniques learned during the war in Detroit factories and elsewhere would force major changes in materials for boat builders in the very near future.

Michigan within the National Context

Despite the large number of boats built, only about 2 percent of the wartime shipbuilding contracts for the navy and Maritime Commission were awarded in the Great Lakes region.[82] While the plethora of boat types produced by Michigan boat builders may not have been especially unique and of far lower dollar value than the large warships and cargo ships built at the great shipyards of the East and West Coasts, their impact on the overall war effort made a substantive difference. Without the thousands of landing craft built by Chris-Craft, Defoe's destroyer escorts on convoy duty, the Gar Wood picket boats guiding the D-Day invasion, hundreds of air-sea rescue boats to save downed pilots, and even the harbor tugs for pushing heavily loaded freighters around, the war might have been much different in its outcome and duration. American forces took the war to the enemy by water, and Michigan-built boats helped deliver them to where they were needed.

CHAPTER SEVEN

Prosperity and Problems, 1950–60

Introduction

In the mid-1950s the nation entered a period of prosperity when the industrial might that came of age during World War II was transformed into an individual and family consumer-driven market economy, unlike any seen before or since. Products generated in a golden age of industrial design looked new and fresh and fulfilled every perceived need, and some beyond need to excess. Most boat styling quickly took after automotive styling, which in turn reflected the aviation industry in the new Jet Age. Cockpits with Plexiglas canopies or windshields, a multiplicity of gauges, high tailfins, and gleaming chrome or polished aluminum all evoked images of the new jets seen at the airports and racing across the skies at speeds inconceivable only decades earlier.

G.I.s and sailors returning home from the war soon started new families, invested in new homes, and tried to ease their way back into civilian life as they remembered it, including forms of outdoor recreation they remembered from earlier times. Material shortages in the first few years after their return stymied the boat builders in trying to fulfill the immediate desire for more boats. As more material became available, the builders ramped up production to meet the new demand. Where once one had to be relatively wealthy to afford a boat of significant speed and comfort, the new materials coming into use in boat building, combined with advances in the power and durability of the outboard motor, created a new enthusiasm for recreational boating at prices affordable to nearly everyone. Boat builders tried to understand what the customers really wanted and offered products to best meet those expectations such as smaller cruisers, outboard-powered boats, and attractive, up-to-date (if not futuristic) runabouts.

Chris-Craft Dominates the Marketplace

The already giant Chris-Craft Corporation in the 1950s sped quickly away into a class of its own in terms of numbers of boats built and sold. The organization did not rest on its laurels after the war, launching into a wide variety of acquisitions, new product offerings, and experiments with new construction materials and techniques. By the late 1950s the company operated nine plants across the nation with an annual output of about eight thousand boats per year, generating forty million dollars in sales.[1] Chris-Craft, however, did not take the initiative in developing the new technologies, letting other firms take the lead in figuring out what would be useful. The company, for instance, never adopted small aluminum boats when others around it grew rapidly in that niche market, and likewise the firm slowly moved into plywood boats after others, like Wagemaker, had already captured a significant share of the market.

Industrial designer Don Mortrude worked out of his own Detroit studio as the stylist for Chris-Craft, making its boats distinctive and fresh with the most recent innovations in automotive styling carefully blended with traditional wooden construction. The bottom designs of the boats remained the realm of naval architects and engineers led by William MacKerer. A Chris-Craft boat of the mid-1950s still vaguely resembled the mahogany-planked, bright finished boats from before the war, but it showed enough difference in materials and styling to provoke a buying decision based on a new-looking boat. The "bull-nose" bow, bleached mahogany king plank, and wraparound windshield of the 1955 Capri model offered a modern look compared to the traditional wooden boats of days past.

One of the longest-lasting model lines in the company's history, the Constellation cruiser series, first offered in 1954, attracted the attention of cruiser buyers due to its large single deck, which provided a means of entertaining large groups of guests. The Constellation came in several different lengths and engine options, frequently varying over the years, the first being a 53-footer in five models priced between $42,860 and $53,560.[2]

Chris-Craft may have been inspired by the many years of success of knockdown boats in Bay City and Saginaw as it introduced a new Kit Boat Division in 1950. The new boats helped attract younger people to boatbuilding with plywood kits consisting of precut parts and assembly instruc-

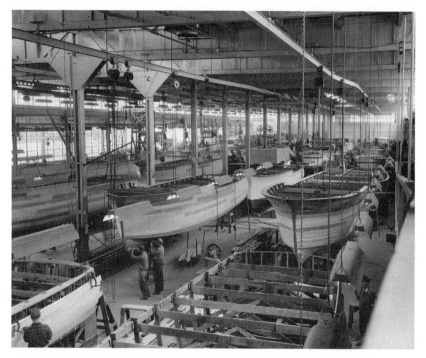

Fig. 23. Chris-Craft cruisers on the assembly line at the Holland plant in the 1950s. The assembly line system brought the boats to the workers via overhead conveyors before moving on to the next process. Chris-Craft bought the Roamer Boat Company in Holland to diversify into steel construction. (Mariners' Museum, Newport News, Virginia.)

tions. Although the Kit Boat Division only lasted eight years, by 1955 it offered twenty-eight models of varying complexity and cost, selling on the low end for only forty-two dollars. The Kit Boat Division also offered unrelated home-built items such as gun cabinets, toy boxes, and trailers.[3] Chris-Craft even produced its own water skis to go with its boats for a short time in the 1950s.

The company made a strong effort to move into the entry-level boating sector by also offering its own line of outboard motors in 1949, built at a factory in Grand Rapids. Chris-Craft inadvertently got into a patent infringement dispute over the bearing design of its 10-horsepower model with Kiekhafer, manufacturers of Mercury outboards, so the company ultimately sold the outboard business to the Oliver Corporation in late 1953.

Making use of the skills developed during the war on landing craft in using the adhesive and sealant Thiokol, Chris-Craft started the Sea Skiff Division in 1954. The Lyman Boat Company of Sandusky, Ohio, on Lake Erie built a sturdy lapstrake boat that sold exceptionally well in the 1950s, and Chris-Craft followed its lead with the Sea Skiff lapstrake. Its round-bottom hulls created a visual break from the traditional Chris-Craft double-planked hulls and the strong construction was advertised as much by word of mouth as by print media. These hulls created so much demand for the new boats that the new factory in Salisbury, Maryland, could barely keep up.[4]

When rival builders started to diversify into materials other than wood, Chris-Craft stepped in with its own new products. Beginning in 1955, Chris-Craft acquired the Roamer Boat Company, builders of steel cruisers in Holland, Michigan, as part of a strategic move into steel construction to compete for a larger share of the growing cruiser market. The company built a brand new 200,000-square-foot factory to construct the welded steel (and later welded aluminum) yachts.[5] At the same time Chris-Craft started the Plywood Division, which within a few years became so successful that it forced the abandonment of the Kit Boat program. A third area of new materials involved the use of fiberglass. Don Mortrude designed a new, elegant-looking boat called the Cobra, featuring a high, gold-colored, dorsal fiberglass tail fin and stern deck area on a varnished mahogany-planked wooden boat that not only looked fast but really could deliver the goods at 55 miles per hour.[6] In the late 1950s, the company's Silver Arrow used fiberglass over spruce and mahogany, complete with winglike tail fins and an automotive-style dashboard. The combination of the fiberglass over the wood made the boat heavier by 400 pounds than a comparably sized wooden boat.[7]

Chris-Craft Corporation, so long a fixture in the village of Algonac, decided to move its corporate headquarters to Pompano Beach, Florida, in 1957. The local populace, stunned by the loss of the leadership role of its largest business, discovered that they would no longer be the center of all the important business decisions. The company issued statements that the new location would be great for testing boats year-round and that more and more boats were being delivered to the Florida market than ever before, but the significance of the loss hit hard in Michigan. The ongoing labor disputes that had soured the relationship between the Smiths and their home community were also a contributing factor in the move.[8] The Algonac plant would remain the company's largest branch, but the loss of the important research, engineering, and administrative functions resulted in a brain drain that would affect the local business climate for years. In a second move two years later, the Smith family decided to sell Chris-Craft to National Automotive Fibers, Inc. (NAFI), a major supplier of automotive interior trim materials, for forty million dollars. At the time, the company employed thirty-five hundred workers and sales exceeded forty million dollars, three times more than the next largest competitor, Owens Yacht Company of Baltimore, Maryland. A split developed within the family over selling the company or retaining it. The deal finalizing the sale, though agreed to by Chairman of the Board Harsen Smith, was against his wishes to hold on to the firm, but Owen Smith, one of Chris Smith's sons and an original incorporator of the firm, wanted to sell his shares. The Brunswick-Balke-Collender Company, the leading recreational equipment producer, complicated the sale by acting as a competing bidder, although it never made a formal offer for the company.[9] Michigan's largest boat manufacturer made its first step down a long, sometimes rocky road of future sales to other corporations.

Century and Styling

The Century Boat Company of Manistee launched itself into a new era of success in the 1950s with a combination of stylish boats of outstanding color selection and design features. In a great return to civilian craft coming out of the war, the company worked its way through the wood, engine, and steering gear shortages by reprioritizing order fulfillment for small boats first, then larger boats as more material became available. The company expanded to a second plant in Manistee in 1947 and opened a third plant, devoted to small plywood boats, in Chattanooga, Tennessee. In the following year Overlakes Corporation purchased the company, the fifth time its ownership had changed in slightly more than two decades.[10] Century also offered a new look—bleached or "blonde" mahogany on the decks presented a striking contrast in color to the formerly dark red stain of previous years. The year 1948 turned out to be a banner year, with over nine hundred units built at a single plant, more than Gar Wood's entire output in its best year. The postwar recession that slowed boat purchasing and material supply problems that hampered manufacturing had largely been resolved. Century introduced a new branding element with the "Thoroughbred Fleet," created by the Jacqua Advertising agency of Grand Rapids, which gave the company a strong identity for years afterward.

Of the major builders of runabouts, Century took automotive styling to a new level of sophistication in boats with the Arabian, designed by Richard Arbib of New York, who trained in his craft at the Harley Earl studios. Blending color and beautiful lines, Arbib's creation had the look and feel of a fast sports car on water. Century combined the new look with a high-performance engine to match, the Cal Connell Crusader, a modified Cadillac V-8. Through the late 1950s Century introduced new features such as a white vinyl foredeck, wraparound windshields, and two-tone paint jobs with spearlike side detailing, making its models easily recognizable amid a blossoming number of boats on the water. Everything about the styling looked as if it were derived from automobiles of the era. These automotive-style elements were attached to a single-planked wooden hull with batten strips. The cutaway landau tops, which offered the full breeze at speed and some sun protection as well, resembled those of popular convertibles. The dashboards, with Stewart-Warner gauges trimmed in fluted aluminum, also reflected the latest in design in automobiles. Arbib's stylish boats culminated with the new Coronado in 1959, with a retractable roof and fiberglass accents on the sides and even a jetlike, strictly decorative, air-intake bow device. Just as the 1959 Cadillac automobile represented the height of excess in tail fins, so did the Coronado in boat styling. On one of its lines, the Resorter, the company retained a more traditional, stained mahogany finish with newer-looking automotive-style upholstery and windshields. Like Chris-Craft and other firms, Century adopted the Lyman-style utility lapstrake hull with a boat named the Viking, one of its most successful products in the mid-1950s. Because of their small size with high-performance speed, water skiers frequently chose Century models as towboats. One of the reasons that Century became one of the rising stars of the boating world in the 1950s was that the company could keep its prices down with cheaper labor and materials costs, due in part to its location in Manistee, a small city in the northern Lower Peninsula.

The End of Hacker

While the Chris-Craft and Century seemed to be in the ascendancy, the Hacker Boat Company had reached maturity and showed its age in terms of the originality of its designs. It continued to build fine boats for several more years in Mount Clemens, but the company's output lacked the innovation of its earlier years and cost-cutting took its toll on the quality of the construction. In the early 1950s, the company built about 8 to 10 boats per month and employed sixteen people, virtually a shell of the once large operation. During the Korean conflict, the company received a contract to build 25 picket boats and served as the lead design firm for a group of five companies that shared in building 123 boats altogether.[11] Unlike the World War II years, Hacker continued to build civilian boats alongside its military work. As in prior wars, the navy canceled the contract, leaving the company with materials to build another 20 boats, causing more financial hardship.[12] The company's superintendent, John Tesmer, decided to retire, and Russell Pouliot took his place.

Customers still wanted traditional-looking mahogany-planked runabouts and utilities, and the Hacker Boat Company kept producing them, but in fewer numbers. Hacker offered a 26-foot triple-cockpit runabout in 1954, although the bottom was made of Port Orford cedar and the sides and decks of mahogany. More and more often the boats seemed to be available either as individual custom boats or as mostly standard boats but only built to order. Working with naval architect John Deering, the company's boats began to look more like the popular Chris-Craft models than its former boats with flattened sides and slight tumble home at the stern. One of the company's last production models, the 22-foot Sport Dolphin utility, introduced in 1950, had a white-painted finish on the sides and varnished decks. Customers thought the overall quality of the boats had dropped, so sales dried up, forcing the closure of the business in the spring of 1957.[13] The rising cost of skilled labor and high-quality materials helped cause the demise. Hacker, once known worldwide for its excellence in craftsmanship and reputation for luxury, had built its last traditional mahogany-planked boat under its original corporate form.

New Arrivals

A typical Michigan boat-building firm in the mid-1950s looked a lot like LaCross Boat Works, which started operations at Alpena as a three-man partnership in 1947. A decade later the company employed twelve men and was building over three hundred boats a year, ranging from rowboats to cabin cruisers. It occupied a 10,500-square-foot building.[14] New startups in Michigan typically were incorporated for about fifty thousand dollars and employed fifteen people or less on average for their operations. Typical of these small startups were Afco, Inc., of Belding; Arena Craft of Mount Clemens, founded by racing boat driver Danny Arena; and the Gada Boat Manufacturing Company of Detroit.

The Big Decision: New Materials

Perhaps the greatest decisions facing postwar boat builders were the selection of hull material and the changing techniques for building them. Each material offered advantages and disadvantages that needed to be carefully evaluated by the builders before starting down that path. Nevertheless, boat builders throughout the state jumped from the standard mahogany, cedar strip, and other forms of wood planking to the relatively new technologies of molded plywood, magnesium and aluminum fabrication, steel welding, and fiberglass. As the popularity of varied hull materials grew by the late 1950s, the larger builders tried to cover all the bases by buying new, struggling, or marginal firms already building with the new materials. In each instance, the companies chose materials that offered alternatives to high-maintenance wooden construction. As the number of choices increased rapidly, the risks of failure caused by choosing an untested technology could quickly ruin a company. Not all were successful, particularly those experimenting with fiberglass.

Aluminum and Magnesium

As a construction material, aluminum as a lightweight metal made excellent sense for boats after World War II production techniques made it readily available. Aluminum did not corrode in the same way as steel, only oxidizing on the surface. When alloyed with other metals such as copper, manganese, magnesium, or zinc, the strength increases substantially over that of the pure metal itself. For fabrication purposes it can be cut and drilled easier and faster than steel and can also be formed, welded, and riveted quickly.[15] Above all else, from a boat owner's perspective, the material is very low maintenance as it does not even require painting unless desired. Spring fit-out usually means a quick cleaning, with no scraping, caulking, or painting. Place the boat in the water and you are good to go.

In Michigan experimental work on lightweight metal boats preceded large-scale postwar production by a decade. Charles W. Stiver, the former president of the Saginaw Shipbuilding Company during World War I, designed and patented a lightweight Dowmetal magnesium alloy canoe, which gained some popularity in the late 1930s. Late in life, he formed a company bearing his name in about 1936 with his office in the Schirmer Building in Saginaw. Stiver advertised his boats as "Dowmetal Water Crafts, Lightest, Strongest, Most Buoyant and Seaworthy." He received a patent for his boat construction technique, U.S. Patent 2,083,410, on June 8, 1937. Stiver's canoe interestingly had a hollow rib design similar in appearance to the wooden canoes of the era. He started a factory at 304 Mackinaw in 1938, and later that year or by 1939 the plant moved to 2100 Holland Avenue, where the firm built approximately one hundred Dowmetal magnesium alloy canoes. In 1940 he employed six people. Stiver never realized the potential success of his invention. He died in December 1941 at age seventy, ending the first small-scale, lightweight metal boat-manufacturing operation in the state and possibly in the nation. Only a short time would pass before lightweight aluminum boats would become immensely popular in the post–World War II era.[16]

Experience gained in the aviation industry during World War II pushed the change to metal boat-building after the war when aircraft companies looked to adapt their technologies to other products. For the manufacturers, the constant pressure during the war to reduce weight and increase structural integrity in aircraft led to innumerable changes in structures and designs. Designers quickly learned new ways to efficiently arrange sheet metal layout and create the necessary tooling for the ever-growing production of the bombers and fighters so desperately needed. Boats, while mostly far simpler than aircraft in design, could be easily fabricated using the same tooling and the skills learned quickly during the war years by the work force.

Even the huge Dow Chemical Company, with all its resources, tried to get into the boat-building business after searching for new ways to market products made of magnesium, its most important wartime product. The company began brainstorming ideas in 1945 to sell more magnesium and decided that portable boats, along with thirty-four other products, made good sense for new small business startups, as Dr. Willard H. Dow stated to the Special Committee of the U.S. Senate to Study Problems of American Small Business. With a potential market estimated at fifty thousand units per year and a relatively low initial capital outlay of fifteen thousand dollars and up, the boats would be a great way to add demand for magnesium while boosting the economy.[17] In a postwar experiment to market its own small magnesium boats and canoes, the company built Dowcraft brand boats and canoes at its Dow Special Products Division in Bay City beginning in mid-1946. The company manufactured 12-foot, 75-pound Deluxe and 73-pound Utility dinghy model boats, as well as a 16-foot canoe. Allen Carr and Delbert Case, paddling a Dowcraft canoe, won the grueling 1947 Au Sable River Canoe Marathon, paddling 120 miles in twenty-one hours.[18] The light weight made a big difference as five Dowcraft canoes placed in the top ten finishers. Despite the successful launch, the products failed to live up to expectations. The company preferred to sell bulk magnesium or its alloys to manufacturers rather than build the boats itself. Despite the substantially lighter weight of magnesium, the disadvantage of its slightly greater cost over cheaper and more abundant aluminum caused the product's demise in the face of broad competition from aircraft manufacturers and other companies marketing aluminum boats. Dow sold the boat line in late 1948 to Star Boat & Tank Company of Goshen, Indiana, and the boats became part of the beginning of the corporate giant Starcraft.[19]

The first high-volume aluminum boat producer in the world, Harwill, Inc., of St. Charles, emerged out of Dow's failure when Dow experimental engineer Lothair Bernard (L. B.) Harkins, along with Douglas Wiltse, became convinced that the boats could be built for far less money. Harkins took a class in aircraft sheet metal work in Detroit and started building aircraft component sections at the Briggs Manufacturing Company early in World War II. In August 1942 he moved to Bay City to join the Dow Special Products Division, again working on aircraft parts. While working for Dow, he wrote a book entitled *Magnesium Fabrication*. Harkins left Dow and joined his brother Leon Harkins and Wiltse to form Harwill, Inc., a startup aluminum-boat-building firm formed in March 1946. The Harkins brothers and Wiltse combined their last names for the corporate name. L. B. Harkins served as president and general manager, Leon Harkins as production manager, and Douglas Wiltse as director of sales. The men leased an old water treatment plant in St. Charles, near Saginaw, as their manufacturing facility. Marketing their boats as Aero-Craft, the company's products became an immediate hit. By January 1947 they were employing forty-three workers and turning out fifty-four boats a week, or over three thousand in their first year of production. The company purchased a new 8-acre site on the outskirts of St. Charles later that year for a new factory location.[20]

Harwill, Inc./Aero-Craft enjoyed great success in the early years of the aluminum boat industry. Soon the company started to offer a wider range of models, including cruisers. The company subcontracted the final assembly and finishing work on the cruisers to the Tittabawassee Manufacturing Company, recently moved to St. Charles, because it did not have enough floor space of its own to complete both the cruisers and its car-top boats at the same time.[21] The Montgomery Ward Company placed orders for 300 of Harwill's 12-foot rowboats and 150 of the 14-footers in November 1952, to be built to Ward's specifications and shipped throughout the country.[22] Sales for the company topped $655,000 in 1953, and twenty-nine different models appeared in its catalog for 1954.[23]

Like most boat builders, Harwill tried to diversify as advances in other hull materials and manufacturing technologies challenged its business in aluminum boats. Acquisitions served as insurance to be able to shift direction quickly to meet consumer demand if needed. The company purchased the fiberglass boat manufacturer Water Wonderland Boat Company of Grand Rapids in late 1956, later moving the operation to St. Charles and giving it the Aero-Glas brand name. The Water Wonderland Company built seven models of fishing and runabout boats prior to the purchase.[24] The majority of the company's work, however, remained with aluminum boats. By 1960 Harwill's line of Aero-Craft boats had grown to include twenty-eight outboards and ten more models in the budget Aero-Line series, and it continued to slowly increase over the years.

Allen H. Meyers formed the Meyers Aircraft Company of Tecumseh in the late 1930s and built an all-aluminum open-cockpit biplane trainer, the OTW (Out To Win), during the war. Like other aircraft builders, he started to look at boat construction as a way to keep his business going. Meyers started building duckboats and small fishing boats of aluminum in 1955 after the early aluminum boat builders became well established. On its 112 WR model the company offered a forward and center wheel deck, a motor well, and also seats with backs built in, all somewhat unique for their time. Built slightly heavier than contemporary boats, Meyers boats proved to be very durable, and the firm enjoyed good success for decades as a regional builder.[25] The Squires Manufacturing Company of Milan and other southern Michigan builders produced thousands of aluminum rowboats and other craft in the late 1950s. The Milco Tank & Boat Company of White Pigeon, builder of the Milco Aqua-Swan, presented aluminum simulated lapstrake boats with extruded gunwales, welded seams, vinyl flooring and tinted windshields in 1963.[26] The material was not solely conducive to constructing small outboard-powered craft. Ferdinand Eichner, an engineer in General Motors' GMC Truck Division, designed and built a novel aluminum sailboat after the war at his home business in Pontiac, called the Trail-A-Boat Company, applying for a patent as early as July 1944.[27]

Pontoon boats as a style took on new popularity for more leisurely cruising on inland lakes and rivers. Where previously speed, durability, and a smooth ride were the most desirable characteristics, the pontoon boat, in contrast, offered a platform for parties and movement around the craft that was not possible with standard hull forms. The Freeland Sons Company of Sturgis, known for its galvanized steel farm tanks since 1893, started building aluminum rowboats by 1953 and galvanized steel pontoon boats in 1958. The aptly named Aqua-Patio Pontoon Boat Company, formed by the Freeland family in approximately 1966, indicated the design intent as a gathering place for a different kind of cruising experience.

Steel

Steel remained a prominent boat-building material for cruisers in the post-war era. Stronger than wood, fiberglass, or aluminum, the advantages of steel for cruisers lie in its ability to take a pounding in the heavy seas of open waters, additional fire resistance, and the minimal annual mainte-nance of painting. Steel lends itself very well to high-precision construc-tion, although it is harder to fix if mistakes are made.[28] While not as labor free as the fiberglass or aluminum construction to which the industry even-tually turned, steel still worked well as an interim step in larger recreational boats because of its lower cost. Until improved manufacturing techniques in the other materials caught up with and superseded it, steel remained an excellent choice for larger boats.

Robert R. Linn of Holland started the largest of the state's postwar steel boat builders, the Roamer Boat Company, after apprenticing with Kenneth Campbell for two years. Linn built his first steel-hulled cruiser in 1946, a 32-footer, probably built at Campbell's yard. He formed the Roamer Boat Company, named after a second boat built at the same location. Some of the early steel hulls could be finished by the owners as "handyman spe-cials" or sold to other builders, such as the Roland E. Ladewig Company. Linn also produced a number of commercial craft such as fishing boats and workboats for governmental agencies. Naval architect A. M. Deering of Chicago supplied several of the Roamer designs in 33- to 48-foot lengths. During the Korean War, Linn obtained a contract for $500,000 to build ten 45-foot tugboats for the navy.[29] Additional tugboat contracts followed, with thirty-one produced overall. So successful in its output, the company was acquired by Chris-Craft for $117,000 as a wholly owned division in March 1955, retaining its name as the Roamer Steel Boats Division.[30] For Chris-Craft, the move made good sense because it already owned a large facility in the community and the new division would help the company diversify its product line. While other steel boat-building firms such as Safti-Craft and Steeliner competed with Roamer for market share, because of Chris-

Craft's dominance, Roamer advertising appeared more prominently than that of any other company in steel boat-building. Roamer began building aluminum-hulled cruisers in addition to its steel boats in 1962 and eventually switched to the material completely.

Thomas Dale Vinette returned to his Upper Peninsula roots after World War II, forming the T. D. Vinette Company, a steel-boat-building firm, in Escanaba in 1947. Born in nearby Nahma in 1915, he graduated from the Merchant Marine Academy in King's Point, New York. During the war he worked as deep-sea diver and diving instructor for the U.S. Navy. Though best known as a builder of fishing boats and workboats, the company built 30-foot cruisers for recreational use. In February 1955 the company expanded into a new 7,000-square-foot plant, serviced by the Escanaba and Lake Superior Railroad. A typical production snapshot in May of that year included two steel-hulled boats under construction, one a 60-foot commercial vessel and the other a 40-foot yacht. Ornamental architectural and structural steel for buildings, school furniture, and miscellaneous steel products also kept the firm busy when its boat work hit slack times.[31]

One of the later steel builders, John Kehrig's Kehrig Manufacturing Company of Utica, metal fabrication specialists of a wide variety of automotive and aircraft products, briefly built 30- and 32-foot Kehrig-Hackerform express cruisers designed by John L. Hacker between 1955 and 1961 using electric welding. Initially the number of orders required the company to increase the size of its factory by 12,000 square feet in 1956.[32] The Detroit Police Department purchased one of its boats for working on the Detroit River, as did Chrysler Corporation's Marine Engine Division for engine testing purposes.[33] The company produced several boats before deciding to leave the boat business in the economic downturn of the early 1960s.

Molded Veneers to Molded Plywood

Growing out of Henry L. Haskell's pioneering work in Ludington before World War I with molded veneer canoes, the Haskelite Manufacturing Corporation's innovative products, such as Haskelite and Plymetl, began appearing in various parts of boats and ships of all kinds, from racing craft to ocean liners. In 1937 the company worked with the Duramold Division of Fairchild Airplane & Engine Manufacturing Corporation to produce the first plywood with compound curves, using a cast-iron mold, steam injection, and a pressurized rubber bag. Water-resistant phenol-formaldehyde resin served as the adhesive between the layers. A different process developed by the U.S. Plywood Corporation, molded Weldwood, used a similar method called Vidal, patented in 1942.[34] Molded plywood vessels offered many unique properties compared to plank-type boats. The boats could readily be shaped to take compound curves. The hulls' extraordinary durability and puncture resistance made them an excellent choice for hard usage by young families. The flat hull bottoms eliminated the ribs typical of most wooden boats.

The Wagemaker Company of Grand Rapids began in 1897 as a manufacturer of wooden flattop and rolltop desks, filing cabinets, filing supplies, and other specialty cabinet work. The company produced an incredibly diverse range of boats, from cedar strip outboards to molded plywood, aluminum, and fiberglass models. The company's line of molded veneer and molded plywood boats became famous under the Wagemaker Wolverine brand name. Ray O. Wagemaker, the company's president and general sales manager, saw the possibilities of boats in 1931 as a way to diversify when the company's furniture sales faltered, and the company produced its first models for national sale in 1933 just when the Great Depression struck at its worst. Sales picked up afterward as conditions slowly improved. In 1939 the company manufactured more than fifty different models, making it one of the national leaders in the production of small boats.[35] Using a phenol-formaldehyde Bakelite-type binding agent applied under high heat and pressure in an autoclave, the company built Weldwood skiffs in several sizes and hull varieties for use with outboard motors. Grand Rapids, as the home of the mass-produced furniture industry, made for a unique, inventive environment for boat-building and furniture. During World War II, the molded plywood designs of Charles and Ray Eames for glider shells, splints, and stretchers led to their famous chairs after the war, some of the ultimate masterpieces of furniture design that showed the world the flexibility of the material and popularized it. World War II interrupted the flow at Wagemaker and set the company to idle as the stocks of plywood were diverted to building warcraft such as landing boats at Higgins and Chris-Craft.

After the war, when the market distress caused by shortages settled down, Wagemaker began a long string of acquisitions for its boat lines. The company purchased the Algoma Plywood & Veneer Company boat operation of Algoma, Wisconsin, and renamed it U.S. Molded Shapes, Inc., a subsidiary of Wagemaker.[36] The new company sold unfinished hulls in bulk to other boat-building firms to complete or also as kits flattened for shipment. The company started its own line of marine hardware with a new Hardware Division where workers made lifting rings, windshields, rowlocks, chocks and cleats, or anything needed for a small boat at its own foundry.

Wagemaker organized the Wagemaker Realty Company for the purpose of acquiring the former Northern Michigan Chair Company plant in Cadillac, Michigan, in order to provide housing for a subsidiary to build metal boats.[37] The Wagemaker Company then formed the Cadillac Boat Company (later renamed Cadillac Marine and Boat Company), in September 1953 as a wholly owned subsidiary to build aluminum boats as a means of diversifying, trying to compete with Aero-Craft and other successful firms in that segment of the marketplace. General Motors Corporation sued the company over its name, which resembled its own Cadillac automotive division, but GM lost the suit as the products could not be considered related.[38] Eventually Wagemaker cross-marketed the different hull material models through each division of the firm, blending the lines of Cadillac and Wagemaker to include cedar strip and molded plywood boats in addition to the aluminum craft under the brand names.

The Wagemaker Company introduced its "Ply-Lap" hulls in 1955, which simulated in molded plywood the lapstrake form of boat construction. New "Boat-A-Ramic" styling, with bold paint colors and sweeping side spears directly derived from the automobile industry's studios, soon found its way into Wagemaker boats. The company started the Empire Boat Company of Frankfort, New York, in 1956 to likewise gain an entry into the fiberglass boat market.[39] The Cadillac Marine and Boat Company achieved some fame when it arranged with industrial designer Brooks Stevens to build a few editions of the 1956 Evinrude Lark, created to promote the motor of the same name, as the Cadillac Sea Lark for the New York and Chicago international boat shows. The Sea Lark, an extreme example of jetlike styling, with a high-tail-finned fiberglass body over a molded plywood hull, looked so futuristic that it even made the cover of *Newsweek* magazine.[40]

The company suffered one of the worst fates to befall a boat firm when fire struck the Wagemaker Company storage yards in February 1957, destroying over fifteen hundred boats awaiting spring delivery at a cost of over $750,000.[41] The following year the company consolidated its well-known brand names so that each of the brands could become identifiable by the three materials of plywood, aluminum, and fiberglass. Wolverine remained for molded plywood and ply-lap boats, Cadillac for aluminum, and the new Empire line, taking the name of the boat company, for fiberglass.[42]

Fig. 24. Industrial designer Brooks Stevens designed the Evinrude Lark
as a concept boat, integrating the tail fins and cockpits of the Jet Age
into a boat, just as automobile manufacturers were doing. The Cadillac
Marine and Boat Company built a few called Cadillac Sea Larks with a
combination of wooden hulls and fiberglass decks for trade shows in 1956.
(© Mystic Seaport, Rosenfeld Collection, no. 150513F.)

The year 1960 proved to be fateful for Wagemaker as the company and
its subsidiaries were purchased for $650,000 by the Walter E. Schott Invest-
ment Company of Cincinnati on April 15. Eight days later a second major
fire struck the U.S. Molded Shapes operation, causing $250,000 in dam-
age, which in turn influenced another transition. The company announced
that it planned to move to Cadillac in June 1960 when the Cadillac City
Commission approved the transfer of control of a former B. F. Goodrich
Company plant to Wagemaker. Walter E. Schott Jr., the new president of
the company, had announced the move, as well as a major reorganization of
the Wagemaker, Empire and Cadillac subsidiaries, two weeks earlier.[43] The
Wagemaker-Schott Company was sold out to Harrison O. Ash, an industrialist of Cincinnati for his Ash-Craft Company in 1961, which he in turn
merged into the New-Kanawha Industrial Corporation of West Virginia.[44]
The latter firm fell into bankruptcy two years later, ending Wagemaker's
long run of over thirty years as a boat-building firm.[45]

Fiberglass

Fiberglass reinforced plastic (FRP), the mixture of glass fibers with plastic resin (abbreviated here to the generic term *fiberglass*), slowly increased in significance as a hull construction material immediately after World War II and then skyrocketed in popularity into the 1950s, changing the very nature of the boat-building industry. Accounting for much of the surge in the popularity of boating after the war, fiberglass offered huge possibilities for change in the boat-building industry because it could be formed into virtually any shape and colored to any tone. The material's durability could be better than wood with only minimal care, and it could be quickly and easily repaired when damaged. Most boat owners wanted to eliminate or reduce the high cost in time and money of hull maintenance of any kind. As a flexible material well suited for mass production, fiberglass had no equal, and for many builders it offered the best choice for future growth. The cost of tooling for fiberglass could be lower compared to the woodworking machinery of a wooden boat manufacturer.

Fiberglass found slightly slower acceptance at first than the lightweight metal and molded plywood boats because problems of many kinds kept popping up, mostly having to do with the bonding materials. Some builders applied fiberglass over wood frames or other materials to which it did not adhere well, so it worked fine until leaks started and the wood rotted beneath the material. Others used inappropriate filler material between the layers. Chris-Craft, the largest small craft manufacturer in the world at the time, purchased a fiberglass boat company in Boca Raton, Florida, named Lake-N-Sea, which turned out to be a near disaster. The hulls, built of fiberglass over plywood and Styrofoam, delaminated and quickly earned the nickname "Leak-N-Sink," much to the chagrin of the company's management. Chris-Craft soon sold its recent acquisition to the Parsons Corporation of Traverse City, manufacturers of helicopter blades. Parsons continued to operate the firm for a few more years. The bad experience had long-lasting results as Chris-Craft did not return to fiberglass boats until quite late in the early generation era, and even then at the cost of a significant amount of market share.

Like most of the other postwar construction materials, fiberglass boat builders had their prewar and wartime predecessors, although none appears to have been located in Michigan. Most of the earliest fiberglass boat manufacturers started in other areas of the country such as California. Because of the extensive recreational boating market in the Great Lakes region, a few looked at Michigan as a good place for branch plants when expansion could be merited. Wizard Boats, Inc., of Costa Mesa, California, briefly opened a branch factory in St. Joseph, Michigan, at the former Robinson plant in October 1954, although it closed four years later and moved to Dickson, Tennessee.[46] Sabre-Craft of Tacoma, Washington, opened a new plant in Niles in 1961 to serve the Midwest and the Great Lakes regional market. A skeleton crew operated the plant for the first couple of weeks after it opened, but the company expected to employ about seventy-five people when at full production. It expected to produce about a thousand boats at the plant in 1961.[47]

The Glasspar Boat Company, one of the largest manufacturers of fiberglass boats prior to 1960, started operations in Sturgis in 1961 in a new plant built after local citizens raised one hundred thousand dollars in bonds for its construction. Internally, the company had been falling apart following its acquisition by Larson Industries of Minnesota the same year.[48] Larson cut back drastically on research and development and merged Glasspar with another division. When the outboard boat market reached saturation, Glasspar failed to bring new, attractive products out when it needed them most. The company announced in September 1962 that it was ceasing operations and putting its plant up for sale after idling fifty-five employees earlier in July. Officials publicly said that the Great Lakes market for boats had turned from the "best" to one of the "worst" in the nation, although mismanagement probably played a larger role in the plant's demise.[49]

Early fiberglass boat manufacturing could be a rough-and-tumble business. By the end of the 1950s, new startups could be found in virtually any space, be it a garage, a rented warehouse, or any kind of building. When the new company did not have its own designer, or even a mold on which to build, it sometimes either borrowed a mold or "splashed" a new one from an existing boat of a manufacturer they liked.[50] As few of the hull designs could be patented, infringement could not be prosecuted easily.

Once fiberglass boats became established as a viable product, several Michigan businesses started new factories in the state to build them. The Pere Marquette Fibre Glass Boat Company of Ludington and Scottville succeeded for a time as one of the state's pioneering fiberglass boat firms. Starting in a garage in Ludington, Charles Wallace incorporated the firm with capital of fifty thousand dollars in August 1954. At the instigation of the Industrial Development Corporation, a group of businessmen in nearby Scottville, the Pere Marquette Company moved into a new factory built for it, which it subsequently purchased. Pere Marquette started production of fiberglass boats in January 1955. Richard Rudysill, the company's president, figured that full production could be reached by June 1 of about fifty to seventy-five boats per week.[51] Pere Marquette produced both boats and canoes and employed up to fifty people at a time. One of its fiberglass canoes was approved by the Health and Safety Council of the Boy Scouts of America for use in its camps throughout the United States. Over four hundred canoes were purchased by the Boy Scouts Supply Division in 1956–57.[52] Models with names such as Vacationer, Cyclone, Tornado, Scout, Woodsman, and Explorer made up some of the product line in 1958–59, all of them in the 12- to 18-foot range.

By 1962 the company had fallen into financial difficulty and the property was auctioned off under the auspices of the Small Business Administration. Thomas C. Billig Jr. either acquired or merged the company with his own firm, the Industrial Fiber Glass Products Company, retaining the Pere Marquette trade name and product line as a division.[53] A year later he increased the number of dealers to fifty, located mostly in the Midwest but also in eastern states, including Pennsylvania, Massachusetts, North Carolina, and Virginia. Sales grew large enough for the company to build an addition to its factory in 1965, as it planned to expand the business by 600 percent.[54] The company lasted until about 1971.

One of the most successful manufacturing stories in Michigan is that of the Slick Craft Boat Company, formed by Leon Slikkers of Holland, Michigan. Slikkers worked at Chris-Craft's Holland plant in the joiner department constructing cabin tops, starting as an eighteen-year-old fresh off the family farm. Over the next few years, Slikkers perfected his craft, moving up to become assistant foreman of the department. Frustrated by a 1952 labor strike at the plant, he joined with another Chris-Craft employee, Jason Petroelje, to build a few boats of their own, selling them out of Slikkers's garage. Although the partnership broke up after the strike, Slikkers continued to build boats on the side and established a network of contacts. Seeking a chance to go out on his own as his side business became increasingly successful, Slikkers departed Chris-Craft in January 1955 and began making boats on his own. He purchased his first molded plywood hulls from U.S. Molded Shapes in Grand Rapids, finishing them as double-cockpit runabouts with mahogany plywood decks. Moving his family into a rented factory with an apartment above, Slikkers shortly afterward started experimenting with fiberglass construction for boats. He managed to build thirty-five boats in his first model year with help from his brother Paul. Slikkers contracted with local fiberglass boat builder Clyde Poll to build fifty boat hulls for his new Wonder Craft Boat Company in December 1955. The Slick Craft Boat Company was off and running.[55]

For the 1958 model year Slikkers contracted with Camfield Manufacturing, a fiberglass company in nearby Zeeland, to build between twenty-five and fifty hulls for his own firm. These boats, the 16-foot Victoria runabout model, mixed color into the gel coat for the first time, giving the boats more distinction in the market. Later deck molds simulated the striped planking of wooden runabouts. All along the path of his early boats, Slikkers continued to build molded plywood models in addition to the fiberglass ones, although he finally dropped the wooden hulls in 1960, and fiberglass boats with wooden decks a year later, shifting to entirely fiberglass construction. "It intrigued me because we were always trying to bend wood that didn't want to bend to some of the curves, and so you'd have to saw it out," he told an interviewer. "And I was thinking, if you could just lay this material in, wow, you could really come up with some fantastic shapes that are more conducive to a boat than to have to bend wood—or cut wood or shape wood. Plus the fact is that the talk was that it would last forever. And I knew that the boating business required a lot of personal attention. You know, when I was making wooden boats, the people actually spent more time working with their boats than using their boats. But that is what they enjoyed. People were craftsmen themselves; they like to tinker and all that stuff. You know that's what made that industry—I'm convinced, the small boat industry. The person could take care of the boat himself."[56]

Powered by the Automobile Industry

New and improved power plants from Detroit formed one of the greatest contributions of the automotive industry to boat-building, aside from styling. Chrysler Corporation, Ford Motor Company, General Motors Detroit Diesel, Chevrolet and Cadillac Divisions, Eaton Corporation's Dearborn Marine Engine Division, and Gray Motor Company's Graymarine, the oldest actual marine engine survivor, all played a very important role in the growth of powerboating, enhancing high-speed performance in large cruisers and runabouts alike. Older, well-established companies such as Kermath and Scripps, though strong in the immediate postwar era, eventually fell by the wayside as the automotive engines dominated the market. More powerful and reliable outboard motors offered speed and flexibility for smaller, inexpensive boats, although a few firms even marketed cabin cruisers powered by outboards. Of all the automobile manufacturers, Chrysler made the biggest jump into the boat-building industry. The company started building marine engines in 1927, shortly after it was founded, and just after World War II it captured an estimated 40 percent of the marine engine market, a tremendous accomplishment.[57] Following its long interest in marine products, the company purchased the Lone Star Boat Company of Plano, Texas, and acquired the West Bend Aluminum Company's outboard motor division to go with it in 1965.[58]

Sailing into the Future

Sailboat development in Michigan in the 1950s took advantage of the new, lightweight materials, as well as the older wooden forms. A few Michigan firms pushed new types of small one-design boats, including the Gibbs Boat Company of LaSalle (and later Erie), near the Ohio border. Dick Gibbs formed the company in about 1954, starting with the Y-Flyer, designed by Alvin M. Youngquist, Gibbs's mentor in boat construction. He later built the Rhodes Bantam in both fiberglass and wood. Gibbs worked with designer James Roderick "Rod" MacAlpine-Downie, a Scotsman, after reading about MacAlpine-Downie's Thai Mk. 4 catamaran, which cleaned up in races in Europe. MacAlpine-Downie licensed Gibbs to build the boat, and shortly afterward, in 1964, the men started a business partnership based on a handshake. MacAlpine-Downie created the hull designs and Gibbs provided the technical expertise for the production in fiberglass and sailmaking. Between the two men they created about eighty types of boats, mostly daysailers and catamarans, including some of the best-known one-designs in the country, the Mutineer and their most successful, the Buccaneer 18. For twenty-two years, some thirty-five thousand boats of the two men's designs were built by an assortment of boat-building firms, including Gibbs, MFG (Molded Fiber Glass), Monark, Chrysler, and Marine Starcraft.[59] After building some six thousand boats at his own firm, Gibbs sold his company to the MFG Boat Company of Union City, Pennsylvania, in 1972 and became the head of SailMFG.[60] The company also bought another Michigan sailboat builder, Anchor Reinforced Plastics of Hazel Park, which offered the Teal fiberglass daysailer. When the Chrysler Corporation started in the boat business with its acquisition of the Lone Star Boat Company of Plano, Texas, its first sailboats failed to meet both sailors' and corporate expectations in light of the rising sales of one-design boats, so Chrysler turned to the partners to produce several of the Gibbs/ MacAlpine-Downie designs for its smaller sailboat line, the Pirateer, Mutineer, Buccaneer, and Dagger.[61]

The Crescent, the world's first fiberglass one-design sailboat class, started as a boat construction project among friends in a driveway in 1953 nicknamed the Dearborn Navy Yard. Designed by Richard Carl "Dick" Hill, a model maker in the styling department at the Ford Motor Company, Hill found some fiberglass and resin at work and made a quarter-scale model of the first boat from a plaster mold, rigging it as a sloop. Taking the wooden-hulled 24-foot sailboat of Dr. Lyndon Babcock, Hill and his friends made a plaster cast of the hull and then built up several layers of fiberglass to form the new boat hull, carefully waxing the plaster mold night after night. Hill's wife Martha remembered, "We had one neighbor, who was an engineer, who came over. He thought some sort of weird thing was going on because he smelled it; he thought it might be rocket fuel." Finished in a peacock blue with white rails, the first hull was named *We Do Tu*. The first production boats, built at Detroit by Abbott Industries, trickled out slowly, with two boats in 1956, five in 1957, and two in 1958. In the mid-1960s and afterward, the boats were built at Custom-Flex, a boatyard in nearby Toledo, Ohio, until 1976. The Crescent fleet consisted of about twenty-seven boats raced competitively on the Detroit River through the Detroit Sail Club and Bayview Yacht Club.[62]

Unlimited Racing Revisited, 1950s Style

After the war, many of the twelve-cylinder Allison V-1710 and Packard-built Rolls-Royce Merlin aircraft engines became available as war surplus, which in turn led to a renewed interest in racing, just as the Liberty engines of World War I had once powered the fastest boats. The Gold Cup class merged with the Unlimited class in 1946 to bring the two back together after a long separation of many years. John L. Hacker continued to design racing boats late in his life, creating the last successful large stepped-type hydroplanes in the late 1940s and early 1950s with two racers, *My Sweetie* and *Miss Pepsi*. Hacker designed *My Sweetie* in 1947 for owners Ed Schoenherr and Ed Gregory, the son of Edgar M. Gregory of Belle Isle company fame. "Wild" Bill Cantrell drove the boat in the 1948 season, but it proved to be very difficult to control. The Allison engine drove a propeller mounted on a shaft extending from nearly amidships on the boat. Hacker redesigned the bottom, and the craft racked up victory after victory in 1949, winning almost all its races, though not the Harmsworth Trophy. Horace Dodge, enamored with the boat's success, purchased it for an attempt to win the Gold Cup a year later. Hacker's last major winner, *Miss Pepsi*, nicknamed "The Mahogany Cigar," was a stretched-out version of

My Sweetie driven by two Allison engines mounted in tandem. The Dossin family of Detroit commissioned Les Staudacher to build the boat in 1950 as a floating advertisement for its Pepsi soft drink distribution company. *Miss Pepsi* won five races in 1951, including the Detroit Memorial and the Silver Cup, and won the national championship that year. The boat ran in the Gold Cup race in 1956 after being brought out of retirement, and it finished second only after an eighty-five-day legal battle determined the winner to be *Miss Thriftway*, driven by former Detroiter Bill Muncey.

One of the greatest rivalries in the history of motor sports pitted the Unlimited boats of Detroit against those emanating from Seattle, in a battle for supremacy among the fastest competition boats in the world. Contested with three-point racing hulls, the "rooster tails" of spray thrown by the boats as they rounded the courses made for spectacular and sometimes dangerous racing events. Jack Schafer's series of boats named *Such Crust* and the Schoenith family's *Gale* racing boats led the charge for the Detroit teams.

At the center of it all stood one of the most important boat designers and builders in the nation of 1950s and 1960s Unlimited racing craft, Frank Lester "Les" Staudacher of the village of Kawkawlin near Bay City. Staudacher got his start in boat construction working at the Eddy Shipbuilding Corporation in Bay City and building a few cruisers for John Hacker, then the racing boats *My Sweetie* and *Miss Pepsi*. He made his living as a church pew builder, earning him a reputation for fine craftsmanship and novel construction capability.[63] Boat designer Ted Jones of Seattle designed a unique hull in 1947 typically called a three-pointer, based on the fact that the hull body, supported by two large sponsons on each side of the bow and a small flat area at the stern, rested on three points at speed. At very high speeds the whole boat lifted out of the water, riding only on its partially submerged propeller as air-water surface effects worked on it. Jones's incredibly successful three-pointer, *Slo-Mo-Shun IV*, astonished the racing world with its speed when the boat blasted past the competition in 1950, first setting a world water speed record in Seattle of 160.32 miles per hour and then seizing the Gold Cup in Detroit. *Slo-Mo-Shun IV*, driven by Jones, beat Dodge's *My Sweetie* by a full lap, infuriating the Detroiters, who accused the Seattle team of bad sportsmanship.[64] Jones approached Staudacher's shop to build his boat designs in 1955 as he had already built the three-pointers *Such Crust III* and *IV* for Jack Schafer. Although the Jones-Staudacher collaboration only lasted about a year, Les Staudacher went on to build three-point hydroplane boats to race in the Gold Cup, Silver Cup,

Fig. 25. Les Staudacher of Kawkawlin (*left*) and his crew working on the hydroplane *Shanty I* in 1956. Staudacher's hydroplanes of the 1950s dominated the sport of unlimited racing, and the contests between Detroit- and Seattle-based boat teams remained an outstanding rivalry for years. (Bay County Historical Society.)

President's Cup, and Harmsworth Trophy contests, with his boats winning fifty-one races between 1953 and 1971 according to H1 Unlimited historian Fred Farley.[65] Clients included the bandleader Guy Lombardo with his *Tempo* series of boats, Henry and Edgar Kaiser with their coral pink *Hawaii Kai III*, and Bill Harrah's *Tahoe Miss*. Famous boats such as *Miss Thriftway*, *Maverick*, and *Nitrogen Too* all came out of the shop in the 1950s, constructed by Staudacher ably assisted by Don Morin, Joe Chosay, Lawrence Fouchea, and a small group of talented craftsmen. On April 17, 1962, Roy Duby drove the Staudacher-built *Miss U.S. I* on Lake Guntersville in Alabama to a mile-straightaway speed of 200.419 miles per hour, a world record for a piston-powered, propeller-driven craft that still stands today.[66]

Staudacher even experimented with jet engines for establishing new world water speed records for boat owners Joe and Lee Schoenith of Detroit and Guy Lombardo. Lombardo's aluminum-hulled *Tempo Alcoa*, with Staudacher himself driving, took a wild ride across rock-strewn Pelican Point on Pyramid Lake near Reno, Nevada, when he lost control of the boat after the water surface shifted from flat to a slight ripple, ending in a crumpled wreck on dry land. Staudacher later said, "When I saw that rocky shore coming at me I said to myself, 'This is a heck of a way to end this thing. I just hope I hit hard enough to do a good job.' I believed this was the end of my life . . . Then I did hit, and I was airborne. I felt a great relief. I was about 20 feet above the peninsula, and that aerial view looked good to me. I knew I hadn't hit too hard. My jet pilot's helmet saved my head when I smashed into the windshield coming down. I'll say one thing. The boat runs much better on water than it does on land."[67] After taking the boat back to Kawkawlin and making repairs, a year later, in 1960, it went to pieces during testing on Saginaw Bay while under remote radio control. Flying water droplets entering the air intake acted like stones on the delicate turbine blades, causing an explosion that destroyed the engine. Undaunted, Staudacher built yet another aluminum-hulled jet boat, *Miss Stars and Stripes II* for Nash Motor Company president Robert B. Evans. A test run of the Evans boat on May 16, 1963, on Hubbard Lake in the northern Lower Peninsula nearly cost Staudacher his life. Traveling at a speed of about 280 miles per hour, the rudder assembly failed. Zooming ever closer to shore, Staudacher somehow managed to eject himself just before the boat careened onto shore and into the woods, leaving him severely injured and unconscious in the shallow water 100 feet from shore with two broken legs, a broken hip, a broken left arm and a dislocated right shoulder.[68] The shop continued to build racing boats for years, with Staudacher's son Jon eventually taking over the operation.

Hanging in There: Knockdown Boats and Folding Canvas Boats

Bay City Boats, Inc., Harry Defoe's old knockdown boat company, was revived after World War II after he sold it to new owners Russell F. Beck and Leonard C. Humes. The company gradually diversified its Bay Craft product line to include eighteen different models in 1954, ranging from a 17-foot runabout to a 54-foot motor sailer. Larger boats up to 90 feet could be special-ordered if desired. Although the number of models dropped substantially from the hundred offered prior to World War II, they nonetheless provided an important lineup of products for do-it-yourselfers. Each Bay Craft boat featured a white oak frame that had been erected, beveled, and fastened before being knocked down into crated portions for shipment. The company supplied all the hardware, planking, decking, and engines necessary to complete the boat in addition to the frame service.[69] In 1962 the company offered boats in sizes from 17 to 34 feet in length, and also a 22-foot sloop. The motorboats could be adapted to use the new inboard-outboard drive systems popular in other boats.

Based on growing demand for the one-design sailboats, Bay City Boats may have forced its own demise by moving out of powerboats completely. In a letter to prospective powerboat owners issued sometime in 1964, according to Jack Woliston, writing for United Press International, the company stated, "Today we are experiencing a terrifically strong move in our pre-fab field toward sailboats. This is involving more and more of our factory floor space and frame erection area, and in fact an ever increasing percentage of our total available facilities. This trend is so great that as we move into this fall we can see that it is very quickly going to involve our total output at our present size and capacity. We have had some 'top level' policy meetings on this matter, and just plain hard business sense points toward a rather rapid elimination of all power boat models from our advertising and production and the conversion of this space and manufacturing ability to the rapidly growing sailboat influx." The company went on to state that it had decided to accept no further powerboat orders after September 30.[70]

Combined with the transition to fiberglass cutting so deeply into the market for all wooden boats, regardless of type, even those built by the owners themselves became less attractive by comparison. Bay City Boats, Inc., dropped out of existence by 1968, ending a run of over thirty-four years.[71]

Pauline S. Winans guided the Kalamazoo Canvas Boat Company through the worst of times in the Depression and World War II after the death of her husband, George, in 1927. She turned over the operation to her son, Paul, by the mid-1950s, who continued to build the unique folding canvas boats in much the same manner as the firm had always done. He carefully sewed the canvas skin pieces together on an ancient industrial sewing machine. Ron Little hammered in metal pockets for the umbrellalike metal ribs. August Peterson, the company's jack-of–all trades, who first started working for the company in 1922 and managed its production, placed the ribs and installed the folding keel. By 1964 the company was still building about two hundred boats a year in three different styles, and three to five sizes in each, ranging in price between $90 and $250 for standard sizes. Larger boats of up to 20 feet in length could be produced on special order. Gross revenue for the little company reached about forty thousand dollars annually, earning Winans and his coworkers a comfortable living. Winans knew his market well. "In running the business," he said, "the main thing I try to do is to keep in touch with a changing market. We used to sell mainly to sport fishermen and hunters. Now we're aiming at family campers, many of them city dwellers who like to take advantage of the increasing number of parks and campsites throughout the country, but who don't have enough storage space for owning rigid boats."[72]

Paul Winans's brother-in-law, Edward D. George, purchased the company in 1967 after Pauline's death. He ran into difficulty running it and sold it to James P. Ash, one of his employees. A fire in 1979 destroyed many of the valuable tools and wooden patterns, but fortunately paper patterns for the boats were stored elsewhere. Ash marketed the boats as Duffelboats, in styles of canoes, square-stern canoes, double-end boats, V-hulls, prams, and a Surf-Yak, a surfing craft that Ash designed himself.[73] The company folded, literally, sometime after 1980, ending over ninety years in the boat-building business.

CHAPTER EIGHT

Epilogue: The 1960s and Beyond

Introduction

To bring the story of Michigan boat-building into the recent past, the period can best be defined as rough waters. At first the recession years of the early 1960s and the growing dominance of fiberglass construction overtaking wooden boat builders forced several Michigan builders out of business. *The Directory of Michigan Manufacturers* listed ninety-four boat-building firms in 1960 but only sixty-four in 1965 and sixty-seven in 1969.[1] Although the national economy had rebounded by the late 1960s, the next major crisis struck with the Arab oil embargo of 1973, which triggered changes in Michigan's manufacturing landscape for decades afterward. Double-digit inflation combined with a stagnating economy to create "stagflation." Interest in environmental protection for natural resources gained strength, forcing new regulations for both building and using boats. Entering the 1980s, waves of recession, growth, and renewed recession caused massive shifts within the recreational boat industry worldwide, and Michigan-based firms or companies that had originated in the state found themselves at the forefront of the changes. As a general trend, Michigan's largest boat builders became acquisition targets for large recreation industry conglomerates. The Outboard Marine Corporation (OMC), Brunswick Corporation, and American Machine and Foundry Corporation (AMF), all seeking to increase their holdings in the recreational boat market, purchased as many of the most valuable companies as they could. What started first as company names devolved into corporate divisions, then into brand names within the larger organizations, gradually changing their identity as time went on.

A smaller, less significant trend in the mid- to late 1960s showed a number of the smaller boat builders in the state establishing themselves near the burgeoning recreational vehicle industry of South Bend and Elkhart, Indiana, and adjacent to the state borders with northern Indiana and northwestern Ohio. Sabre-Craft in Niles, Aqua-Patio in Sturgis, the Geneva Boat Company in Hudson, and the Dowagiac Steel Tank Company in Dowagiac are representative of some of these operations. The modern boat factory just as likely overlooked nearby farm fields as a lake because most smaller boats were shipped by truck. Boat builders had once established their plants on waterfronts for testing and delivery, but now access to expressways became just as important for getting the boats to the dealers and having materials and parts shipped in for construction.

With the consolidation among the largest companies, the number of firms shrank overall, but the number of employees and value of the shipments increased dramatically. By 1963 the nation had 1,626 boat-building and repairing establishments, employing 24,861 employees, and sending out shipments valued at $360,208,000, of which about $338,000,000 consisted of new boats. In Michigan there were 53 establishments, of which 12 employed 20 or more people. The industry employed 1,894 employees earning $9,079,000 for their work. Michigan's value of shipments totaled $30,649,000, or just over 8.5 percent of the nation's total, consisting of about $29,000,000 in new boats.[2]

By contrast, just twenty years later, in 1982, the number of establishments in Michigan had been reduced to forty-five, of which ten employed twenty people or more, but the large companies employed sixteen thousand people and spent $26.9 million on payroll. The value of shipments increased to a whopping $119.4 million, though just over 5 percent of the national total.

By the late 1960s, Michigan's boat builders were shipping thousands of recreational watercraft of all kinds around the world each year, with something for every opportunity to play on the water. Within the state, good wages in the automobile industry and other kinds of manufacturing enabled workers to enjoy a high standard of living not possible in other regions of the country because for decades unions had secured the best available benefits and wage packages for their members. For assembly line workers, skilled tradesmen, and young executives, the high wages and salaries enabled them to build or purchase the vacation homes lining the state's Great Lakes and inland lakeshores and the boats of their dreams to go with them.

When the Arab oil embargo struck in 1973, Michigan, as the home of the automobile industry, experienced several painful changes in direction as the auto manufacturers struggled with downsizing the weight of vehicles to improve gasoline mileage. The short-term wake-up call of skyrocketing gasoline prices led to a gradual questioning and change of perception about American-made vehicles, as people began to ask why the gas-guzzler of old could not be made better and cheaper. As people tried to figure out what was wrong with Detroit, the domestic automobile industry watched, virtually helplessly, as the Japanese in the 1980s made enormous gains in market share based on consumers' perceptions of the quality of their cars and lower prices. "Detroit iron" no longer held the cachet that it once had, and while the products met the transport needs of many, more and more people felt that the cars were increasingly sloppily built. Misaligned hoods, runs in the paint, and plastic parts that quickly broke all surfaced as symptoms of a larger problem of quality control. Planned obsolescence, in which annual styling changes brought out a slightly changed grille or chromed bumper design to maintain freshness and sales levels, seemed no longer desirable.

The changes hurt as the workers suffered layoffs in waves as plants closed, downsized their work force, or automated with robotic equipment, eliminating the need for the humans that had formerly performed every little job with mind-numbing repetition. None of the robots called in sick or showed up drunk or suffered from attitude problems. As the layoffs increased, the first impact was on a family's discretionary spending, especially for recreation. Boats served as expensive toys, and often they came first on the family budget chopping block as they could not substitute for putting food on the table or paying the mortgage.

The state's boat builders suffered similar consequences as these events were repeated endlessly throughout the Midwest and anyplace where manufacturing was prevalent, with residents leaving the "Rust Belt" for the "Sun Belt" in droves, taking their money with them. A glut of used boats on the market similarly drove down prices and cut deeply into sales of new craft. In the years immediately following the oil embargo, just one event in a tumultuous era, total domestic recreational boat shipments reached 729,000 in 1974, only to tumble to less than 600,000 in the following year.[3] A great deal of consolidation in the recreational boating industry nationally led to the elimination of small individual firms and the growth of large conglomerates, which brought together over a dozen brand names at once. *The Directory of Michigan Manufacturers* listed sixty boat-building and repair companies in 1971 and a sharp decrease to only forty-six in 1976.

Just as the automobile industry headed south in the 1980s for cheaper labor costs and less influence by the strong labor unions, a few of the largest boat companies in Michigan likewise left the state completely, destined for Sun Belt locations, for the same reasons. They desired to be closer to locations where the boats could be tested year-round and more efficient marketing could be targeted to a larger customer base. For small communities such as Algonac, Oxford, and St. Charles, where boat-building had provided a significant number of high-paying manufacturing jobs, the losses distressed the local economies for years afterward until the void could be filled.

Fiberglass construction quickly gained ground in the boat-building industry in the 1960s to become the dominant form of material for hull construction. Advancements in construction techniques included the development of the chopper gun, which applied a coating of fiberglass sprayed onto the mold while wetting it with resin and catalyst at the same time. Prior to this development, workers typically laid woven fabriclike sheets of fiberglass over the molds by hand and then sprayed on the resin. Resins that cured at room temperature further sped the construction of boats and other fiberglass products.[4]

Trouble at Chris-Craft

Chris-Craft Corporation, by now headquartered in Pompano Beach, Florida, started a long roller-coaster ride through a number of different corporations between the 1960s and 1980s.

The company gradually left behind the business of building small runabouts and utilities, concentrating its work instead on large cruisers, more luxurious craft with better profit margins. The change took place slowly over the decades. Chris-Craft made one of its biggest acquisitions when it purchased the assets and designs of the Thompson Boat Company of Cortland, New York, in 1962. With the Thompson purchase, Chris-Craft reentered the field of outboard runabouts and small fiberglass cruisers, diversifying the business and forming what later became known as the Corsair Division.[5]

Cornelius Shields of Shields and Company, a major stockholder in Chris-Craft's new owners, the NAFI organization, took the company down several new paths in changing the product lineup to meet the customers' new interests in fiberglass and vinyl. The era of the wooden enclosed cockpit runabouts ended with the last Capri model in 1961, although wooden utilities lasted a while longer, ending in 1968. One of the company's diversions into a short-lived venture in the world of sailing craft started in 1964 with the introduction of the 35-foot fiberglass Sail Yacht or Motor Sailer. Shields had sailed competitively for years and wanted to give Chris-Craft a role in the burgeoning fiberglass sailboat industry. The company eventually produced eight models, but with a change of ownership the sailboats were gone after 1976.[6]

Chris-Craft introduced its first completely fiberglass cruiser model, the 38-foot Commander, at the National Motor Boat Show in New York in January 1964. The largest fiberglass production boat built to date, the Commander was equipped with a pair of Chris-Craft engines and sold for $29,900. The boat marked a major departure for the firm and put it at the forefront of fiberglass technology after careful study of fiberglass construction at the Fiberglass and Tooling Activity Division located in Holland. Successful from the very start, the Commander Series Fiberglass Division was created to guide future development of the boat.[7]

After guiding the transition of the company to the age of fiberglass, William MacKerer decided to retire in 1965 after forty years of service. As the corporate visionary with the incredible organizational skills so critical to the firm's survival and key to its success, "Mr. Chris-Craft," as he came to be known, stepped away, having brought both the boats and the corporate structure to the pinnacle of the industry. After coming to Michigan decades earlier to work for the best in the business, earning his living as a sometimes-employed, sometimes-not young apprentice with a passion for boats, MacKerer epitomized the professional boat builder in all facets as a craftsman, businessman, and teacher.

Despite the growing significance of fiberglass construction in the industry, the wooden construction techniques were not ignored and were actually improved on a regular basis. A mid-1960s Chris-Craft still used steam-bent white oak ribs between bolted Philippine mahogany frames. Marine plywood in large sheets on the inner hull served as a stiffener to prevent the frames from shifting under stress. Philippine mahogany planking over the plywood, separated by a gasket layer of canvas saturated in bedding compound, finished the outside skin of the hull, secured to battens at the seams. Screws were still covered with bungs, matched for grain and color to the planks to make them disappear. All bare wood was sealed, painted, or varnished on every model without exception. The Roamer Division also improved its steel and aluminum fabricating methods with enhancements such as the Capac electronic electrolysis protection system.

Chris-Craft, at the height of its manufacturing capability by 1965, operated plants in five states, as well as Stratford, Ontario, and Flumicino, Italy, with a total of well over 1.9 million square feet of production space.[8]

After many decades of incredible achievements, dark years at Chris-Craft, now known as Chris-Craft Industries, Inc., appeared on the horizon by the late 1960s. Herbert J. Siegel launched a successful financial takeover of the corporation in late 1967. Chris-Craft as a corporation moved into many other commercial avenues outside its core business of boats such as broadcast media outlets. Siegel, seeking to increase the value of those, isolated the boat-building operations in a single Boat Division, reducing the significance of the original industry giant within the corporate entity. The corporate headquarters was shifted to New York, and with its leadership lacking interest in boats, the Boat Division quickly felt the impact as its portion of the company began a long downward spiral since it drastically downsized the offerings in its various lines.[9]

The older Michigan plants suffered greatly with the reductions in a series of closures. The Cadillac plant, dating back to 1941, shut down in 1968. Worse yet, the original Algonac plant shut down boat construction operations in mid-1970, and the engine portion of the business was moved to Gallipolis, Ohio. The plant remained the home of the corporation's Parts Division, but its glory years as the heart and soul of the world's largest boat-building firm had long since passed. Chris-Craft historian Jeffrey Rodengen determined that the last boat to leave the Algonac plant was a 46-foot Aqua-Home houseboat in March 1972. The same year, Chris-Craft turned completely to fiberglass boat-building with its last fully wooden boat produced as a 57-foot Constellation for National Football League commissioner Alvin R. "Pete" Rozelle, who also served on the company's board of directors.[10]

Chris-Craft Industries struggled mightily in the early 1970s after the oil embargo, with sales in 1974 down 50 percent compared to the same quarters in 1973. The company lost five million dollars in 1975 on sales of under forty million, with a nearly equal loss of just less than five million the following year.[11] In a number of cost-cutting moves meant to help the company recover from the economic crisis, it shut down its plant in Chattanooga, Tennessee, and merged its operations with the main Holland, Michigan, plant. Siegel closed the Holland Roamer facility in 1976, shifting production to a new aluminum cruiser plant in Pompano Beach, Florida. Herbert Siegel brought in a turnaround specialist, Richard Genth, as president of the Boat Division in 1978 to set a new direction for the floundering company. Genth closed the money-losing plant in Pompano Beach and whittled down the operations to just two manufacturing plants, the cruiser production facility in Holland, and a new plant in Bradenton, Florida, built to produce the new Scorpion sport boat line. Genth also moved the Boat Division headquarters to Bradenton.[12]

Shortly after the Boat Division turned profitable again, George Dale Murray and Richard Genth, along with prominent attorney F. Lee Bailey and Walt Schumacher purchased the Chris-Craft Boat Division from Chris-Craft Industries for about five million dollars in December 1981, renaming it Murray Chris-Craft. The purchase included the Bradenton and Holland plants, as well as licensing of the Chris-Craft name, still highly valued and respected as a brand.[13] By the late 1980s, competition between the conglomerates Outboard Marine Corporation and Brunswick Corporation for purchases of smaller boat companies led to their combined control of one-third of American pleasure craft production. Murray sold the company to the Outboard Marine Corporation in 1989, which operated it successfully for just over a decade before going bankrupt in 2000. Chris-Craft's operations went on hiatus until a new suitor arrived in Stellican, Ltd., an investment group, which purchased the firm and introduced three new Heritage models in 2001, along with a 43-foot Roamer yacht. The company celebrated its 140th anniversary in 2014.[14]

Struggling with Century

The Century Boat Company suffered a dramatic drop in sales in 1960 and following years, particularly in the Coronado and Arabian lines, where sales declined by 60 percent. In an effort to attract younger customers, the company offered the new plywood Ski Dart in bright yellow and black. Advancements in plywood construction initiated by designer Robert Hobbs simplified the inner structure of the hulls to just four stringers and four full frames, a reinforced keel, and a laminated stem.[15] The company decided to move into the small cruiser market in the early 1960s with its acquisition of the CruisAlong Boat Company, but in the end it found that it just did not fit what the company wanted to be. Cruisers, because of their size, did not take well to the stylistic lines of the runabouts, and the owners seemed far more interested in interior space and amenities. The cruisers lost money because of outdated manufacturing equipment, and each one was essentially handcrafted with minimal tooling. Century sold the cruiser business to the Ventnor Boat Company of New Jersey in 1966.[16]

Finally conceding to the changing times, Century introduced its first fiberglass boat in 1966, the Fibersport model. In two more years, the company built its last wooden boat, converting entirely to fiberglass. Allan Hegg, formerly the vice president of manufacturing for Larson Industries, purchased Century in 1969. He brought in people experienced in fiberglass construction, revamped the dealer network, and enlarged the Manistee plant. Hegg moved its headquarters and main production facility from Manistee to Panama City, Florida, in 1983. More tumultuous times followed, with new owners and a foreclosure of the property after Hegg sold the business.[17] The Yamaha Motor Corporation purchased Century and Cobia boats in 1995, linking the two firms together as C & C Manufacturing. In 2012 Yamaha sold the company to Allcraft Marine, LLC, an American firm based in of Zephyrhills, Florida, which manufactures saltwater sport fishing boats in lengths from 17 to 32 feet.[18]

Harwill Closes Down

Harwill Inc./Aero-Craft, like most of the rest of Michigan's largest boat builders, went through traumatic times in the late 1960s and early 1970s. Always relatively successful, the company looked attractive to the Browning Arms Company, which bought the firm in April 1969 for two million dollars.[19] What started well quickly turned out to be a bad fit. With the oil embargo of 1973 in full swing, causing the company severe losses, Browning drastically cut personnel to mitigate the damage. Browning sold the boat company portion of its business to Fuqua Industries' subsidiary Signa Corporation of Atlanta, Georgia, in August 1974.[20] A serious fire in 1976 caused a loss of four hundred thousand dollars from which the company never really recovered. The last Aero-Craft built in St. Charles left the factory in 1979, and Signa moved the operation to Decatur, Indiana, where it folded entirely shortly afterward.[21] By the mid-1980s, the former St. Charles boat factory, since abandoned, was considered a toxic waste Superfund site by the federal Environmental Protection Agency because of barrels of fiberglass resin and other materials left at the site after the closing. The venerable Wisconsin boat-building firm Thompson, itself having gone through bankruptcy, was purchased by Dale and Dave Anderson and moved to the Browning-Aerocraft plant in the summer of 1980. The combination of an old plant, expensive site cleanup, and two fires in 1987 forced the company to move to a new site in St. Charles the following year. Building about three thousand boats a year in 1987 and 1988, sales dropped by a third in 1989. Thompson declared bankruptcy in May 1993, only to be resurrected once again before closing for good in 2001.[22]

Slick Craft Stays Afloat

Leon Slikkers of the Slick Craft Boat Company moved his fiberglass boat-building operation in Holland into an old skating rink in 1962. Business in fiberglass boats picked up substantially for him during a time when other builders struggled. He knew he needed help, so he brought in Robert Egan to build up the dealer network. Egan had recently left Skee-Craft of Pennsylvania, and he saw Slick Craft's boats at the Chicago show and noticed their high-quality detailing. Slikkers also hired Ed Wennersten away from Chris-Craft to run the research and development functions for Slick Craft.[23] In 1964 Slick Craft produced a very successful deep V-bottom trailerable boat with a cuddy cabin named the SS235, which quickly became its top seller. Slikkers built a new plant in 1966 to handle the ever-increasing business. In a unique switch, Slikkers used his expertise in fiberglass to work with the Century Boat Company, much larger than his own, to supply their first Cheetah fiberglass boat hulls.[24]

Like several Michigan boat builders, Slikkers's company found itself the acquisition target of a large conglomerate seeking to diversify into the recreational market. Slikkers sold Slick Craft to AMF, of White Plains, New York, in September 1969 and remained as president of the AMF Slickcraft Division. The conglomerate also owned Crestliner, Alcort, and Hatteras as its other boat lines. Shortly afterward, Slikkers became increasingly disenchanted with the new owners' lack of interest in using the high-quality materials and careful craftsmanship he had used in his Slick Craft boats, so he left AMF in November 1973. A non-competition clause in the AMF contract to purchase Slick Craft prohibited Slikkers from building powerboats for five years after the date of the sale, so he started experimenting with fiberglass sailboat design. He formed a new company, S2 Yachts (which stood for "Slikkers's second company") in February 1974, after the height of the Arab oil embargo. Slikkers family members that worked at AMF soon joined him in the new venture, as did former employees Robert Egan and Ed Wennersten. The new company grossed $1.6 million in sales its first year and managed to keep fifty-three employees working on the 23-foot and 26-foot sailboats. Reentering the powerboat field in 1976 because of its greater return on investment, Slikkers formed the Tiara Division of S2 Yachts, followed by the Pursuit fishing boat line a year later.[25]

Fig. 26. Leon Slikkers's Slick Craft factory interior in 1968. After he was bought out by the recreational conglomerate AMF in 1969, Slikkers reinvented his company as a sailing yacht manufacturer called S2 Yachts and eventually returned to building power yachts with the Tiara brand. (Joint Archives of Holland, Michigan.)

When AMF stopped building Slickcraft boats in 1980, Slikkers reacquired the brand name from AMF in 1983 and continued production of small sport boats under that name through the late 1980s when it was merged into the Tiara line. Production of S2 sailboats ended in 1987 when a glut of used boats hit the market.[26] Among the numerous awards and recognition earned by Leon Slikkers and his companies, he was inducted into the Michigan Boating Hall of Fame in 2000. Leon Slikkers elevated his son Tom to become president and chief executive officer of S2 Yachts in 2012, stepping back from his leadership role after sixty-six years in the business.[27] Tiara produces exceptional motor yachts to this day made with great pride by the company's owners and great craftsmanship by the employees alike.

Sea Ray Moves

Sea Ray, one of Michigan's largest boat manufacturers of the 1970s, got its start when Cornelius N. Ray III of Oxford, Michigan, a young man fresh out of college at the University of California, Los Angeles, wanted to get into a new business. Having worked in the aggregates and charcoal industry where his family had made its fortune in Oxford area gravel pits as United Fuel and Supply, later named Ray Industries, the firm provided the material for Michigan's growing network of improved roads. In October 1959, Ray purchased the assets of a small fiberglass boat company, Carr-Craft of Detroit, and started his new venture, Sea Ray, as a part of the existing Ray Industries. Bringing in a friend from college, Arch Mehaffey, and Carr-Craft's designer, Jerry Michalak, to assist in running the new business, Ray moved the operation to his hometown of Oxford, setting up shop in a former potato warehouse. The company produced six different outboard-powered runabout models ranging in length from 12 to 17 feet.

Sea Ray raised the bar for most fiberglass boat manufacturers with the styling of the interiors. Earlier fiberglass boat builders put minimal effort into making the interiors look and feel interesting and comfortable. They figured that the exterior is what people saw at the boat shows and that hull design and speed meant more than the interior fit and finish. In one of its first steps, Sea Ray contracted with Harley Earl Associates, the private design firm of General Motors' leading stylist, to create the interiors of some of its boats.[28]

Ray's business started to take off. To keep up with orders, he built a new factory on Stony Lake just north of Oxford in 1962. Sea Ray introduced deep-vee hulls to its lineup in 1964 after C. Ray Hunt's series of offshore ocean racing boats built for Richard Bertram popularized the hull form.[29] Michalak added a distinctive reverse sheer line to the styling of Sea Ray's boats by the mid-1960s for the deep-vee hulls. Drawing on the new technology of stern drives, the company redesigned its hulls to integrate powertrains from OMC and Mercury Mercruiser. Charles Strang and Jim Wynne's inboard-outboard drives for speeding through rough seas completely changed the way boats and power plants were packaged for sale.[30]

The Oxford plant continued to flourish during the company's first ten years while the boats grew in size and sophistication. Two-thirds of the offerings featured stern drives by 1969, and in the following model years they gradually reduced the number of outboards. Sea Ray added dealerships in the western United States, and fearing the strength of the unions in Southeast Michigan, the company moved to new corporate headquarters in Phoenix, Arizona, in May 1971. It added a new production facility on Merritt Island, near Cape Canaveral, Florida, which opened in 1973. The Oxford plant also expanded to 120,000 square feet to accommodate more boat orders. Sea Ray gambled on the introduction of a new 30-foot boat, its largest yet, just when the oil embargo effects began to be felt, and dealers found them difficult to move in the environment of outrageous fuel costs and staggering inflation that followed. The company issued layoff notices to get through the crisis.[31]

Cornelius Ray briefly left the firm's presidency in 1979 with Arch Mehaffey taking over, but he returned in 1984 to reorganize the company. Brunswick Corporation, seeking an opportunity to grow and beat rival Outboard Marine Corporation in the acquisitions game, purchased both Sea Ray and Bayliner within weeks of each other in 1986.[32] The Sea Ray purchase alone cost an approximate $350 million. At the time Sea Ray was the second-largest recreational boat manufacturer in the United States, controlling about 12 percent of its market.[33] Sales bounced back, with Sea Ray delivering 23,686 boats in 1988 for sales of $518 million. Cornelius Ray left the presidency of Sea Ray for a good two years after the deal with Brunswick, ascending instead to Sea Ray's chairmanship. The good times would not last. Sales dropped precipitously in 1989, hampered by a recession nationally. As a further complication, the imposition of the federal 10 percent luxury tax on boats selling for $100,000 or more hurt Sea Ray as it sold larger boats. Brunswick shut down the Oxford, Michigan, plant in 1991, ending its long-standing Michigan connection. The plant built over one hundred thousand boats during the time it operated, but as the oldest plant in the Sea Ray system, it became expendable when only fifteen boats left the factory each week.[34]

Sea Ray continued to survive and prosper over time. In 1995 it purchased Baja Boats, Inc., and the Boston Whaler brand a year later and expanded its factory operations worldwide. Sales surpassed $1 *billion* in 2005, and the company celebrated its fiftieth anniversary in 2009.[35] Not bad for a little fiberglass boat company from Oxford.

Four Winns Makes Waves

Four Winns, Inc., started in a furniture and appliance store in Cadillac, Michigan, when the store owner, George Spicer, started selling Clipper Craft boats. Clipper Craft, Inc., was incorporated in Indiana in 1962, and Spicer purchased the entire operation and moved it to Cadillac in 1963. Spicer became involved in a lawsuit over the trademark with a company of the same name in Florida, so he later incorporated the business as the Saf-T-Mate Company, manufacturers of fiberglass boats, in 1967.[36]

Desiring to sell his business as he approached retirement, Spicer looked for someone to buy his firm. Meeting with two independent sales representatives who sold his boats, John and William Winn Jr., in 1975, Spicer told them to "buy the company or you're fired." The purchase turned out to be a family affair as brothers John, William, and Charlie Winn arranged with their father, William Winn Sr., to cosign for a working capital loan to buy the company because of their youthful age. The elder Winn, vice president of Triumph/BSA motorcycles in Los Angeles, resigned his position and joined the sons in their new venture. The family moved to Cadillac where the company soon started to grow. The firm's first boats produced under the new ownership were named Saf-T-Mate by Four Winns and the Captain, a 16-footer with an open bow for seating. These boats led the company's lineup of six different models. The family later shortened the name to Four Winns.

Getting through the late 1970s proved to be very difficult. A fire on May 1, 1978, destroyed their plant, although the Cadillac community helped the firm get back into operation within a few months, temporarily working out of its warehouse. Finished boats rescued from the disaster served as the plugs for new molds.[37] Slowly the company bounced back, adding the popular Sundowner line of cuddy cabin models and the Horizon line of open-bow boats in 1984. Just six years after the fire in 1985, the company added a new cruiser plant to handle the construction of larger craft. It started building its own custom welded-steel trailers a year later, each one color matched to the boat. By the mid-1980s, the company was thriving on sales of about thirteen thousand boats a year, built and serviced by more than sixteen hundred employees.[38]

The Winn family sold Four Winns, Inc., to the Outboard Marine Corporation in 1986 as part of an OMC buying spree that added several new boat companies to its holdings during the ongoing consolidation of the industry. The new owners continued to invest in the future of the company as Four Winns opened a new Engineering and Research Center in 1989.

For the Four Winns brand, the future would become a dark roller-coaster ride from one corporate giant to another. Banks tightened credit, and in 1990 Congress imposed the 10 percent luxury tax on any boat sold for more than one hundred thousand dollars. Dick Austin, director of operations in 1998, commented that the constant ups and downs, takeover talk, and rumors had led to poor morale: "It's been a tough couple of years. A lot of our workers started looking for other jobs. That hurt because it takes up to a month to train new people to do the jobs in our plant."[39] The parent company, the massive Outboard Marine Corporation, builders of Evinrude and Johnson outboards and owner of a host of boat companies, filed for bankruptcy in December 2000. At the time the firm commanded one-third of the entire outboard boat and motor market. The collapse of the conglomerate, with its heritage dating back to 1929, shook the entire boating industry to its core.[40]

Irwin Jacobs's Genmar Holdings, Inc., purchased Four Winns from the Outboard Marine Corporation in early 2001, shortly after OMC's bankruptcy, acquiring the Javelin, Stratos, Hydra-Sports, Seaswirl, and Lowe boat lines. With the company's total of eighteen different brands and approximately 20 percent of the market, Genmar overtook Brunswick Corporation as the nation's largest boat-building conglomerate.[41] Genmar Holdings fell into bankruptcy a decade later, in 2010, and Four Winns was salvaged out of the remains, along with Wellcraft and Glastron, by Platinum Equity. Platinum Equity formed a new company, Rec Boat Holdings, LLC, the corporate entity that owned and operated the Four Winns brand.[42] In June 2014, Platinum Equity sold Rec Boat Holdings to Groupe Beneteau, a French sailboat and powerboat manufacturer. Its boats range in size from 16 to 48 feet in length.

Leisure Life Limited: Slow Speed Ahead

One of Michigan's largest boat manufacturers did not produce the high-powered craft running through the water at top speed. Instead, Leisure Life Limited of Grand Rapids soared to great heights financially through slow speed in something much more mundane—pedal boats. The company started as the brainchild of Charles E. Billmayer in 1977 when he wanted to build a better pedal boat than the versions currently available. In his first year, he built 540 of a single-model pedal boat in a 4,200-square-foot plant. The company shifted into building its boats out of thermo-formed polyethylene plastic in 1981. Philip Globig, vice president of sales and marketing, stated, "It is resistant to chemicals, does not corrode, resists fading and cracking, is five times more impact-resistant than fiberglass and is maintenance free and—it never needs to be painted." Globig added, "In addition, polyethylene allows minimal moisture absorption, has excellent electrical insulating properties, has a low-coefficient of friction and is much less costly than an FRP or aluminum material. From a production standpoint, polyethylene is easier to process." The company merged with Johnson Worldwide Associates (now Johnson Outdoors, Inc.) on February 10, 1998, whose products included Old Town Canoes and Minn Kota electric outboard motors. In 1999 the company employed eighty people, working in a 152,000-square-foot plant, and producing twenty-four models of boats, including pontoon boats, kayaks, fishing boats, canoes, tenders, and dinghies, all in addition to the pedal boats.[43] One unique product, the Eldebo (Electric Deck Boat) pontoon, driven by a battery-powered electric motor, reflects the company's interest in quiet, nonpolluting boats. By means of the sheer number of units built, the company became one of the larger boat manufacturers in the United States at the time. Johnson eliminated Leisure Life Limited as a brand name in 2001.

Meyers Boat Company

Allen H. Meyers of Tecumseh sold the aircraft portion of his business to North American Rockwell in 1965 in order to concentrate on the wide range of boats the company offered. After Meyers died in 1976, Alan Beatty purchased the company the following year and assumed the presidency, with Wayne Seagraves as vice president. In 1978 the company expanded, purchasing the Sportpal Canoe Company of Johnstown, Pennsylvania, and moving the operation to a recently renovated plant in nearby Blissfield, Michigan. The company purchased another factory in Newport, Washington, in 1980. Products in 1981 included aluminum boats, aluminum canoes, inflatable boats, aluminum jeep tops, and military contract items, all built by about seventy-five employees.[44] Meyers acquired the Aerocraft Boat Company of Coldwater in 1985, builders of fiberglass boats. The company also announced a joint venture with Kemco Unit Control of Maitland, Florida, to build boats in its plant to meet growing demand in the Southeast.[45] Just over six months later, it purchased Michi-Craft Corporation of Ligonier, Indiana, one of the nation's leading canoe manufacturers.[46] Unfortunately, Meyers Industries, Inc., bid too low on an unspecified government contract, forcing it to file for Chapter 11 bankruptcy protection in April 1986 for itself and its new Aerocraft Boat Company subsidiary. Union members at Meyers agreed to a series of concessions in July to keep their workplace alive.[47]

Meyers boats were formed starting with a 3,500-pound coil of aluminum, cut to length, then stretch-formed on a 32-foot press to create the hull. After stretch-forming, the boats were heliarc-welded. The process left a single seam in the hull, which minimized leakage. Teams of workers added seats, keels, ribs, and gunwales to complete the boats. During the company's fiftieth anniversary in 1987, it produced fourteen different models from 10 to 16 feet in length, including a variety of styles for recreational and utility use, totaling five thousand units a year.[48]

Meyers changed to new ownership in 1991 and moved to Adrian, Michigan.

Maurell Products

Crest Pontoon Boats, initially built by Maurell Products of Owosso, Michigan, started as an idea with Maurice E. Schell in 1957, who built his first boat for personal use as a motorized, steerable platform for diving. He incorporated the firm in December 1968, capitalized at fifty thousand dollars.[49] After Schell's death in 1999, the operation continued under the guidance of his daughter, Linda Schell Tomczak. The company survives today after more than fifty years in the industry by building only one form of boat, pontoons, and doing it exceptionally well. The company has been operated as Crest Marine, LLC, since 2010, employing nearly fifty people and operating a 100,000-square-foot factory. What the company excels at is variety within the pontoon type, offering seven different models with at least two sizes in each model. In recent years, some of its pontoons have been specialized for fishing and adapted for water-skiing.[50]

Yar-Craft

One of the better-known boat builders of the Upper Peninsula in the late twentieth century was Yar-Craft Boat Company, Inc., of Menominee, formed on May 22, 1969, by Jack Dallman. Dallman, former general manager of the Thompson Boat Company, decided to go out on his own. The company manufactured fiberglass pleasure boats used mostly in the upper Great Lakes states. Over thirteen years the company grew to a staff of forty and shifted its location to a plant on 20th Street. Early in 1978, the company introduced a full line of fishing boats, transitioning out of runabouts and into deep-vee-hulled craft advertised as "The Dry One." Its five thousandth boat came out of the plant in the spring of 1982. Dallman died in 1996, and Bob Schuette purchased the company from the family. Schuette started the Storm series line of his own design. Corey Suthers, a young businessman of Wausau, Wisconsin, acquired the company as part of Norlen, Inc., itself part of Tomcor Industries, in 2004 and moved it to Wausau. Suthers sold the firm to Ron and Rick Pierce and family on December 8, 2011, who moved the operations to Mountain Home, Arkansas, where they produced their first Yar-Craft in February 2012. The Yar-Craft company became a division of Challenger, Inc., and merged as a brand with Bass Cat Boats.[51]

Gougeon Brothers

Jan, Meade, and Joel Gougeon pioneered a new form of wooden boat technology with their invention of the WEST System of epoxy fabrication. As young boys growing up in Bay City, they built and raced wooden boats on Saginaw Bay on Lake Huron. At age thirteen, Jan Gougeon decided that he wanted to become a professional boat builder. He apprenticed under Vic Carpenter at Superior Sailboats in Montrose to learn the craft. Carpenter introduced the young men to the use of epoxy resins in 1958. Carpenter, one of the earliest users of the material as a structural adhesive in wooden boats, learned about it from pattern makers. Meade Gougeon earned a business administration degree in 1960 and started working for various industries as a sales representative. Both he and Jan experimented with epoxies for trimarans he built in Erie, Pennsylvania, in the early 1960s, learning how it could bond most woods, metals, and fiber reinforcement with the added benefit of exceptional water resistance.

Meade and Jan Gougeon moved back to Bay City and started their new business, Gougeon Brothers, Inc., in 1969, building DN (Detroit News) class iceboats for winter racing. The Gougeons, with help from some friends at Dow Chemical Company, formulated their own epoxy resins as an adhesive laminating system over wood called the WEST (Wood Epoxy Saturation Technique) System. Their DN iceboats became immensely successful, with both Gougeons earning numerous championships of their own and emerging as the nation's largest iceboat builder between 1970 and 1975. The Gougeon brothers' uncle, Ben Huskin, operated a boatyard in the city and became a noted builder of catamarans. The boatyard burned in April 1966, and Huskin, seventy years old at the time, had no desire to start over, so he sold the property to the young men, who moved their operation to the Huskin boatyard site in 1971. Another brother, Joel, joined the company the same year to help market the new product. Selling the iceboat business in 1975 to concentrate on developing the WEST System, the Gougeon brothers saw the product's use soar in the repairing of older wooden-hulled boats and even aging fiberglass hulls because of the adhesive's ability to bond to virtually any substrate.[52] Boat restoration shops felt that it provided the strongest, safest solution for preserving original bottoms and structural elements.

As boat builders, the Gougeon brothers focused on building custom racing sailboats, such as the *Rogue Wave*, a 60-foot trimaran designed by Dick Newick for owner Phil Weld and launched at the Gougeon yard in 1977. Jan Gougeon designed a 32-foot, trailerable racing/cruising catamaran, the G32, in 1989. The company produced fourteen of them between 1990 and 1994. Using a similar technology to its boat-building system, the company received a contract from the National Aeronautics and Space Administration (NASA) to build an experimental wind turbine blade, and under a subsequent contract it produced forty-three hundred blades between 1979 and 1993.[53] The company celebrated forty years of "sticking together" in 2009. As Meade Gougeon said on the anniversary, "We got in this business because it's kind of in our DNA to do this sort of thing. When I was a kid, we always built boats, and I just thought it was the funnest thing."[54]

Coming About: Almost Full Circle

The interest in wooden boats never really went away. With large numbers of old wooden hulls ending up on beaches as nighttime bonfires, the increasing rarity of the wooden craft did not go unnoticed. Even the Chris-Craft corporation, so long affiliated with mahogany-planked boats, searched for its oldest wooden boat in 1969, locating *Miss Belle Isle*, a 1923-vintage 26-foot runabout, still with its Smith-Curtiss OX-5 marine conversion aircraft engine, which it restored at Algonac and donated to the Mariners' Museum at Newport News, Virginia, as one step in preserving its wooden boat legacy.[55]

Wooden boats, by their very nature, are extremely labor intensive to maintain and require an extensive skill set to do the work. Despite this, as the age of wooden boats slowly faded away, the perseverance of the style, design, and materials led to a number of companies offering reproductions, custom designs using older aesthetics of famous brands and model forms, and boat restorations.

Turning Old into New

Not surprisingly, a renewed interest in wooden boats in Michigan centered in Holland, home to more than fifty different boat companies over the years. Descendants of Dutch craftsmen who honed their woodworking skills in the nearby furniture industry developed the sense of craftsmanship and strong work ethic that run deep in the area. The new builders of wooden boats powered them with high-performance automotive engines, improved the bottoms with updated materials, and added modern electronics and controls. Macatawa Bay Boat Works of Holland started building reproductions of 1930 Chris-Craft boats in 1979. Steve Northuis, the founder of the firm, wanted to build a "new old boat" and called them "Grand-Craft." Employing many of the skilled craftsmen from the local Chris-Craft plant, the company built 24- and 27-foot Chris-Craft-styled triple-cockpit runabouts, as well as sport boats in 20- and 23-foot sizes. The first Grand-Craft, a 24-foot Chris-Craft design, was sold to Theron Van Putten of Grand Rapids. Richard and Marti Sligh bought the firm's brand name and assets in February 1984 and formed Grand-Craft Corporation. "On the classics," Sligh said, "we use the same construction techniques that Chris-Craft used years ago, like the double-planked mahogany bottom, but we've gone with modern sealants and adhesives that bond the entire bottom together so well that preseason soak-up is virtually unnecessary. Still overall, we're committed to retaining Chris-Craft's traditional look and values."[56] Grand-Craft produced over two hundred wooden boats in its Classic and Sport lines by 2007.[57] Sligh sold the company in 2005, and, after a brief closing and new ownership in 2009, the organization is still in business well after thirty years.[58]

Taking a slightly different tack, Doug Morin's Morin Boats of Bay City carries on the tradition of building custom wooden high-speed runabouts such as *Amy Ann*, a sleek 30-footer. Although it is not a replica, the boat is styled after the 1930s era Chris-Crafts and Hackers, constituting a resurgence of the design elements with the class and glamour of fine-crafted boats of an earlier time. Powered by an Italian BPM V-12 marine engine, the boat is capable of 65 miles per hour. The boat is equipped with a bow thruster for maneuvering in tight spaces.[59]

The intergenerational nature of the boat-building business is carried on by several firms. One of the oldest is the Mayea Boat & Aeroplane Company, Louis Mayea's firm from the Hacker partnership days, which survives in Fair Haven. The work is carried on by the fourth generation, Larry and Don Mayea, who build Mays-Craft boats. Working on custom-made wooden boats in the same vein as Morin, the Mayeas still use Philippine mahogany and Michigan white oak to create their boats. One of their boats, *Temptation*, built for Detroit entrepreneur Michael Malik in 2004, is believed to be the longest mahogany speedboat. A 47- by 12-foot all-mahogany speedboat powered by twin SeaTec 850-horsepower diesels, the detailing on the boat includes interior seating wrapped in ostrich skin, teak floors inlaid with black walnut, granite countertops, and a push-button-operated disappearing tabletop.[60]

Steve and Jean Van Dam's passion for excellence in craftsmanship led them to form Van Dam Custom Boats in 1977, with Steve acting as the company's president and team leader, and his wife Jean as the marketing and chief financial officer. Their son Ben serves as the firm's vice president and project manager. Steve learned the craft as an apprentice to Vic Carpenter, the same man who taught the Gougeon Brothers about epoxy formulation, although Carpenter had since moved to Ontario. Van Dam started his own four-year apprenticeship program to teach his employees the trade. "Each apprentice must first create his own toolbox as part of the process of learning how to use hand tools," says Steve, "and the process continues through the four years as they learn boat-building skills and the skills needed to install the complex mechanical systems that go into many of the boats."[61]

Preserving Boats

Boat restoration shops, including Don Danenberg's Danenberg Boatworks, not only restore and preserve the antique and classic wooden boats but also provide a wide variety of useful information to owners on how to preserve their craft through publications and a community forum.[62] Enthusiasm for boat-building is best illustrated today by the interest in traditional boat-building programs and preservation groups. The Great Lakes Boat Building School of Cedarville, which opened in 2007, also devotes time and effort to the preservation of wooden boat-building with a full-fledged academic and vocational training program.[63] The Pine Lake chapter of the Traditional Small Craft Association in Lansing meets regularly to demonstrate sailing and rowing craft on Michigan's inland lakes and offers instruction on how to take lines off existing boats in museums and elsewhere to preserve the record of how they were built.

Numerous boat clubs for owners of Chris-Craft, Century, Dodge, Wagemaker, Gar Wood, and other makes help to preserve the memory of how the boats were built, marketed, and used. The Antique and Classic Boat Society, with two chapters in Michigan, hosts antique boat shows and cruises on both the east and west sides of the state.[64]

Fiberglass boats are relatively new to the boat preservation movement;

Fig. 27. Steve and Ben Van Dam, father and son, working on a part together. The intergenerational aspect of passing along boat-building craftsmanship and business skills remains an important element in the work today. Ben is now the firm's project manager. (Van Dam Custom Boats.)

in addition, both collectors and marine historians must come to terms with the rapidly growing hobby that was once considered the bane of boat shows. Wooden boat acquisition and restoration costs became too expensive for young, boat-loving hobbyists, so they formed their own niche. Websites such as Fiberglassics.com have produced a huge amount of historical data about these boats of the recent past and valuable tips on how to preserve and restore them.[65]

An Enduring Legacy

The boat-building industry nationally grew to include approximately 1,117 boat-building establishments in 2007. Of these, only twenty-two were located in Michigan. The Michigan firms employed 2,019 people and had an annual payroll of $77,741,000.[66]

In Michigan we still love our boats, even if we do not make as many here as we did in decades past. Despite the lack of companies locally producing them, Michigan boat registrations alone reached a peak of 1,000,049 in 2000, topping all the other states in the nation. Registrations vary significantly from state to state for the size of boats and why they need to be registered, which complicates the calculation of which state has the most boats in use. Although the number dropped to 812,066 in 2010 during the "Great Recession," Michigan still ranked third in the United States, behind Florida and Minnesota but ahead of California.[67] If small boats not required to be registered by law because of their size are included, the number would still place the state among the national leaders. The recreational boating industry in all forms in the state constituted an estimated $3.9 billion in economic activity in 2010.

In essence, Michigan boat builders produced not just boats but loads of fun for generation after generation of Americans in the boats they offered. From early resorters and workers seeking a respite from a hard day's labor to the first yachtsmen experimenting with a cantankerous motor in a boat, Michigan craftsmen created the boats essential for their experimentation and recreation. From the budget-restricted backyard builder with his knockdown kit boat to the wealthy racers with their gleaming hydroplanes powered by marine-conversion aircraft engines, Michigan builders created new hull forms and ways to construct boats that could be shipped anywhere—and made them go faster than any other boat in the world. For rumrunners crossing the Detroit River and the rum chasers trying to catch them, Michigan-built boats not only popularized the need for speed but served as tools for changing social trends in respect to law enforcement and personal freedom. Even during the height of the Depression years, the runabouts and sailing craft built in Michigan's factories and boat shops reached a new level of elegance and stately appearance while still serving the practical needs of the budget minded with utility boats. Michigan-built landing craft, along with many other boat types, led the way to victory in World War II. In a celebration of styling, the 1950s and 1960s Michigan boat builders adapted the look of automobiles at the pinnacle of their creative achievements, on both the interiors and exteriors of the boats. Despite economic distresses in the late twentieth century, boat builders originating in the state figured out ways to survive through mergers or acquisitions to become the national and international leaders in the field.

What one cannot fathom is the millions of hours of joy found on the water due to the efforts of the builders and their customers, and how they made the pleasure of boating all the more important to our recreation and family life.

Appendixes

Geographic Distribution and Employment Statistics of Michigan Boat Builders, 1890–95

The following list in the 1891 *Michigan State Gazetteer and Business Directory* of boat builders and their home cities reflects the division between the urban boat builders and those more reliant on resort traffic on the inland lakes and rivers.

Smith, C. C. & Co.	Algonac
Sutherland, G. G. & L. C.	Argentine
Willis, W. J.	Au Sable
Pennock, N. S.	Baraga
Osgood, N. A. (canvas)	Battle Creek
Van Dusen, C. W. (metallic)	Battle Creek
Heath, E. W.	Benton Harbor
Cook, M. G.	Boyne
Randles, W. G.	Cadillac
Towle, H. R.	Cadillac
Beauvais, Joseph	Charlevoix
Campbell, Smith	Charlevoix
Washburn, James	Charlevoix
Canfield, B.	Crystal
Boston, Charles	Delray
Allen, Thomas	Detroit
Coller Steam Yacht and Engine Works	Detroit
Davis Boat and Oar Co., The	Detroit
Dean, James & Co.	Detroit
Detroit Boat Works	Detroit
Schmidt, H. A.	Detroit
Schweikart, Carl	Detroit
Steinbrecher, W. H.	Detroit

Thurston, Thomas	Detroit
Bross, John	Dexter
Dougherty, Archibald	Elk Rapids
Hazen, D. E.	Escanaba
McCovey, F. G.	Ferrysburg
Brown, Daniel	Gibralter
Truscott, T. H. & Sons	Grand Rapids
Johnson, D. E.	Grosse Ile
Wallace, Joseph	Houghton
Dagwell, H. T.	Indian River
Thorsen, R. & Co.	Manistee
Anderson, Alexander	Marine City
Demont, Thomas	Marine City
Langell, Thomas	Marine City
Freeman, A. J.	Marquette
Oudotte, Jean	Marquette
Prior, George	Marquette
Weston, Harry	Marquette
Renier, Enis	Menominee
Cooper Bros.	Monroe
Lundy, Robert	Orion
Cook, J. W. & Son	Petoskey
Forbes, John	Plainwell
LeBlanc, William	Port Huron
Pace, W. B.	Port Huron
Fish, F. L. P. & Sons	Saginaw (east side)
Langell & Sons	St. Clair
Chenier, Hyacinthe	St. Ignace
McCann, John	St. Ignace
Smith, G. H.	Sand Beach
Brittain, R. C.	Saugatuck
Rogers & Bird	Saugatuck
Stillson, A. H.	Saugatuck
Martel, J. B.	South Haven
Gain, John	Sparta
Spring Lake Boat Manufacturing Co.	Spring Lake
Parent, F. A.	Trenton
Burnham, S. E.	West Bay City
Friend, G. W.	West Bay City
Demass, Martin	Whitehall

According to the 1894 Census of Michigan for manufactories, the following geographic distribution, capital outlay and employment statistics were determined for small craft builders.

Table 3. Manufactories: Boat, launch, sail, steam yacht, and canoe

County where located	No. of establishments	Capital, real and personal, invested in the business—dollars	Avg. no. of hands employed, males over age 15	Avg. no. of hands employed, females over age 15
State	21	$63,100	147	1
Allegan	2	$3,000	25	
Alpena	1	$2,000	5	
Berrien	1	$10,000	24	1
Charlevoix	3	$21,000	15	
Chippewa	1	$300	2	
Emmet	1	$2,000	2	
Genesee	1	$3,000	2	
Grand Traverse	1	$2,000	2	
Muskegon	1	$500	1	
Ottawa	2	$11,000	6	
Saginaw	1	$500	3	
Sanilac	1	$200	1	
St. Clair	3	$6,400	53	
Wayne	2	$1,200	6	

Sources

Michigan, Secretary of State, *Census of the State of Michigan, 1894, Agriculture, Manufactories, Mines, and Fisheries,* vol. 2 (Lansing: Secretary of State, 1896), table 66, "Other Manufactories," 850.

R. L. Polk & Co., *Michigan State Gazetteer and Business Directory, 1891–92* (Detroit: R. L. Polk, 1891), 1606.

Employment and Boat Production
of Michigan Boat Builders, 1905

In 1905, State of Michigan factory inspectors recorded the following employment and production figures and product values for small boat manufacturers, merged here in a single table. The *Michigan State Gazetteer and Business Directory* for 1905–6 listed seventy-five boat-building firms in the state. Most of these were either individual builders or partnerships for which no data were collected, but the names and locations were recorded as they existed at the same time. Additional entries can be found in *The American Boating Directory, 1906*.

Sources:

Michigan, Bureau of Labor and Industrial Statistics, *Twenty-Third Annual Report of the Bureau of Labor and Industrial Statistics* (Lansing: Bureau of Labor and Industrial Statistics, 1906.), "Chapter III—Names of Factories with Locations, etc." and "A table giving list of boat building establishments canvassed in Michigan, together with locations, names of managers, number of boats built in 1905, with approximate value of the same," 29–154, 373–75. Note: Names and data of known shipbuilding firms have been deleted to clarify the presentation of small craft manufacturers. Company names have been corrected to their actual or advertised names where known variations are listed.
Penton Publishing Company, *The American Boating Directory, 1906* (Cleveland: Penton Publishing, 1906), 9–12.
R. L. Polk & Co., *Michigan State Gazetteer and Business Directory, 1905–06* (Detroit: R. L. Polk, 1905), 1973.

Table 4. Boat building companies in Michigan in 1905

Company name	City or village	County	Name of manager	No. of males employed	No. of females employed	Whole number	No. of boats built in 1905	Approximate value of boats built
Allen, M. A.	Allegan	Allegan	M. A. Allen				8	$100
Allen, Robert	Detroit	Wayne	Robert Allen				8	$4,000
Allen, William J.	Delray	Wayne						
Allen Brothers	Detroit	Wayne		3	0	3		
American Motor Boat Works	Grand Rapids	Kent						
Baldwin, Arthur	Port Huron	St. Clair						
Beebe Bros. & Salsbury	Marine City	St. Clair						
Belgard, Joseph	Manistee	Manistee						
Belle Isle Launch & Power Company	Detroit	Wayne	Cyrus B. Merriam	5	0	5	12	$2,500
Bird Boat Company	Saugatuck	Allegan						
C. H. Blomstrom Motor Company	Detroit	Wayne	Carl H. Blomstrom				200	$12,000
Boston, Charles & Sons	Delray	Wayne						
Brooks Boat Manufacturing Company	Bay City	Bay	Clifford C. Brooks	26	8	34	6,000	$240,000
Bross, John	Dexter	Washtenaw						
Brown, Solomon	Port Sanilac	Sanilac						
Bryan, Edward C.	Wyandotte	Wayne	Edward C. Bryan	6	0	6	21	$7,000
Carpenter, Frank A.	Sebewaing	Huron						
Carpenter, George	Houghton	Houghton						
Charlevoix Boat & Motor Company	Charlevoix	Charlevoix						
Christie, Henry	Alpena	Alpena						
Central Lake Boat Company	Central Lake	Antrim	C. S. Frost	2	0	2	9	$1,500
Chenier, Hyacinthe	St. Ignace	Mackinac						
Chippewa Engine Works	Sault Ste. Marie	Chippewa						

Name	City	County	Proprietor			Employees	Value
Clark, George	Ecorse	Wayne				1	$140
Convery, Hugh	Detroit	Wayne	Hugh Convery				
Cooper, John E.	Monroe	Monroe					
Cottrell Boat & Oar Works	Marine City	St. Clair					
Cummins, James E.	Detroit	Wayne				4	$1,200
Cunningham, J. R.	Detroit	Wayne	J. R. Cunningham				
Dagwell, Harry T.	Indian River	Cheboygan					
Dakin, Henry A.	Grand Rapids	Kent					
Dean, James	Detroit	Wayne					
Detroit Boat Company	Detroit	Wayne					
Detroit Canoe & Oar Works	Detroit	Wayne	Jasper N. Dodge	11	0	75	$3,750
Detroit River Boat & Oar Company	Wyandotte	Wayne	David N. Perry	6	0	21	$4,000
Detroit Steel Boat Works	Detroit	Wayne					
Dougherty, Archibald K.	Elk Rapids	Antrim					
Drake & Wallace	St. Joseph	Berrien					
John East	Algonac	St. Clair	John East	2	0	25	$750
Eclipse Boat Works	Walloon Lake	Charlevoix					
Edgley, O. C.	Hubbard Lake	Alcona					
Fetterley, William M.	Traverse City	Grand Traverse					
Fish, Frank L. P.	Saginaw	Saginaw					
Frame, John	Harbor Beach	Huron					
Freeman, Andrew J.	Marquette	Marquette					
French, C. M.	Waterford	Oakland					
Grand Rapids Gas Engine & Yacht Company	Grand Rapids	Kent	Willis J. Perkins	5	0	75	$30,000
Great Lakes Boat Works	Detroit	Wayne	John Bolio	9	0	183	$15,000
Harper, John	Houghton	Houghton					
Ingleston, Capt. Frank A.	Beulah	Benzie	Capt. Frank A. Ingleston	9	9	43	$4,095
Jesiek Brothers	Grand Rapids	Kent	Jesiek Bros.			12	$1,650

Table 4.—*Continued*

Company name	City or village	County	Name of manager	No. of males employed	No. of females employed	Whole number	No. of boats built in 1905	Approximate value of boats built
Johnston Brothers	Ferrysburg	Ottawa	Thomas Johnston				3	$65,000
King Folding Canvas Boat Company	Kalamazoo	Kalamazoo	George H. Winans	5	4	9	400	$15,000
Lake Shore Engine Works	Marquette	Marquette						
Leland Boat & Supply Company	Leland	Leelanau	Leland Boat & Supply Co.				3	$1,200
Lesperance, Alexander	Delray	Wayne						
Lewis, M. M. & Sons	Battle Creek	Calhoun	Morgan M. Lewis	82	0	82	200	$4,000
Life-Saving Folding Canvas Boat Company	Kalamazoo	Kalamazoo	Ira O. Perring	3	1	4	300	$7,200
Manistee Skiff Works	Manistee	Manistee						
Marine City Boat Works	Marine City	St. Clair						
Marine Manufacturing Company	Detroit	Wayne	James H. House				8	$8,000
Mason, Oscar D.	Charlevoix	Charlevoix						
McDonald, George	Hubbard Lake	Alcona						
McEwen & Butler	Alanson	Emmet						
Melching, Henry W.	Harbor Springs	Emmet						
Michigan Consolidated Boat Company	Battle Creek	Calhoun		13	0	13		
Michigan Steel Boat Company [1st plant]	Detroit	Wayne	Frederick E. Wadsworth	36	2	38		
Michigan Steel Boat, Company [2nd plant]	Detroit	Wayne	Frederick E. Wadsworth	236	7	243	1,200	None given
Michigan Yacht & Power Company	Detroit	Wayne		80	2	82		

Company	City	County				Owner		
Modern Boat Pattern Company, Ltd.	Bay City	Bay	38	4	42			
Mosher, Leo	Provemont	Leelanau	2	0	2	Leo Mosher	12	$1,000
Nelson & Finch	Traverse City	Grand Traverse				Nelson & Finch	6	$1,200
Ouellette, W.J.	Bay City	Bay	3	0	3	Winslow J. Ouellette		
Parent, Frank A.	Trenton	Wayne						
Peck, L. R.	Northport	Leelanau						
Petoskey Boat Company	Petoskey	Emmet	8	0	8	Lyman R. Merrill	35	$5,000
Pungs-Finch Auto & Gas Engine Company	Detroit	Wayne						
Racine Boat Manufacturing Company	Muskegon	Muskegon	320	2	322	Walter J. Reynolds	3,005	$300,000
Randolph Copper and Steel Motor Boat Company	Detroit	Wayne						
Ranger, Roy	Charlevoix	Charlevoix						
Rankin, Ronald	St. Ignace	Mackinac						
Reade & VanDamme	Detroit	Wayne				W. W. Reade	2	$800
Renaud, Maurice	Detroit	Wayne				Maurice Renaud	2	$500
Rice Boat Works	Detroit	Wayne				Lewis J. Rice	8	$5,540
St. Joseph Boat Manufacturing Company	St. Joseph	Berrien						
Schweikart, Carl	Detroit	Wayne						
Schweikart Boat Works	Detroit	Wayne	9	0	9	John Schweikart	14	$4,500
Seidel & Mulder	Grand Rapids	Kent				Charles W. Seidel	68	$2,670
Seymour, Alfred	Detroit	Wayne						

243

Table 4. —Continued

Company name	City or village	County	Name of manager	No. of males employed	No. of females employed	Whole number	No. of boats built in 1905	Approximate value of boats built
Smith, C. C. & Company	Algonac	St. Clair	Christopher C. Smith	7	0	7	40	$9,375
Smith, George H.	Harbor Beach	Huron						
Spring Lake Clinker Boat Company	Spring Lake	Ottawa	William M. Barrett	8	0	8	9	$1,100
Stanton, Thomas W.	Traverse City	Grand Traverse						
Studer, Peter H.	Detroit	Wayne	Peter H. Studer	7	0	7	29	$55,000
Superior Launch Company	Kalamazoo	Kalamazoo						
Sweeney, Alexander	Grand Rapids	Kent						
Truscott Boat Manufacturing Company	St. Joseph	Berrien	James M. Truscott	194	10	204	600	$500,000
Washburn, William W.	Charlevoix	Charlevoix						
White Bros.	Lexington	Sanilac						
Wolverine Motor Works	Grand Rapids	Kent	Charles L. Snyder	26	0	26	11	$14,000
Wood, John W.	Three Rivers	St. Joseph						
Wright, Charles H.	Belleville	Wayne						

Notes

Chapter One

1. Brian Leigh Dunnigan, *Frontier Metropolis: Picturing Early Detroit, 1701–1838* (Detroit: Wayne State University Press, 2001).

2. Timothy J. Kent, *Birchbark Canoes of the Fur Trade* vol. 1 (Ossineke, MI: Silver Fox Enterprises, 1997), 64.

3. Ibid., 5.

4. James P. Barry, *Ships of the Great Lakes: 300 Years of Navigation* (Holt, MI: Thunder Bay Press, 1996), 15.

5. U.S. Commission of Fish and Fisheries, part 2, *Report of the Commissioner for 1872 and 1873* (Washington, DC: Government Printing Office, 1874), A—"Inquiry into the Decrease of the Food-Fishes," I.—"Report on the Fisheries of the Great Lakes: The Result of Inquiries Prosecuted in 1871 and 1872 by James W. Milner," 3–4, 13–14.

6. Ruth Robbins Montieth, *Michigan Census, 1850, Counties of Houghton, Marquette, Michilimackinac, Schoolcraft, Ontonagon* (Allegan, MI: by author, 1956), 34.

7. Jesse Wells Church Collection, GLMS-10, Historical Collections of the Great Lakes, Bowling Green State University, Folders 2 and 4.

8. William Ratigan, "Last of the Mackinaw Boat Builders," *The Boating Industry*, Vol. 21, No. 6, August 10, 1958, 52.

9. Elam E. Branch, *The History of Ionia County, Michigan* (Indianapolis: B. F. Bowen, 1916), 189–90, 213; Albert Baxter, *History of the City of Grand Rapids, Michigan* (New York and Grand Rapids: Munsell, 1891), 518.

10. Mount Clemens Public Library, *The Clinton-Kalamazoo Canal* (Mount Clemens, MI: Mount Clemens Public Library, 2008), http://www.mtclib.org/local%20 history/canal.pdf, accessed April 6, 2013.

11. Donna R. Braden, *Leisure and Entertainment in America* (Dearborn, MI: Henry Ford Museum and Greenfield Village, 1988), 9–13.

12. *Detroit Morning Tribune*, June 10, 1886, 5.

13. Frank N. Elliott, *When the Railroad Was King* (Lansing: Michigan History

Division, Michigan Department of State, 1977), 43, 45; Michigan Department of Transportation, *150 Years of Michigan's Railroad History* (Lansing: Michigan Department of Transportation, c. 1987), 9–13.

14. Jeffrey L. Rodengen, *The Legend of Chris-Craft* (Fort Lauderdale, FL: Write Stuff Syndicate, 1998), 10–13.

15. C. Kurt Dewhurst and Marsha MacDowell, *Downriver and Thumb Area Michigan Waterfowling: The Folk Arts of Nate Quillen and Otto Misch* (East Lansing: The Museum, Michigan State University, 1981), 3–6.

16. Thaddeus Norris, "The Michigan Grayling," *Scribner's Monthly*, Vol. 19, No. 1, November 1879, 17–23, Making of America Series, Cornell University digital library collection.

17. Franklin Ellis, *History of Livingston County, Michigan* (Philadelphia: Everts & Abbott, 1880), 107; U.S. Bureau of the Census, Ninth Census of the United States, 1870, Michigan, Livingston County, Cohoctah, Roll 687, 31-R; *Crawford County Avalanche* (Grayling, MI), May 12, 1881, June 5, 1884; "Extractions from the 'Avalanche,' a Crawford Co., MI, Newspaper, 1879–1940s," http://stoliker.tripod.com/pafn02.htm, accessed December 11, 2009.

18. "Extractions from the 'Avalanche'"; *Michigan Conservation*, Vol. 31, No. 3, May–June 1962, 14–16.

19. Nathaniel A. Osgood, Improvement in Portable Folding Boats, U.S. Patent 200,664, filed February 11, 1878, patented February 26, 1878; R. L. Polk & Co., *Michigan State Gazetteer and Business Directory, 1889–90* (Detroit: R. L. Polk, 1889), 277; Chadwyck-Healey, Inc., *The Sanborn Fire Insurance Maps: Battle Creek, Michigan, June 1887* (3920) (Teaneck, NJ: Chadwyck-Healey, 1983–90), Sheet 3.

20. *Brockett v. Lewis*, 144 Mich. 560, Michigan Reports, July 1906.

21. Michigan Bureau of Labor and Industrial Statistics, *Sixteenth Annual Report of the Bureau of Labor and Industrial Statistics* (Lansing: Bureau of Labor and Industrial Statistics, 1899), 73; Michigan Bureau of Labor and Industrial Statistics, *Twenty-Third Annual Report of the Bureau of Labor and Industrial Statistics* (Lansing: Bureau of Labor and Industrial Statistics, 1906), 77.

22. Ihling Bros. & Everard, *Ihling Bros. & Everard's Kalamazoo City and County Directory for the Year Ending November 1st, 1904* (Kalamazoo, MI: Ihling Bros. & Everard, 1903), 327; Michigan Department of Commerce, Corporations and Securities Division, Corporation Annual Reports, 1906, Life Saving Folding Canvas Boat Company, Archives of Michigan, RG 61-11-A, Box 129, No. 319, Reel 1463.

23. Life Saving Folding Canvas Boat Company catalog, 1906, Michigan Maritime Museum Collection.

24. Robert D. Fisher (ed.), *Marvyn Scudder Manual of Extinct or Obsolete Companies, vol. 4: 1934* (New York: Marvyn Scudder Manual of Extinct or Obsolete Companies, 1934), 1410.

25. *Detroit Free Press*, October 2, 1910, 14.

26. Cliff Warner, *Detroit Boat Club Centennial Book* (Wayne, MI: Warner, 1939?), 16.

27. Talcott E. Wing (ed.), *History of Monroe County, Michigan* (New York: Munsell, 1890), 401–2.

28. Charles Pierre Goldey, *The Sportsman's Directory and Yearbook* (New York: Pond and Goldey, 1893), 168–74.

29. George W. Hawes, *George W. Hawes' Michigan State Gazetteer and Business Directory for 1860* (Detroit: F. Raymond, 1859), 359; Charles F. Clark (comp. and pub.), *Michigan State Gazetteer and Business Directory for 1863–4* (Detroit: Charles F. Clark, 1863), 261; Montague T. Platt, *Michigan State Business Directory, 1870–71* (Detroit: Tribune Book & Job Office, 1870), 167; R. L. Polk & Co., *Michigan State Gazetteer and Business Directory, 1875* (Detroit: Tribune Printing, 1875), 345, 748.

30. Wing, *History of Monroe County, Michigan*, 391.

31. *Rudder*, Vol. 1, No. 1, May 1890, Advertising Section, 8.

32. Michigan State Board of Agriculture, *Eighteenth Annual Report of the Secretary of the State Board of Agriculture of the State of Michigan for the Year Ending August 31st, 1879* (Lansing: State Board of Agriculture, 1880), 408; Detroit International Fair and Exposition Association, *Official Catalogue of the Entries and Exhibits at the Fourth Annual Detroit International Fair and Exposition* (Detroit: Detroit International Fair and Exposition Association, 1892), 161.

33. Michigan Secretary of State, *Census of the State of Michigan, 1894: Agriculture, Manufactories, Mines and Fisheries, vol. 2* (Lansing: Secretary of State, 1896), 850.

34. Joseph Gribbins, *Wooden Boats: From Sculls to Yachts* (New York: Grove Press, 1991), 14.

35. Record Publishing Company, *Portrait and Biographical Record of Northern Michigan* (Chicago: Record Publishing, 1895), 275–76.

36. *Detroit Free Press*, February 6, 1908, 5; U.S. Bureau of the Census, *Ninth Census of the United States, 1870*, Michigan, Wayne County, City of Detroit, Tenth Ward, 372 (Washington, DC: National Archives and Records Service, General Services Administration, 1965) Roll 715, Michigan, Vol. 29 (209–508A), Wayne County (pt.) Detroit City Wards 9 and 10; J. E. Scripps and R. L. Polk (comps.), *Michigan State Gazetteer and Business Directory for 1873* (Detroit: Tribune Book and Job Office, 1873), 230, 650; R. L. Polk & Co., *Michigan State Gazetteer and Business Directory, 1879* (Detroit: R. L. Polk, 1879), 438, 1082.

37. Robert F. Eldredge, *Past and Present of Macomb County, Michigan, Together with Biographical Sketches of Many of Its Leading and Prominent Citizens and Illustrious Dead* (Chicago: S. J. Clarke, 1905), 702.

38. "Charles Plass, Designer of Keewahdin Sailboat," http://www.gwbhs.org/object/charles-plass-designer-of-keewahdin-sailboat/, accessed April 12, 2013.

39. Chapin & Brother, *Michigan State Gazetteer and Business Directory, 1867–68* (Detroit: Chapin & Brother, 1867), 52, 495; Burch & Hamilton, *Burch & Hamilton's Gazetteer of the Detroit & Milwaukee and Flint & Pere Marquette Railroads, 1870–71* (Detroit: Burch & Hamilton, 1870), 428, 431, 440; Biographical Publishing Company, *Portrait and Biographical Record of Saginaw and Bay Counties, Michigan* (Chicago: Biographical Publishing, 1892), 383–84; H. R. Page & Co., *History of Bay County, Michigan* (Chicago: H. R. Page, 1883), 206.

40. R. L. Polk & Co., *East Saginaw and Saginaw City Directory for 1886* (Detroit: R. L. Polk, 1886), 167.

41. J. H. Beers & Co., *Commemorative Biographical Record of the Upper Lake Region* (Chicago,: J. H. Beers, 1905), 91.

42. Michigan Bureau of Labor and Industrial Statistics, *First Annual Report of Inspection of Factories in Michigan* (Lansing: Bureau of Labor and Industrial Statistics, 1894), 49.

43. R. L. Polk & Co., *Michigan State Gazetteer and Business Directory, 1877* (Detroit: R. L. Polk, 1877), 274, 327, 873; *Detroit Free Press*, May 12, 1878, 3.

44. Richard Edwards (comp.), *Industries of Michigan: City of Detroit, Historical and Descriptive Review—Industries, Institutions, Commercial, and Manufacturing Advantages, 1880* (New York: Historical Publishing, 1880), 190; *Detroit Free Press*, September 1, 1880, 8.

45. U.S. Coast Guard and U.S. Life-Saving Service, *Annual Report of the Operations of the United States Life-Saving Service for the Fiscal Year Ending June 30, 1883* (Washington, DC: Government Printing Office, 1884), Addenda 1, "Daily Record of the Proceedings of the Board, September 3, 1883," 417, 496–97.

46. R. L. Polk & Co., *Michigan State Gazetteer and Business Directory, 1881* (Detroit: R. L. Polk, 1881), 362, 443, 1157; R. L. Polk & Co., *Michigan State Gazetteer and Business Directory, 1883* (Detroit: R. L. Polk, 1883), 480, 611, 1517.

47. *Detroit Free Press*, December 24, 1883, 6.

48. *Detroit Free Press*, October 21, 1884, 8; R. L. Polk & Co., *Michigan State Gazetteer and Business Directory, 1885* (Detroit: R. L. Polk, 1885), 538, 597, 1629.

49. R. L. Polk & Co., *Michigan State Gazetteer and Business Directory, 1891–92* (Detroit: R. L. Polk, 1891), 484, 595, 1606.

50. Michigan Bureau of Labor and Industrial Statistics, *Third Annual Report of Inspection of Factories in Michigan* (Lansing: Bureau of Labor and Industrial Statistics, 1896), 16–17; Michigan Death Certificates, 1897–1920, James Dean, Wayne County, 1905, No. 579, www.seekingmichigan.org, accessed November 23, 2009; R. L. Polk & Co., *R. L. Polk & Co.'s Detroit City Directory, 1906–1907* (Detroit: R. L. Polk, 1906), 3159.

51. R. L. Polk & Co., *Michigan State Gazetteer and Business Directory, 1887* (Detroit: R. L. Polk, 1887), 526, 1728.

52. R. L. Polk & Co., *Michigan State Gazetteer and Business Directory, 1891* (Detroit: R. L. Polk, 1891), 486, 1606.

53. *Detroit Free Press*, May 15, 1892, 7.

54. *Detroit Free Press*, June 10, 1890, 7; Bowling Green State University, Historical Collections of the Great Lakes, Great Lakes Vessels Index, *Helen*, US96290; Bowling Green State University, Historical Collections of the Great Lakes, Great Lakes Vessels Index, *Cynthia*, US127106.

55. *Detroit Free Press*, July 14, 1891, 3; August 11, 1891, 2.

56. *Detroit Free Press*, November 29, 1891, 6; April 30, 1892, 6.

57. Gary W. McCue, "The Baker Boat," http://www.geocities.ws/gwmccue/Competition/Baker.html, accessed April 10, 2013.

58. *St. Lawrence Republican* (New York), March 8, 1893, 3.

59. Michigan Bureau of Labor and Industrial Statistics, *First Annual Report of Inspection of Factories in Michigan* (Lansing: Bureau of Labor and Industrial Statistics, 1894), 11; Michigan Bureau of Labor and Industrial Statistics, *Third Annual Report of Inspection of Factories in Michigan* (Lansing: Bureau of Labor and Industrial Statistics, 1896), Inspection Book No. 1, p. 4.

60. *Detroit Free Press*, January 21, 1900, 11; Robert D. Fisher (ed.), *Marvyn Scudder Manual of Extinct or Obsolete Companies, vol. 3: 1930* (New York: Marvyn Scudder Manual of Extinct or Obsolete Companies, 1930), 516; *Detroit Free Press*, October 24, 1901, 10.

61. *Detroit Evening News*, March 26, 1901, 9.

62. Rogers & Thorpe, *Detroit in History and Commerce* (Detroit: Rogers & Thorpe, 1891), 156–57.

63. Evening News Association, *Quarterly Register of Current History*, Vol. 2, No. 6, May 1892, ii.

64. *Detroit Free Press*, January 15, 1893, 24; *Detroit Free Press*, April 16, 1893, 7; *Detroit Free Press*, November 15, 1893, 8; *Detroit Free Press*, February 1, 1894, 5; Michigan Bureau of Labor and Industrial Statistics, *First Annual Report of Inspection of Factories in Michigan* (Lansing: Bureau of Labor and Industrial Statistics, 1894), 13.

65. Michigan Department of Commerce, Corporations and Securities Commission, Abstracts of Reports of Corporations, Lot 3, Vol. 3 (1899–1904), Archives of Michigan, RG 61-11, 280; Fisher, *Marvyn Scudder Manual of Extinct or Obsolete Companies*, vol. 3: 1930, 1467.

66. Robert B. Ross and George B. Catlin, revised by Clarence W. [*sic*] Burton, *Landmarks of Detroit, Michigan: A History of the City* (Detroit: Evening News Association, 1898), 683–84.

67. H. R. Page & Co., *The Traverse Region, Historical and Descriptive . . .* (Chicago: H. R. Page, 1884), 196.

68. Michigan Secretary of State, *Census of the State of Michigan, 1884, vol. 2: Agriculture and Manufactories* (Lansing: Secretary of State, 1886), 392; Michigan Secretary of State, *Census of the State of Michigan, 1894: Agriculture, Manufactories, Mines, and Fisheries*, vol. 2 (Lansing: Secretary of State, 1896), 850.

69. Announcement, Rescue Life Boat Company, Muskegon, MI, Rescue Life Boat Company, 1900?, Library of Michigan. Rare Book Collection.

70. Edwin Verburg, Boat, U.S. Patent 597,595, filed June 9, 1897, issued January 18, 1898.

Chapter Two

1. Stan Grayson, *Engines Afloat: From Early Days to D-Day*, vol. 1, *The Gasoline Era* (Marblehead, MA: Devereux Books, 1999), x–xi, 1–8.

2. *Detroit Free Press*, July 9, 1905, part 4, 5.

3. D. W. Fostle, *Speedboat* (Mystic, CT: Mystic Seaport Museum Stores, 1988), 13.

4. *Scientific American*, Vol. 77, No. 1, January 1, 1898, 13.

5. Grayson, *Engines Afloat*, 1:10.

6. *Detroit Free Press*, August 11, 1891, 2; Stan Grayson, *Beautiful Engines: Treasures of the Internal Combustion Century* (Marblehead, MA: Devereux Books, 2001), 37.

7. Stan Grayson, "Time Machine: Exploring America's Oldest Marine Engine," *WoodenBoat*, No. 213, March–April 2010, 62–69.

8. *Scientific American*, Vol. 45, No. 20, November 14, 1891, 316.

9. Michigan Department of Commerce, Corporation and Securities Division, Corporation Annual Reports, Sintz Gas Engine Company Corporation Annual Report, 1894, Archives of Michigan, RG 61-11-A, Box 32, Vol. 1, No. 42, Reel 1353.

10. Michigan Bureau of Labor and Industrial Statistics, *First Annual Report of In-*

spection of Factories in Michigan (Lansing: Michigan Bureau of Labor and Industrial Statistics, 1894), table 1, inspection no. 1286, 27; Michael M. Dixon, *Motormen and Yachting: The Waterfront Heritage of the Automobile Industry* (St. Clair Shores, MI: Mervue Publications, 2005), 91.

11. Robert D. Fisher (ed.), *Marvyn Scudder Manual of Extinct or Obsolete Companies*, vol. 3, 1930 (New York: Marvyn Scudder Manual of Extinct or Obsolete Companies 1930), 1259.

12. R. L. Polk & Co., *R. L. Polk & Co.'s Grand Rapids City Directory, 1900* (Grand Rapids, MI: Grand Rapids Directory Co., 1900), 580.

13. Grayson, *Beautiful Engines*, 37; Grayson, *Engines Afloat*, 1:14–15; Dixon, *Motormen and Yachting*, 93–98; R. L. Polk & Co., *Michigan State Gazetteer and Business Directory, 1897* (Detroit: R. L. Polk, 1897), 891, 1722; R. L. Polk & Co., *Michigan State Gazetteer and Business Directory, 1899* (Detroit: R. L. Polk, 1899), 905, 1741; R. L. Polk & Co., *Michigan State Gazetteer and Business Directory, 1901* (Detroit: R. L. Polk, 1901), 885, 939, 994, 1780.

14. Michigan Bureau of Labor and Industrial Statistics, *Twenty-Third Annual Report of the Bureau of Labor and Industrial Statistics* (Lansing: Bureau of Labor and Industrial Statistics, 1906), 373; R. L. Polk & Co., *Michigan State Gazetteer and Business Directory, 1903–1904* (Detroit: R. L. Polk, 1903), 895, 1810.

15. Dixon, *Motormen and Yachting*, 96–99.

16. H. G. Diefendorf, "The Extent of the Marine Gasoline Engine Business," *Gas Power*, Vol. 9, No. 2, August 1911, 60.

17. *Horseless Age*, Vol. 5, No. 25, March 21, 1900, 14; Fisher, *Marvyn Scudder Manual of Extinct or Obsolete Companies*, 3:966.

18. Dixon, *Motormen and Yachting*, 99–103.

19. *Marine Engineering*, Vol. 5, No. 4, April 1900, 150–54; Lloyd's Register of American Yachts, 1903, *Amalie*, Annual No. 38, 52.

20. Dixon, *Motormen and Yachting*, 103–11.

21. Helen Jones Earley and James R. Walkinshaw, *Setting the Pace: Oldsmobile's First Hundred Years* (Lansing, MI: Oldsmobile Division of General Motors, 1996), 25, 29.

22. Michigan Department of Commerce, Corporations and Securities Commission, Michigan Yacht & Power Company Corporation Annual Report, 1900, Archives of Michigan, RG 61-11-A, Box 67, Vol. 1, No. 220, Reel 1384.

23. Albert Nelson Marquis (ed.), *The Book of Detroiters*, 2nd ed. (Chicago: A. N. Marquis & Co., 1914), 360, 39899.

24. *Detroit Free Press*, January 21, 1900, 11.

25. Dixon, *Motormen and Yachting*, 106.

26. Michigan Bureau of Labor and Industrial Statistics, *Eighteenth Annual Report of the Bureau of Labor and Industrial Statistics* (Lansing: Michigan Bureau of Labor and Industrial Statistics, 1901), 24, 46.

27. Lloyd's Register of Shipping, *Lloyd's Register of American Yachts, 1907* (New York: Lloyd's Register of Shipping, 1907), 61, Annual no. 301, and 109, Annual No. 1013; Lloyd's Register of Shipping, *Lloyd's Register of American Yachts, 1903* (New York: Lloyd's Register of Shipping, 1903), 101, Annual No. 480, and 138, Annual No. 817; *Detroit Free Press*, June 4, 1901, 10–11; *Detroit Free Press*, April 12, 1903, A5.

28. Fisher, *Marvyn Scudder Manual of Extinct or Obsolete Companies*, 3:945.

29. *Rudder*, Vol. 12, No. 5, May 1901, 246.

30. Albert Stegmeyer, Detroit, Michigan, to the Buick Manufacturing Company, Detroit, Michigan, November 30, 1901, collection of Terry B. Dunham, quoted in Dixon, *Motormen and Yachting*, 131.

31. Penton Publishing Co., *The American Boating Directory, 1906* (Cleveland: Penton Publishing, 1906), 13–14.

32. Marquis, *The Book of Detroiters*, 65–66.

33. Frederick Stonehouse, *Wreck Ashore: The United States Life-Saving Service on the Great Lakes* (Duluth, MN: Lake Superior Port Cities, 1994), 108–11; Tim Dring, "Summary of the Development of Early Motorized Lifeboats for the USLSS and USCG," U.S. Coast Guard History Program, http://www.uscg.mil/history/articles/DringDevelopmentEarlyMotorizedLifeboats.pdf, accessed March 22, 2012.

34. C. H. Blomstrom Motor Company, *The C. H. Blomstrom Motor Company: Builders of Gasoline Launches, Marine Gasoline Engines, Solid and Reversing Propeller Wheels* (catalog) (Detroit: C. H. Blomstrom Motor Co., 1903?), Library of Michigan, Rare Book Collection; Michigan Bureau of Labor and Industrial Statistics, *Twenty-Third Annual Report of the Bureau of Labor and Industrial Statistics* (Lansing: Bureau of Labor and Industrial Statistics, 1906), 373, 375.

35. *Sail and Sweep*, Vol. 3, No. 1, January 1904, 40–41.

36. R. L. Polk & Co., *Detroit City Directory for 1889* (Detroit: R. L. Polk, 1889), 1096.

37. *Detroit Free Press*, July 25, 1899, 6; November 4, 1900, B3.

38. *Michigan Investor*, Vol. 2, No. 15, January 9, 1904, 8.

39. Ohio Secretary of State, *Annual Report of the Secretary of State to the Governor of the State of Ohio, for the Year Ending Nov. 15, 1904* (Springfield, OH: Secretary of State, 1905), 857.

40. R. L. Polk & Co., *Michigan State Gazetteer and Business Directory, 1909–1910* (Detroit: R. L. Polk, 1909), 698, 2318; R. L. Polk & Co., *Detroit City Directory, 1909* (Detroit: R. L. Polk, 1909), 791, 1362, 1895, 1728, 2825; R. L. Polk & Co., *Michigan State Gazetteer and Business Directory, 1911–1912* (Detroit: R. L. Polk, 1911), 695, 2167; Michigan, Corporation and Securities Division, Abstracts of Reports of Corporations, Lot 3, Vol. 4 (1903–1909), 431, Archives of Michigan, RG 61-11; Michigan, Corporation and Securities Division, Abstracts of Reports of Corporations, Lot 3, Vol. 5 (1910–1914), 478, Archives of Michigan, RG 61-11; Fisher, *Marvyn Scudder Manual of Extinct or Obsolete Companies*, 3:1145.

41. Julius Frederick Stone, *Canyon Country: The Romance of a Drop of Water and a Grain of Sand* (New York: G. P. Putnam, 1932), 45–107; William C. Suran, "With the Wings of an Angel: A Biography of Ellsworth and Emery Kolb, Photographers of Grand Canyon," manuscript, 1991, chap. 2, p. 3, http://www.grandcanyonhistory.org/Publications/Kolb/kolb.html, accessed April 17, 2013.

42. *Detroit Free Press*, October 2, 1910, 14.

43. *Detroit Free Press*, July 13, 1896, 3.

44. "Racine Boat Manufacturing Company," http://www.coachbuilt.com/bui/r/racine_boat/racine_boat.htm, accessed March 28, 2012.

45. *Michigan Investor*, Vol. 3, No. 52, September 30, 1905, 14; Vol. 6, No. 31, May 9, 1908, 12.

46. *Muskegon Chronicle*, September 27, 1952, sec. 3, 5.

47. *Marine Review*, Vol. 19, No. 2, January 12, 1899, 35.

48. *Heritage Journal, the Newsletter of the Fort Miami Heritage Society*, Vol. 4, No. 2, Summer 2004, 6–7.

49. Sanborn Map Company, *Sanborn Fire Insurance Maps, Michigan* (Teaneck, NJ: Chadwyck-Healey, 1983–90), St. Joseph, Michigan (4184), Aug. 1892, 6; Oct. 1896, 5; July 1902, 9.

50. Penton Publishing Company, *The American Boating Directory, 1906* (Cleveland: Penton Publishing, 1906), 7.

51. Sanborn Map Company, *Sanborn Fire Insurance Maps, Michigan*, Wyandotte, Michigan (4238), April 1895, July 1900.

52. Truscott Boat Manufacturing Company Catalog, January 1898, Library of Michigan, Rare Book Collection; Truscott Boat Manufacturing Company, Advance Catalogue, 1905, reprinted by the Vestal Press, Vestal, New York (n.d., c. 1982), from an original in the collection of Carl Fila.

53. *Michigan Investor*, Vol. 2, No. 48, September 3, 1904, 14; Vol. 3, No. 9, December 3, 1904, 7.

54. U.S. Department of the Interior, U.S. Census Office, *Twelfth Census of the United States Taken in the Year 1900: Census Reports, vol. 10, Manufactures, part 4, Special Reports on Selected Industries (Continued)* (Washington, DC: U.S. Census Office, 1902), table 17, "Establishments Engaged in the Construction and Repair of Small Boats, with Capital and Value of Products, by States: 1900," 226; table 20, "Small Boats, by States: 1900," 227.

55. U.S. Department of Commerce and Labor, Bureau of the Census, *Manufactures, 1905, part 4, Special Reports on Selected Industries* (Washington, DC: Government Printing Office, 1908), table 26, "Number and Value of Boats under Five Tons, by States: 1905 and 1900," 342.

56. Michigan Secretary of State, *Census of the State of Michigan, 1894, Agricultural, Manufactories, Mines, and Fisheries*, vol. 2 (Lansing: Secretary of State, 1896), 850.

57. Michigan Bureau of Labor and Industrial Statistics, *Third Annual Report of Inspection of Factories in Michigan* (Lansing: Bureau of Labor and Industrial Statistics, 1896), 16–17, 30–31, 38–39, 74–75, 156–57.

58. Michigan Bureau of Labor and Industrial Statistics, *Fifth Annual Report of Inspection of Factories in Michigan* (Lansing: Bureau of Labor and Industrial Statistics, 1898), 40, 86; Michigan Bureau of Labor and Industrial Statistics, *Sixteenth Annual Report of the Bureau of Labor and Industrial Statistics* (Lansing: Bureau of Labor and Industrial Statistics, 1899), 78; Michigan Bureau of Labor and Industrial Statistics, *Seventeenth Annual Report of the Bureau of Labor and Industrial Statistics* (Lansing: Bureau of Labor and Industrial Statistics, 1900), 61, 66; Michigan Bureau of Labor and Industrial Statistics, *Eighteenth Annual Report of the Bureau of Labor and Industrial Statistics* (Lansing: Bureau of Labor and Industrial Statistics, 1901), 24, 78.

59. *St. Joseph Saturday Herald*, July 28, 1900, 5.

60. *St. Joseph Saturday Herald*, December 1, 1900, 5.

61. Michigan Bureau of Labor and Industrial Statistics, *Twentieth Annual Report of the Bureau of Labor and Industrial Statistics* (Lansing: Bureau of Labor and Industrial Statistics, 1903), 213.

Chapter Three

1. *Motor Boat*, Vol. 2, No. 1, January 10, 1905, 24; *Michigan Investor*, Vol. 2, No. 2, September 26, 1903, 10.

2. *Business Man's Magazine*, Vol. 19, No. 10, April 1907, 71–76.

3. Bernard A. Weisberger, *The Dream Maker: William C. Durant, Founder of General Motors* (Boston: Little, Brown, 1979), 139, citing Lawrence H. Seltzer, *A Financial History of the American Automobile Industry* (Boston, H. Mifflin, 1928), 157.

4. *Michigan Manufacturer*, Vol. 7, No. 12, September 16, 1911, 2.

5. Poor's Railroad Manual Co., *Poor's Manual of Industrials, 1913* (New York: Poor's Railroad Manual Co., 1913), 1721–22.

6. Willard Flint, *Lightships of the United States Government: Reference Notes* (Washington, DC: U.S. Coast Guard Historian's Office, 1989), LV82, LV95.

7. *Michigan Manufacturer and Financial Record*, Vol. 17, No. 16, April 15, 1916, 18.

8. *Gas Power*, Vol. 10, No. 11, May 1913, 106.

9. R. L. Polk & Co., *Michigan State Gazetteer and Business Directory, 1901* (Detroit: R. L. Polk, 1901), 1100, 1780.

10. Arthur E. Chambers, Boat, U.S. Patent 681,363, filed March 26, 1900, patented August 27, 1901.

11. *Detroit Free Press*, December 30, 1901, 3; September 27, 1905, 1.

12. Helen Jones Earley and James R. Walkinshaw, *Setting the Pace: Oldsmobile's First Hundred Years* (Lansing, MI: Oldsmobile Division of General Motors, 1996), 51; *Detroit Evening News*, January 12, 1902, part 2, 14; "Detroit Boat Company," http://www.antiquengines.com/DBC_Literature.htm, accessed July 4, 2012; *Detroit Free Press*, September 27, 1905, 1.

13. Joseph J. Schroeder Jr., *Sears, Roebuck & Co. 1908 Catalogue, No. 117, the Great Price Maker* (Northfield, IL: DBI Books, 1971), 756.

14. Michigan, Bureau of Labor and Industrial Statistics, *Twenty-Third Annual Report of the Bureau of Labor and Industrial Statistics* (Lansing: Bureau of Labor and Industrial Statistics, 1906), 373, 375.

15. *New York Times*, February 24, 1910, 11.

16. *Dun's Review*, Vol. 16, No. 6, February 1911, 63.

17. Robert D. Fisher (ed.), *Marvyn Scudder Manual of Extinct or Obsolete Companies, vol. 3, 1930* (New York: Marvyn Scudder Manual of Extinct or Obsolete Companies, 1930), 944.

18. Wadsworth Manufacturing Company, http://www.coachbuilt.com/bui/w/wadsworth/wadsworth.htm, accessed July 10, 2012.

19. *Michigan Investor*, Vol. 5, No. 10, December 8, 1906, 18; Vol. 5, No. 14, January 5, 1907, 3; Vol. 5, No. 16, January 19, 1907, 11; Vol. 6, No. 37, June 20, 1908, 17.

20. *Michigan Investor*, Vol. 3, No. 17, January 28, 1905, 9; Fisher, *Marvyn Scudder Manual of Extinct or Obsolete Companies*, 3:1214.

21. *Michigan Investor*, Vol. 4, No. 5, November 4, 1905, 14; *Michigan Investor*, Vol. 4, No. 9, December 2, 1905, 15; *Automobile*, Vol. 13, No. 22, November 30, 1905, 618; *Michigan Investor*, Vol. 5, No. 16, January 19, 1907, 2; *Michigan Investor*, Vol. 6, No. 11, December 14, 1907, 23; *Power Boating*, Vol. 3, No. 12, December 1908, 63;

Foote v. Greilick, 166 Mich. 636, Supreme Court of Michigan, September 29, 1911, 132 NW 473.

22. Matthew J. Friday, *The Inland Water Route* (Mount Pleasant, SC: Arcadia Publishing, 2010), 34–35; *Michigan Investor*, Vol. 6, No. 34, May 30, 1908, 3; *Northern Michigan Skipper*, July 1957, 3, 21.

23. Jeffrey L. Rodengen, *The Legend of Chris-Craft* (Fort Lauderdale, FL: Write Stuff Syndicate, 1998), 25–29; Anthony Mollica Jr. and Jack Savage, *Chris-Craft Boats* (St. Paul, MN: MBI Publishing, 2001), 12–13.

24. D. W. Fostle, *Speedboat* (Mystic, CT: Mystic Seaport Museum Store, 1988), 99.

25. *Motor Way*, Vol. 17, No. 3, April 1907, 42; *Motor World*, Vol. 24, No. 3, July 21, 1910, 160; *Motor World*, Vol. 25, No. 6, November 10, 1910, 365; Max F. Homfeld, *753 Manufacturers of Inboard Marine Engines* (St. Michaels, MD: Max F. Homfeld, 1991), 1; Howard A. Pike, *How to Build an 18-Ft. Launch* (Detroit: Belle Isle Motor Company, 1907), Library of Michigan, Rare Book Collection.

26. *Michigan Manufacturer*, Vol. 6, No. 13, January 28, 1911, 3.

27. *Fore 'N' Aft*, Vol. 3, No. 2, July 1907, 69.

28. Ibid.; *Motor Boat*, Vol. 5, No. 10, May 25, 1908, 52; Michigan Bureau of Labor and Industrial Statistics, *Twenty-Sixth Annual Report of the Bureau of Labor and Industrial Statistics* (Lansing: Bureau of Labor and Industrial Statistics, 1909), 239.

29. *Michigan Manufacturer*, Vol. 6, No. 19, March 11, 1911, 11; James P. Barry, *Hackercraft* (St. Paul, MN: MBI Publishing, 2002), 14.

30. Barry, Hackercraft, 14.

31. Fostle, *Speedboat*, 99; Stan Grayson, "The Man from Motor Boat Lane: Joe Van Blerck and the Van Blerck Motor Company," *WoodenBoat*, No. 197, July–August 2007, 82.

32. Chad E. Mayea, *Since the Beginning: Mayea Boats* (Fairhaven, MI: by author, 2005), 24–25.

33. Ron Bloomfield for the Bay County Historical Society, *Maritime Bay County* (Charleston, SC: Arcadia Publishing, 2009), 7–8.

34. Edgar Werner Coleman, *Advertising Development: A Brief Review of and Commentary upon Various Phases of Advertising Development as influenced by the Advertising Manager and Advertising Agent as Factors in Creating National and International Markets for American Products* (Milwaukee: by author, 1909), 74–75; Robert Schweitzer and Michael W. R. Davis, *America's Favorite Homes: Mail-Order Catalogues as a Guide to Popular Early 20th-Century Houses* (Detroit: Wayne State University Press, 1990), 82; *Michigan Investor*, Vol. 2, No. 48, September 3, 1904, 13.

35. Michigan, Department of Commerce, Corporations and Securities Commission, Brooks Boat Manufacturing Company Corporation Annual Report, 1903, Archives of Michigan, RG 61-11, Box 91, No. 150, Reel 1409; R. L. Polk & Co., *Bay City Directory, 1902–1903* (Detroit: R. L. Polk, 1902), 145, 418, 533.

36. Postcards of catalogue orders, Brooks Boat Manufacturing Company, 1905–1908, Bay County Historical Society, Historical Museum of Bay County, Accession No. 89-93.1-.15; *Scientific American*, Vol. 88, No.14, April 4, 1903, 250.

37. *Michigan Investor*, Vol. 2, No. 48, September 3, 1904, 13.

38. Michigan Bureau of Labor and Industrial Statistics, *Twenty-Third Annual Re-

port of the Bureau of Labor and Industrial Statistics (Lansing: Bureau of Labor and Industrial Statistics, 1906), 373, 375.

39. *Motor Boat*, Vol. 3, No. 14, July 25, 1906, 65.

40. Coleman, *Advertising Development*, 74–75.

41. R. L. Polk & Co., *Michigan State Gazetteer and Business Directory, 1905–06* (Detroit: R. L. Polk & Co., 1905), 402, 1973; *Iron Age*, Vol. 74, August 25, 1904, 25.

42. R. L. Polk & Co., *Michigan State Gazetteer and Business Directory, 1905–06*, 402, 1973; R. L. Polk & Co., *R. L. Polk & Co.'s Bay City Directory, Year Ending October 15, 1906* (Detroit: R. L. Polk, 1905), 532, 807; *Motor Boat*, Vol. 2, No. 23, December 10, 1905, 75; Archives of Michigan, Abstracts of Reports of Corporations, RG 61-11, Lot 3, Vol. 4 (1903–1909), 613; Michigan Bureau of Labor and Industrial Statistics, *Twenty-Third Annual Report of the Bureau of Labor and Industrial Statistics* (Lansing: Bureau of Labor and Industrial Statistics, 1906), 39; Fisher, *Marvyn Scudder Manual of Extinct or Obsolete Companies*, 962.

43. Michigan Department of Commerce, Corporations and Securities Commission. Pioneer Boat & Pattern Co. Corporation Annual Report, 1906, Archives of Michigan, RG 61-11-A, Box 131, Vol. 1, No. 354, Reel 1466.

44. Michigan Bureau of Labor and Industrial Statistics, *Twenty-Fifth Annual Report of the Bureau of Labor and Industrial Statistics, 1908* (Lansing: Bureau of Labor and Industrial Statistics, 1908), 32.

45. Bloomfield, *Maritime Bay County*, 68–70.

46. *Power Boating*, Vol. 4, No. 3, March 1908, 152, Advertising Section, 25.

47. Schweitzer and Davis, *America's Favorite Homes*, 81–82.

48. Coleman, *Advertising Development*, 74–75.

49. *Detroit Free Press*, August 14, 1905, 7; October 8, 1906, 9.

50. R. L. Polk & Co., *Polk's Saginaw City Directory, 1921–1943*, various annual issues.

51. *Saginaw News*, July 2, 1941, part 2, 13.

52. *Motor Boat*, Vol. 6, No. 23, December 10, 1909, 220; Vol. 5, No. 7, April 10, 1908, 74.

53. *Michigan Investor*, Vol. 8, No. 16, January 22, 1910, 11; *Michigan Investor*, Vol. 10, No. 2, October 21, 1911, 7; *Michigan Investor*, Vol. 10, No. 21, March 2, 1912, 16; Bruce Hall, "Valley Boat & Engine Company of Baldwinsville, NY," *Brightwork*, newsletter of the Finger Lakes Chapter of the Antique & Classic Boat Society, December 2000, 5-6.

54. University of Michigan, Department of Engineering, "General Announcement of Courses in Engineering and Architecture, 1913–1917," *University Bulletin*, new series, Vol. 14, No. 18, April 1913, 317; James Cooke Mills, *History of Saginaw County, Michigan: Historical, Commercial, Biographical, Profusely Illustrated with Portraits of Early Pioneers, Rare Pictures and Scenes of Olden Times, and Portraits of Representative Citizens of Today* (Saginaw: Seemann & Peters, 1918), 160.

55. Beverly Rae Kimes et al., *Standard Catalog of American Cars, 1895–1942* (Iola, WI: Krause Publications, 1996), 1318.

56. *Michigan Investor*, Vol. 18, No. 14, November 15, 1919, 3; *Michigan Manufacturer and Financial Record*, Vol. 33, No. 20, May 17, 1924, 28.

57. *Forest and Stream*, Vol. 48, No. 6, February 6, 1897, 120; *Marine Engineering*, Vol. 2, No. 1, January 1898, 34.

58. *Power Boating*, Vol. 4, No. 3, March 1908, Advertising Section, 25; *Popular Mechanics*, May 1908, Advertising Section.

59. *Power Boating*, Vol. 4, No. 3, March 1908, 152.

60. *Sail and Sweep*, Vol. 3, No. 11, November 1904, 529–30.

61. R. L. Polk & Co., *Michigan State Gazetteer and Business Directory, 1931–1932* (Detroit: R. L. Polk, 1931), 146, 1649.

62. Bloomfield, *Maritime Bay County*, 69.

63. *Michigan Sportsman*, Vol. 4, No. 1, July 1917, 44; R. L. Polk & Co., *Polk's Saginaw City Directory, 1941* (Detroit: R. L. Polk, 1941), 161, 682; R. L. Polk & Co., *Polk's Saginaw City Directory, 1950* (Detroit: R. L. Polk & Co., 1950), 177, 764.

64. *Michigan Manufacturer and Financial Record*, Vol. 53, No. 19, May 12, 1934, 10.

65. Peter Hunn, *The Old Outboard Book* (Camden, ME: International Marine and Ragged Mountain Press, 1994), 3–5.

66. Grosse Ile Historical Society, Cameron D. Waterman file, cited in "Scream and Fly Powerboats and High Performance Powerboating Discussion Forums>Main>Outboard and Racing History>where was the outboard invented U ask," Scream and Fly, www.screamandfly.com/archive/index.php/t-25897.html, accessed April 16, 2013.

67. Hunn, *The Old Outboard Book*, 5–7.

68. Hu Maxwell, *Wood-Using Industries of Michigan* (Lansing: Michigan Public Domain Commission, State Land Office, 1912), 54–55.

69. Gilbert C. Klingel, *Boatbuilding with Steel* (Camden, ME: International Marine Publishing, 1973), 16–28.

70. Frank Passic, "Darrow Boats Once Made in Albion," *Albion Recorder*, April 12, 1999, 4, http://www.albionmich.com/history/histor_notebook/R990412.shtml, accessed June 28, 2013; Darrow Steel Boat Company, Inc., *The Darrow Boat Book* (Albion, MI: Darrow Steel Boat Co., 1926).

71. Michigan Department of Labor, *First Annual Report of the Department of Labor of the State of Michigan* (Lansing: Department of Labor, 1910), 105.

72. Walter Smith Miscellaneous Ship Drawing Collection, Kingsbury, S. B., Naval Architect—Designs, GLMS-74 mf, Historical Collections of the Great Lakes, Bowling Green State University, Bowling Green, Ohio; *Michigan Alumnus* (University of Michigan), Vol. 22, No. 214, May 1916, 441.

73. Charles Moore, *History of Michigan*, vol. 2 (Chicago: Lewis Publishing, 1915), 1064–65; *Ludington Chronicle*, November 24, 1909, 1.

Chapter Four

1. *Michigan Manufacturer and Financial Record*, Vol. 19, No. 14, March 31, 1917, 21.

2. *Michigan Manufacturer and Financial Record*, Vol. 20, No. 6, August 11, 1917, 12.

3. Navy Department, Construction and Repair Bureau, *Ships' Data, U.S. Naval*

Vessels, November 1, 1918 (Washington, DC: Government Printing Office, 1919), 368–73, entry 213.

4. *Michigan Manufacturer and Financial Record*, Vol. 20, No. 5, August 4, 1917, 30.

5. U.S. Congress, Senate, Committee on Military Affairs, "Aircraft Production: Hearings," Sixty-Fifth Congress, 2nd session, parts 1 and 2, (Washington, DC: Government Printing Office, 1918), 676.

6. U.S. Congress, Public Act 254, Revenue Act of 1918, Sixty-Fifth Congress, section 900, subsection 20, and section 1003.

7. *Michigan Manufacturer and Financial Record*, Vol. 20, No. 3, July 21, 1917, 17; Vol. 21, No. 18, May 4, 1918, 12; Vol. 22, No. 19, November 9, 1918, 37.

8. *Michigan Manufacturer and Financial Record*, Vol. 21, No. 21, May 25, 1918, 39.

9. *Michigan Manufacturer and Financial Record*, Vol. 22, No. 12, September 21, 1918, 45.

10. *Michigan Manufacturer and Financial Record*, Vol. 22, No. 2, July 13, 1918, 38.

11. Ibid., 42.

12. *Michigan Manufacturer and Financial Record*, Vol. 22, No. 21, November 23, 1918, 19.

13. *Michigan Manufacturer and Financial Record*, Vol. 20, No. 5, August 4, 1917, 8.

14. *Michigan Manufacturer and Financial Record*, Vol. 19, No. 12, March 17, 1917, 17.

15. *Michigan Manufacturer and Financial Record*, Vol. 22, No. 13, September 28, 1918, 39.

16. Peter Van Der Linden, "The Art of Ship Repair . . . McLouth of Marine City," *Telescope*, May–June 1976, 69; *Popular Mechanics*, Vol. 38, No. 3, September 1922, 165.

17. R. L. Polk & Co., *Michigan State Gazetteer and Business Directory, 1917* (Detroit: R. L. Polk, 1917), 2022; R. L. Polk & Co., *Michigan State Gazetteer and Business Directory, 1923* (Detroit: R. L. Polk, 1923), 2001–2; *Michigan Manufacturer and Financial Record*, Vol. 28, No. 1, July 2, 1921, 35.

18. Allan Nevins and Frank Ernest Hill, *Ford: Expansion and Challenge, 1915–1933* (New York: Charles Scribner's Sons, 1957), 68–71.

19. David A. Hounshell, "Ford Eagle Boats and Mass Production during World War I," in *Military Enterprise and Technological Change: Perspectives on the American Experience*, ed. Merritt Roe Smith (Cambridge: Massachusetts Institute of Technology Press, 1985), 175–202.

20. Randy Leffingwell, *Ford Farm Tractors* (Osceola, WI: MBI Publishing, 1998), 72.

21. *Michigan Manufacturer and Financial Record*, Vol. 35, No. 20, May 16, 1925, 20; *Motor Boat*, Vol. 17, No. 1, January 10, 1920, 36.

22. D. W. Fostle, *Speedboat* (Mystic, CT: Mystic Seaport Museum Stores, 1988), 120–22.

23. Anthony S. Mollica Jr., *Gar Wood Boats: Classics of a Golden Era* (Osceola, WI: MBI Publishing, 1999), 17.

24. Philip P. Mason, *Rumrunning and the Roaring Twenties: Prohibition on the Michigan-Ontario Waterway* (Detroit: Wayne State University Press, 1995), 39.

25. Andrew Lefebvre, "Prohibition and the Smuggling of Intoxicating Liquors between the Two Saults," *Northern Mariner*, Vol. 11, No. 3, July 2001, 33–40, http://www.cnrs-scrn.org/northern_mariner/vol11/nm_11_3_33to40.pdf, accessed September 1, 2012.

26. Paul R. Kavieff, *Detroit's Infamous Purple Gang* (Charleston, SC: Arcadia Publishing, 2008), 19.

27. Chad E. Mayea, *Since the Beginning: Mayea Boats* (Fairhaven, MI: by author, 2005), 42.

28. Larry Engelmann, *Intemperance: The Lost War against Liquor* (New York: Free Press, 1979), 84.

29. James P. Barry, *American Powerboats: The Great Lakes Golden Years* (St. Paul, MN: MBI Publishing, 2003), 82.

30. Fostle, *Speedboat*, 133, 138.

31. *State Trooper*, Vol. 5, No. 10, June 1924, 1.

32. Engelmann, *Intemperance*, 82–83.

33. Ibid., 80–81.

34. Scott M. Peters, "Roar on the Water: Gar Wood Searches for Speed," *Michigan History*, Vol. 81, No. 5, September–October 1997, 64.

35. Mollica, *Gar Wood Boats*, 13–14.

36. Ibid., 25–26.

37. Ibid., 25, 27.

38. J. Lee Barrett, *Speed Boat Kings: 25 Years of International Speedboating* (Ann Arbor: Historical Society of Michigan; Berrien Springs, MI: Hardscrabble Press, 1986), 69–76, reprint of the 1939 edition published by Arnold-Powers, Inc.

39. Fostle, *Speedboat*, 168–69.

40. Peters, "Roar on the Water," 67.

41. "Gar Wood's Mystery Boat," *Popular Mechanics*, Vol. 64, No. 3, September 1935, 407–9.

42. Barrett, *Speedboat Kings*, 119–20, 131–32.

43. Anthony Mollica Jr. and Jack Savage, *Chris-Craft Boats* (St. Paul, MN: MBI Publishing, 2001), 16–17; Joseph Gribbins, *Chris-Craft: A History, 1922–1942* (Marblehead, MA: Devereux Books, 2001), 39.

44. Philip B. Ballantyne and Robert Bruce Duncan, *Classic American Runabouts: Wood Boats, 1915–1965* (Osceola, WI: MBI Publishing, 2001), 29–31.

45. Gribbins, *Chris-Craft*, 41–42.

46. Chris-Craft Financial Ledger entries, June 1922–December 1924, personal correspondence, Jerry Conrad, Mariner's Museum, Chris-Craft Collection, to the author, August 22, 2005. The owners' occupations were drawn from the 1924 *Detroit City Directory*.

47. Jeffrey L. Rodengen, *The Legend of Chris-Craft* (Fort Lauderdale, FL: Write Stuff Syndicate, 1998), 59.

48. Mollica and Savage, *Chris-Craft Boats*, 67.

49. Gribbins, *Chris-Craft*, 42.

50. Ibid., 44, 46.

51. Mollica, *Gar Wood Boats*, 41–43.

52. Ballantyne and Duncan, *Classic American Runabouts*, 11.

53. James P. Barry, *Hackercraft* (St. Paul, MN: MBI Publishing, 2002), 20–23.

54. *Michigan Manufacturer and Financial Record*, Vol. 25, No. 9, February 28, 1920, 58; Vol. 25, No. 20, May 15, 1920, 42.

55. Anthony S. Mollica Jr., *The American Wooden Runabouts* (St. Paul, MN: MBI Publishing, 2002), 57; *Michigan Manufacturer and Financial Record*, Vol. 35, No. 8, February 21, 1925, 34.

56. Michigan Department of Commerce, Corporations and Securities Division, Hacker & Fermann, Inc., Corporation Annual Report, 1925, Archives of Michigan, RG 61-11-A, Box 573, No. 151, Reel 5795.

57. *Michigan Manufacturer and Financial Record*, Vol. 41, No. 21, May 26, 1928, 48–53; Barry, *Hackercraft*, 35; *Michigan Manufacturer and Financial Record*, Vol. 42, No. 8, August 25, 1928, 23.

58. Robert Speltz, *The Real Runabouts V* (Lake Mills, IA: Graphic Publishing, 1984), 95.

59. Barry, *Hackercraft*, 58–59.

60. Anthony S. Mollica Jr., *Dodge Boats* (St. Paul, MN: MBI Publishing, 2003), 12–29.

61. Ibid., 30–41.

62. Ibid., 56–59.

63. Ibid., 60, 105, 118–19.

64. *Michigan Manufacturer and Financial Record*, Vol. 43, No. 20, May 18, 1929, 28; Robert Speltz, *The Real Runabouts III* (Lake Mills, IA: Graphic Publishing, 1980), 4–6.

65. Lloyd's Register of Shipping, *Lloyd's Register of American Yachts, 1922* (New York: Lloyd's Register of Shipping, 1922), 60, 107, 141.

66. Alan E. Dinn, *Boats by Purdy* (St. Michaels, MD: Tiller Publishing, 2003), 19–32.

67. Ibid., 46–49.

68. Ibid., 64–65.

69. *Michigan Manufacturer and Financial Record*, Vol. 19, No. 15, April 7, 1917, 68; Vol. 41, No. 21, May 26, 1928, 48–53.

70. John F. Polacsek, "Yachts of the Auto Barons," in *Tonnancour, vol. 2: Life in Grosse Pointe and along the Shores of Lake St. Clair*, edited by Arthur M. Woodford (Detroit: Grosse Pointe Historical Society and Omnigraphics, Inc., 1996), 159–60.

71. *Michigan Manufacturer and Financial Record*, Vol. 41, No. 21, May 26, 1928, 48–53.

72. *Michigan Manufacturer and Financial Record*, Vol. 43, No. 9, March 2, 1929, 28; Vol. 42, No. 5, August 4, 1928, 28.

73. Department of Commerce, Bureau of the Census, *Fourteenth Census of the United States Taken in the Year 1920*, vol. 10, *Manufacturers, 1919: Reports for Selected Industries* (Washington, DC: Government Printing Office, 1923), "Shipbuilding, Including Boat Building," 1006–25.

74. U.S. Department of Commerce, Bureau of the Census, *Biennial Census of Manufacturers, 1927* (Washington, DC: Government Printing Office, 1930), table 11, "Number of Power Boats Built (Less Than 5 Gross Tons), for the United States . . . by States, 1927," 1166; U.S. Department of Commerce, Bureau of the

Census, *Fifteenth Census of the United States, Manufactures, 1929*, vol. 2, *Reports by Industries* (Washington, DC: Government Printing Office, 1933), "Ship and Boat Building," table 11, "Number of Power Boats Built (Less Than 5 Gross Tons), for the United States . . . by States, 1929," 1238.

Chapter Five

1. Jack Savage, *Chris-Craft* (Osceola, WI: MBI Publishing, 2000), 31.

2. U.S. Department of Commerce, Bureau of the Census, *Fifteenth Census of the United States, Manufactures, 1929*, vol. 2, *Reports by Industries* (Washington, DC: Government Printing Office, 1933), table 2, "General Statistics by States, 1929, 1927, and 1919," 1233; U.S. Department of Commerce, Bureau of the Census, *Biennial Census of Manufacturers, 1933* (Washington, DC: Government Printing Office, 1936), table 1, "Summary for the United States, 1927 to 1933, and for States, 1933 and 1931," 615; U.S. Department of Commerce, Bureau of the Census, *Biennial Census of Manufacturers, 1937, part 1* (Washington, DC: Government Printing Office, 1939), table 2, "Summary by States, 1937," 1218.

3. Anthony S. Mollica Jr., *The American Wooden Runabout* (St. Paul, MN: MBI Publishing, 2002), 17–18.

4. *Michigan Manufacturer and Financial Record*, Vol. 41, No. 24, June 16, 1928, 42; Vol. 43, No. 12, March 23, 1929, 34.

5. *Motor Boat*, Vol. 27, No. 9, September 1930, 12–13.

6. U.S. Department of Commerce, Bureau of the Census, *Fifteenth Census of the United States, Manufactures, 1929*, vol. 2, *Reports by Industries* (Washington, DC: Government Printing Office, 1933), table 11, "Number of Power Boats Built (Less Than 5 Gross Tons), for the United States, 1923 to 1929, and by States, 1929," 1238; U.S. Department of Commerce, Bureau of the Census, *Biennial Census of Manufactures, 1931* (Washington, DC: Government Printing Office, 1935), table 6, "Number of Power Boats Built (Less than 5 Gross Tons), for the United States, 1925 to 1931, and for States, 1931," 1065; U.S. U.S. Department of Commerce, Bureau of the Census, *Biennial Census of Manufactures, 1935* (Washington, DC: Government Printing Office, 1938), table 4, "Number of Vessels Launched . . . 1929 to 1935," 1166.

7. Jeffrey L. Rodengen, *The Legend of Chris-Craft* (Fort Lauderdale, FL: Write Stuff Syndicate, 1998), 93–95.

8. Joseph Gribbins, *Chris-Craft: A History, 1922–1942* (Marblehead, MA: Devereux Books, 2001), 49–50, 52.

9. Rodengen, *The Legend of Chris-Craft*, 96, 99.

10. Anthony S. Mollica Jr., *Gar Wood Boats* (Osceola, WI: MBI Publishing, 1999), 63–64.

11. Mollica, *The American Wooden Runabout*, 58.

12. Rodengen, *The Legend of Chris-Craft*, 100; Mollica, *Gar Wood Boats*, 65.

13. Gribbins, *Chris-Craft*, 79.

14. Pat Zacharias, "Sailing on Lake St. Clair's Icy Winds," *Detroit News*, February 8, 1998, http://blogs.detroitnews.com/history/1998/02/07/sailing-on-lake-st-clairs-icy-winter-winds/, accessed June 29, 2013.

15. *Motor Boat*, Vol. 26, No. 18, December 1929, 14.

16. *Michigan Manufacturer and Financial Record*, Vol. 43, No. 16, April 20, 1929, 8; Chester Dorman Kelly, "Boat Builders for the World," *Magazine of Michigan*, Vol. 2, Nos. 5–6, May–June 1930, 5–6.

17. Russell J. Pouliot, Outboard Motor Boat, U.S. Patent 1,818,273, filed June 14, 1929, patented August 11, 1931.

18. Robert Speltz, *The Real Runabouts* (Lake Mills, IA: Graphic Publishing, 1977), 42.

19. *New York Times*, November 16, 1930, sec. 2, 2.

20. Philip B. Ballantyne and Robert Bruce Duncan, *Classic American Runabouts: Wood Boats, 1915–1965* (Osceola, WI: MBI Publishing, 2001), 68, 71.

21. *Michigan Manufacturer and Financial Record*, Vol. 46, No. 19, November 8, 1930, 28.

22. *Michigan Manufacturer and Financial Record*, Vol. 48, No. 3, July 18, 1931, 5.

23. Ballantyne and Duncan, *Classic American Runabouts*, 88–90.

24. Michigan Department of Commerce, Corporations and Securities Commission, Dee-Wite, Inc., Corporation Annual Report, 1933, Archives of Michigan, RG 64-6-A, Box 25, Vol. 1, No. 182, Reel 7201.

25. *Michigan Manufacturer and Financial Record*, Vol. 43, No. 17, April 27, 1929, 13; Vol. 45, No. 3, January 18, 1930, 171; Vol. 45, No. 13, March 29, 1930, 6.

26. *Michigan Manufacturer and Financial Record*, Vol. 64, No. 13, September 30, 1939, 15.

27. Rodengen, *The Legend of Chris-Craft*, 101–3.

28. Mollica, *Dodge Boats*, 98–99.

29. Gribbins, *Chris-Craft*, 81; Mollica, *Gar Wood Boats*, 78.

30. U.S. Department of Commerce, Bureau of the Census, *Fifteenth Census of the United States, Manufactures, 1929*, vol. 2, *Reports by Industries* (Washington, DC: Government Printing Office, 1933), table 14, "Wage Earners by Months for the United States . . . and by States, 1929," 1241; U.S. Department of Commerce, Bureau of the Census, *Biennial Census of Manufacturers, 1933* (Washington, DC: Government Printing Office, 1936), table 1, "Summary for the United States, 1927 to 1933 and for States, 1933 and 1931," 615; U,S, Department of Commerce, Bureau of the Census, *Biennial Census of Manufacturers, 1937, part 1* (Washington, DC: Government Printing Office, 1939), table 2, "Summary by States, 1937," 1218.; U.S. Department of Commerce, Bureau of the Census, *Sixteenth Census of the United States, Manufactures, 1939*, vol. 2, part 2, *Reports by Industries, Groups 11 to 20* (Washington, DC: Government Printing Office, 1942), table 5, "Wage Earners Engaged in Manufacturing . . . by States, 1939," 550.

31. Mollica, *Gar Wood Boats*, 66.

32. Gribbins, *Chris-Craft*, 80–81, 88.

33. *Michigan Manufacturer and Financial Record*, Vol. 48, No. 10, September 5, 1931, 6; Vol. 48, No. 11, September 12, 1931, 3.

34. James P. Barry, *Hackercraft* (St. Paul, MN: MBI Publishing, 2002), 83.

35. Ibid., 96–98.

36. Rodengen, *The Legend of Chris-Craft*, 107–9.

37. Geoffrey Reynolds, "Jesiek Brothers Shipyard: From Minnows to Marina," *Joint Archives Quarterly*, Vol. 2, No. 22, Summer 2012, 1–3.

38. Chad E. Mayea, *Since the Beginning: Mayea Boats* (Fairhaven, MI: by author, 2005), 43–44, 53, 87.

39. *Michigan Manufacturer and Financial Record*, Vol. 48, No. 3, July 18, 1931, 16; *Motor Boat*, Vol. 27, No. 9, September 1930, 26.

40. *Michigan Manufacturer and Financial Record*, Vol. 53, No. 8, February 24, 1934, 4.

41. Patrick Lapinski, "The Long Journey of the *Voyageur I*," *Nor'Easter* (Lake Superior Marine Museum Association), Vol. 32, No. 1, First Quarter, 2007.

42. Neil Thornton, *Around the Bay* (Tawas City, MI: Printer's Devil Press, 1991), 150–57.

43. Robert Speltz, *The Real Runabouts II* (Lake Mills, IA: Graphic Publishing, 1978), 89; Gribbins, *Chris-Craft*, 88–89.

44. *Michigan Manufacturer and Financial Record*, Vol. 53, No. 26, June 30, 1934, 9.

45. *Iron Age*, Vol. 136, No. 5, August 1, 1935, 23.

46. *Popular Mechanics*, Vol. 72, No. 2, August 1939, 187.

47. *Securities and Exchange Commission v. Gilbert*, 29 F. Supp. 654 (1939).

48. Milo Bailey, "Arc Welded Steel Pleasure Cruisers," in *Arc Welding in Design, Manufacture, and Construction*, 377–90 (Cleveland: James F. Lincoln Arc Welding Foundation, 1939).

49. *Motor Boat*, Vol. 36, No. 1, January 1939, 134.

50. *Michigan Investor*, Vol. 32, No. 39, April 21, 1934, 6.

51. *Benton Harbor News-Palladium*, January 14, 1926, 1, 8; January 18, 1926, 1; January 23, 1926, 1; January 13, 1927, 8.

52. *Heritage Journal* (Fort Miami Heritage Society), Vol. 5, No. 2, Summer 2005, 6–7.

53. *Michigan Manufacturer and Financial Record*, Vol. 45, No. 22, May 31, 1930, 9.

54. *Michigan Manufacturer and Financial Record*, Vol. 49, No. 4, January 23, 1932, 80.

55. *Michigan Manufacturer and Financial Record*, Vol. 53, No. 17, April 28, 1934, 23–24.

56. Michael Gillespie, "A Tale of Two Boats," *Lake of the Ozarks Business Journal*, September 2005, http://www.lakehistory.info/excursionboats.html, accessed November 14, 2012.

57. *Michigan Manufacturer and Financial Record*, Vol. 52, No. 20, November 18, 1933, 6; Vol. 53, No. 15, April 14, 1934, 4.

58. *Michigan Investor*, Vol. 34, No. 10, September 28, 1935, 5.

59. *Michigan Investor*, Vol. 32, No. 45, June 2, 1934, 6. See also *Michigan Manufacturer and Financial Record*, Vol. 53, No. 19, May 12, 1934, 10.

60. *Michigan Manufacturer and Financial Record*, Vol. 62, No. 4, July 23, 1938, 9.

61. Peter Hunn, *The Old Outboard Book* (Camden, ME: International Marine Publishing and McGraw-Hill Professional, 1994), 108–9, 141–42.

62. *Michigan Manufacturer and Financial Record*, Vol. 42, No. 26, December 29, 1928, 45; Vol. 43, No. 8, February 23, 1929, 16.

63. *Michigan Manufacturer and Financial Record*, Vol. 43, No. 17, April 27, 1929, 21; Paul Miklos, Frank Miklos, and Trudi Miklos, *Classic Century Powerboats* (St. Paul, MN: MBI Publishing, 2002), 13.

64. Miklos, Miklos, and Miklos, *Classic Century Powerboats*, 14.

65. *Michigan Manufacturer and Financial Record*, Vol. 46, No. 26, December 27, 1930, 25; Vol. 47, No. 18, May 2, 1931, 3.

66. *Michigan Manufacturer and Financial Record*, Vol. 49, No. 25, June 18, 1932, 10.

67. Miklos, Miklos, and Miklos, *Classic Century Powerboats*, 18.

68. *Michigan Manufacturer and Financial Record*, Vol. 56, No. 23, December 7, 1935, 3.

69. *Michigan Investor*, Vol. 34, No. 23, December 28, 1935, 6.

70. Robert Speltz, *The Real Runabouts IV* (Lake Mills, IA: Graphic Publishing Co., 1982), 173–174.

71. Peter Hunn, *The Golden Age of the Racing Outboard* (Marblehead, MA: Devereux Books, 2000), 164–65.

72. Weston Farmer, *From My Old Boat Shop: One-Lung Engines, Fantail Launches, and Other Marine Delights* (Camden, ME: International Marine Publishing, 1979), 129, 325.

73. Michigan Department of Commerce, Corporations and Securities Commission, Russell J. Pouliot, Inc., Corporation Annual Report, 1934, Archives of Michigan, RG 65-20A, Box 41, Vol. 1, No. 112, Reel 7274.

74. D. W. Barton, "The Northern Michigan (NM) Racing Sloop: Its Design, Builders and Similar Boats" (retyped from a draft document dated March 4, 1992), Little Traverse Yacht Club, http://ltyc.org/sailing/club-racing/fleet-directory/nm/, accessed June 13, 2012.

75. *Michigan Manufacturer and Financial Record*, Vol. 49, No. 5, January 30, 1932, 5.

76. *Michigan Manufacturer and Financial Record*, Vol. 60, No. 1, July 3, 1937, 14.

77. Donald F. Prather, "Yachting at Chicago," in *Sailing Craft: Mostly Descriptive of Smaller Pleasure Sail Boats of the Day*, ed. Edwin J. Schoettle (New York: Macmillan, 1937), 389.

78. Miklos, Miklos, and Miklos, *Classic Century Powerboats*, 20–21.

79. John S. Bowdidge, "Toys and Sporting Goods, 39.4," in *Manufacturing: A Historiographical and Bibliographical Guide*, ed. David O. Whitten and Bessie E. Whitten (New York: Greenwood Press, 2000), 398–99.

80. Rodengen, *The Legend of Chris-Craft*, 110–11.

81. Fred P. Bingham, *Boat Joinery and Cabinet Making Simplified* (Camden, ME: International Marine Publishing and McGraw-Hill Professional, 1993), ix–x.

Chapter Six

1. U.S. Department of Commerce, Bureau of the Census, *Sixteenth Census of the United States, 1940, Manufactures, 1939*, vol. 2, part 2, *Reports by Industries, Groups 11 to 20* (Washington, DC: Government Printing Office, 1942), 548–50.

2. Anthony S. Mollica Jr., *Gar Wood Boats: Classics of a Golden Era* (Osceola, WI: MBI Publishing, 1999), 96–101.

3. *Michigan Manufacturer and Financial Record*, Vol. 66, No. 9, August 31, 1940, 10; Vol. 66, No. 19, November 9, 1940, 10; Vol. 65, No. 9, March 2, 1940, 10.

4. K. Jack Bauer, "Inland Seas and Overseas: Shipbuilding on the Great Lakes during World War II," *Inland Seas*, Vol. 38, No. 2, Summer 1984, 84.

5. *Michigan Manufacturer and Financial Record*, Vol. 63, No. 24, June 17, 1939, 3; Vol. 64, No. 16, October 21, 1939, 50.

6. James P. Barry, *Hackercraft* (St. Paul, MN: MBI Publishing, 2002), 99–100.

7. Norman Polmar and Samuel Loring Morison, *PT Boats at War: World War II to Vietnam* (Osceola, WI: MBI Publishing, 1999), 10–20; Curtis L. Nelson, *Hunters in the Shallows: A History of the PT Boat* (Washington, DC: Brassey's, 1998), 114; Frank D. Johnson, *United States PT-Boats of World War II in Action* (Poole, Dorset: Blandford Press Ltd., 1980), 21–22, 27, 33, 154.

8. Stan Grayson, *Engines Afloat: From Early Days to D-Day*, vol. 2, *The Gasoline/Diesel Era* (Marblehead, MA: Devereux Books, 1999), 162–63.

9. U.S. Congress, Senate, Committee on Interstate Commerce, *Expediting Loading and Unloading of Railroad Freight Cars: Hearings before a Subcommittee of the Committee on Interstate Commerce, United States Senate, Seventy-Seventh Congress, Second Session, on S.J. Res. 147, a Joint Resolution Providing for the More Effective Prosecution of the War by Expediting the Loading and Unloading of Railroad Freight Cars, June 30 and July 1, 1942*, part 1 (Washington, DC: Government Printing Office, 1942), 170.

10. Jeffrey L. Rodengen, *The Legend of Chris-Craft* (Fort Lauderdale, FL: Write Stuff Syndicate, 1998), 122–23.

11. Anthony S. Mollica Jr., *Gar Wood Boats: Classics of a Golden Era* (Osceola, WI: MBI Publishing, 1999), 104–7; Joseph Gribbins, *Chris-Craft: A History, 1922–1942* (Marblehead, MA: Devereux Books, 2001), 117; James P. Barry, *Hackercraft* (St. Paul, MN: MBI Publishing, 2002), 100–101.

12. Chad E. Mayea, *Since the Beginning: Mayea Boats* (Fairhaven, MI: by author, 2008), 54–60.

13. *Benton Harbor News-Palladium*, February 6, 1941, 1, 9.

14. *Great Lakes Journal*, Vol. 10, No. 6, October–November 1941, 8.

15. *The Boating Industry*, Vol. 4, No. 2, March 1941, 34.

16. *Michigan Manufacturer and Financial Record*, Vol. 59, No. 6, February 6, 1937, 15.

17. *Michigan Manufacturer and Financial Record*, Vol. 66, No. 5, August 3, 1940, 3.

18. Mayea, *Since the Beginning*, 60.

19. *Michigan Manufacturer and Financial Record*, Vol. 59, No. 16, April 17, 1937, 14.

20. Rodengen, *The Legend of Chris-Craft*, 110; *Michigan Manufacturer and Financial Record*, Vol. 59, No. 16, April 17, 1937, 14; *Michigan Manufacturer and Financial Record*, Vol. 65, No. 5, February 3, 1940, 10.

21. Rodengen, *The Legend of Chris-Craft*, 124.

22. Ibid.

23. Gribbins, *Chris-Craft*, 118.

24. Bauer, "Inland Seas and Overseas," 166.

25. Anthony S. Mollica, with Chris Smith, *Building Chris-Craft: Inside the Factories* (Minneapolis: Voyageur Press and MBI Publishing, 2010), 61.

26. Defoe Shipbuilding Company, *The Defoe Story* (Bay City, MI: Defoe Shipbuilding Company, n.d. [c. 1970]), 4–7.

27. *Defoe Rollover*, Vol. 3, No. 3, February 1945.

28. Barry, *Hackercraft*, 99–100; Mollica, *Gar Wood Boats*, 103–9.

29. Theodore R. Treadwell, *Splinter Fleet: The Wooden Subchasers of World War II* (Annapolis, MD: Naval Institute Press, 2000), 40.

30. Barry, *Hackercraft*, 100.

31. Geoffrey D. Reynolds, "Almost Famous: The Foster Boat Company," *Rudder*, (Antique and Classic Boat Society), Vol. 19, No. 3, Winter 2010, 17–19.

32. *Great Lakes Journal*, Vol. 10, No. 6, October–November 1941, 2.

33. Donald L. van Reken, *Macatawa Park: A Chronicle* (Holland, MI: by author, 1991), 175–76.

34. *Benton Harbor News-Palladium*, December 15, 1942, 3.

35. Tim Colton, "Eddy Shipbuilding, Bay City," http://shipbuildinghistory.com/history/shipyards/4emergencysmall/eddy.htm, accessed January 2, 2013; Barry, *Hackercraft*, 101.

36. John R. Phillips, "Kalamazoo Canvas Boat at 75," *Kalamazoo Magazine*, April 1964, 17, 38.

37. *Defoe Rollover*, Vol. 2, No. 4, March 1944, 1.

38. *Benton Harbor News-Palladium*, February 25, 1942, 1.

39. *Benton Harbor News-Palladium*, June 10, 1949, 1.

40. *St. Joseph Herald-Press*, March 1, 1944, 1, 8.

41. *St. Joseph Herald-Press*, November 16, 1944, 1.

42. Neil Thornton, *Around the Bay* (Tawas City, MI: Printer's Devil Press, 1991), 156.

43. Rodengen, *The Legend of Chris-Craft*, 127; *Benton Harbor News-Palladium*, December 31, 1942, 15.

44. Jean Blashfield Black, "Wood at War," *Wood and Wood Products*, January 1, 1995, http://www.thefreelibrary.com/Wood+at+war.-a017796175, accessed January 4, 2012.

45. Rodengen, *The Legend of Chris-Craft*, 130.

46. Alan Clive, *State of War: Michigan in World War II* (Ann Arbor: University of Michigan Press, 1979), 37.

47. *Benton Harbor News-Palladium*, December 31, 1942, 14.

48. Clive, *State of War*, 36.

49. *Benton Harbor News-Palladium*, December 31, 1941, 14.

50. Mercer Fisher to Jane Granzow Miles, undated, with sample of wooden plugs, Heritage Museum and Cultural Center, St. Joseph, Michigan, 78.11.34-901.

51. *Benton Harbor News-Palladium*, January 7, 1943, 3.

52. Van Reken, *Macatawa Park*, 175–76.

53. Ibid.

54. *Defoe Rollover*, Vol. 1, No. 7, June 1943, 16.

55. Rodengen, *The Legend of Chris-Craft*, 130.

56. Bert C. Brennan, "Fighting Ships from Bay City," *Inland Seas*, Vol. 1, No. 3, July 1945, 23–24.

57. Program, Presentation of the U.S. Navy E-Pennant to Robinson Marine Construction Company, ceremony March 5, 1942, collection of the Heritage Museum and Cultural Center, St. Joseph, Michigan; *Benton Harbor News-Palladium*, March 6, 1942, 1.

58. Rodengen, *The Legend of Chris-Craft*, 130.

59. Ibid.

60. Bauer, "Inland Seas and Overseas," 92, 166.

61. Mollica, *Gar Wood Boats*, 109.

62. *The Boating Industry, American Boatbuilders for Victory, December 10th, 1943* (St. Joseph, MI: *The Boating Industry*, 1943).

63. Jack Savage, *Chris-Craft* (Osceola, WI: MBI Publishing, 2000), 52.

64. *Defoe Rollover*, Vol. 4, No. 2, January 1946, 1.

65. *Defoe Rollover*, Vol. 2, No. 1, December 1943, 1–2.

66. Mollica, *Gar Wood Boats*, 112–13.

67. Ibid., 115–18.

68. Ibid., 120–26.

69. *St. Joseph Herald-Press*, December 31, 1945, 10.

70. Michelle Hill, "Recapturing a Fading Maritime Consciousness: Shipyards in St. Joseph, Michigan," paper prepared for Dr. Michael Chiarappa in his Seminar in Local History, Western Michigan University, 9; Harold Conklin, oral history interview with the author, St. Joseph, Michigan, March 3, 1998, Collection of the Heritage Museum and Cultural Center, St. Joseph, Michigan.

71. *Motor Boating*, Vol. 80, No. 5, November 1947, 121.

72. *Benton Harbor News Palladium*, April 16, 1948, 1.

73. *Benton Harbor News Palladium*, October 13, 1948, 1.

74. Hill, "Recapturing a Fading Maritime Consciousness," 9; Harold Conklin, oral history interview.

75. *Michigan Manufacturer and Financial Record*, Vol. 78, No. 16, October 19, 1946, 10; Vol. 80, No. 14, October 6, 1947, 4.

76. *St. Joseph Herald-Press*, November 3, 1949, 1, 14; November 17, 1949, 1.

77. Reginald Crabtree, *The Luxury Yacht from Steam to Diesel* (New York: Drake Publishers, 1974), 187–88.

78. Sparkman & Stephens Design 509, Brasil and Mackinac Classes, http://sparkmanstephens.blogspot.com/2011/04/design-509-brasil-and-mackinac-classes.html, accessed January 12, 2013.

79. *Defoe Rollover*, Vol. 4, No. 2, January 1946, 6–7.

80. Dale Patrick Wolicki, *The Historic Architecture of Bay City, Michigan* (Bay City: Bay County Historical Society, 1998), 258; *Defoe Rollover*, Vol. 4, No. 2, January 1946, 6–7.

81. Mollica, *Chris-Craft Boats*, 22.

82. Bauer, "Inland Seas and Overseas," 170.

Chapter Seven

1. Jack Savage, *Chris-Craft* (Osceola, WI: MBI Publishing, 2000), 83.

2. Ibid., 70.

3. Jeffrey L. Rodengen, *The Legend of Chris-Craft* (Fort Lauderdale, FL: Write Stuff Syndicate, 1998), 180–85.

4. Anthony Mollica Jr. and Jack Savage, *Chris-Craft Boats* (St. Paul, MN: MBI Publishing, 2001), 155–59.

5. Rodengen, *The Legend of Chris-Craft*, 159, 165–67.

6. Savage, *Chris-Craft*, 70–71.

7. Mollica and Savage, *Chris-Craft Boats*, 61.

8. Savage, *Chris-Craft*, 74.

9. Rodengen, *The Legend of Chris-Craft*, 187–93.

10. Paul Miklos, Frank Miklos, and Trudi Miklos, *Classic Century Powerboats* (St. Paul, MN: MBI Publishing, 2002), 51.

11. *St. Joseph Herald-Press,* January 23, 1952, 12.

12. James P. Barry, *Hackercraft* (St. Paul, MN: MBI Publishing, 2002), 110.

13. Ibid., 110–11, 122–23; Philip B. Ballantyne and Robert Bruce Duncan, *Classic American Runabouts: Wood Boats, 1915–1965* (Osceola, WI: MBI Publishing, 2001), 136–37.

14. *Michigan Manufacturer and Financial Record,* Vol. 101, No. 5, May 1958, 22.

15. Thomas Colvin, "Boatbuilding with Aluminum," in *Boatbuilding with Steel,* ed. Gilbert C. Klingel (Camden, ME: International Marine Publishing, 1973), 206.

16. R. L. Polk & Co., *Polk's Saginaw City Directory, 1936* (Detroit: R. L. Polk, 1936), 432; Charles W. Stiver, Boat Construction, U.S. Patent 2,083,410, filed May 4, 1935, patented June 8, 1937.

17. Dow Chemical Company, *Thirty-Five Opportunities for Small Business with Magnesium: Report by Dr. Willard H. Dow, President of the Dow Chemical Company, to the Special Committee of the United States Senate to Study Problems of American Small Business* (Midland, MI: Dow Chemical Company, March 1945); *Dow Diamond,* July 1946, 22–27.

18. *The Brine Well,* Vol. 4, No. 24, September 16, 1947, 1, 4.

19. Peter Hunn, *Tail Fins and Two-Tones: The Guide to America's Classic Fiberglass and Aluminum Runabouts* (Marblehead, MA: Devereux Books, 2006), 36.

20. Andreas Jordahl Rhude, "AeroCraft-Harwill," http://www.fiberglassics.com/library/Aerocraft, accessed February 23, 2013; *St. Charles Union,* November 24, 1949, 1.

21. *St. Charles Union,* March 31, 1949, 1.

22. *St. Charles Union,* November 27, 1952, 1.

23. *St. Charles Union,* May 6, 1954, 1.

24. *Lakeland Boating,* Vol. 12, No. 1, January 1957, 30–31.

25. Hunn, *Tail Fins and Two-Tones,* 47–48.

26. Ibid., 41.

27. Ferdinand R. Eichner, Metal Boat Construction, U.S. Patent 2,500,279, filed July 26, 1944, patented March 14, 1950.

28. Gilbert C. Klingel (ed.), *Boatbuilding with Steel* (Camden, ME: International Marine Publishing, 1973), 16–28.

29. *Michigan Manufacturer and Financial Record,* Vol. 88, No. 2, August 1951, 10.

30. Geoffrey D. Reynolds, "Roamer, before Chris-Craft," Faculty Publications, paper 424, http://digitalcommons.hope.edu/faculty_publications/424; *Classic Boating,* No. 167, May 1, 2012, 6–7. Accessed August 10, 2014.

31. *Michigan Manufacturer and Financial Record,* Vol. 95, No. 5, May 1955, 28.

32. *Michigan Manufacturer and Financial Record,* Vol. 96, No. 5, November 1955, 105; Vol. 98, No. 2, August 1956, 37.

33. *Lakeland Boating,* Vol. 13, No. 10, October–November 1958, 25.

34. Daniel Spurr, *Heart of Glass: Fiberglass Boats and the Men Who Made Them* (Camden, ME: International Marine Publishing and McGraw-Hill Professional, 2000), 7–8.

35. *The Boating Industry,* Vol. 2, No. 1, January 1939, 85.

36. *The Boating Industry,* Vol. 13, No. 1, January 10, 1950, 153.

37. *Holland Evening Sentinel,* September 15, 1953, 2.

38. *General Motors Corporation v. Cadillac Marine & Boat Co., and Ash Craft Co.*, 1964, DC Mich. DCWD (WD Mich. 1964) 226 F. Supp. 716, 737–38.

39. *Yachting*, January 1956, 158.

40. *Newsweek*, April 15, 1957.

41. *Ludington Daily News*, February 20, 1957, 1.

42. *Lakeland Boating*, Vol. 13, No. 10, October–November 1958, 29.

43. *Benton Harbor News-Palladium*, June 11, 1960, 4.

44. *Raleigh Register* (Beckley, WV), April 10, 1961, 1–2.

45. *Charleston Gazette* (Charleston, WV), September 27, 1963, 1.

46. *Benton Harbor News-Palladium*, December 31, 1954, 12; *Michigan Manufacturer and Financial Record*, Vol. 102, No. 2, August 1958, 33.

47. *Michigan Manufacturer and Financial Record*, Vol. 107, No. 1, January 1961, 14.

48. Spurr, *Heart of Glass*, 89–92.

49. *Michigan Manufacturer and Financial Record*, Vol. 110, No. 3, September 1962, 58; Vol. 110, No. 6, December 1962, 30.

50. Spurr, *Heart of Glass*, 159.

51. *Michigan Manufacturer and Financial Record*, Vol. 94, No. 2, August 1954, 14; Vol. 95, No. 2, February 1955, 35.

52. *Ludington Daily News*, July 26, 1957, 7.

53. *Ludington Daily News*, July 28, 1962, 8.

54. *Michigan Manufacturer and Financial Record*, Vol. 116, No. 3, September 1965, 58.

55. Geoffrey D. Reynolds, "Fifty Years of Making Fun: The Story of the Slick Craft Boat Company," *Joint Archives of Holland Quarterly*, Vol. 14, No. 4, Winter 2005, 1–5.

56. Geoffrey D. Reynolds, "Slick Craft: The Quality Name in Boating," *Classic Boating*, No. 127, September 1, 2005, 6–11.

57. Terry Parkhurst, "Chrysler Marine: Chrysler on Water," http://www.allpar.com/history/marine.html, accessed February 26, 2013.

58. Peter Hunn, *The Old Outboard Book* (Camden, ME: International Marine Publishing and McGraw-Hill Professional, 1994), 112–13.

59. Claas van der Linde, "James Roderick 'Rod' MacAlpine-Downie," in Lucia del Sol Knight and Daniel Bruce MacNaughton, *The Encyclopedia of Yacht Designers* (New York: W. W. Norton & Company, Inc., 2006), 293.

60. Mutineer 15 Class Association, "Men behind the Mutineeer," http://www.mutineer15.org/men-behind-the-mutineer.html, accessed March 2, 2013.

61. Chrysler Historical Information Page, http://chryslersailing.lizards.net/sail_history.html, accessed March 2, 2013.

62. Tim Moran, Mid-American Shore Report, "The Amazing Crescent Boat," *Great Lakes Sailor*, November–December 1988, http://goatyard.com/crescent-sailing/, accessed June 29, 2013.

63. Barry, *Hackercraft*, 111–18.

64. David D. Williams, *Hydroplane Racing in Detroit, 1946–2008* (Charleston, SC: Arcadia Publishing, 2009), 21–22.

65. Fred Farley, "Les Staudacher Remembered," Hydroplane and Raceboat Museum, http://www.thunderboats.org/history/history0418.html, accessed February 2, 2013.

66. *Miss U.S. I* Official Site, http://missus1.com/, accessed February 2, 2013.

67. "I Felt a Great Relief," *Sports Illustrated*, December 7, 1959, http://www.si.com/vault/1959/12/07/604521/events--discoveries, accessed August 10, 2014.

68. *Traverse City Record-Eagle*, May 17, 1963, 18.

69. *Motor Boating*, Vol. 93, No. 1, January 1954, 204.

70. *Mount Carmel Daily Republican Register* (Mount Carmel, IL), October 15, 1964, B3.

71. Ron Bloomfield for the Bay County Historical Society, *Maritime Bay County* (Charleston, SC: Arcadia Publishing, 2009), 108.

72. John R. Phillips, "Kalamazoo Canvas Boat at 75," *Kalamazoo Magazine*, April 1964, 17.

73. *Kalamazoo Gazette*, February 17, 1980, 11.

Chapter Eight

1. Michigan Manufacturer and Financial Record, *The Directory of Michigan Manufacturers, 1960* (Detroit: Manufacturer Publishing Company, 1960), 410; Michigan Manufacturer and Financial Record, *The Directory of Michigan Manufacturers, 1965* (Detroit: Manufacturer Publishing Company, 1965), 395; Michigan Manufacturer and Financial Record, *The Directory of Michigan Manufacturers, 1969* (Detroit: Manufacturer Publishing Company, 1969), 427.

2. U.S. Department of Commerce, Bureau of the Census, *1963 Census of Manufactures*, vol. 2, *Industry Statistics*, part 2, *Major Groups 29 to 39 and 19* (Washington, DC: Government Printing Office, 1966), 37C-21 to 37C-22, 37C-26.

3. Jeffrey L. Rodengen, *Commanding the Waterways: The Story of Sea Ray* (Fort Lauderdale, FL: Write Stuff Enterprises, 2008), 48–49, citing statistics of the National Marine Manufacturers Association, Market Statistics Division, January 1999.

4. Daniel Spurr, *Heart of Glass: Fiberglass Boats and the Men Who Made Them* (Camden, ME: International Marine Publishing and McGraw-Hill Professional, 2000), 167–68.

5. Anthony Mollica Jr. and Jack Savage, *Chris-Craft Boats* (St. Paul, MN: MBI Publishing, 2001), 25.

6. Jack Savage, *Chris-Craft* (Osceola, WI: MBI Publishing, 2000), 88–89.

7. Jeffrey L. Rodengen, *The Legend of Chris-Craft* (Fort Lauderdale, FL: Write Stuff Syndicate, 1998), 200, 202.

8. Ibid., 193, 201, 204.

9. Savage, *Chris-Craft*, 89.

10. Rodengen, *The Legend of Chris-Craft*, 206, 218, 220.

11. Savage, *Chris-Craft*, 90; Rodengen, *The Legend of Chris-Craft*, 223.

12. Savage, *Chris-Craft*, 90.

13. Rodengen, *The Legend of Chris-Craft*, 234–37.

14. "Chris-Craft History," http://www.chriscraft.com/main/company/history.aspx, accessed August 10, 2014.

15. Paul Miklos, Frank Miklos, and Trudi Miklos, *Classic Century Powerboats* (St. Paul, MN: MBI Publishing, 2002), 89–92.

16. Ibid., 105.

17. James P. Barry, *American Powerboats: The Great Lakes Golden Years* (St. Paul, MN: MBI Publishing, 2003), 112–13.

18. "Century Boats—History," http://centuryboats.com/about/histor/, accessed August 10, 2014.

19. *Saginaw News*, April 9, 1969, A9.

20. *Saginaw Valley News*, August 30, 1974, 1.

21. Peter Hunn, *Tail Fins and Two-Tones: The Guide to America's Classic Fiberglass and Aluminum Runabouts* (Marblehead, MA: Devereux Books, 2006), 19.

22. Andreas Jordahl Rhude, "Thompson's Fiberglass Boats," http://www.fiber-glassics.com/library/Thompson_Bros, accessed March 15, 2013.

23. Geoffrey D. Reynolds, "Slick Craft: The Quality Name in Boating," *Classic Boating*, No. 127, September 1, 2005, 10.

24. Barry, *American Powerboats*, 115, 118.

25. Geoffrey D. Reynolds, "Fifty Years of Making Fun: The History of the Slik-kers Family and Boat Building, Part Two," *Joint Archives of Holland Quarterly*, Vol. 15, No. 3, Fall 2005, 1–4.

26. Spurr, *Heart of Glass*, 158.

27. Tiara Yachts Press release, "S2 Yachts Re-tools for the Future," July 3, 2012, http://www.tiarayachts.com/tiara-news/2012-press-releases/s2-yachts-re-tools-for-the-future.aspx, accessed March 4, 2013.

28. Jeffrey L. Rodengen, *Commanding the Waterways: The Story of Sea Ray* (Fort Lauderdale, FL: Write Stuff Enterprises, 2008), 10–14.

29. D. W. Fostle, *Speedboat* (Mystic, CT: Mystic Seaport Museum Stores, 1988), 208–13.

30. Rodengen, *Commanding the Waterways*, 29–31.

31. Ibid., 36, 48, 50–51.

32. Peter A. Jannsen, "The Booming Boating Business," *Motor Boating & Sailing*, February 1987, 11.

33. Rodengen, *Commanding the Waterways*, 79–81.

34. Ibid., 86, 96.

35. Ibid., 113, 149.

36. *Michigan Manufacturer and Financial Record*, Vol. 119, No. 5, May 1967, 68.

37. Alexandria Lopez, "A Legacy of Success: Four Winns Goes the Distance," *North American Composites*, Fall 2011, http://www.nacomposites.com/delivering-performance/page.asp?issueid=18&page=cover, accessed March 2, 2013; John Winn, personal correspondence with the author, June 28, 2013.

38. Bill Halls, "Boat Maker Builds Hope in Quality, Price," *Detroit News*, January 29, 1998, B1; John Winn, personal correspondence with the author, June 28, 2013.

39. *Detroit News*, January 29, 1998, B1.

40. Pete McDonald, "Engine Failure: The Slow, Painful Death of Once-Proud OMC," *Boating*, May 2001, 152–56.

41. "Genmar Holdings, Inc., History," http://www.fundinguniverse.com/com-pany-histories/genmar-holdings-inc-history/, accessed March 17, 2013.

42. Kris Verhage, "Four Winns to Be Sold," *Cadillac News*, December 11, 2009 http://cadillacnews.com/news_story/?story_id=1273652&year=2009&issue=20091211, accessed August 19, 2014.

43. Karen M. Koenig, "Boat Maker 'Pedals' Thermoforming Technique," *Plastics Machining*, July 1999, http://www.plasticsmachining.com/magazine/199907/leisurelife.html, accessed March 9, 2013.

44. *Adrian Daily Telegram,* June 26, 1981, D10.

45. *Adrian Daily Telegram,* June 21, 1985, C7.

46. *Tecumseh Herald,* January 30, 1986, 1.

47. *Adrian Daily Telegram,* April 29, 1986, A1; July 25, 1986, A1.

48. "Meyers Industries Celebrates 50 Years," *Tecumseh Herald,* September 10, 1987, 1, 10.

49. *Michigan Manufacturer and Financial Record,* Vol. 123, No. 1, January 1969, 26.

50. "Crest Pontoon Boats," http://crestpontoonboats.com/crest/, accessed March 23, 2013.

51. City of Menominee Centennial Corporation, *History of the City of Menominee, Michigan: The Past with Remembrance . . . the Future with Longing, 1883–1983* (Dallas: Taylor Publishing, 1983), 267; "Yar-Craft—History," http://yarcraft.com/history.html, accessed March 23, 2013.

52. Meade Gougeon, *The Gougeon Brothers on Boat Construction: Wood and WEST System® Materials,* 5th ed. (Bay City, MI: Gougeon Brothers, 2005), 1–3.

53. Ibid., 3; Ron Bloomfield for the Bay County Historical Society, *Maritime Bay County* (Charleston, SC: Arcadia Publishing, 2009), 114–15.

54. *Flint Journal,* August 30, 2009, E1.

55. Savage, *Chris-Craft,* 90.

56. Tim Cole, "Splash from the Past," *Popular Mechanics,* June 1986, 77.

57. "Wings and Water: First Loves," *Robb Report,* April 1, 2007, http://robbreport.com/Boating-Yachting/Wings--Water-First-Loves, accessed August 10, 2014.

58. Jeremy Gonsior, "Classic Boat Maker Beached," *Holland Sentinel,* June 12, 2009, http://www.hollandsentinel.com/news/x2122534558/Classic-boat-maker-beached, accessed March 16, 2013; "Grand Craft," http://www.grandcraft.com/, accessed March 16, 2013.

59. "*Amy Ann,* a Custom One-Off Creation from Morin Boats," http://www.woodyboater.com/communityweb/amy-ann-a-custom-one-off-creation-from-morin-boats/, accessed March 16, 2013.

60. Chad Mayea, *Since the Beginning: Mayea Boats* (Fairhaven, MI: by author, 2005), 72.

61. "Van Dam History," http://vandamboats.com/about-us/history/, accessed March 16, 2013.

62. "Danenberg Boatworks," http://www.danenbergboatworks.com/index.html, accessed March 16, 2013.

63. "Great Lakes Boat Building School History," http://www.glbbs.org/History, accessed March 16, 2013.

64. "Antique and Classic Boat Society," http://www.acbs.org/, accessed March 16, 2013.

65. "Fiberglassics," http://www.fiberglassics.com/, accessed March 16, 2013.

66. U.S. Department of Commerce, Bureau of the Census, *Industry Statistics Sampler, NAICS 336612, Boat Building,* https://www.census.gov/econ/isp/sampler.php?naicscode=336612&naicslevel=6, accessed accessed August 16, 2014.

67. "NMMA Releases 2010 U.S. Recreational Boat Registration Statistics Report," http://www.nmma.org/news.aspx?id=18028, accessed March 23, 2013.

Selected Bibliography

Because the subject of boat-building in Michigan is covered by a wide array of sources far beyond strictly maritime historical works, I have attempted to focus the materials listed herein as being the most useful examples for the study of the business of boat-building in the state. They are a mixture of company histories, articles, county and regional histories containing biographical sketches, trade periodicals and catalogs, city and state directories, newspapers, and government records. Other sources used in the work for particular factual information are included in the endnotes.

Books

Abos Publishing Company. *1962 Blue Book Boat & Trailer Trade-In Guide, 1956 through 1961*. Columbia, MO: Abos Publishing, 1961.

Ballantyne, Philip B., and Robert Bruce Duncan. *Classic American Runabouts: Wood Boats, 1915–1965*. Osceola, WI: MBI Publishing, 2001.

Barrett, J. Lee. *Speed Boat Kings*. Ann Arbor: Historical Society of Michigan; Berrien Springs, MI: Hardscrabble Books, 1986.

Barry, James P. *American Powerboats: The Great Lakes Golden Years*. St. Paul, MN: MBI Publishing, 2003.

Barry, James P. *Hackercraft*. St. Paul, MN: MBI Publishing, 2002.

Barry, James P. *Ships of the Great Lakes: 300 Years of Navigation*. Holt, MI: Thunder Bay Press, 1996.

Baxter, Albert. *History of the City of Grand Rapids, Michigan*. New York and Grand Rapids: Munsell, 1891.

Beers, J. H., & Co. *Commemorative Biographical Record of the Upper Lake Region*. Chicago: J. H. Beers, 1905.

Bingham, Fred P. *Boat Joinery and Cabinet Making Simplified*. Camden, ME: International Marine Publishing and McGraw-Hill Professional, 1993.

Biographical Publishing Co. *Portrait and Biographical Record of Saginaw and Bay Counties, Michigan*. Chicago: Biographical Publishing, 1892.

Bloomfield, Ron, for the Bay County Historical Society. *Maritime Bay County*. Charleston, SC: Arcadia Publishing, 2009.

Boating Industry, The. *American Boatbuilders for Victory, December 10th, 1943*. St. Joseph, MI: The Boating Industry, 1943.

Braden, Donna R. *Leisure and Entertainment in America*. Dearborn, MI: Henry Ford Museum and Greenfield Village, 1988.

Branch, Elam E. *The History of Ionia County, Michigan*. Indianapolis: B. F. Bowen, 1916.

City of Menominee Centennial Corporation. *History of the City of Menominee, Michigan: The Past with Remembrance . . . the Future with Longing, 1883–1983*. Dallas: Taylor Publishing, 1983.

Clive, Alan. *State of War: Michigan in World War II*. Ann Arbor: University of Michigan Press, 1979.

Cochrane, Timothy, and Hawk Tolson. *A Good Boat Speaks for Itself: Isle Royale Fishermen and Their Boats*. Minneapolis: University of Minnesota Press, 2002.

Coleman, Edgar Werner. *Advertising Development: A Brief Review of and Commentary upon Various Phases of Advertising Development as Influenced by the Advertising Manager and Advertising Agent as Factors in Creating National and International Markets for American Products*. Milwaukee: Coleman, 1909.

Colvin, Thomas. "Boatbuilding with Aluminum." In *Boatbuilding with Steel*, edited by Gilbert C. Klingel, 204–43. Camden, ME: International Marine Publishing, 1973.

Conrad, Jerry. *Chris-Craft: The Essential Guide*. Newport News, VA: The Mariners' Museum, 2002.

Crabtree, Reginald. *The Luxury Yacht: From Steam to Diesel*. New York: Drake Publishers, 1974.

Defoe Shipbuilding Company. *The Defoe Story*. Bay City, MI: Defoe Shipbuilding, c. 1970.

Detroit International Fair and Exposition Association. *Official Catalogue of the Entries and Exhibits at the Fourth Annual Detroit International Fair and Exposition*. Detroit: Detroit International Fair and Exposition Association, 1892.

Dewhurst, C. Kurt, and Marsha MacDowell. *Downriver and Thumb Area Michigan Waterfowling: The Folk Arts of Nate Quillen and Otto Misch*. East Lansing: The Museum, Michigan State University, 1981.

Dinn, Alan E. *Boats by Purdy*. St. Michaels, MD: Tiller Publishing, 2003.

Dixon, Michael M. *Motormen and Yachting: The Waterfront Heritage of the Automobile Industry*. St. Clair Shores, MI: Mervue Publications, 2005.

Dow Chemical Company. *Thirty-Five Opportunities for Small Business with Magnesium: Report by Dr. Willard H. Dow, President of the Dow Chemical Company, to the Special Committee of the United States Senate to Study Problems of American Small Business*. Midland, MI: Dow Chemical Company, 1945.

Dunnigan, Brian Leigh. *Frontier Metropolis: Picturing Early Detroit, 1701–1838*. Detroit: Wayne State University Press, 2001.

Earley, Helen Jones, and James R. Walkinshaw. *Setting the Pace: Oldsmobile's First Hundred Years*. Lansing, MI: Oldsmobile Division of General Motors, 1996.

Edwards, Richard (comp.). *Industries of Michigan: City of Detroit, Historical and Descriptive Review—Industries, Institutions, Commercial, and Manufacturing Advantages, 1880*. New York: Historical Publishing, 1880.

Eldredge, Robert F. *Past and Present of Macomb County, Michigan, Together with Biographical Sketches of Many of Its Leading and Prominent Citizens and Illustrious Dead*. Chicago: S. J. Clarke, 1905.

Elliott, Frank N. *When the Railroad Was King*. Lansing: Michigan History Division, Michigan Department of State, 1977.

Ellis, Franklin. *History of Livingston County, Michigan*. Philadelphia: Everts & Abbott, 1880.

Engelmann, Larry. *Intemperance: The Lost War against Liquor*. New York: Free Press, 1979.

Farmer, Weston. *From My Old Boat Shop*. Portland, OR: Boat House, [1979] 1996.

Fisher, Robert D. (ed.). *Marvyn Scudder Manual of Extinct or Obsolete Companies*. Vol. 3: 1930. New York: Marvyn Scudder Manual of Extinct or Obsolete Companies, 1930.

Fisher, Robert D. (ed.). *Marvyn Scudder Manual of Extinct or Obsolete Companies*. Vol. 4: 1934. New York: Marvyn Scudder Manual of Extinct or Obsolete Companies, 1934.

Flint, Willard. *Lightships of the United States Government: Reference Notes*. Washington, DC: United States Coast Guard Historian's Office, 1989.

Fostle, D. W. *Speedboat*. Mystic, CT: Mystic Seaport Museum Stores, 1988.

Friday, Matthew J. *The Inland Water Route*. Mount Pleasant, SC: Arcadia Publishing, 2010.

Goldey, Charles Pierre, *The Sportsman's Directory and Yearbook*. New York: Pond and Goldey, 1893.

Gougeon, Meade. *The Gougeon Brothers on Boat Construction: Wood and WEST System® Materials*, 5th ed. Bay City, MI: Gougeon Brothers, 2005.

Grayson, Stan. *American Marine Engines, 1885–1950*. Marblehead, MA: Devereux Books, 2008.

Grayson, Stan. *Beautiful Engines: Treasures of the Internal Combustion Century*. Marblehead, MA: Devereux Books, 2001.

Grayson, Stan. *Engines Afloat: From Early Days to D-Day*. Vol. 1: *The Gasoline Era*. Marblehead, MA: Devereux Books, 1999.

Grayson, Stan. *Engines Afloat: From Early Days to D-Day*. Vol. 2: *The Gasoline/ Diesel Era*. Marblehead, MA: Devereux Books, 1999.

Gribbins, Joseph. *Chris-Craft: A History, 1922–1942*. Marblehead, MA: Devereux Books, 2001.

Gribbins, Joseph. *Wooden Boats: From Sculls to Yachts*. New York: Grove Press, 1991.

Grover, David H. *U.S Army Ships and Watercraft of World War II*. Annapolis, MD: Naval Institute Press, 1987.

Guétat, Gérald G. *Classic Speedboats: The Summit, 1945–1962*. Osceola, WI: MBI Publishing, 2000.

Guétat, Gérald G., and Éric Ledru. *Classic Speedboats, 1916–1939*. Osceola, WI: MotorBooks International, 1997.

Homfeld, Max F. *753 Manufacturers of Inboard Marine Engines*. St. Michaels, MD: by author, 1991.

Hunn, Peter. *The Golden Age of the Racing Outboard*. Marblehead, MA: Devereux Books, 2000.

Hunn, Peter. *The Old Outboard Book*. Camden, ME: International Marine Publishing and McGraw-Hill Professional, 1994.

Hunn, Peter. *Tail Fins and Two-Tones: The Guide to America's Classic Fiberglass and Aluminum Runabouts*. Marblehead, MA: Devereux Books, 2006.

Johnson, Frank D. *United States PT-Boats of World War II in Action*. Poole, Dorset: Blandford Press, 1980.

Jones, Gregory O. *The American Sailboat*. St. Paul, MN: MBI Publishing, 2002.

Kavieff, Paul R. *Detroit's Infamous Purple Gang*. Charleston, SC: Arcadia Publishing, 2008.

Kent, Timothy J. *Birchbark Canoes of the Fur Trade*. Vol. 1. Ossineke, MI: Silver Fox Enterprises, 1997.

Kimes, Beverly Rae, and Henry Austin Clark et al. *Standard Catalog of American Cars, 1895–1942*. Iola, WI: Krause Publications, 1996.

Klingel, Gilbert C. *Boatbuilding with Steel*. Camden, ME: International Marine Publishing, 1973.

Knight, Lucia del Sol, and Daniel Bruce MacNaughton. *The Encyclopedia of Yacht Designers*. New York: W. W. Norton, 2006.

Lane, Kit. *Built on the Banks of the Kalamazoo*. Douglas, MI: Pavilion Press, 1993.

Leffingwell, Randy. *Ford Farm Tractors*. Osceola, WI: MBI Publishing, 1998.

Marquis, Albert Nelson (ed.). *The Book of Detroiters*. Chicago: A. N. Marquis, 1908.

Marquis, Albert Nelson (ed.). *The Book of Detroiters*. 2nd ed. Chicago: A. N. Marquis, 1914.

Mason, Philip P. *Rumrunning and the Roaring Twenties: Prohibition on the Michigan-Ontario Waterway*. Detroit: Wayne State University Press, 1995.

Maxwell, Hu. *Wood-Using Industries of Michigan*. Lansing: Michigan Public Domain Commission, State Land Office, 1912.

Mayea, Chad E. *Since the Beginning: Mayea Boats*. Fair Haven, MI: by author, 2005.

Miklos, Paul, Frank Miklos, and Trudi Miklos. *Classic Century Powerboats*. St. Paul, MN: MBI Publishing, 2002.

Mills, James Cooke. *History of Saginaw County, Michigan; Historical, Commercial, Biographical, Profusely Illustrated with Portraits of Early Pioneers, Rare Pictures and Scenes of Olden Times, and Portraits of Representative Citizens of Today*. Saginaw, MI: Seemann & Peters, 1918.

Mollica, Anthony, Jr., and Jack Savage. *Chris-Craft Boats*. St. Paul, MN: MBI Publishing, 2001.

Mollica, Anthony S., with Chris Smith. *Building Chris-Craft: Inside the Factories*. Minneapolis: Voyageur Press and MBI Publishing, 2010.

Mollica, Anthony S., Jr. *The American Wooden Runabout*. St. Paul, MN: MBI Publishing, 2002.

Mollica, Anthony S., Jr. *Dodge Boats*. St. Paul, MN: MotorBooks International and MBI Publishing, 2003.

Mollica, Anthony S., Jr. *Gar Wood Boats: Classics of a Golden Era*. Osceola, WI: MBI Publishing, 1999.

Montieth, Ruth Robbins. *Michigan Census, 1850, Counties of Houghton, Marquette, Michilimackinac, Schoolcraft, Ontonagon*. Allegan, MI: Montieth, 1956.

Moore, C. Philip. *Yachts in a Hurry*. New York: W. W. Norton, 1993.

Moore, Charles. *History of Michigan*. Vol. 2. Chicago: Lewis Publishing, 1915.

Neal, Robert J. *Packards at Speed*. Kent, WA: Aero-Marine History Publishing, 1995.

Nelson, Curtis L. *Hunters in the Shallows: A History of the PT Boat*. Washington, DC: Brassey's, 1998.

Nevins, Allan, and Frank Ernest Hill. *Ford: Expansion and Challenge, 1915–1933*. New York: Charles Scribner's Sons, 1957.

O'Brien, T. Michael. *Guardians of the Eighth Sea: A History of the U.S. Coast Guard on the Great Lakes*. Washington, DC: U.S. Coast Guard, 1976.

Page, H. R., & Co. *History of Bay County, Michigan*. Chicago: H. R. Page, 1883.

Page, H. R., & Co. *The Traverse Region, Historical and Descriptive . . .* Chicago: H. R. Page, 1884.

Penton Publishing Company. *The American Boating Directory, 1906*. Cleveland: Penton Publishing, 1906.

Pike, Howard A. *How to Build an 18-Ft. Launch*. Detroit: Belle Isle Motor Company, 1907.

Polmar, Norman, and Samuel Loring Morison. *PT Boats at War: World War II to Vietnam*. Osceola, WI: MBI Publishing, 1999.

Poor's Railroad Manual Co. *Poor's Manual of Industrials, 1913*. New York: Poor's Railroad Manual Co., 1913.

Record Publishing Company. *Portrait and Biographical Record of Northern Michigan*. Chicago: Record Publishing, 1895.

Rodengen, Jeffrey L. *Commanding the Waterways: The Story of Sea Ray*. Fort Lauderdale, FL: Write Stuff Enterprises, 2008.

Rodengen, Jeffrey L. *The Legend of Chris-Craft*. 3rd ed. Fort Lauderdale, FL: Write Stuff Syndicate, 1998.

Rogers & Thorpe. *Detroit in History and Commerce*. Detroit: Rogers & Thorpe, 1891.

Ross, Robert B., and George B. Catlin, revised by Clarence W. [*sic*] Burton. *Landmarks of Detroit, Michigan: A History of the City*. Detroit: Evening News Association, 1898.

Savage, Jack. *Chris-Craft*. Osceola, WI: MBI Publishing, 2000.

Schroeder, Joseph J., Jr. *Sears, Roebuck & Co. 1908 Catalogue No. 117: The Great Price Maker*. Northfield, IL: DBI Books, 1971.

Schweitzer, Robert, and Michael W. R. Davis. *America's Favorite Homes: Mail-Order Catalogues as a Guide to Popular Early 20th-Century Houses*. Detroit: Wayne State University Press, 1990.

Speltz, Robert. *The Real Runabouts*. Lake Mills, IA: Graphic Publishing, 1977.
Speltz, Robert. *The Real Runabouts II*. Lake Mills, IA: Graphic Publishing, 1978.
Speltz, Robert. *The Real Runabouts III*. Lake Mills, IA: Graphic Publishing, 1980.
Speltz, Robert. *The Real Runabouts IV*. Lake Mills, IA: Graphic Publishing, 1982.
Speltz, Robert. *The Real Runabouts V*. Lake Mills, IA: Graphic Publishing, 1984.
Speltz, Robert. *The Real Runabouts VI*. Lake Mills, IA: Graphic Publishing, 1987.
Speltz, Robert. *The Real Runabouts VII*. Mason City, IA: Stoyles Graphic Services, 1996.
Spurr, Daniel. *Heart of Glass: Fiberglass Boats and the Men Who Made Them*. Camden, ME: International Marine Publishing and McGraw-Hill Professional, 2000.
Stone, Julius Frederick. *Canyon Country: The Romance of a Drop of Water and a Grain of Sand*. New York and London: G. P. Putnam, 1932.
Stonehouse, Frederick. *Wreck Ashore: The United States Life-Saving Service on the Great Lakes*. Duluth, MN: Lake Superior Port Cities, 1994.
Thornton, Neil. *Around the Bay*. Tawas City, MI: Printer's Devil Press, 1991.
Treadwell, Theodore R. *Splinter Fleet: The Wooden Subchasers of World War II*. Annapolis, MD: Naval Institute Press, 2000.
van Reken, Donald L. *Macatawa Park: A Chronicle*. Holland, MI: by author, 1991.
Warner, Cliff. *Detroit Boat Club Centennial Book*. Wayne, MI: Warner, 1939?
Weisberger, Bernard A. *The Dream Maker: William C. Durant, Founder of General Motors*. Boston: Little, Brown, 1979.
Williams, David D., and the Hydroplane and Race Boat Museum. *Hydroplane Racing in Detroit, 1946–2008*. Charleston, SC: Arcadia Publishing, 2008.
Wing, Talcott E. (ed.). *History of Monroe County, Michigan*. New York: Munsell, 1890.
Wittig, William G. *The Story of the Century*. Manistee, MI: Century Boat Company, 1984.
Wolicki, Dale Patrick. *The Historic Architecture of Bay City, Michigan*. Bay City: Bay County Historical Society, 1998.

Articles and Essays

Bailey, Milo. "Arc Welded Steel Pleasure Cruisers." In James F. Lincoln Arc Welding Foundation, *Arc Welding in Design, Manufacture, and Construction*, 377–90. Cleveland: James F. Lincoln Arc Welding Foundation, 1939.
Bauer, K. Jack. "Inland Seas and Overseas: Shipbuilding on the Great Lakes during World War II." *Inland Seas*, Vol. 38, No. 2, Summer 1984, 84–94; Vol. 38, No. 3, Fall 1984, 165–70.
Bowdidge, John S. "Toys and Sporting Goods, 39.4." In *Manufacturing: A Historiographical and Bibliographical Guide*, edited by David O. Whitten and Bessie E. Whitten, 398–99. New York: Greenwood Press, 2000.
Brennan, Bert C. "Fighting Ships from Bay City." *Inland Seas*, Vol. 1, No. 3, July 1945, 21–25.
Cole, Tim. "Splash from the Past." *Popular Mechanics*, June 1986, 77.

Diefendorf, H. G. "The Extent of the Marine Gasoline Engine Business." *Gas Power*, Vol. 9, No. 2, August 1911. 377–80.

Grayson, Stan. "The Man from Motor Boat Lane: Joe Van Blerck and the Van Blerck Motor Company." *WoodenBoat*, No. 197, July–August 2007, 82–91.

Grayson, Stan. "Time Machine: Exploring America's Oldest Marine Engine." *WoodenBoat*, No. 213, March–April 2010, 62–69.

Hall, Bruce. "Valley Boat & Engine Company of Baldwinsville, NY." *Brightwork: Newsletter of the Finger Lakes Chapter of the Antique & Classic Boat Society*, December 2000, 5–6.

Halls, Bill. "Boat Maker Builds Hope in Quality, Price." *Detroit News*, January 29, 1998, B1.

Hounshell, David A. "Ford Eagle Boats and Mass Production during World War I." In *Military Enterprise and Technological Change: Perspectives on the American Experience*, edited by Merritt Roe Smith, 175–202. Cambridge, MA: Massachusetts Institute of Technology Press, 1985.

Jannsen, Peter A. "The Booming Boating Business." *Motor Boating & Sailing*, February 1987, 11.

Kelly, Chester Dorman. "Boat Builders for the World." *Magazine of Michigan*, Vol. 2, Nos. 5–6, May–June 1930, 5–6.

Lapinski, Patrick. "The Long Journey of the *Voyageur I*." *Nor'Easter* (Lake Superior Marine Museum Association), Vol. 32, No. 1, First Quarter, 2007, 1–6.

McDonald, Pete. "Engine Failure: The Slow, Painful Death of Once-Proud OMC." *Boating*, May 2001, 152–56.

Norris, Thaddeus. "The Michigan Grayling." *Scribner's Monthly*, Vol. 19, No. 1, November 1879, 17–23.

Peters, Scott M. "Roar on the Water: Gar Wood Searches for Speed." *Michigan History*, Vol. 81, No. 5, September–October 1997, 64–68.

Phillips, John R. "Kalamazoo Canvas Boat at 75." *Kalamazoo Magazine*, April 1964, 16–17, 38–41.

Polacsek, John F. "Yachts of the Auto Barons." In *Tonnancour*. Vol. 2: *Life in Grosse Pointe and along the Shores of Lake St. Clair*, edited by Arthur M. Woodford, 156–68. Detroit: Grosse Pointe Historical Society and Omnigraphics, 1996.

Prather, Donald F. "Yachting at Chicago." In *Sailing Craft: Mostly Descriptive of Smaller Pleasure Sail Boats of the Day*, edited by Edwin J. Schoettle, 381–404. New York: MacMillan, 1937.

Ratigan, William. "Last of the Mackinaw Boat Builders." *The Boating Industry*, Vol. 21, No. 6, August 10, 1958, 52.

Reynolds, Geoffrey. "Jesiek Brothers Shipyard: From Minnows to Marina." *Joint Archives Quarterly*, Vol. 2, No. 22, Summer 2012, 1–3.

Reynolds, Geoffrey D. "Almost Famous: The Foster Boat Company." *Rudder* (Antique and Classic Boat Society), Vol. 19, No. 3, January 1, 2010, 17–19.

Reynolds, Geoffrey D. "Fifty Years of Making Fun: The Story of the Slick Craft Boat Company." *Joint Archives of Holland Quarterly*, Vol. 14, No. 4, Winter 2005, 1–5.

Reynolds, Geoffrey D. "Fifty Years of Making Fun: The History of the Slikkers

Family and Boat Building, Part Two." *Joint Archives of Holland Quarterly*, Vol. 15, No. 3, Fall 2005, 1–4.

Reynolds, Geoffrey D. "Slick Craft: The Quality Name in Boating." *Classic Boating*, No. 127, September 1, 2005, 6–11.

University of Michigan, Department of Engineering. "General Announcement of Courses in Engineering and Architecture, 1913–1917." *University Bulletin*, new series, Vol. 14, No. 18, April 1913. 317.

van der Linde, Claas. "James Roderick 'Rod' MacAlpine-Downie." In *The Encyclopedia of Yacht Designers*, edited by Lucia del Sol Knight and Daniel Bruce MacNaughton, 293. New York: W. W. Norton, 2006.

Van Der Linden, Peter. "The Art of Ship Repair . . . McLouth of Marine City." *Telescope*, May–June 1976. 66–74.

Periodicals

Automobile
Boating
The Boating Industry
The Brine Well (Dow Chemical Company)
Business Man's Magazine
Classic Boating
Defoe Rollover (Defoe Shipbuilding Company)
Detroit Marine Historian
The Directory of Michigan Manufacturers
Dow Diamond (Dow Chemical Company)
Dun's Review
The Fisherman
Fore 'N' Aft
Forest and Stream
Gas Power
Great Lakes Fisherman
Great Lakes Journal
Horseless Age
Inland Seas
Iron Age
Kalamazoo Magazine
Lakeland Boating
Lakeland Yachting
Lloyd's Register of American Yachts
Magazine of Michigan
Marine Engineering
Marine Review
Michigan Conservation
Michigan History
Michigan Investor

Michigan Manufacturer
Michigan Manufacturer and Financial Record
Michigan Sportsman
Motor Boat
Motor Boating
Motor Way
Motor World
Newsweek
Northern Michigan Skipper
Outing Magazine
Popular Mechanics
Power Boating
Rudder
Rudder (Antique and Classic Boat Society)
Sail and Sweep
Scientific American
Sports Illustrated
State Trooper
Telescope
WoodenBoat
Yachting
Evening News Association. *The Quarterly Register of Current History*, Vol. 2, No. 6, May 1892.
Fort Miami Heritage Society. *Heritage Journal: The Newsletter of the Fort Miami Heritage Society*, Vol. 4, No. 2, Summer 2004, 6–7.
Heritage Journal, Vol. 5, No. 2, Summer 2005, 6–7.

Trade Catalogs

Ann Arbor Boat Company. *Launches, Rowboats, Canoes: Let Us Build Them Right for You*. Ann Arbor: Ann Arbor Boat Company, 1908, Bentley Historical Library, University of Michigan, Ann Arbor.
Blomstrom, C. H., Motor Company. *The C. H. Blomstrom Motor Company: Builders of Gasoline Launches, Marine Gasoline Engines, Solid and Reversing Propeller Wheels*. Detroit: C. H. Blomstrom Motor Co., 1903?, Library of Michigan, Rare Book Collection, Lansing.
Brooks Boat Manufacturing Company.
Davis Boat & Oar Company.
Kalamazoo Folding Canvas Boat Company.
King Folding Canvas Boat Company
Life-Saving Folding Canvas Boat Company, Michigan Maritime Museum, South Haven.
Modern Boat Pattern Company, Ltd.
Pioneer Boat & Pattern Company.
Racine Boat Manufacturing Company.

Rescue Life Boat Company. Announcement, Rescue Life Boat Company, Muskegon, MI, Rescue Life Boat Company, 1900?, Library of Michigan, Rare Book Collection, Lansing.

Truscott Boat Manufacturing Company. Truscott Boat Manufacturing Company, January 1898, Library of Michigan, Rare Book Collection, Lansing.

Truscott Boat Manufacturing Company. Advance Catalogue, 1905. Reprinted by The Vestal Press, Vestal, New York, from an original in the collection of Carl Fila, n.d., c. 1982.

Business Directories, City Directories, and State Gazetteers

Burch & Hamilton. *Burch & Hamilton's Gazetteer of the Detroit & Milwaukee and Flint & Pere Marquette Railroads, 1870–71.* Detroit: Burch & Hamilton, 1870.

Chapin & Brother. *Michigan State Gazetteer and Business Directory, 1867–68.* Detroit: Chapin & Brother, 1867.

Clark, Charles F. (comp.). *Michigan State Gazetteer and Business Directory for 1863–4.* Detroit: Charles F. Clark, 1863.

Hawes, George W. *George W. Hawes' Michigan State Gazetteer and Business Directory for 1860.* Detroit: F. Raymond, 1859.

Ihling Bros. & Everard. *Ihling Bros. & Everard's Kalamazoo City and County Directory for the Year Ending November 1st, 1904.* Kalamazoo, MI: Ihling Bros. & Everard, 1903.

Michigan Manufacturer and Financial Record. *The Directory of Michigan Manufacturers, 1960.* Detroit: Manufacturer Publishing, 1960.

Michigan Manufacturer and Financial Record. *The Directory of Michigan Manufacturers, 1965.* Detroit: Manufacturer Publishing, 1965.

Michigan Manufacturer and Financial Record. *The Directory of Michigan Manufacturers, 1969.* Detroit: Manufacturer Publishing, 1969.

Platt, Montague T. *Michigan State Business Directory, 1870–71.* Detroit: Tribune Book & Job Office, 1870.

Polk, R. L., & Co. *Bay City Directory, 1902–1903.* Detroit: R. L. Polk, 1902.

Polk, R. L., & Co. *Detroit City Directory for 1889.* Detroit: R. L. Polk, 1889.

Polk, R. L., & Co. *Detroit City Directory, 1909.* Detroit: R. L. Polk, 1909.

Polk, R. L., & Co. *East Saginaw and Saginaw City Directory for 1886.* Detroit: R. L. Polk, 1886.

Polk, R. L., & Co. *Michigan State Gazetteer and Business Directory, 1875.* Detroit: Tribune Printing Company, 1875.

Polk, R. L., & Co. *Michigan State Gazetteer and Business Directory, 1877.* Detroit: R. L. Polk, 1877.

Polk, R. L., & Co. *Michigan State Gazetteer and Business Directory, 1879.* Detroit: R. L. Polk, 1879.

Polk, R. L., & Co. *Michigan State Gazetteer and Business Directory, 1881.* Detroit: R. L. Polk, 1881.

Polk, R. L., & Co. *Michigan State Gazetteer and Business Directory, 1883.* Detroit: R. L. Polk, 1883.

Polk, R. L., & Co. *Michigan State Gazetteer and Business Directory, 1885.* Detroit: R. L. Polk, 1885.

Polk, R. L., & Co. *Michigan State Gazetteer and Business Directory, 1887.* Detroit: R. L. Polk, 1887.

Polk, R. L., & Co. *Michigan State Gazetteer and Business Directory, 1891–92.* Detroit: R. L. Polk, 1891.

Polk, R. L., & Co. *Michigan State Gazetteer and Business Directory, 1897.* Detroit: R. L. Polk, 1897.

Polk, R. L., & Co. *Michigan State Gazetteer and Business Directory, 1899.* Detroit: R. L. Polk, 1899.

Polk, R. L., & Co. *Michigan State Gazetteer and Business Directory, 1901.* Detroit: R. L. Polk, 1901.

Polk, R. L., & Co. *Michigan State Gazetteer and Business Directory, 1903–1904.* Detroit: R. L. Polk, 1903.

Polk, R. L., & Co. *Michigan State Gazetteer and Business Directory, 1905–06.* Detroit: R. L. Polk, 1905.

Polk, R. L., & Co. *Michigan State Gazetteer and Business Directory, 1909–1910.* Detroit: R. L. Polk, 1909.

Polk, R. L., & Co. *Michigan State Gazetteer and Business Directory, 1911–1912.* Detroit: R. L. Polk, 1911.

Polk, R. L., & Co. *Michigan State Gazetteer and Business Directory, 1917.* Detroit: R. L. Polk, 1917.

Polk, R. L., & Co. *Michigan State Gazetteer and Business Directory, 1923.* Detroit: R. L. Polk, 1923.

Polk, R. L., & Co. *R. L. Polk & Co.'s Bay City Directory, Year Ending October 15, 1906.* Detroit: R. L. Polk, 1905.

Polk, R. L., & Co. *R. L. Polk & Co.'s Detroit City Directory, 1906–1907.* Detroit: R. L. Polk, 1906.

Polk, R. L., & Co. *R. L. Polk & Co.'s Grand Rapids City Directory, 1900.* Grand Rapids, MI: Grand Rapids Directory Co., 1900.

Polk, R. L., & Co. *Polk's Saginaw City Directory, 1921–1943.* Various annual issues.

Scripps, J. E., and R. L. Polk (comps.). *Michigan State Gazetteer and Business Directory for 1873.* Detroit: Tribune Book and Job Office, 1873.

Manuscripts

Chris-Craft Financial Ledgers, June 1922–December 1924, Chris-Craft Collection, Mariners' Museum, Newport News, Virginia.

Collection of the Heritage Museum and Cultural Center, St. Joseph, Michigan, 78.11.34—-901.

Frank E. Kirby Collection, Catalog 01437, Burton Historical Collections, Detroit Public Library, Detroit.

Garfield Arthur Wood Collection, MS68-307, Burton Historical Collections, Detroit Public Library, Detroit.

Hill, Michelle. "Recapturing a Fading Maritime Consciousness: Shipyards in St.

Joseph, Michigan." Paper prepared for Dr. Michael Chiarappa in his Seminar in Local History, 9. Western Michigan University.

Jesse Wells Church Collection, GLMS-10, Historical Collections of the Great Lakes, Bowling Green State University, Bowling Green, Ohio, Folders 2 and 4.

John L. Hacker Collection, MS310, Mariners' Museum, Newport News, Virginia.

Mercer Fisher to Jane Granzow Miles, undated, with sample of wooden plugs, Heritage Museum and Cultural Center, St. Joseph, Michigan, 78.11.34-901.

Postcards of catalog orders, Brooks Boat Manufacturing Company, 1905–8, in the collection of the Bay County Historical Society, Historical Museum of Bay County, Bay City, Michigan, Accession No. 89-93.1-.15.

Program, Presentation of the U.S. Navy E-Pennant to the Robinson Marine Construction Company, ceremony held March 5, 1942, collection of the Heritage Museum and Cultural Center, St. Joseph, Michigan.

Walter Smith Miscellaneous Ship Drawing Collection, Kingsbury, S. B., Naval Architect, Designs, GLMS-74mf, Historical Collections of the Great Lakes, Bowling Green State University, Bowling Green, Ohio.

Newspapers

Adrian Daily Telegram
Benton Harbor News-Palladium
Cadillac News
Charleston Gazette (Charleston, WV)
Crawford County Avalanche
Detroit Evening News
Detroit Free Press
Detroit News
Detroit Tribune
Flint Journal
Holland Evening Sentinel
Kalamazoo Gazette
Ludington Daily News
Mount Carmel Daily Republican Register (Mount Carmel, IL)
Muskegon Chronicle
New York Times
Raleigh Register (Beckley, WV)
Saginaw News
Saginaw Valley News
St. Charles Union
St. Joseph Herald-Press
St. Joseph Saturday Herald
St. Lawrence Republican (Ogdensburg, NY)
Tecumseh Herald
Traverse City Record-Eagle

Government Documents

Michigan

Brockett v. Lewis, 144 Mich 560, Michigan Reports, July 1906.

Foote v. Greilick, 166 Mich. 636, Supreme Court of Michigan, September 29, 1911, 132 NW 473.

Michigan Bureau of Labor and Industrial Statistics. *Second Annual Report of the Bureau of Labor and Industrial Statistics, February 1, 1885*. Lansing: Bureau of Labor and Industrial Statistics, 1885.

Michigan Bureau of Labor and Industrial Statistics. *First Annual Report of Inspection of Factories in Michigan*. Lansing: Michigan Bureau of Labor and Industrial Statistics, 1894.

Michigan Bureau of Labor and Industrial Statistics. *Third Annual Report of Inspection of Factories in Michigan*. Lansing: Bureau of Labor and Industrial Statistics, 1896.

Michigan Bureau of Labor and Industrial Statistics. *Fifth Annual Report of Inspection of Factories in Michigan*. Lansing: Bureau of Labor and Industrial Statistics, 1898.

Michigan Bureau of Labor and Industrial Statistics. *Sixteenth Annual Report of the Bureau of Labor and Industrial Statistics*. Lansing: Bureau of Labor and Industrial Statistics, 1899.

Michigan Bureau of Labor and Industrial Statistics. *Seventeenth Annual Report of the Bureau of Labor and Industrial Statistics*. Lansing: Bureau of Labor and Industrial Statistics, 1900.

Michigan Bureau of Labor and Industrial Statistics. *Eighteenth Annual Report of the Bureau of Labor and Industrial Statistics*. Lansing: Michigan Bureau of Labor and Industrial Statistics, 1901.

Michigan Bureau of Labor and Industrial Statistics. *Twentieth Annual Report of the Bureau of Labor and Industrial Statistics*. Lansing: Bureau of Labor and Industrial Statistics, 1903

Michigan Bureau of Labor and Industrial Statistics. *Twenty-Third Annual Report of the Bureau of Labor and Industrial Statistics*. Lansing: Bureau of Labor and Industrial Statistics, 1906.

Michigan Bureau of Labor and Industrial Statistics. *Twenty-Fifth Annual Report of the Bureau of Labor and Industrial Statistics, 1908*. Lansing: Bureau of Labor and Industrial Statistics, 1908.

Michigan Bureau of Labor and Industrial Statistics. *Twenty-Sixth Annual Report of the Bureau of Labor and Industrial Statistics*. Lansing: Bureau of Labor and Industrial Statistics, 1909.

Michigan Department of Commerce. Corporations and Securities Commission. Abstracts of Reports of Corporations, Lot 3, Vol. 3 (1899–1904); Lot 3, Vol. 4 (1903–9); Lot 3, Vol. 5 (1910–14), Archives of Michigan, RG 61-11-A.

Michigan Department of Commerce. Corporations and Securities Commission. Brooks Boat Manufacturing Company Corporation Annual Report, 1903, Archives of Michigan, RG 61-11-A, Box 91, No. 150, Reel 1409.

Michigan Department of Commerce. Corporations and Securities Commission. Dee-Wite, Inc., Corporation Annual Report, 1933, Archives of Michigan, RG 64-6-A, Box 25, Vol. 1, No. 182, Reel 7201.

Michigan Department of Commerce. Corporations and Securities Commission. Hacker & Fermann, Inc., Corporation Annual Report, 1925, Archives of Michigan, RG 61-11-A, Box 573, No. 151, Reel 5795.

Michigan Department of Commerce. Corporations and Securities Commission. Life Saving Folding Canvas Boat Company, Corporation Annual Report, 1906, Archives of Michigan, RG 61-11-A, Box 129, No. 319, Reel 1463.

Michigan Department of Commerce. Corporations and Securities Commission. Michigan Yacht & Power Company, Corporation Annual Report, 1900, Archives of Michigan, RG-61-11-A, Box 67, Vol. 1, No. 220, Reel 1384.

Michigan Department of Commerce. Corporations and Securities Commission. Pioneer Boat and Pattern Co., Corporation Annual Report, 1906, Archives of Michigan, RG 61-11-A, Box 131, Vol. 1, No. 354, Reel 1466.

Michigan Department of Commerce. Corporations and Securities Commission. Russell J. Pouliot, Inc., Corporation Annual Report, 1934, Archives of Michigan, RG 65-20-A, Box 41, Vol. 1, No. 112, Reel 7274.

Michigan Department of Commerce. Corporations and Securities Commission. Sintz Gas Engine Company, Corporation Annual Report, 1894, Archives of Michigan, RG 61-11-A, Box 32, Vol. 1, No. 42, Reel 1353.

Michigan Department of Transportation. *150 Years of Michigan's Railroad History*. Lansing: Michigan Department of Transportation, c. 1987.

Michigan Secretary of State. *Census of the State of Michigan, 1884*. Vol. 2: *Agriculture and Manufactories*. Lansing: Secretary of State, 1886.

Michigan Secretary of State. *Census of the State of Michigan, 1894: Agriculture, Manufactures, Mines, and Fisheries*. Vol. 2. Lansing: Secretary of State, 1896.

Michigan State Board of Agriculture. *Eighteenth Annual Report of the Secretary of the State Board of Agriculture of the State of Michigan for the Year Ending August 31st 1879*. Lansing: State Board of Agriculture, 1880.

Other States

Ohio Secretary of State. *Annual Report of the Secretary of State to the Governor of the State of Ohio for the Year Ending November 15, 1904*. Springfield, OH: Secretary of State, 1905.

United States

General Motors Corporation v. Cadillac Marine & Boat Co., and Ash Craft Co. 1964, DC Mich. DCWD (WD Mich. 1964) 226 F. Supp. 716, 737–38.

Securities and Exchange Commission v. Gilbert, 29 F. Supp. 654 (1939).

U.S. Bureau of the Census. *Ninth Census of the United States, 1870*. Washington, DC: Government Printing Office, 1872.

U.S. Commission of Fish and Fisheries. *Report of the Commissioner for 1872 and 1873, part 2*. Washington, DC: Government Printing Office, 1874, A—

"Inquiry into the Decrease of the Food-Fishes," I.—"Report on the Fisheries of the Great Lakes: The Result of Inquiries Prosecuted in 1871 and 1872 by James W. Milner."

U.S. Congress. Senate. Committee on Military Affairs. "Aircraft Production: Hearings," Sixty-Fifth Congress, 2nd session, parts 1 and 2. 1918.

U.S. Congress. Senate. Committee on Interstate Commerce. *Expediting Loading and Unloading of Railroad Freight Cars: Hearings before a Subcommittee of the Committee on Interstate Commerce, United States Senate, Seventy-Seventh Congress, Second Session, on S.J. Res. 147, a Joint Resolution Providing for the More Effective Prosecution of the War by Expediting the Loading and Unloading of Railroad Freight Cars, June 30 and July 1, 1942, part 1.* Washington, DC: Government Printing Office, 1942.

U.S. Department of Commerce. Bureau of the Census. *Biennial Census of Manufacturers, 1927.* Washington, DC: Government Printing Office, 1930, table 11, "Number of Power Boats Built (Less Than 5 Gross Tons), for the United States . . . by States, 1927," 1166.

U.S. Department of Commerce. Bureau of the Census. *Biennial Census of Manufactures, 1931.* Washington, DC: Government Printing Office, 1935, table 6, "Number of Power Boats Built (Less than 5 Gross Tons), for the United States, 1925 to 1931, and for States, 1931," 1065.

U.S. Department of Commerce. Bureau of the Census. *Biennial Census of Manufacturers, 1933.* Washington, DC: Government Printing Office, 1936. table 1, "Summary for the United States, 1927 to 1933 and for States, 1933 and 1931," 615.

U.S. Department of Commerce. Bureau of the Census. *Biennial Census of Manufactures, 1935.* Washington, DC: Government Printing Office, 1938, table 4, "Number of Vessels Launched . . . 1929 to 1935," 1166.

U.S. Department of Commerce. Bureau of the Census. *Biennial Census of Manufacturers, 1937,* part 1. Washington, DC: Government Printing Office, 1939, table 2, "Summary by States, 1937," 1218.

U.S. Department of Commerce. Bureau of the Census. *Fifteenth Census of the United States, Manufactures, 1929.* Vol. 2: *Reports by Industries.* Washington, DC: Government Printing Office, 1933, "Ship and Boat Building," table 2, "General Statistics by States, 1929, 1927, and 1919," 1233; table 11, "Number of Power Boats Built (Less Than 5 Gross Tons), for the United States . . . by States, 1929; table 14, "Wage Earners by Months for the United States . . . and by States, 1929," 1241.

U.S. Department of Commerce. Bureau of the Census. *Fourteenth Census of the United States Taken in the Year 1920.* Vol. 10: *Manufacturers: 1919, Reports for Selected Industries.* Washington, DC: Government Printing Office, 1923, "Shipbuilding, Including Boat Building," 1006–25.

U.S. Department of Commerce. Bureau of the Census. *Sixteenth Census of the United States, Manufactures: 1939.* Vol. 2, Part 2: *Reports by Industries Groups 11 to 20.* Washington. DC: Government Printing Office, 1942, table 5, "Wage Earners Engaged in Manufacturing . . . by States, 1939," 550.

U.S. Department of Commerce. Bureau of the Census. *Sixteenth Census of the*

United States: 1940, Manufactures 1939. Vol. 2, Part 2: *Reports by Industries Groups 11 to 20.* Washington, DC: Government Printing Office, 1942.

U.S. Department of Commerce and Labor. Bureau of the Census. *Manufactures, 1905.* Part 4: *Special Reports on Selected Industries.* Washington, DC: Government Printing Office, 1908, table 26, "Number and Value of Boats under Five Tons, by States: 1905 and 1900," 342.

U.S. Department of the Interior. U.S. Census Office. *Twelfth Census of the United States Taken in the Year 1900, Census Reports.* Vol. 10: *Manufactures.* Part 4: *Special Reports on Selected Industries (Continued).* Washington, DC: U.S. Census Office, 1902. table 17, "Establishments Engaged in the Construction and Repair of Small Boats, with Capital and Value of Products, by States: 1900," 226; table 20, "Small Boats, by States: 1900," 227.

U.S. Life-Saving Service. *Annual Report of the Operations of the United States Life-Saving Service for the Fiscal Year Ending June 30, 1883.* Washington, DC: Government Printing Office, 1884, addenda 1, "Daily Record of the Proceedings of the Board," September 3, 1883.

U.S. Navy Department. Construction and Repair Bureau. *Ships' Data, U.S. Naval Vessels, November 1, 1918.* Washington, DC: Government Printing Office, 1919.

Patents

Chambers, Arthur E. Boat. U.S. Patent 681,363, filed March 26, 1900, patented August 27, 1901.

Eichner, Ferdinand R. Metal Boat Construction. U.S. Patent 2,500,279, filed July 26, 1944, patented March 14, 1950.

Osgood, Nathaniel A. Improvement in Portable Folding Boats. U.S. Patent 200,664, filed February 11, 1878, patented February 26, 1878.

Pouliot, Russell J. Outboard Motor Boat. U.S. Patent 1,818,273, filed June 14, 1929, patented August 11, 1931.

Stiver, Charles W. Boat Construction. U.S. Patent 2,083,410, filed May 4, 1935, patented June 8, 1937.

Verburg, Edwin. Boat. U.S. Patent 597,595, filed June 9, 1897, patented January 18, 1898.

Online Sources and Websites

"*Amy Ann,* A Custom One-Off Creation from Morin Boats." http://www.woody-boater.com/communityweb/amy-ann-a-custom-one-off-creation-from-morin-boats/. Accessed March 16, 2013.

"Antique and Classic Boat Society." http://www.acbs.org/. Accessed March 16, 2013.

Barton, D. W. "The Northern Michigan (NM) Racing Sloop: Its Design, Builders, and Similar Boats," (retyped from a draft document dated March 4, 1992), Little Traverse Yacht Club. http://ltyc.org/sailing/club-racing/fleet-directory/nm/. Accessed June 13, 2012.

Black, Jean Blashfield. "Wood at War." *Wood and Wood Products*, January 1, 1995. http://www.thefreelibrary.com/Wood+at+war.-a017796175. Accessed 4 January 2012.

Bowling Green State University, Historical Collections of the Great Lakes. Great Lakes Vessels Index. http://www.bgsu.edu/colleges/library/cac/page38714.html. Accessed April 24, 2013.

"Century Boats—History." http://centuryboats.com/about/histor. Accessed August 10, 2014.

"Chris-Craft History." http://www.chriscraft.com/main/company/history.aspx. Accessed August 10, 2014.

"Chrysler Historical Information Page." http://chryslersailing.lizards.net/sail_history.html. Accessed March 2, 2013.

Coachbuilt. "Racine Boat Manufacturing Company." http://www.coachbuilt.com/bui/r/racine_boat/racine_boat.htm. Accessed 28 March 2012.

Coachbuilt. "Wadsworth Manufacturing Company." http://www.coachbuilt.com/bui/w/wadsworth/wadsworth.htm. Accessed July 10, 2012.

"Crest Pontoon Boats." http://crestpontoonboats.com/crest/. Accessed March 23, 2013.

"Detroit Boat Company." http://www.antiquengines.com/DBC_Literature.htm. Accessed July 4, 2012.

Colton, Tim. "Eddy Shipbuilding, Bay City." Shipbuilding History. http://shipbuildinghistory.com/history/shipyards/4emergencysmall/eddy.htm. Accessed 2 January 2013.

"Danenberg Boatworks." http://www.danenbergboatworks.com/index.html. Accessed March 16, 2013.

Dring, Tim. "Summary of the Development of Early Motorized Lifeboats for the USLSS and USCG." U.S. Coast Guard History Program. http://www.uscg.mil/history/articles/DringDevelopmentEarlyMotorizedLifeboats.pdf. Accessed 22 March 2012.

"Extractions from the 'Avalanche', a Crawford Co., MI Newspaper, 1879–1940s." http://stoliker.tripod.com/pafn02.htm. Accessed December 11, 2009.

Farley, Fred. "Les Staudacher Remembered." Hydroplane and Raceboat Museum. http://www.thunderboats.org/history/history0418.html. Accessed February 2, 2013.

"Fiberglassics." http://www.fiberglassics.com/. Accessed March 16, 2013.

"Genmar Holdings, Inc. History." http://www.fundinguniverse.com/company-histories/genmar-holdings-inc-history/. Accessed March 17, 2013.

Gillespie, Michael. "A Tale of Two Boats," *Lake of the Ozarks Business Journal*, September 2005. http://www.lakehistory.info/excursionboats.html. Accessed November 14, 2012.

"Grand Craft." http://www.grandcraft.com/. Accessed March 16, 2013.

"Great Lakes Boat Building School History." http://www.glbbs.org/History. Accessed March 16, 2013.

Greater West Bloomfield Historical Society. "Charles Plass, Designer of Keewahdin Sailboat." http://www.gwbhs.org/object/charles-plass-designer-of-keewahdin-sailboat/. Accessed April 12, 2013.

Gonsior, Jeremy. "Classic Boat Maker Beached." *Holland Sentinel*, June 12, 2009. http://www.hollandsentinel.com/news/x2122534558/Classic-boat-maker-beached. Accessed March 16, 2013.

"I Felt a Great Relief." *Sports Illustrated*, December 7, 1959. http://www.si.com/vault/1959/12/07/604521/events--discoveries. Accessed August 10, 2014.

Koenig, Karen M. "Boat Maker 'Pedals' Thermoforming Technique." *Plastics Machining*, July 1999. http://www.plasticsmachining.com/magazine/199907/leisurelife.html. Accessed March 9, 2013.

Lefebvre, Andrew. "Prohibition and the Smuggling of Intoxicating Liquors between the Two Saults." *Northern Mariner*, Vol. 11, No. 3, July 2001, 33–40. http://www.cnrs-scrn.org/northern_mariner/vol11/nm_11_3_33to40.pdf. Accessed September 1, 2012.

Lopez, Alexandria. "A Legacy of Success: Four Winns Goes the Distance." *North American Composites*, Fall 2011. http://www.nacomposites.com/delivering-performance/page.asp?issueid=18&page=cover. Accessed March 2, 2013.

McCue, Gary W. "The Baker Boat." http://www.geocities.ws/gwmccue/Competition/Baker.html. Accessed April 10, 2013.

Michigan Historical Center. Michigan Death Certificates, 1897–1920, James Dean, Wayne County, 1905, No. 579. www.seekingmichigan.org. Accessed November 23, 2009.

Miss U.S. I Official Site. http://missus1.com/. Accessed February 2, 2013.

Moran, Tim. Mid-American Shore Report, "The Amazing Crescent Boat," *Great Lakes Sailor*, November–December 1988. http://goatyard.com/crescent-sailing/. Accessed June 29, 2013.

Mount Clemens Public Library. *The Clinton-Kalamazoo Canal*. Mount Clemens, MI: Mount Clemens Public Library, 2008. http://www.mtclib.org/local%20history/canal.pdf. Accessed April 6, 2013.

Mutineer 15 Class Association. "Men behind the Mutineeer." http://www.mutineer15.org/men-behind-the-mutineer.html. Accessed March 2, 2013.

NMMA Releases 2010 U.S. Recreational Boat Registration Statistics Report." http://www.nmma.org/news.aspx?id=18028. Accessed March 23, 2013.

Parkhurst, Terry. "Chrysler Marine: Chrysler on Water." http://www.allpar.com/history/marine.html. Accessed February 26, 2013.

Passic, Frank. "Darrow Boats Once Made in Albion." *Albion Recorder*, April 12, 1999, 4. http://www.albionmich.com/history/histor_notebook/R990412.shtml. Accessed June 28, 2013.

Reynolds, Geoffrey D. "Roamer, before Chris-Craft," *Faculty Publications*, paper 424. http://digitalcommons.hope.edu/faculty_publications/424. *Classic Boating*, No. 167, May 1, 2012, 6–7. Accessed August 10, 2014.

Rhude, Andreas Jordahl. "AeroCraft-Harwill." Fiberglassics.com. http://www.fiberglassics.com/library/Aerocraft. Accessed February 23, 2013.

Rhude, Andreas Jordahl. "Thompson's Fiberglass Boats." http://www.fiberglassics.com/library/Thompson_Bros. Accessed March 15, 2013.

Sparkman & Stephens Design 509: Brasil and Mackinac Classes. http://sparkmanstephens.blogspot.com/2011/04/design-509-brasil-and-mackinac-classes.html. Accessed January 12, 2013.

Suran, William C. "With the Wings of an Angel: A Biography of Ellsworth and Emery Kolb, Photographers of Grand Canyon." Manuscript, 1991. http://www.grandcanyonhistory.org/Publications/Kolb/kolb.html. Accessed April 17, 2013.

Tiara Yachts. Press release, "S2 Yachts Re-tools for the Future," July 3, 2012. http://www.tiarayachts.com/tiara-news/2012-press-releases/s2-yachts-re-tools-for-the-future.aspx. Accessed March 4, 2013.

U.S. Department of Commerce. Bureau of the Census. *Industry Statistics Sampler, NAICS 336612, Boat Building.* https://www.census.gov/econ/isp/sampler.php?naicscode=336612&naicslevel=6. Accessed August 16, 2014.

"Van Dam History." http://vandamboats.com/about-us/history/. Accessed March 16, 2013.

Verhage, Kris. "Four Winns to be Sold." *Cadillac News,* December 11, 2009. http://cadillacnews.com/news_story/?story_id=1273652&year=2009&issue=20091211. Accessed August 19, 2014.

"Wings and Water: First Loves." *Robb Report,* April 1, 2007. http://robbreport.com/Boating-Yachting/Wings--Water-First-Loves. Accessed August 10, 2014.

"Yar-Craft—History." http://yarcraft.com/history.html. Accessed March 23, 2013.

Zacharias, Pat. "Sailing on Lake St. Clair's Icy Winds," *Detroit News,* February 8, 1998. http://blogs.detroitnews.com/history/1998/02/07/sailing-on-lake-st-clairs-icy-winter-winds/. Accessed June 29, 2013.

Maps

Battle Creek, Michigan (3920), June 1887.

Chadwyck-Healey, Inc. *The Sanborn Fire Insurance Maps.* Teaneck, NJ: Chadwyck-Healey, 1983–90.

St. Joseph, Michigan (4184), August 1892, October 1896, July 1902.

Wyandotte, Michigan (4238), April 1895.

Index

Note: Pages in italics indicate illustrations and tables.

LCVP (landing craft, vehicle and personnel), 161
LeBaron, Inc., 128
LeGroue, Henry, 44
Leisure Life Limited, 224–25
Lend-Lease projects, 156, 157
Lenoir, Jean-Joseph Etienne, 28
"Level Riding" runabouts, 129
Lewis, Harry, 10
Liberty aircraft engines, 93, 98, 100, 109, 112
Life Saving Folding Canvas Boat Co., 12–13
lifeboats: construction during WWI, 90; folding canvas, 12–13; motorized, 42; patents on, 27; Woolsey's Patent Life Raft, 21
Liggett, Alfred, 69. *See also* A. G. Liggett & Son Co.
Liggett, Louis Kroh, 69, 117, 118
Light Vessel No. 82, 61
Light Vessel No. 95, 60–61
lighthouse service boats, 60–61, 134, 141
Lincoln Motor Co., 93
Linn, Robert, 195
Lippincott, J. Gordon, 180
Lisee, Joseph Napoleon "Nap," 99, 105–7, 178
Little, Ron, 209
Little Jewish Navy, 95
Little Traverse Yacht Club, 146
Lockwood, Andre, 78
Lockwood racing motors, 142
Lockwood-Ash Motor Co., 78–79
Lodge, Alice Dwight Berry, 125, 127
Lodge, Edwin, 125
Lodge, John, 126
Lodge, Joseph Berry, 125, 126, 127, 128
Lodge engines, 127
Lodge Motors, Inc., 128
Lodge Torpedo, 128
Loewy, Raymond, 125
Lombardo, Guy, 207, 208
Lone Star Boat Co., 204
Lone Wolf, 153

Lorimer, Robert, 22
Lotus, 40
Love Construction and Engineering Co., 167
Ludolph's Wildcat, 145
Luke, W. L., 63
lumber, sourcing, 49, 84–85, 177
lumber industry, 5, 69
Lusitania, 88
luxury tax (WWI), 89
Lyman Boat Co., 187
Lyons, Laurence, 97

M. M. Lewis & Sons Co., 10
M. O. Cross Engine Co., 41
MacAlpine-Downie, James Roderick "Rod," 204
Macatawa Bay Boat Works, 229
MacGregor, Charles, 148
MacKerer, William ("Mac" or "Bill"): at C. C. Smith & Sons, 105–7, 108; at Chris-Craft, 130, 155, 161, 185, 215; employment during Great Depression, 130–31, 139; incorporation of Robinson Marine Construction Co., 138–39
Mackinac Island ferries, 139
Mackinac sloop, 181
Mackinaw boats, 3, 4, 27
magnesium alloys, 191–93
mahogany, 21, 49, 84–85, 177, 191
"Mahogany Cigar," 205–6
Malik, Michael, 229
Mallon, Gerald, 135, 169
Mallon Boat Co., 135
Manistee Shipbuilding Co., 143
Mann, William, 60
Maple Leaf series, 100
Margie, 181
marine gasoline engines: advantages over steam launches, 29, *30*; builders in Detroit area, 36–41; builders in smaller cities, 41–43; disadvantages of early models, 29–30; early challenges, 29–30; four-cycle, 31, 37, *38*, 39; Grand Rapids builders, 30–36; innovations in, 28–30; manufactur-